Shojo Beat

St. Dragon Girl

VOLUME SIX

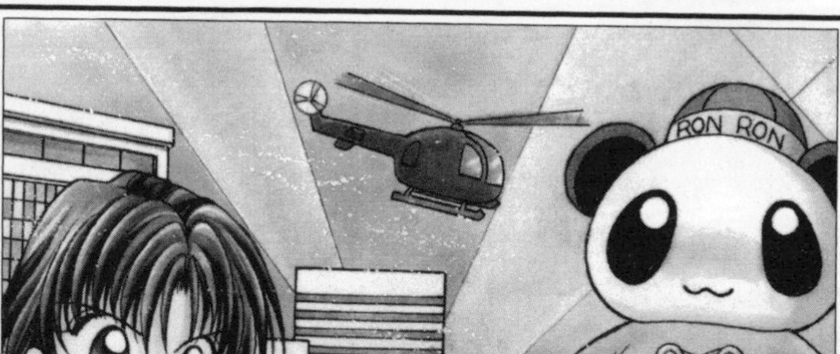
RON RON

Fill in the bubbles with your own dialogue!

Story & Art by **Natsumi Matsumoto**

ST.♥ DRAGON GIRL

CHARACTERS

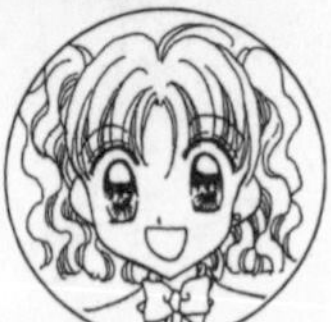

Shunran Kou

Ryuga's cousin and Momoka's best friend. Has psychic abilities.

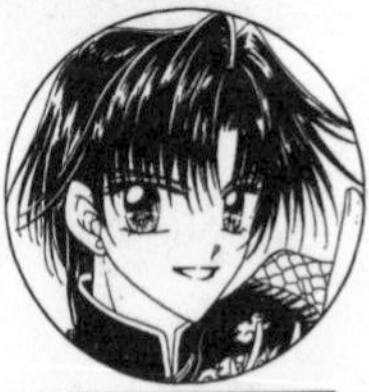

Ryuga Kou

Momoka's childhood friend and magic master.

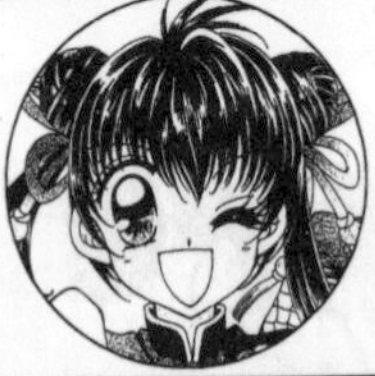

Momoka Sendou

She's possessed by a dragon spirit Ryuga called forth. When the seal on the dragon is broken, she becomes an invincible dragon girl.

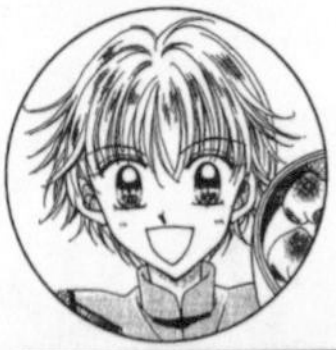

Touya Shirai

He's actually Yutengenyo, but he's reformed now. He loves Momoka. ♥

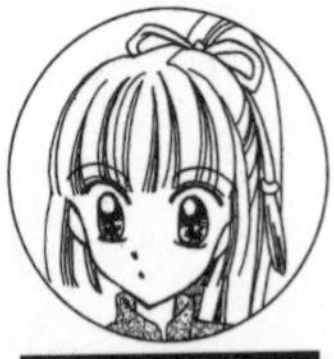

Ageha Inui

Momoka's friend. Member of the kenpo club.

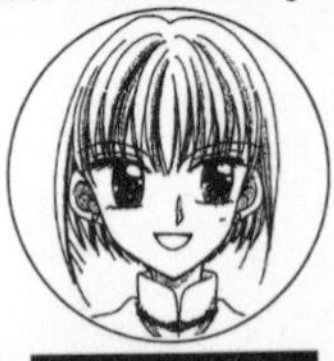

Raika Kou

Ryuga's distant relative. She can summon the Thunder Dragon.

STORY THUS FAR

Momoka is a member of the kenpo club at Yokohama's Tourin Academy. Her friends Ryuga and Shunran belong to a family of magic masters who can control dragons. Ever since the dragon Ryuga summoned possessed Momoka, she's been in danger many times. But every time, they manage to control the dragon and fight together.

One day, after eating "pandango" at the school bazaar, the parents and students are turned into pandas! The Panda King, unable to rest in peace, is the one responsible. He has a grudge against humans, but he changes after witnessing Momoka's kindness. Ryuga casts a spell that seals the Panda King's soul inside of Ron-Ron. From that point on, Momoka and Ron-Ron are best friends! ♥

Unfortunately Momoka's relationship with Ryuga hasn't developed the way she wanted. Not only have Touya and Akira-chan been interfering constantly, but Ryuga and Momoka have been unable to be straightforward with each other. What will happen between them now?

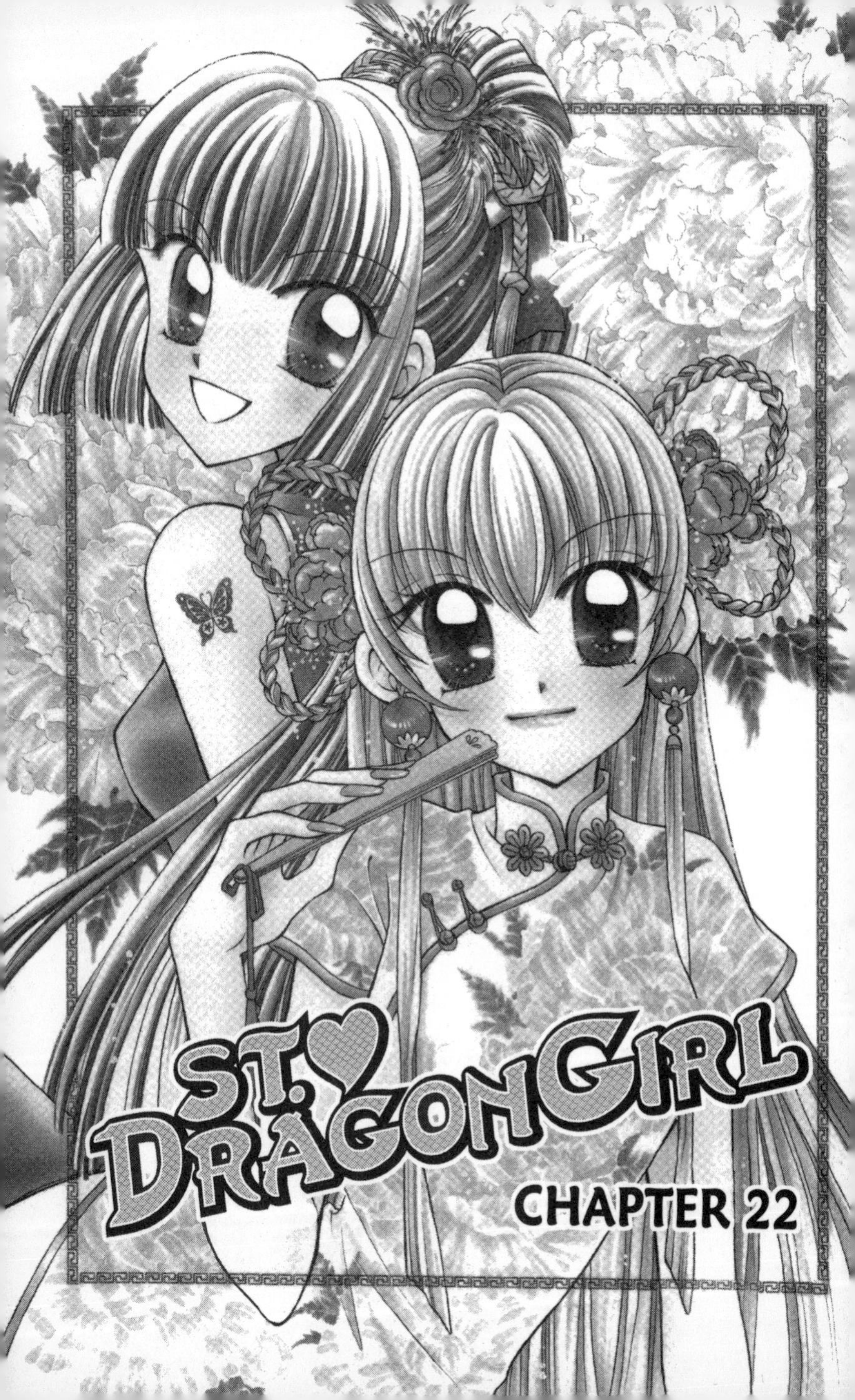
ST. DRAGON GIRL
CHAPTER 22

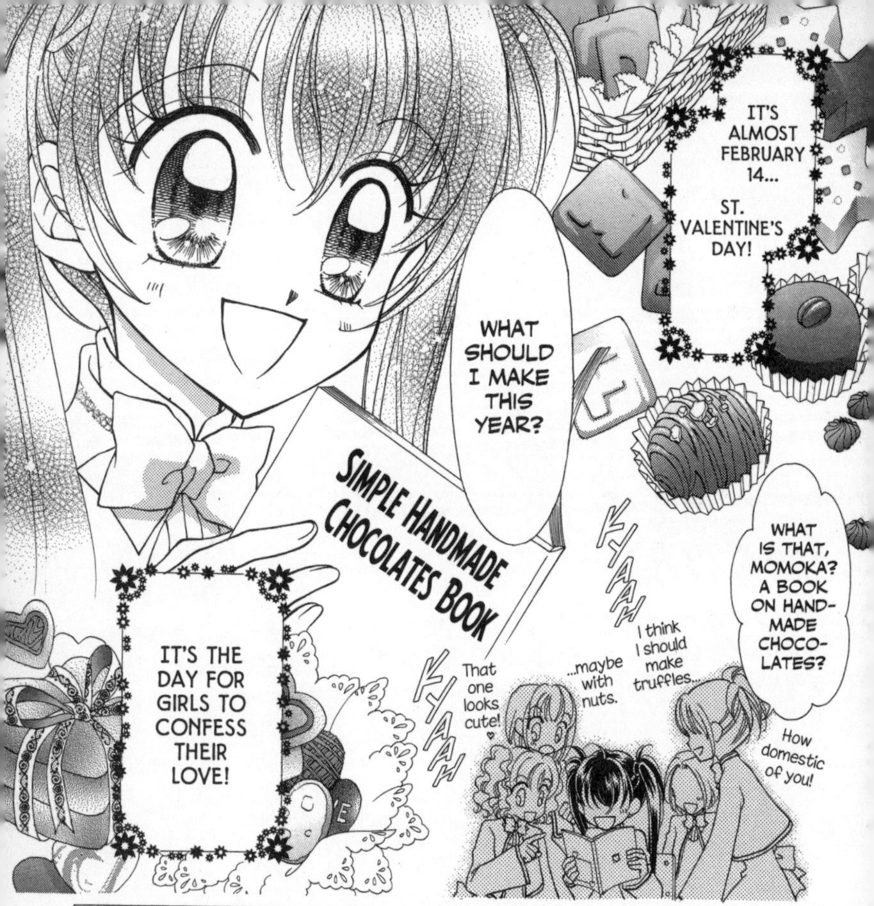
IT'S ALMOST FEBRUARY 14... ST. VALENTINE'S DAY!
WHAT SHOULD I MAKE THIS YEAR?
SIMPLE HANDMADE CHOCOLATES BOOK
WHAT IS THAT, MOMOKA? A BOOK ON HAND-MADE CHOCO-LATES?
How domestic of you!
KYAAAH
I think I should make truffles...
...maybe with nuts.
That one looks cute!♥
KYAAAH
IT'S THE DAY FOR GIRLS TO CONFESS THEIR LOVE!

I got a letter that said, "Matsumoto-san, you usually draw a lot of flowers or food on the title pages." I guess that's true! I love them both so much that I end up drawing them all the time. I often draw peonies for *St.♥Dragon Girl*. They have so many petals, and I think they're gorgeous. (I don't draw all the petals, so I guess mine are fake peonies!) Last year for my birthday, I got a bouquet of flowers with a peony in it.

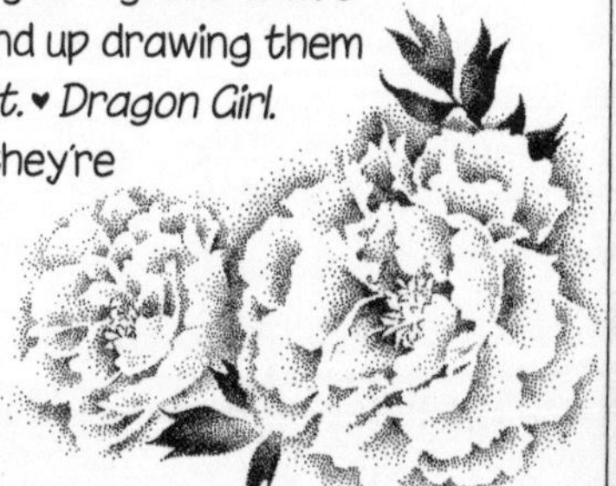

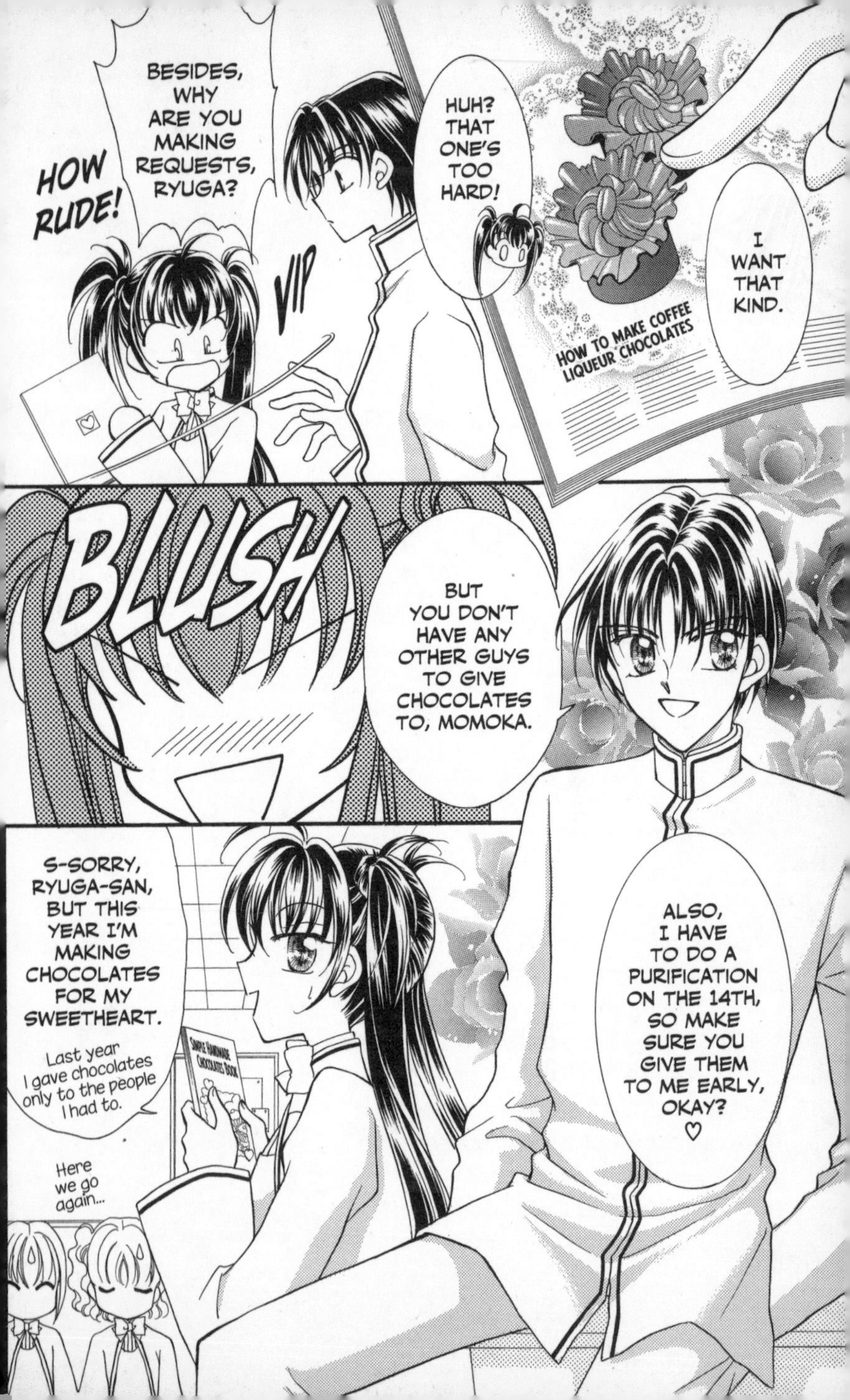
I WANT THAT KIND.
HOW TO MAKE COFFEE LIQUEUR CHOCOLATES
HUH? THAT ONE'S TOO HARD!
BESIDES, WHY ARE YOU MAKING REQUESTS, RYUGA?
HOW RUDE!
VIP
BUT YOU DON'T HAVE ANY OTHER GUYS TO GIVE CHOCOLATES TO, MOMOKA.
ALSO, I HAVE TO DO A PURIFICATION ON THE 14TH, SO MAKE SURE YOU GIVE THEM TO ME EARLY, OKAY? ♡
BLUSH
S-SORRY, RYUGA-SAN, BUT THIS YEAR I'M MAKING CHOCOLATES FOR MY SWEETHEART.
Last year I gave chocolates only to the people I had to.
SIMPLE HANDMADE CHOCOLATES BOOK
Here we go again...

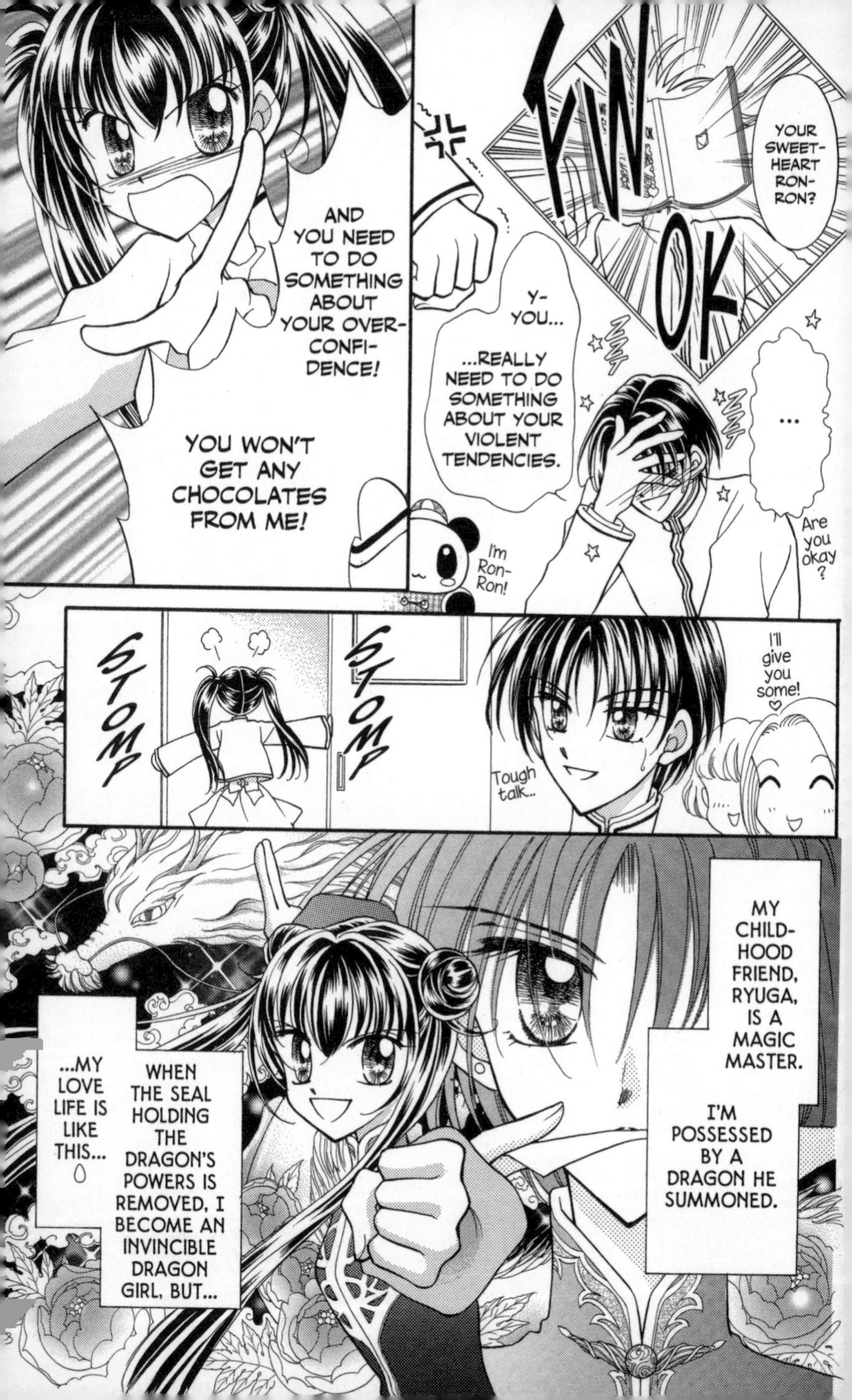
KNOK
YOUR SWEETHEART RON-RON?
Y- YOU...
...REALLY NEED TO DO SOMETHING ABOUT YOUR VIOLENT TENDENCIES.
...
Are you okay?
I'm Ron-Ron!
AND YOU NEED TO DO SOMETHING ABOUT YOUR OVERCONFIDENCE!
YOU WON'T GET ANY CHOCOLATES FROM ME!
I'll give you some!
Tough talk...
STOMP
STOMP
MY CHILDHOOD FRIEND, RYUGA, IS A MAGIC MASTER.
I'M POSSESSED BY A DRAGON HE SUMMONED.
WHEN THE SEAL HOLDING THE DRAGON'S POWERS IS REMOVED, I BECOME AN INVINCIBLE DRAGON GIRL, BUT...
...MY LOVE LIFE IS LIKE THIS...

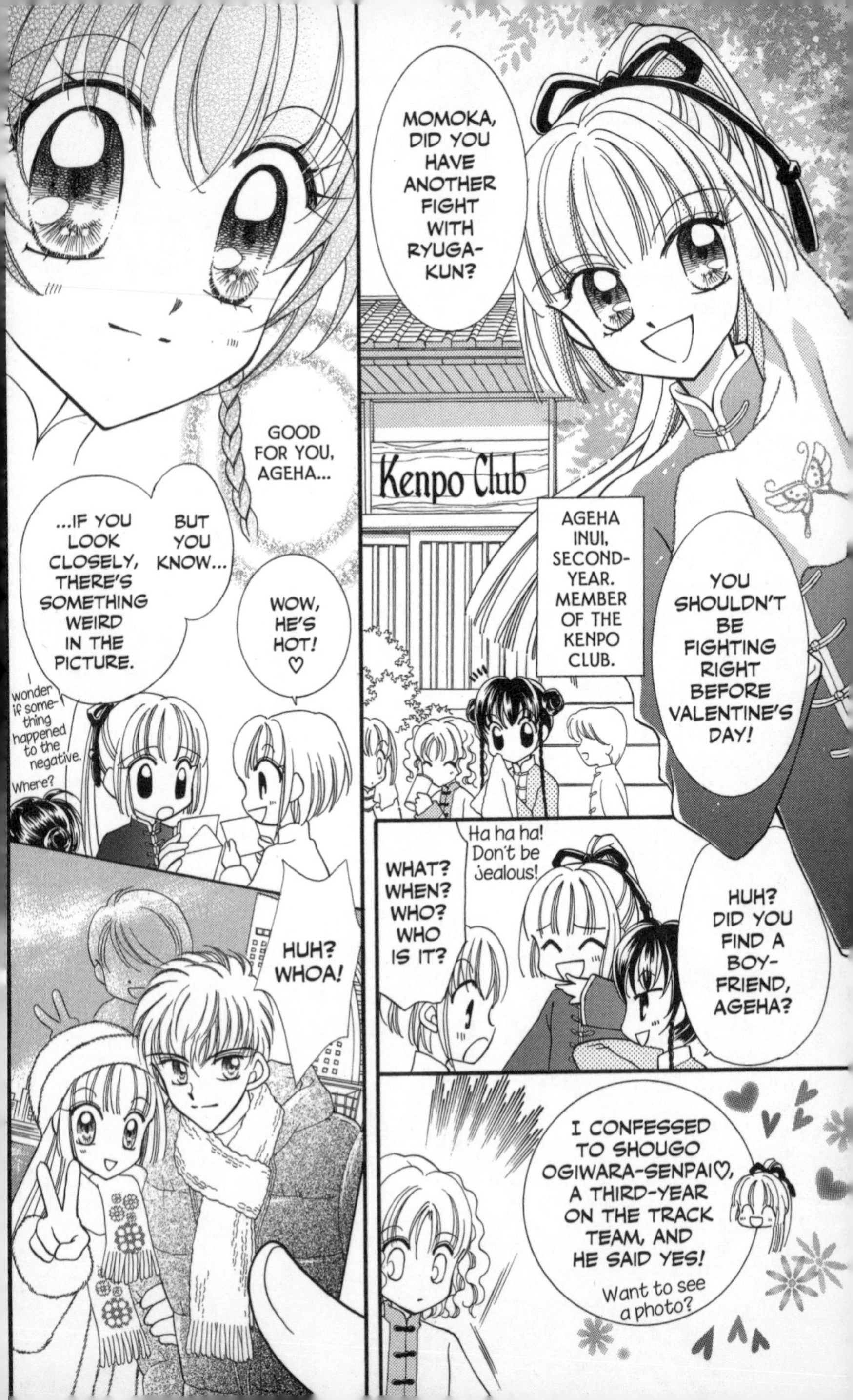
MOMOKA, DID YOU HAVE ANOTHER FIGHT WITH RYUGA-KUN?
YOU SHOULDN'T BE FIGHTING RIGHT BEFORE VALENTINE'S DAY!
Kenpo Club
AGEHA INUI, SECOND-YEAR. MEMBER OF THE KENPO CLUB.
HUH? DID YOU FIND A BOYFRIEND, AGEHA?
Ha ha ha! Don't be jealous!
WHAT? WHEN? WHO? WHO IS IT?
I CONFESSED TO SHOUGO OGIWARA-SENPAI♡, A THIRD-YEAR ON THE TRACK TEAM, AND HE SAID YES!
Want to see a photo?
GOOD FOR YOU, AGEHA...
BUT YOU KNOW...
...IF YOU LOOK CLOSELY, THERE'S SOMETHING WEIRD IN THE PICTURE.
WOW, HE'S HOT! ♡
I wonder if something happened to the negative.
Where?
HUH? WHOA!

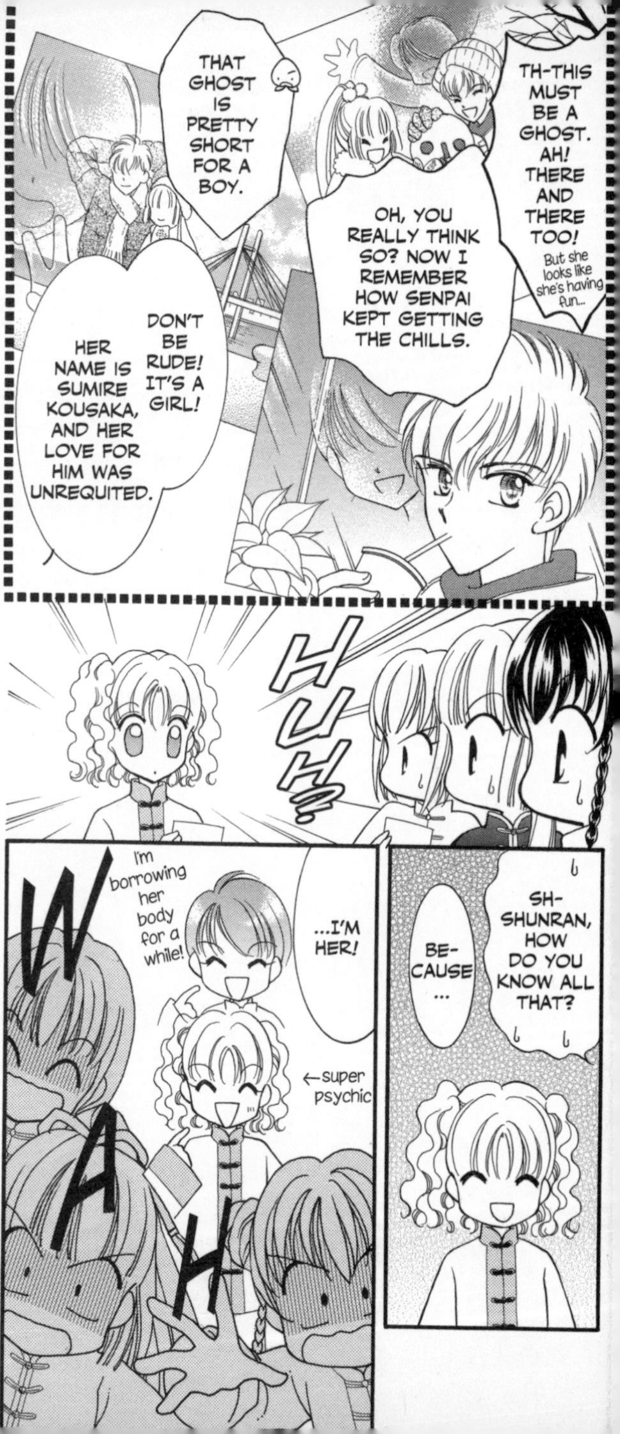
TH-THIS MUST BE A GHOST. AH! THERE AND THERE TOO!
But she looks like she's having fun...
THAT GHOST IS PRETTY SHORT FOR A BOY.
OH, YOU REALLY THINK SO? NOW I REMEMBER HOW SENPAI KEPT GETTING THE CHILLS.
DON'T BE RUDE! IT'S A GIRL!
HER NAME IS SUMIRE KOUSAKA, AND HER LOVE FOR HIM WAS UNREQUITED.
HUH?!
SH-SHUNRAN, HOW DO YOU KNOW ALL THAT?
BE-CAUSE...
...I'M HER!
I'm borrowing her body for a while!
←super psychic
WAAH

1

Good afternoon, Matsumoto here. Thanks for buying *St.♥Dragon Girl* volume 6! If you're standing there in the bookstore reading this, go up to the cash register and buy it! (laugh)

This volume has six stories that appeared in the magazine, so there are a lot of these columns! I'm sitting here at home writing these leisurely. It's really hot outside right now (it's August). I hope when this manga comes out, it will be a lot cooler! After all, it's a Valentine's Day story!

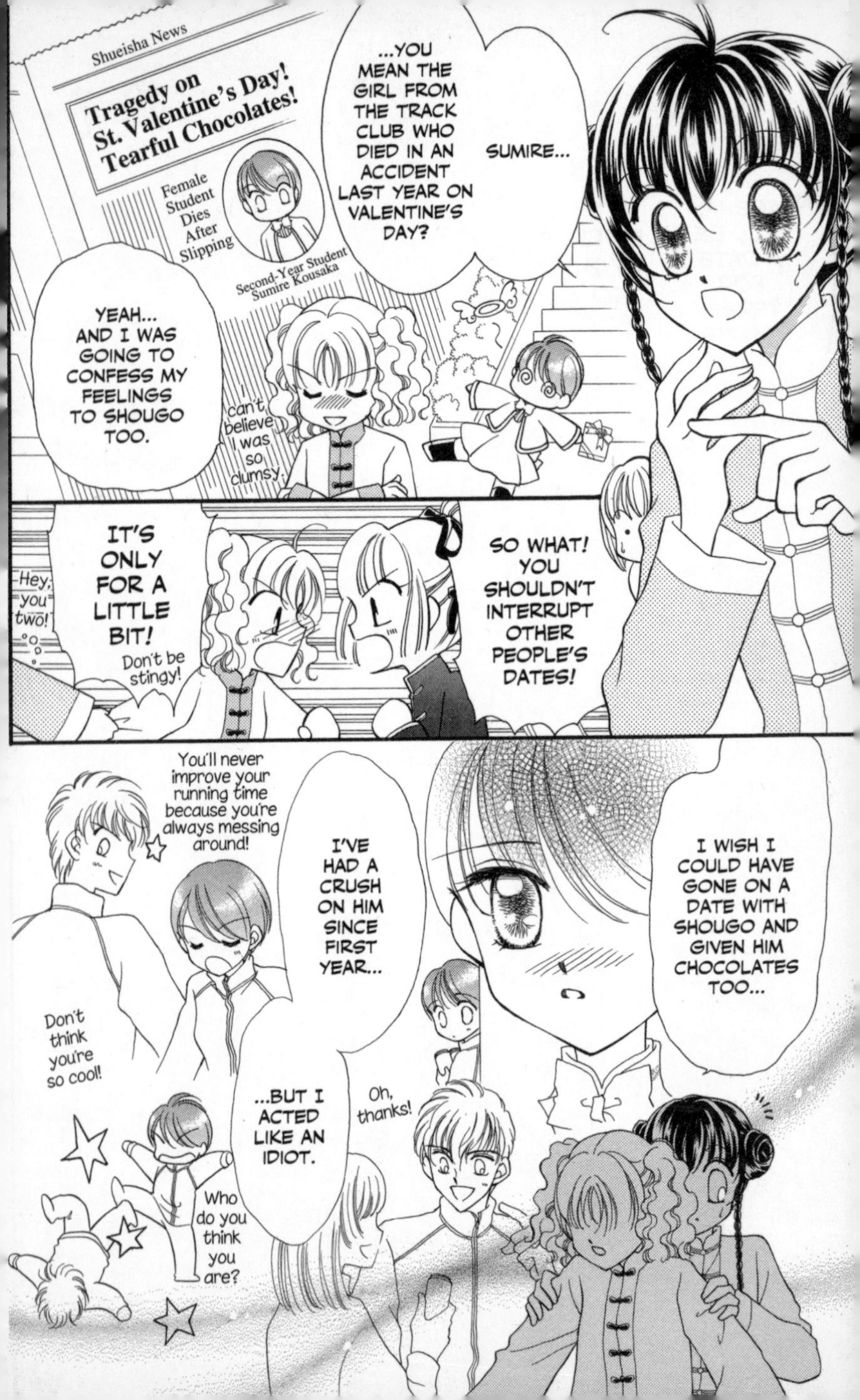
SUMIRE...
...YOU MEAN THE GIRL FROM THE TRACK CLUB WHO DIED IN AN ACCIDENT LAST YEAR ON VALENTINE'S DAY?
Shueisha News
Tragedy on St. Valentine's Day! Tearful Chocolates!
Female Student Dies After Slipping
Second-Year Student Sumire Kousaka
I can't believe I was so clumsy.
YEAH... AND I WAS GOING TO CONFESS MY FEELINGS TO SHOUGO TOO.
SO WHAT! YOU SHOULDN'T INTERRUPT OTHER PEOPLE'S DATES!
IT'S ONLY FOR A LITTLE BIT!
Don't be stingy!
Hey, you two!
I WISH I COULD HAVE GONE ON A DATE WITH SHOUGO AND GIVEN HIM CHOCOLATES TOO...
I'VE HAD A CRUSH ON HIM SINCE FIRST YEAR...
You'll never improve your running time because you're always messing around!
Don't think you're so cool!
...BUT I ACTED LIKE AN IDIOT.
Oh, thanks!
Who do you think you are?

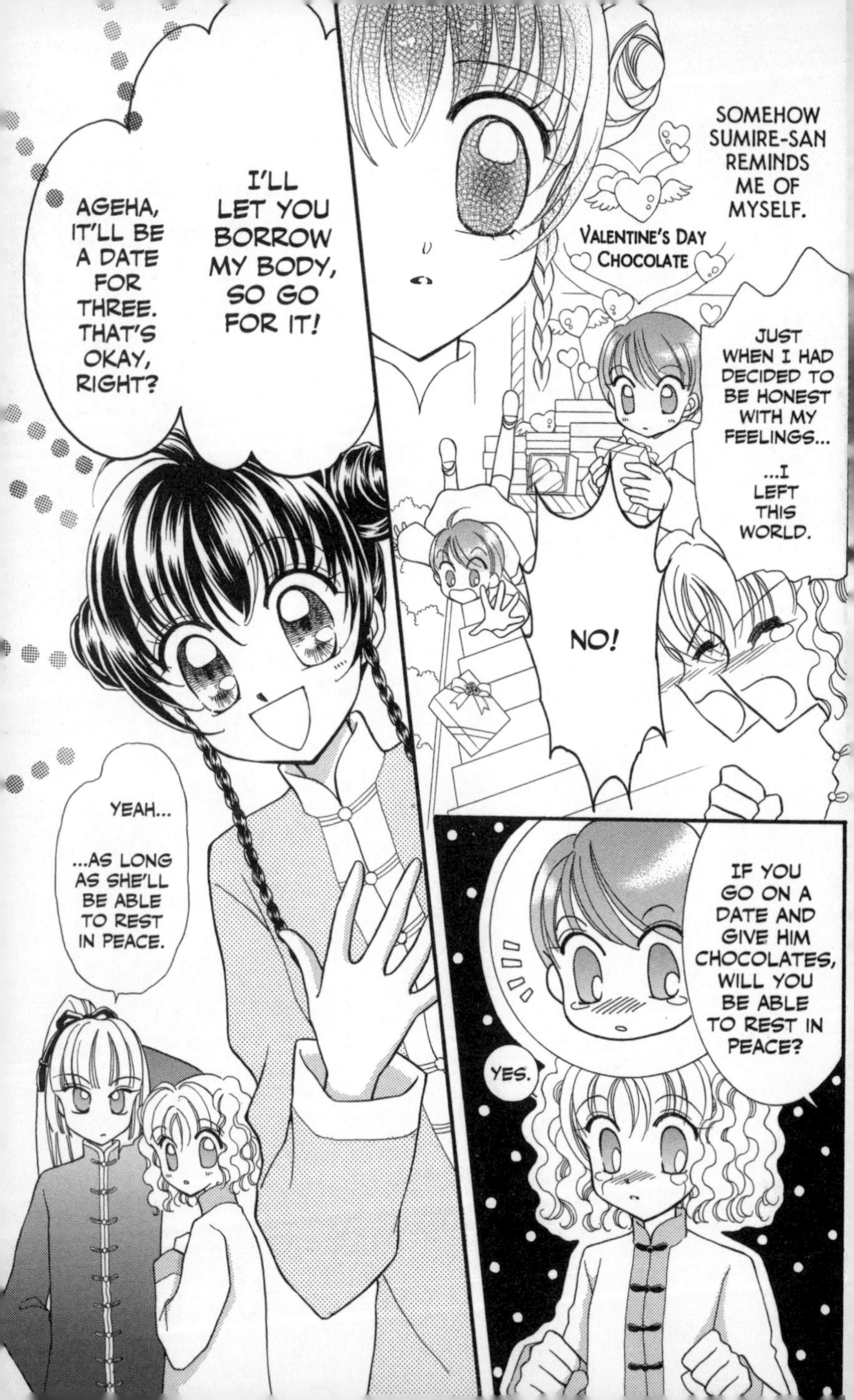
SOMEHOW SUMIRE-SAN REMINDS ME OF MYSELF.
VALENTINE'S DAY CHOCOLATE
JUST WHEN I HAD DECIDED TO BE HONEST WITH MY FEELINGS...
...I LEFT THIS WORLD.
NO!
IF YOU GO ON A DATE AND GIVE HIM CHOCOLATES, WILL YOU BE ABLE TO REST IN PEACE?
YES.
I'LL LET YOU BORROW MY BODY, SO GO FOR IT!
AGEHA, IT'LL BE A DATE FOR THREE. THAT'S OKAY, RIGHT?
YEAH...
...AS LONG AS SHE'LL BE ABLE TO REST IN PEACE.

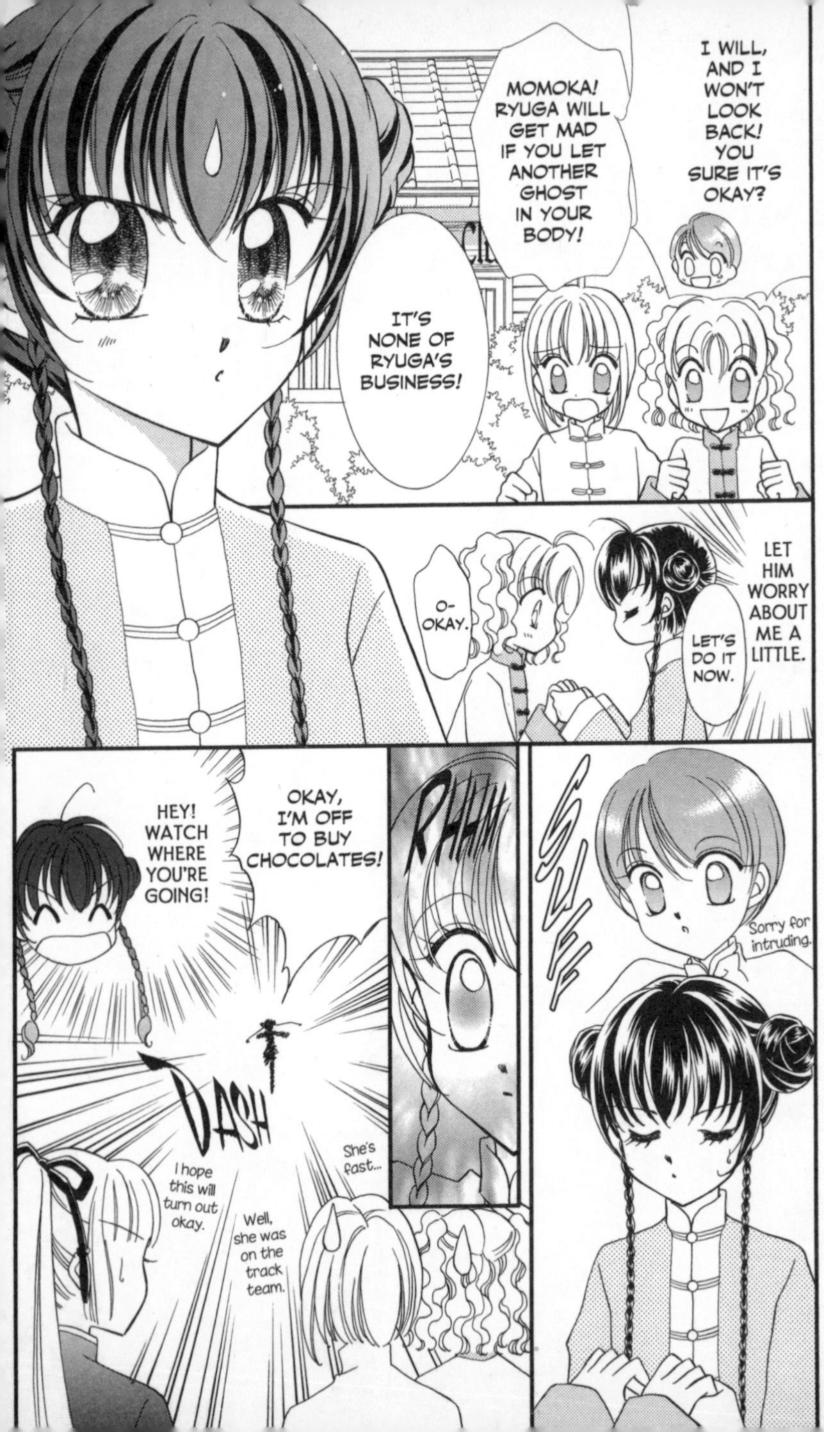
I WILL, AND I WON'T LOOK BACK! YOU SURE IT'S OKAY?
MOMOKA! RYUGA WILL GET MAD IF YOU LET ANOTHER GHOST IN YOUR BODY!
IT'S NONE OF RYUGA'S BUSINESS!
LET HIM WORRY ABOUT ME A LITTLE.
LET'S DO IT NOW.
O-OKAY.
Sorry for intruding.
OKAY, I'M OFF TO BUY CHOCOLATES!
HEY! WATCH WHERE YOU'RE GOING!
DASH
She's fast...
Well, she was on the track team.
I hope this will turn out okay.

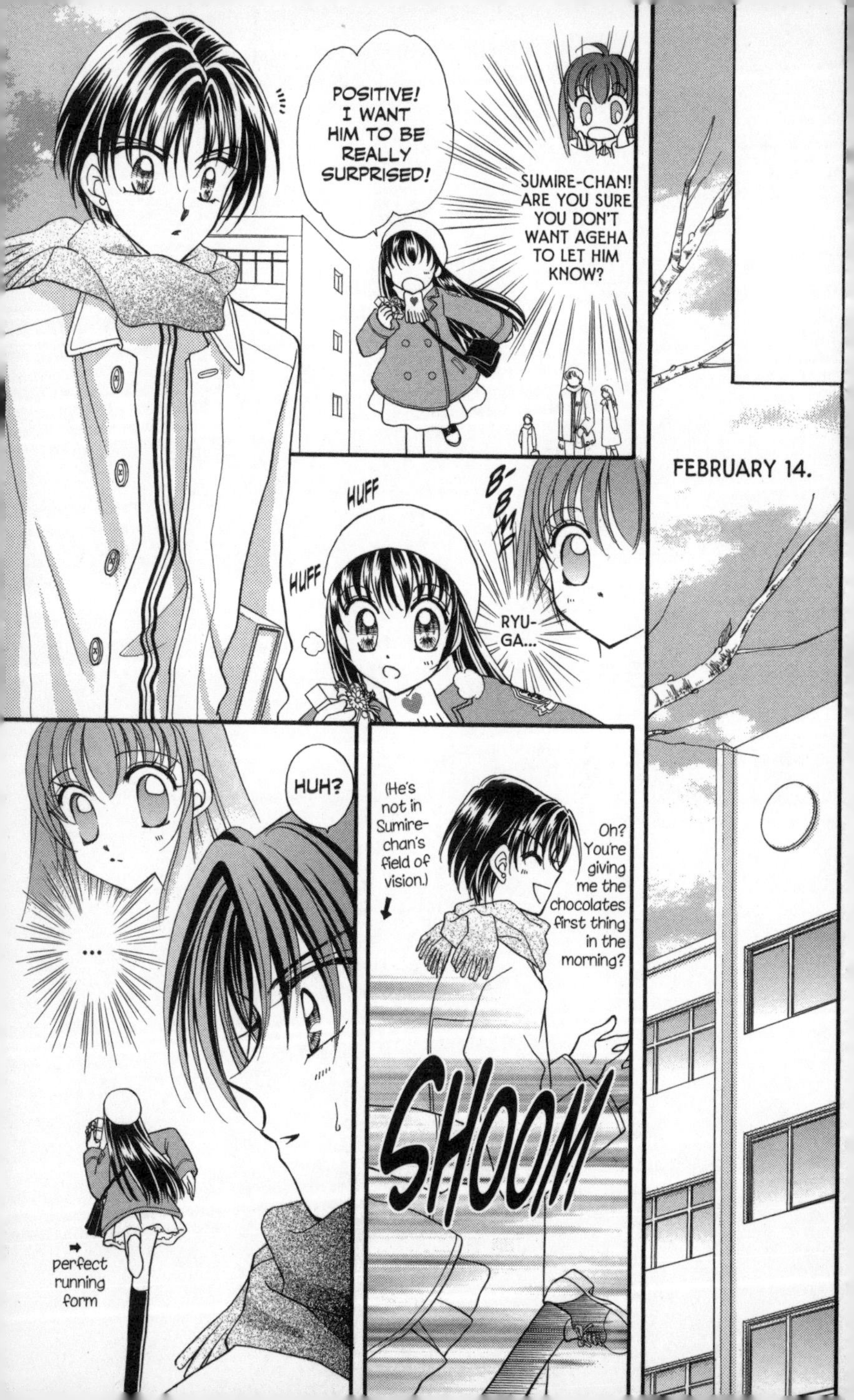
FEBRUARY 14.
SUMIRE-CHAN! ARE YOU SURE YOU DON'T WANT AGEHA TO LET HIM KNOW?
POSITIVE! I WANT HIM TO BE REALLY SURPRISED!
B-BMP
RYUGA...
HUFF
HUFF
Oh? You're giving me the chocolates first thing in the morning?
(He's not in Sumire-chan's field of vision.)
SHOOM
HUH?
...
perfect running form

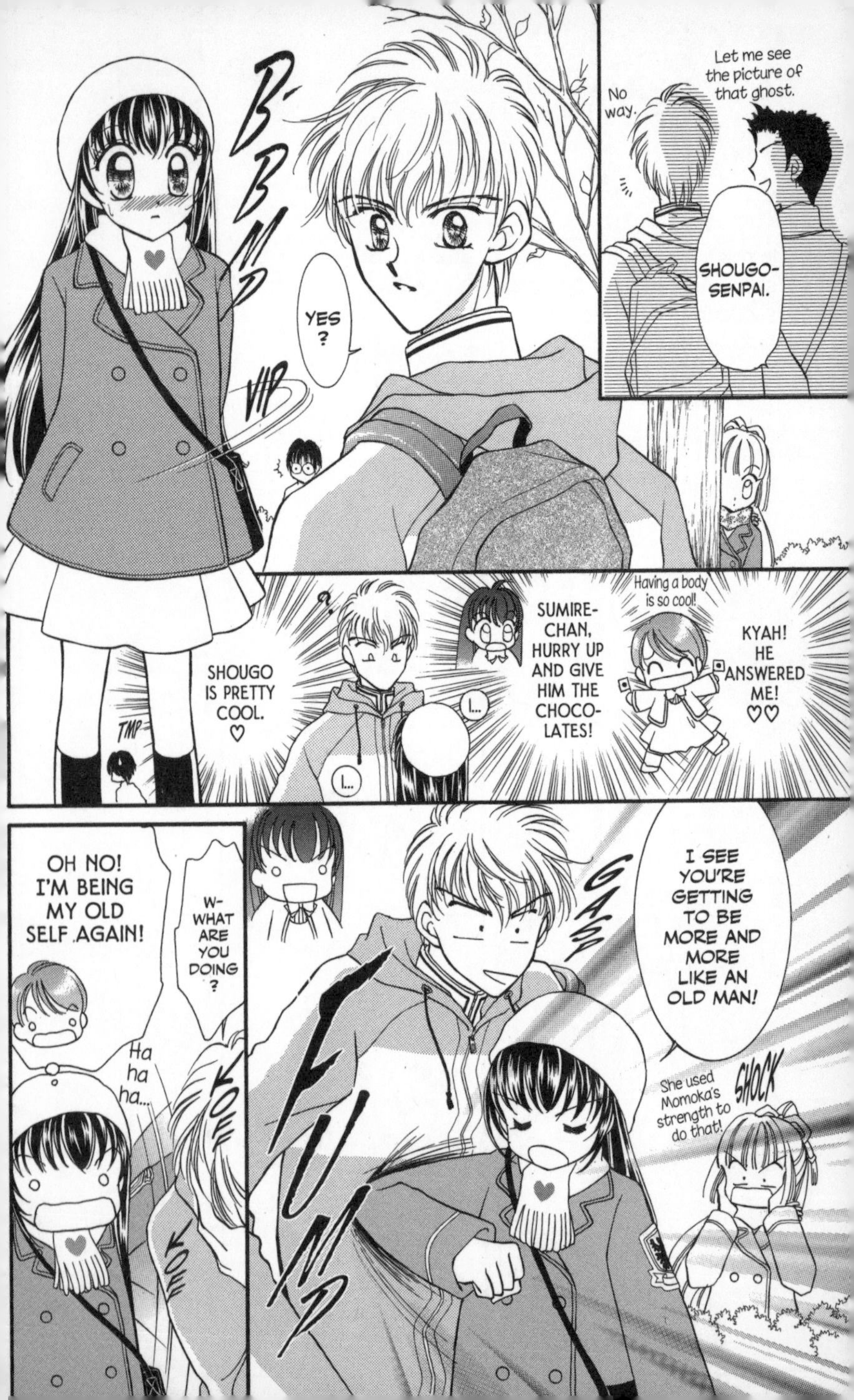

Let me see the picture of that ghost.
No way.
SHOUGO-SENPAI.
YES ?
KYAH! HE ANSWERED ME! ♡♡
Having a body is so cool!
SUMIRE-CHAN, HURRY UP AND GIVE HIM THE CHOCOLATES!
SHOUGO IS PRETTY COOL. ♡
I...
I...
TMP
I SEE YOU'RE GETTING TO BE MORE AND MORE LIKE AN OLD MAN!
SHOCK
She used Momoka's strength to do that!
W-WHAT ARE YOU DOING ?
OH NO! I'M BEING MY OLD SELF AGAIN!
Ha ha ha...
KOFF
KOFF

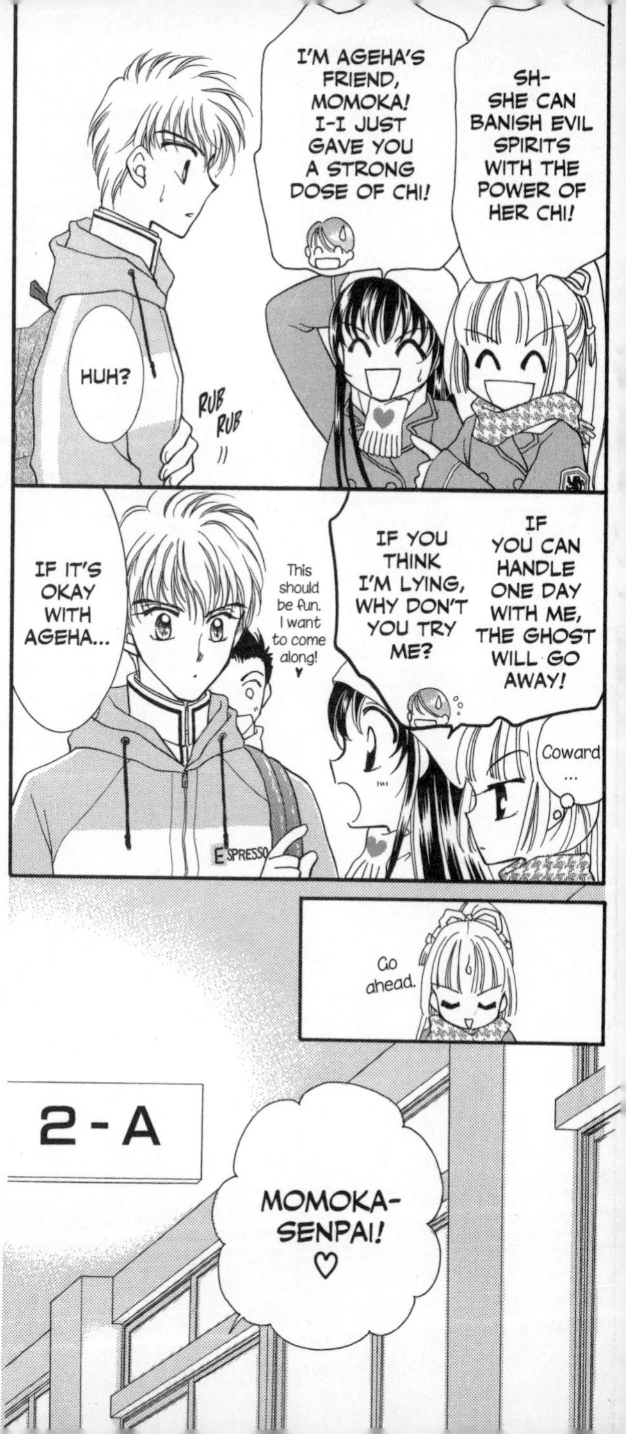
SH- SHE CAN BANISH EVIL SPIRITS WITH THE POWER OF HER CHI!
I'M AGEHA'S FRIEND, MOMOKA! I-I JUST GAVE YOU A STRONG DOSE OF CHI!
HUH?
RUB RUB
IF YOU CAN HANDLE ONE DAY WITH ME, THE GHOST WILL GO AWAY!
IF YOU THINK I'M LYING, WHY DON'T YOU TRY ME?
Coward...
This should be fun. I want to come along! ♥
IF IT'S OKAY WITH AGEHA...
ESPRESSO
Go ahead.
MOMOKA-SENPAI! ♡
2 - A

2

Pi Pi

In this story Ageha suddenly gets a boyfriend! In the first volume she was deceived by a weird teacher. As a result, I got a lot of letters asking for her to have a boyfriend... This guy looks like he's okay. Shougo-senpai is a rare type for me to draw, so it was fun. Sumire-chan is also the first girl for me to draw with short hair, so it was really refreshing. I hope I can draw a girl like her again.

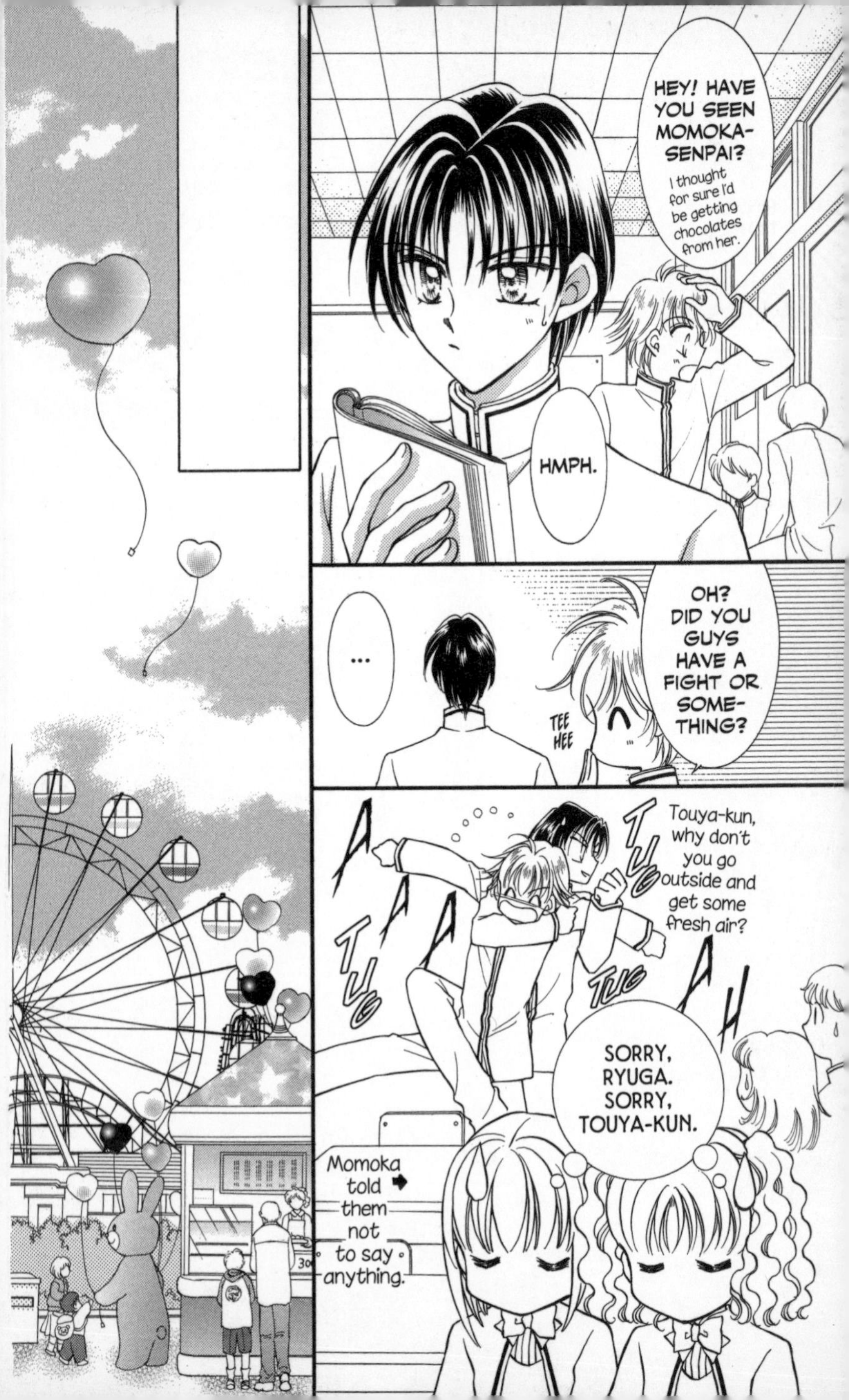
HEY! HAVE YOU SEEN MOMOKA-SENPAI?
I thought for sure I'd be getting chocolates from her.
HMPH.
OH? DID YOU GUYS HAVE A FIGHT OR SOME-THING?
TEE HEE
...
Touya-kun, why don't you go outside and get some fresh air?
AAAA
TUG
TUG
TUG
AH
SORRY, RYUGA. SORRY, TOUYA-KUN.
Momoka told them not to say anything.

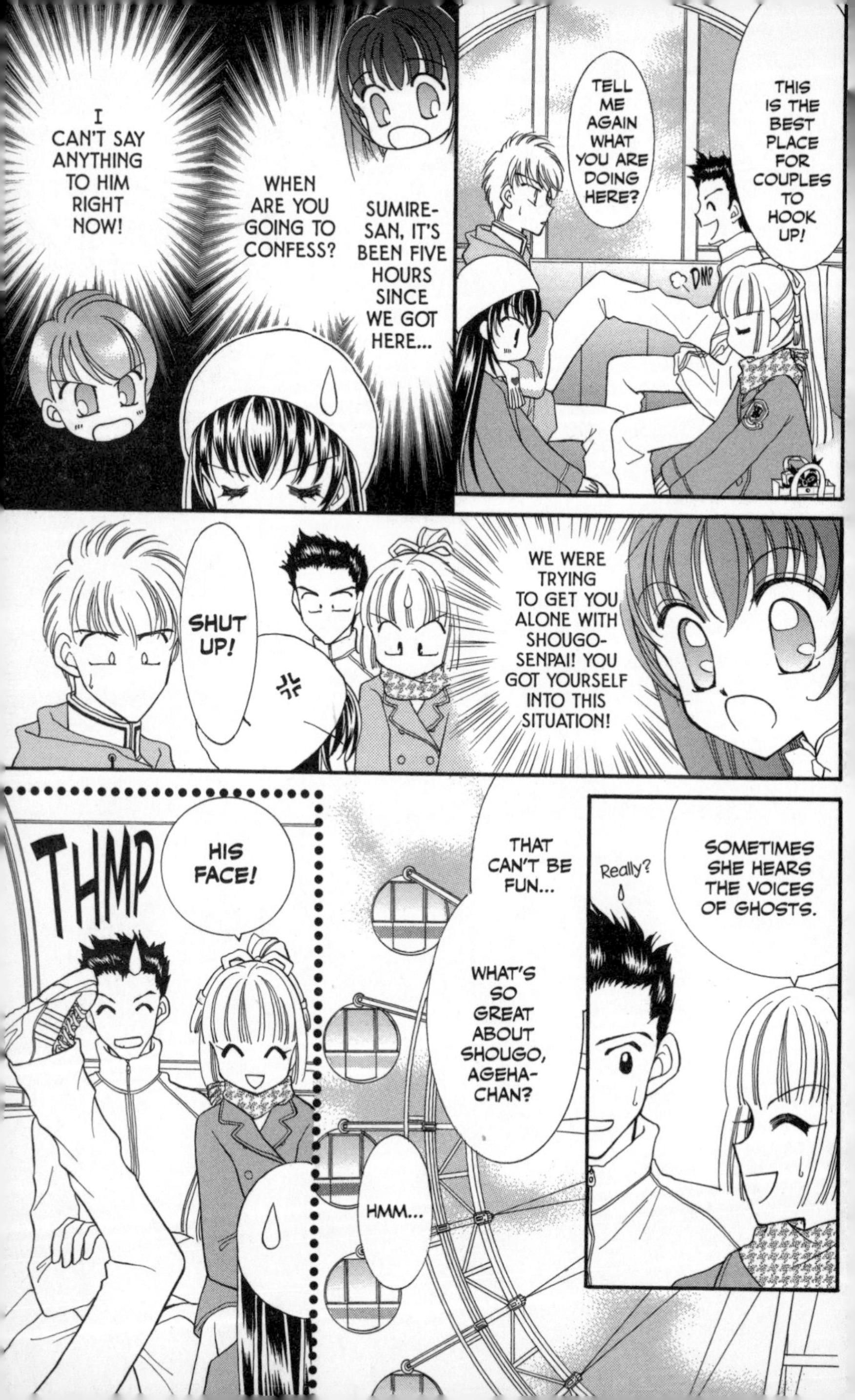
THIS IS THE BEST PLACE FOR COUPLES TO HOOK UP!
TELL ME AGAIN WHAT YOU ARE DOING HERE?
DMP
SUMIRE-SAN, IT'S BEEN FIVE HOURS SINCE WE GOT HERE...
WHEN ARE YOU GOING TO CONFESS?
I CAN'T SAY ANYTHING TO HIM RIGHT NOW!
WE WERE TRYING TO GET YOU ALONE WITH SHOUGO-SENPAI! YOU GOT YOURSELF INTO THIS SITUATION!
SHUT UP!
SOMETIMES SHE HEARS THE VOICES OF GHOSTS.
Really?
THAT CAN'T BE FUN...
WHAT'S SO GREAT ABOUT SHOUGO, AGEHA-CHAN?
HMM...
HIS FACE!
THMP

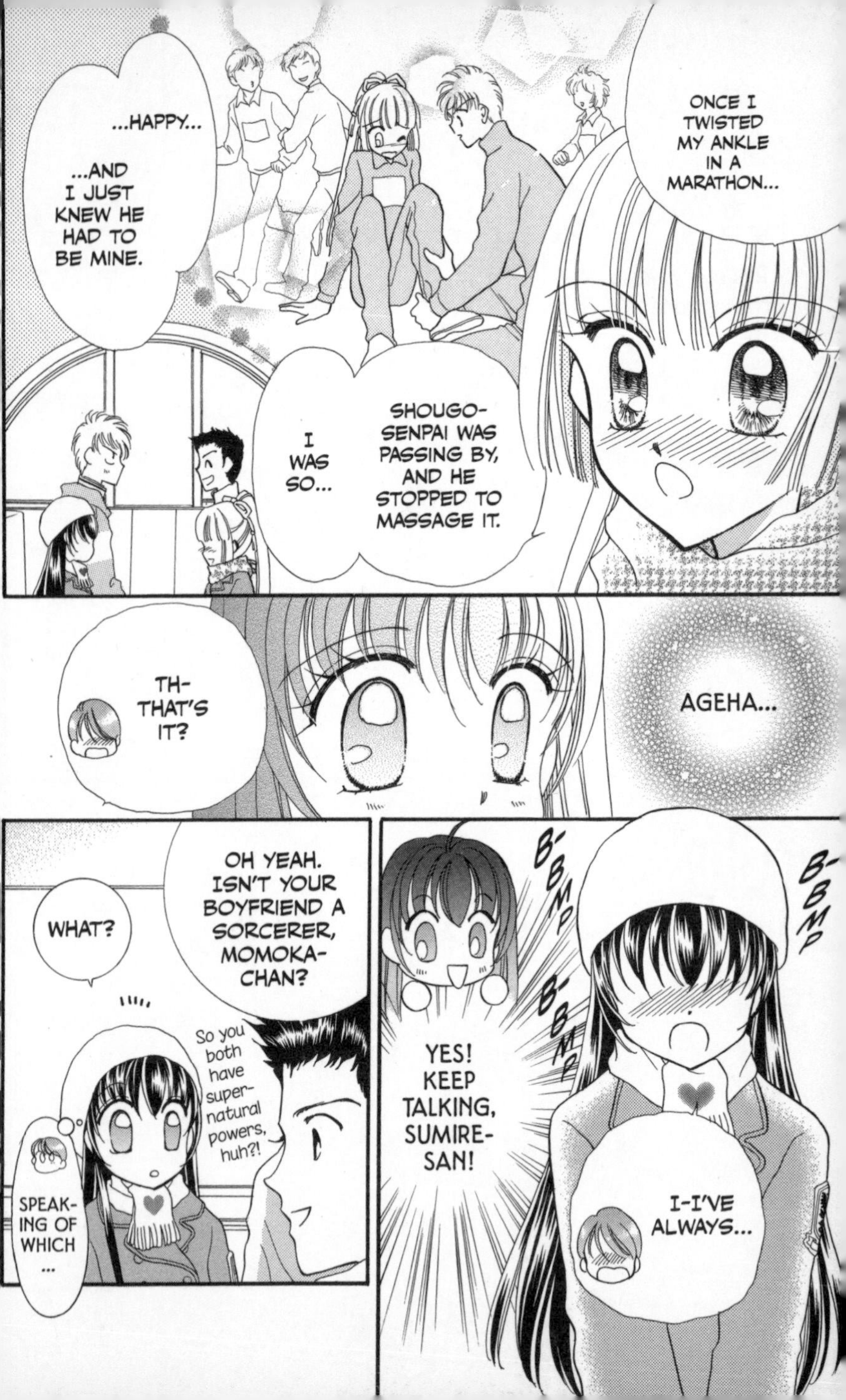
ONCE I TWISTED MY ANKLE IN A MARATHON...
SHOUGO-SENPAI WAS PASSING BY, AND HE STOPPED TO MASSAGE IT.
I WAS SO...
...HAPPY...
...AND I JUST KNEW HE HAD TO BE MINE.
AGEHA...
TH-THAT'S IT?
B-BMP
B-BMP
B-BMP
I-I'VE ALWAYS...
YES! KEEP TALKING, SUMIRE-SAN!
OH YEAH. ISN'T YOUR BOYFRIEND A SORCERER, MOMOKA-CHAN?
WHAT?
So you both have super-natural powers, huh?!
SPEAK-ING OF WHICH ...

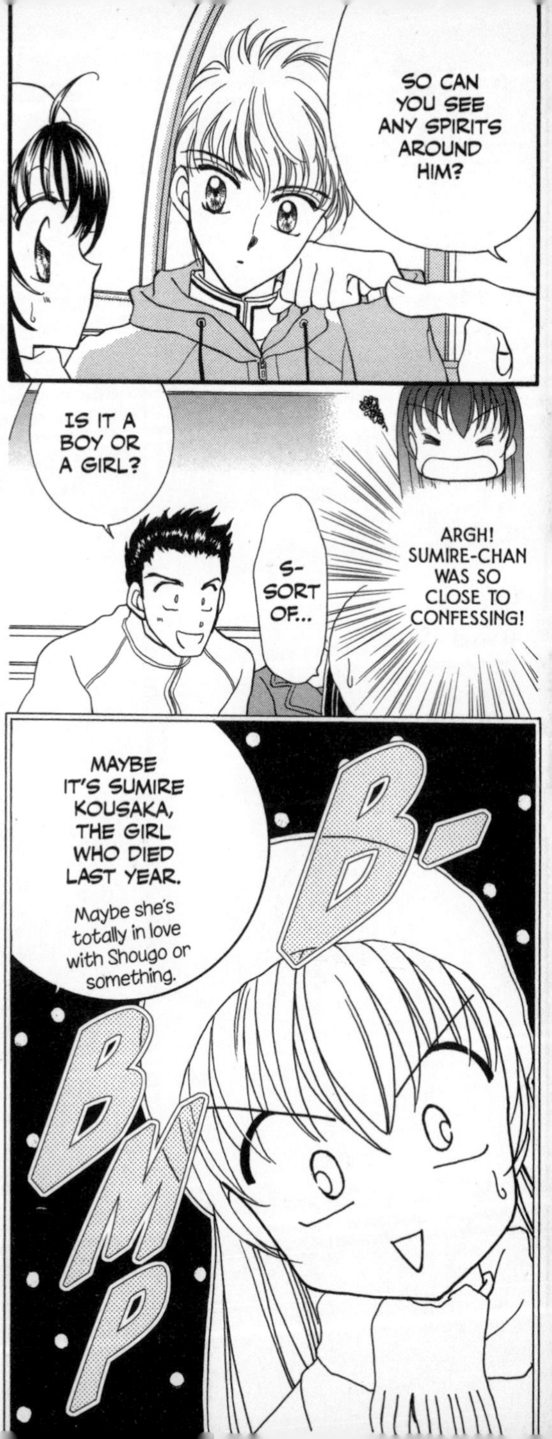
SO CAN YOU SEE ANY SPIRITS AROUND HIM?
IS IT A BOY OR A GIRL?
S-SORT OF...
ARGH! SUMIRE-CHAN WAS SO CLOSE TO CONFESSING!
MAYBE IT'S SUMIRE KOUSAKA, THE GIRL WHO DIED LAST YEAR.
Maybe she's totally in love with Shougo or something.
B-BMP

3

This story was the last one I did this year. After the New Year, I couldn't think of a good story. I like seasonal stories, so I always write stories about Valentine's Day or Christmas. Now I think, "Man, how many Valetine's Day stories have I done??"

Sorry about that. Just think of it as "manga time." Momoka and the others are still second-years in high school, and Touya and Akira are still first-years. Thanks to all the people who gave me chocolate for Valentine's Day!♡ (I loved it!)

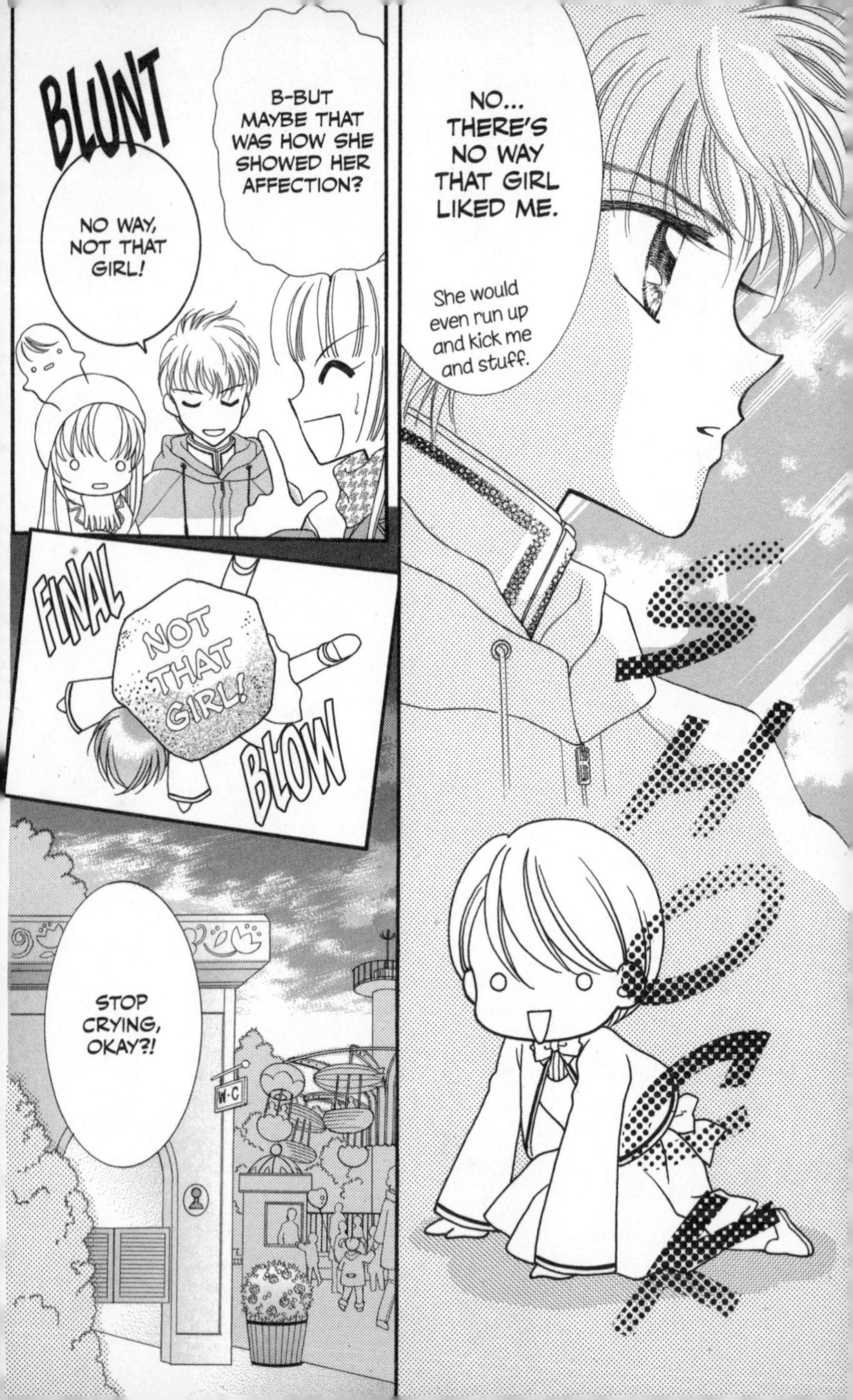
NO... THERE'S NO WAY THAT GIRL LIKED ME.
She would even run up and kick me and stuff.
B-BUT MAYBE THAT WAS HOW SHE SHOWED HER AFFECTION?
BLUNT
NO WAY, NOT THAT GIRL!
FINAL
NOT THAT GIRL!
BLOW
STOP CRYING, OKAY?!
W·C

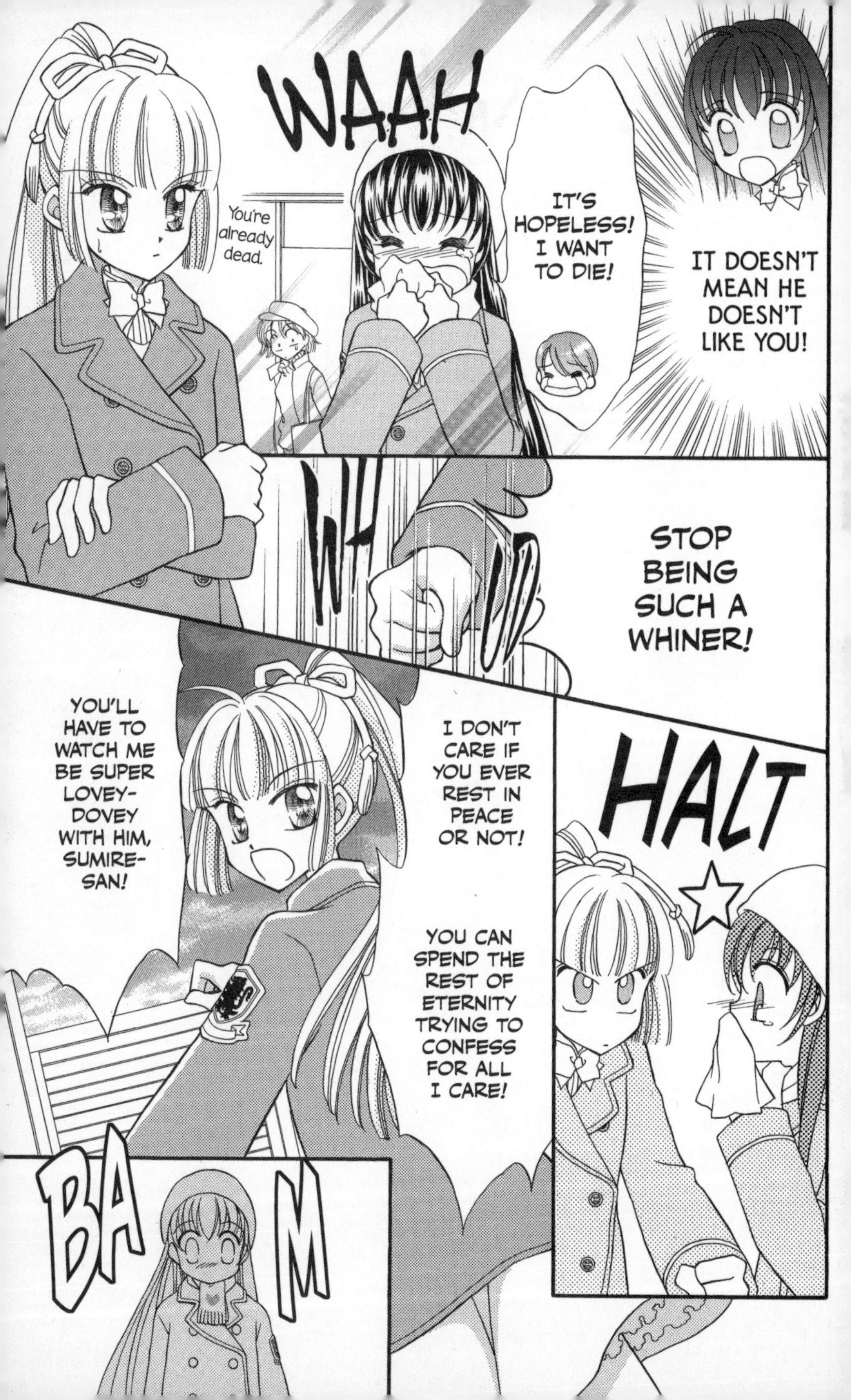
IT DOESN'T MEAN HE DOESN'T LIKE YOU!
IT'S HOPELESS! I WANT TO DIE!
WAAH
You're already dead.
STOP BEING SUCH A WHINER!
WHUD
HALT
I DON'T CARE IF YOU EVER REST IN PEACE OR NOT!
YOU CAN SPEND THE REST OF ETERNITY TRYING TO CONFESS FOR ALL I CARE!
YOU'LL HAVE TO WATCH ME BE SUPER LOVEY-DOVEY WITH HIM, SUMIRE-SAN!
BAM

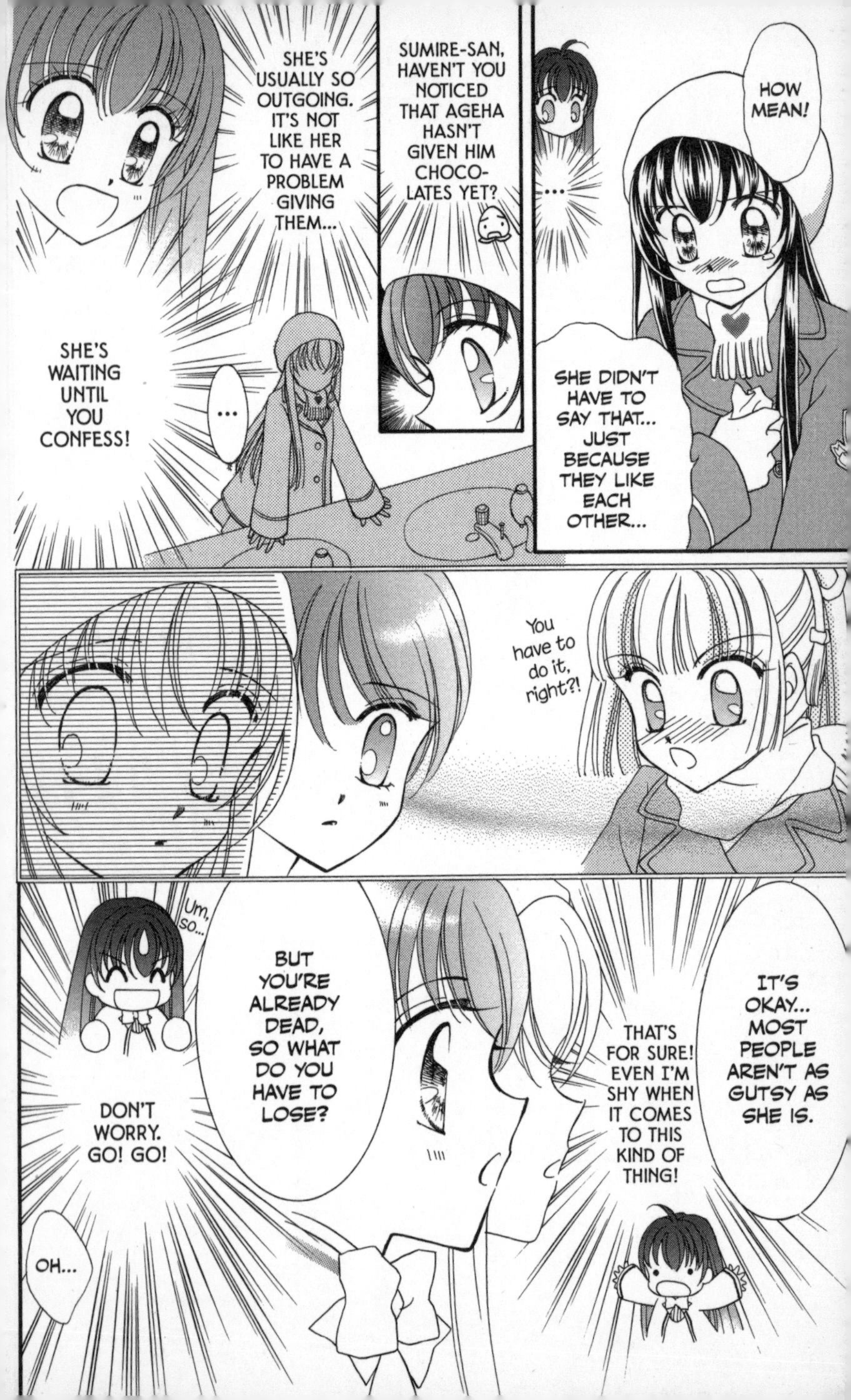
HOW MEAN!
SHE DIDN'T HAVE TO SAY THAT... JUST BECAUSE THEY LIKE EACH OTHER...
...
SUMIRE-SAN, HAVEN'T YOU NOTICED THAT AGEHA HASN'T GIVEN HIM CHOCO-LATES YET?
SHE'S USUALLY SO OUTGOING. IT'S NOT LIKE HER TO HAVE A PROBLEM GIVING THEM...
...
SHE'S WAITING UNTIL YOU CONFESS!
You have to do it, right?!
IT'S OKAY... MOST PEOPLE AREN'T AS GUTSY AS SHE IS.
THAT'S FOR SURE! EVEN I'M SHY WHEN IT COMES TO THIS KIND OF THING!
BUT YOU'RE ALREADY DEAD, SO WHAT DO YOU HAVE TO LOSE?
Um, so...
DON'T WORRY. GO! GO!
OH...

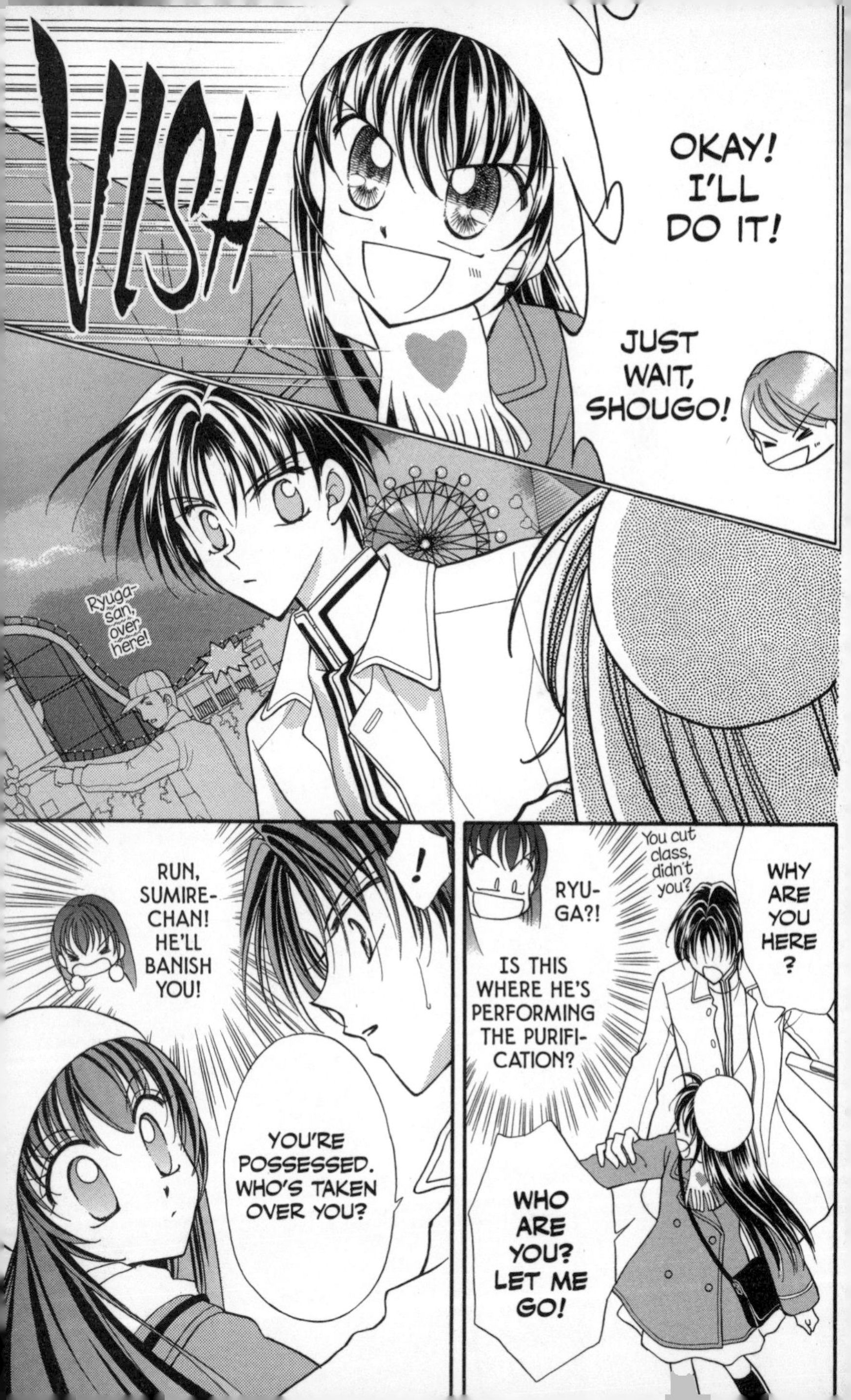
OKAY! I'LL DO IT!
JUST WAIT, SHOUGO!
VISH
Ryuga-san, over here!
WHY ARE YOU HERE?
You cut class, didn't you?
RYU-GA?!
IS THIS WHERE HE'S PERFORMING THE PURIFICATION?
WHO ARE YOU? LET ME GO!
!
RUN, SUMIRE-CHAN! HE'LL BANISH YOU!
YOU'RE POSSESSED. WHO'S TAKEN OVER YOU?

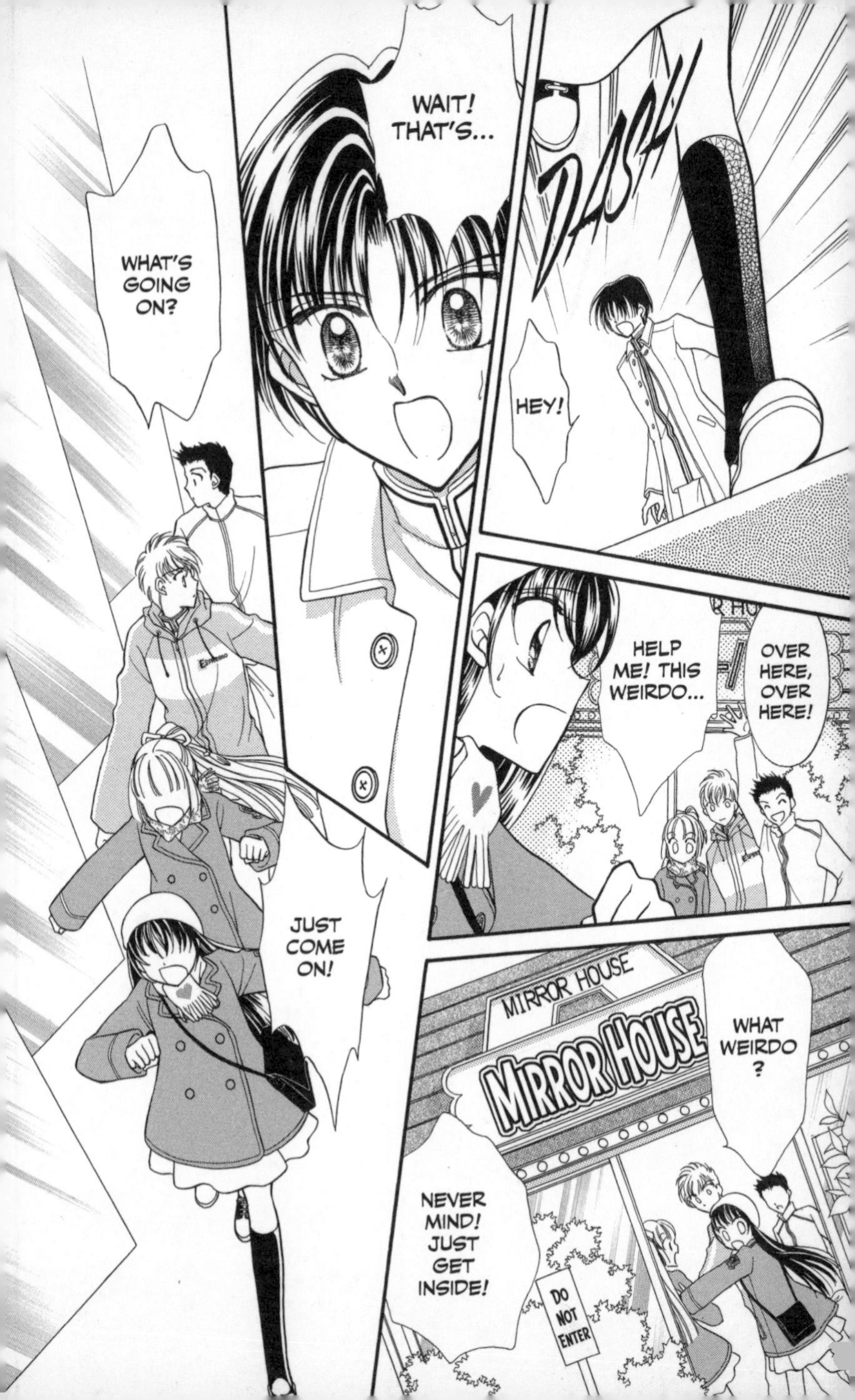
DASH
HEY!
WAIT! THAT'S...
OVER HERE, OVER HERE!
HELP ME! THIS WEIRDO...
WHAT'S GOING ON?
JUST COME ON!
MIRROR HOUSE
MIRROR HOUSE
WHAT WEIRDO?
NEVER MIND! JUST GET INSIDE!
DO NOT ENTER

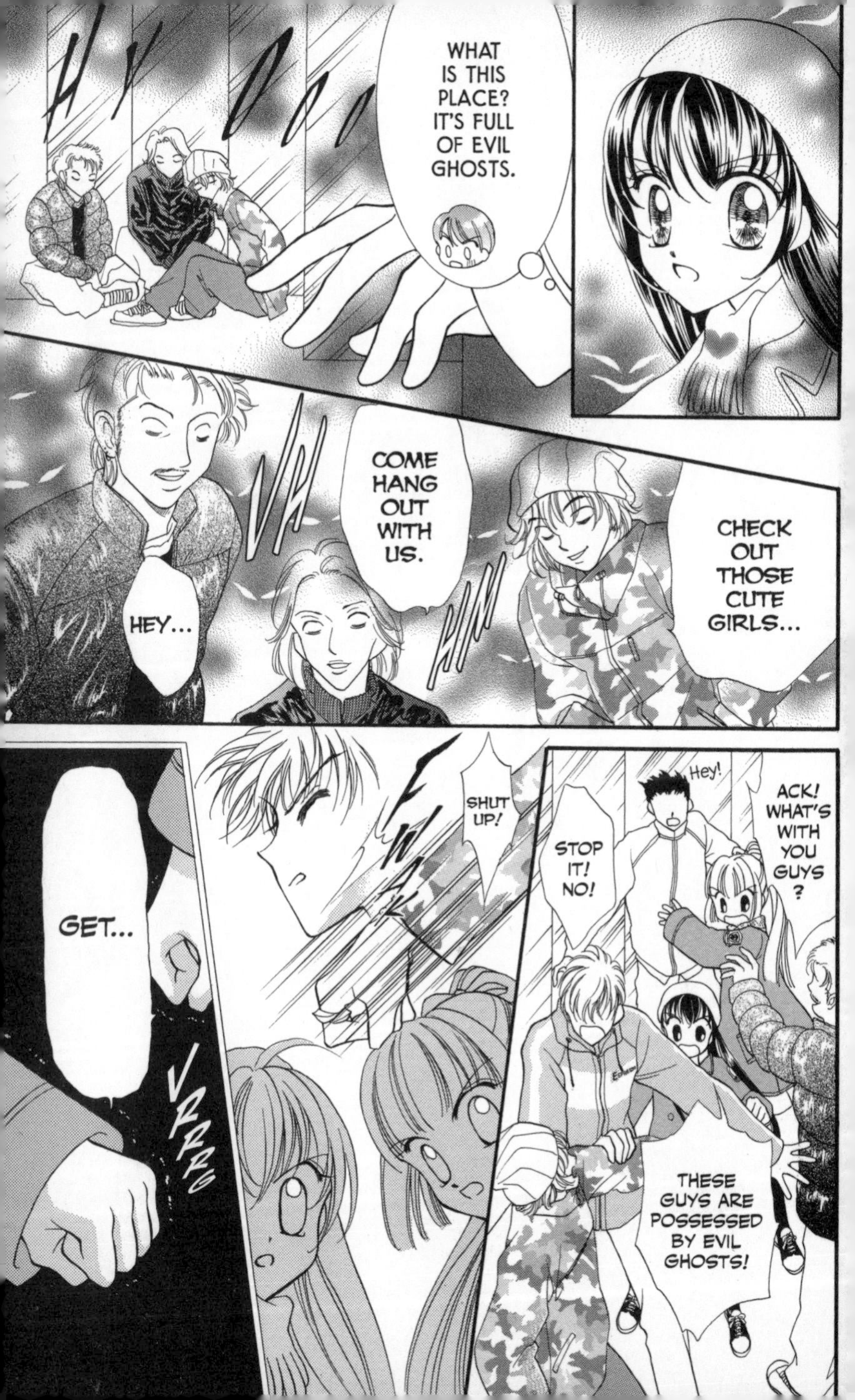
WHAT IS THIS PLACE? IT'S FULL OF EVIL GHOSTS.
CHECK OUT THOSE CUTE GIRLS...
COME HANG OUT WITH US.
HEY...
Hey!
ACK! WHAT'S WITH YOU GUYS?
STOP IT! NO!
THESE GUYS ARE POSSESSED BY EVIL GHOSTS!
SHUT UP!
GET...

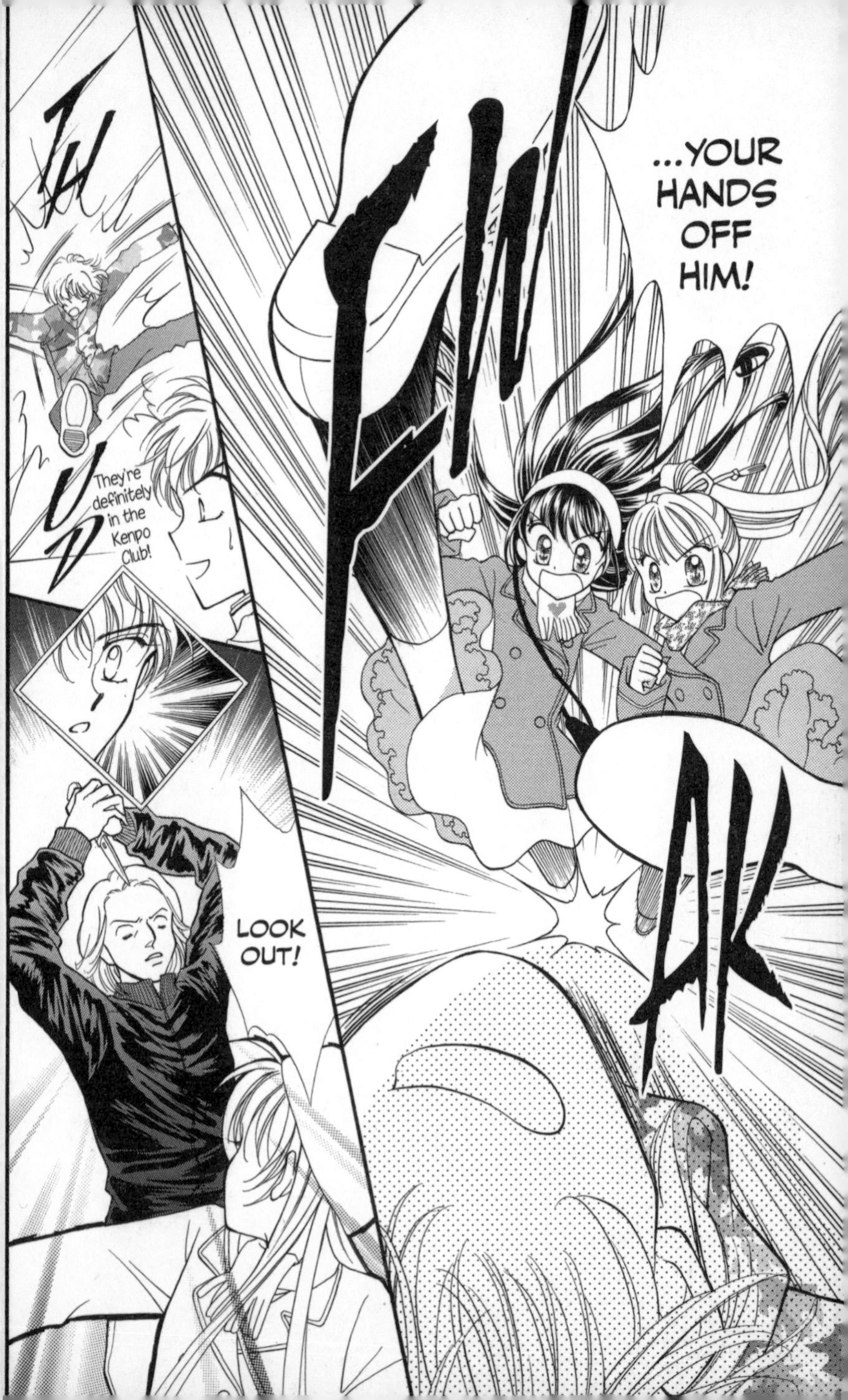
...YOUR HANDS OFF HIM!
They're definitely in the Kenpo Club!
LOOK OUT!

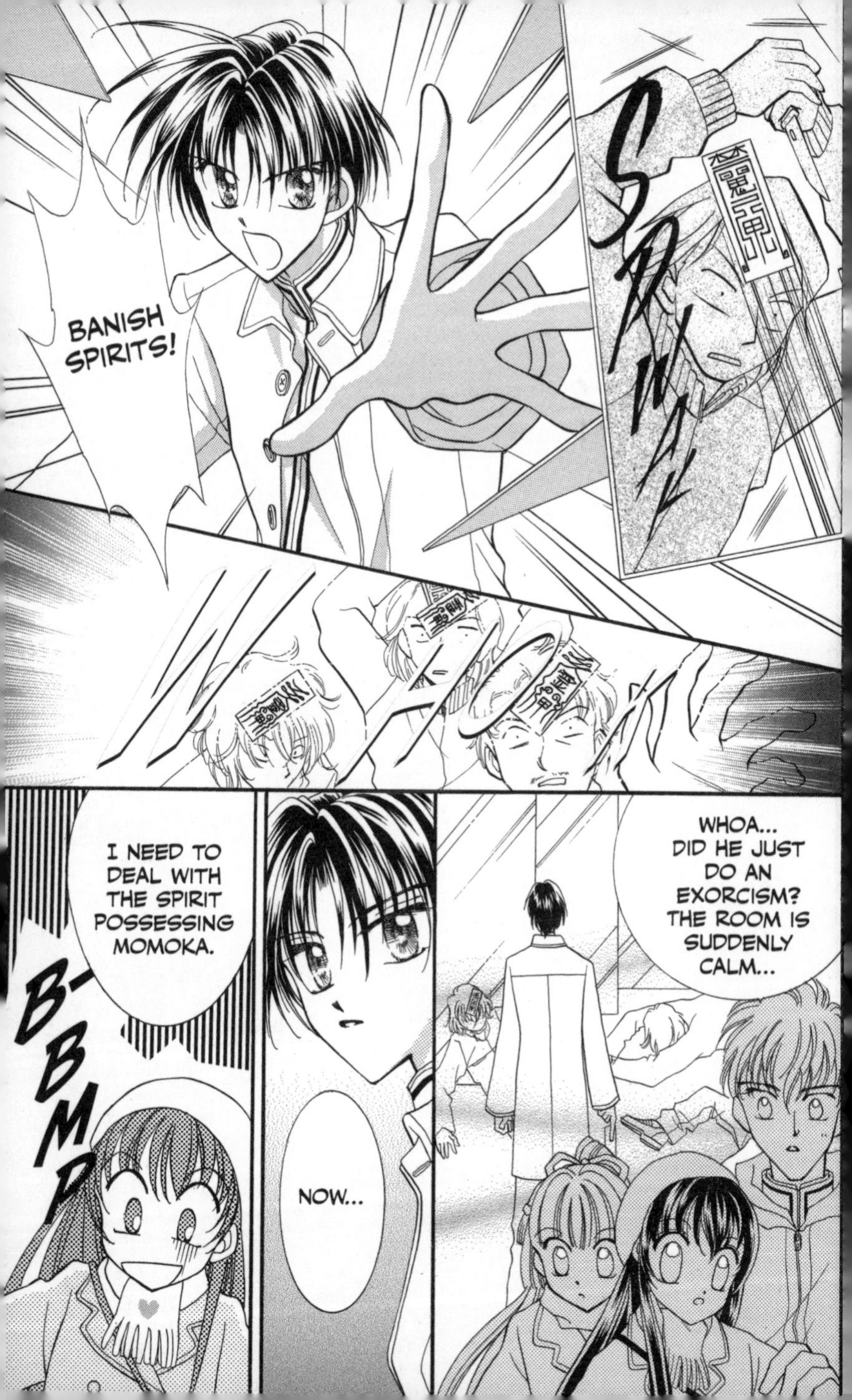
BANISH SPIRITS!
WHOA... DID HE JUST DO AN EXORCISM? THE ROOM IS SUDDENLY CALM...
NOW...
I NEED TO DEAL WITH THE SPIRIT POSSESSING MOMOKA.

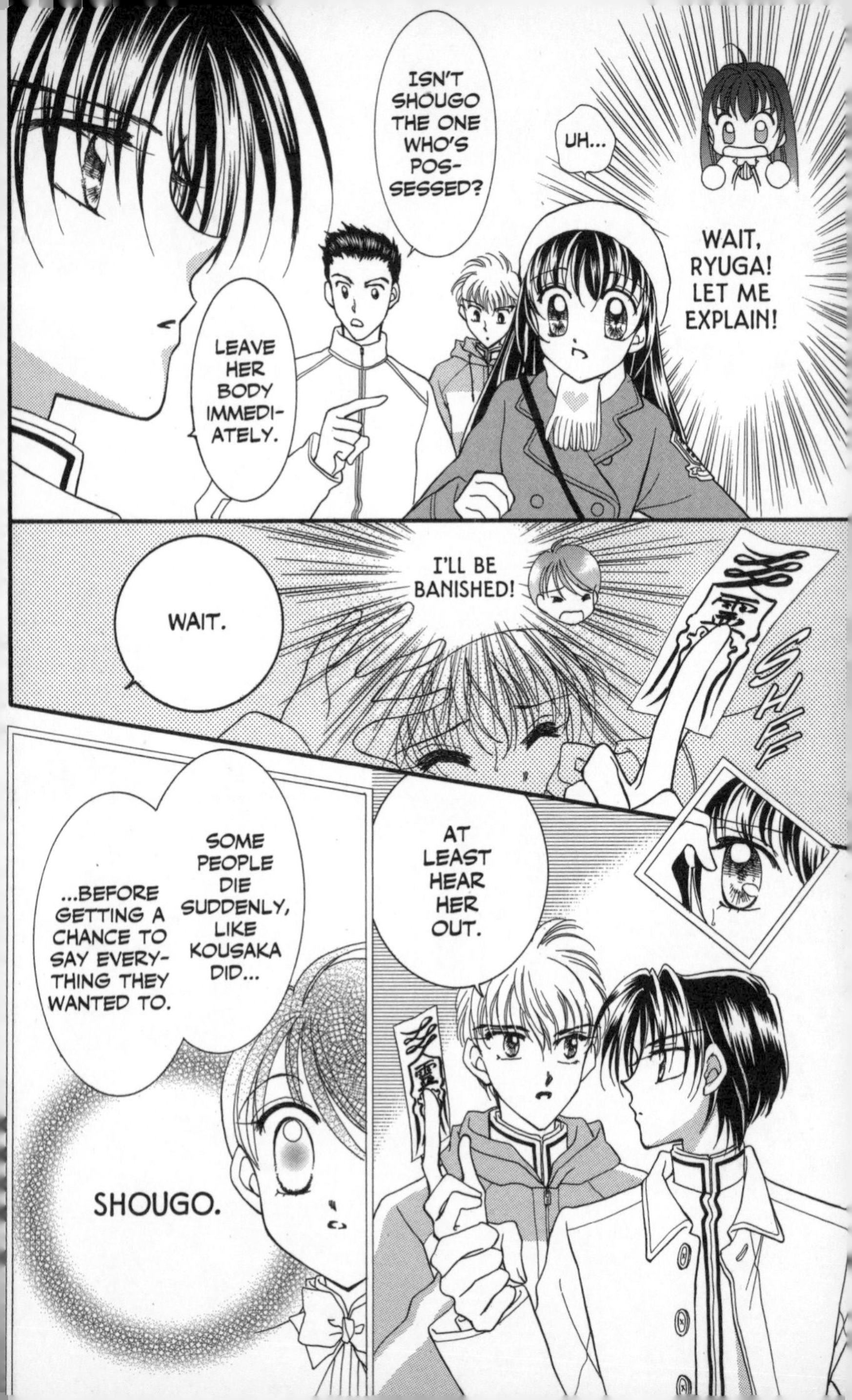
UH...
WAIT, RYUGA! LET ME EXPLAIN!
ISN'T SHOUGO THE ONE WHO'S POS-SESSED?
LEAVE HER BODY IMMEDI-ATELY.
I'LL BE BANISHED!
WAIT.
AT LEAST HEAR HER OUT.
SOME PEOPLE DIE SUDDENLY, LIKE KOUSAKA DID...
...BEFORE GETTING A CHANCE TO SAY EVERY-THING THEY WANTED TO.
SHOUGO.

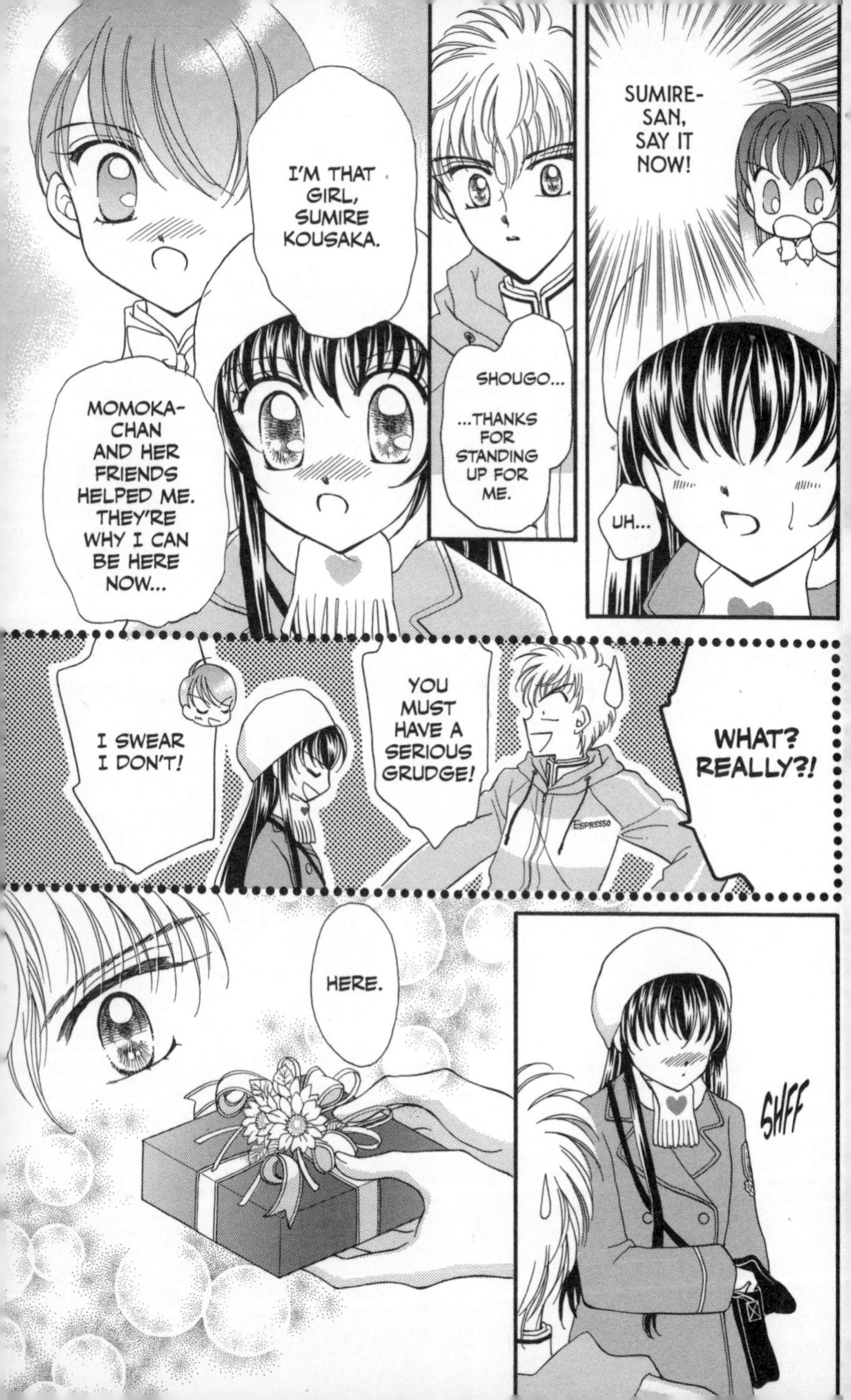
SUMIRE-SAN, SAY IT NOW!
UH...
SHOUGO...
...THANKS FOR STANDING UP FOR ME.
I'M THAT GIRL, SUMIRE KOUSAKA.
MOMOKA-CHAN AND HER FRIENDS HELPED ME. THEY'RE WHY I CAN BE HERE NOW...
WHAT? REALLY?!
YOU MUST HAVE A SERIOUS GRUDGE!
ESPRESSO
I SWEAR I DON'T!
SHFF
HERE.

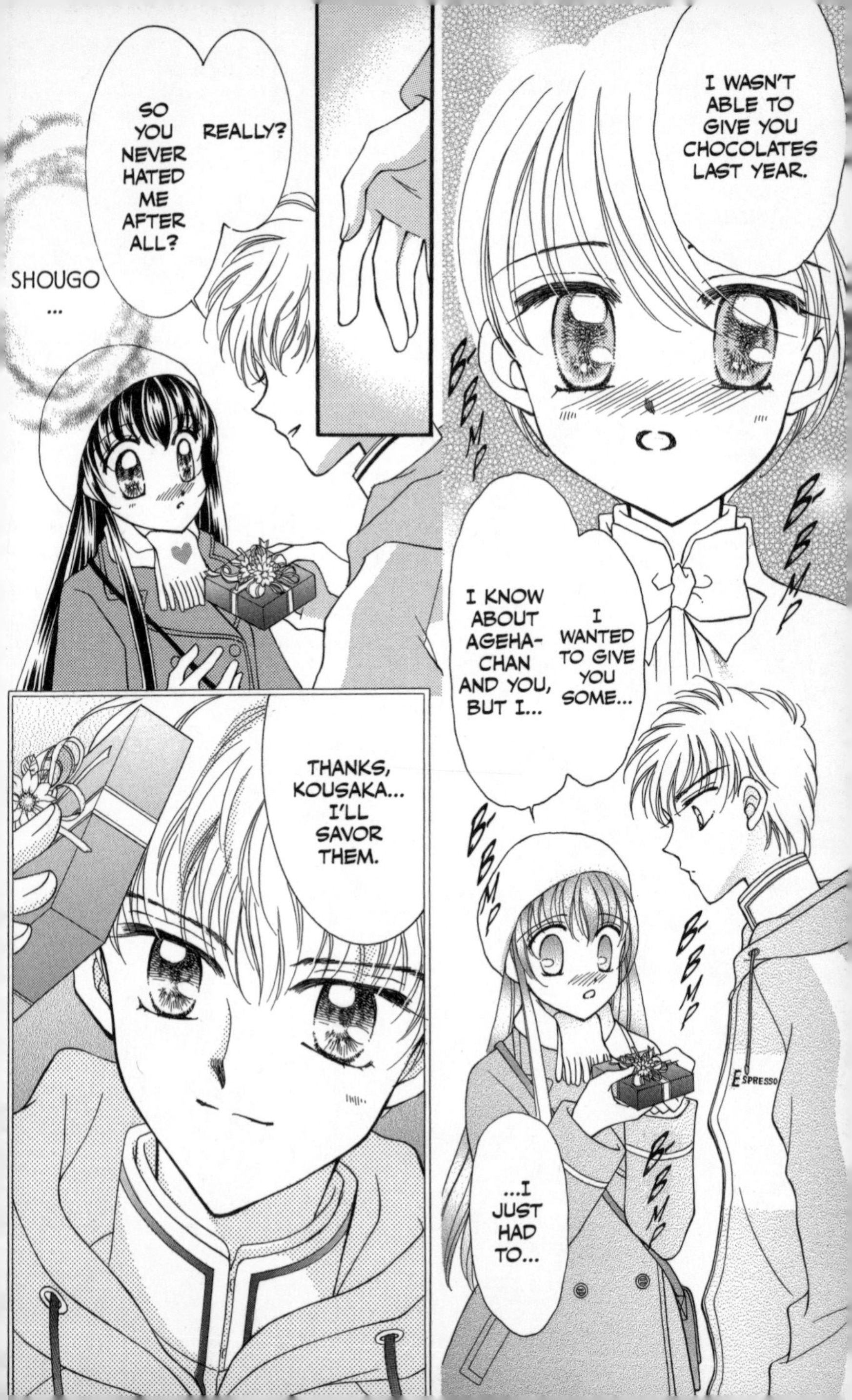
I WASN'T ABLE TO GIVE YOU CHOCOLATES LAST YEAR.
I KNOW ABOUT AGEHA-CHAN AND YOU, BUT I...
I WANTED TO GIVE YOU SOME...
...I JUST HAD TO...
SO YOU NEVER HATED ME AFTER ALL?
REALLY?
SHOUGO...
THANKS, KOUSAKA... I'LL SAVOR THEM.
ESPRESSO

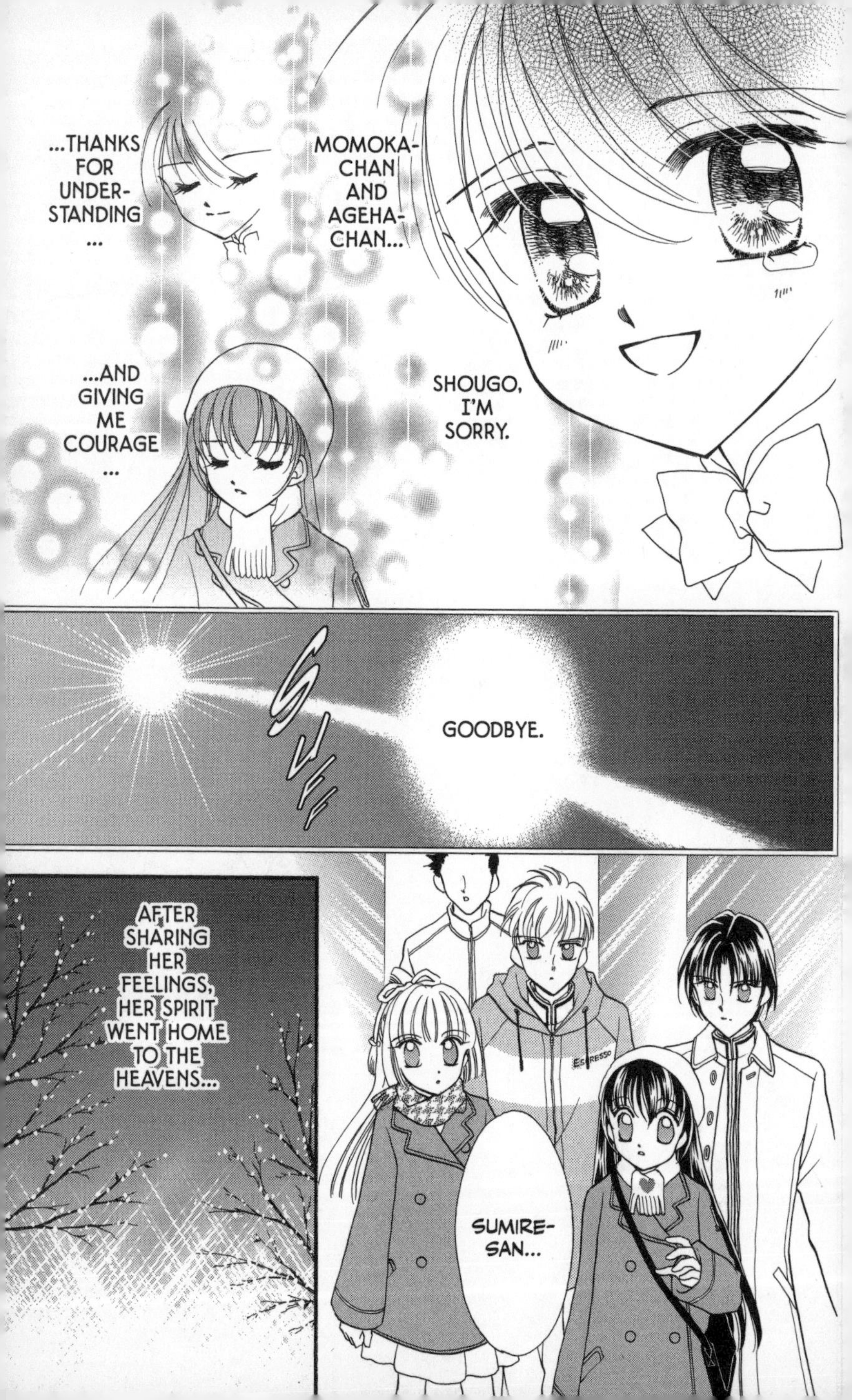
MOMOKA-CHAN AND AGEHA-CHAN...
...THANKS FOR UNDER-STANDING...
...AND GIVING ME COURAGE...
SHOUGO, I'M SORRY.
GOODBYE.
SUMIRE-SAN...
AFTER SHARING HER FEELINGS, HER SPIRIT WENT HOME TO THE HEAVENS...

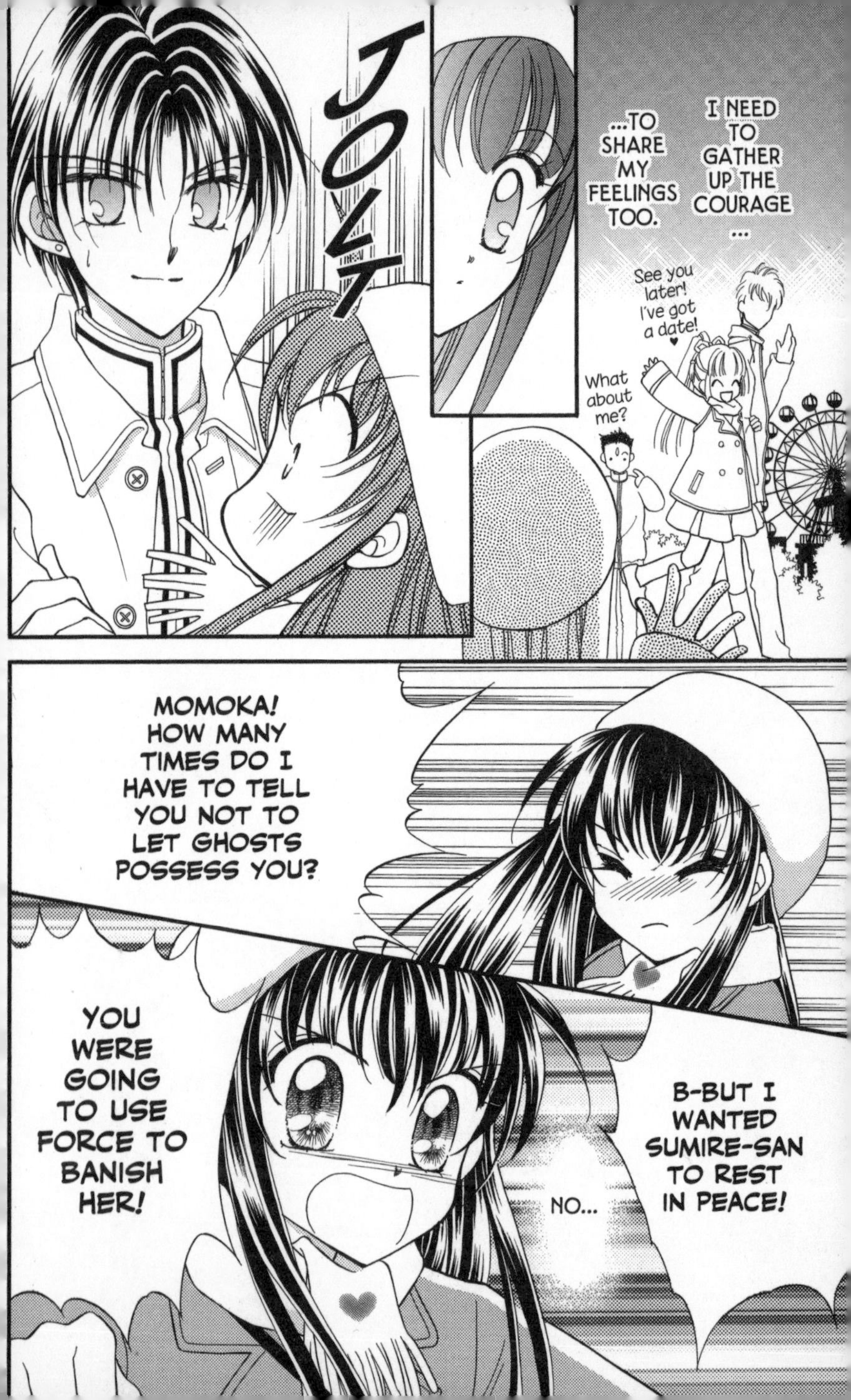
I NEED TO GATHER UP THE COURAGE...
...TO SHARE MY FEELINGS TOO.
See you later! I've got a date! ♥
What about me?
JOLT
MOMOKA! HOW MANY TIMES DO I HAVE TO TELL YOU NOT TO LET GHOSTS POSSESS YOU?
B-BUT I WANTED SUMIRE-SAN TO REST IN PEACE!
NO...
YOU WERE GOING TO USE FORCE TO BANISH HER!

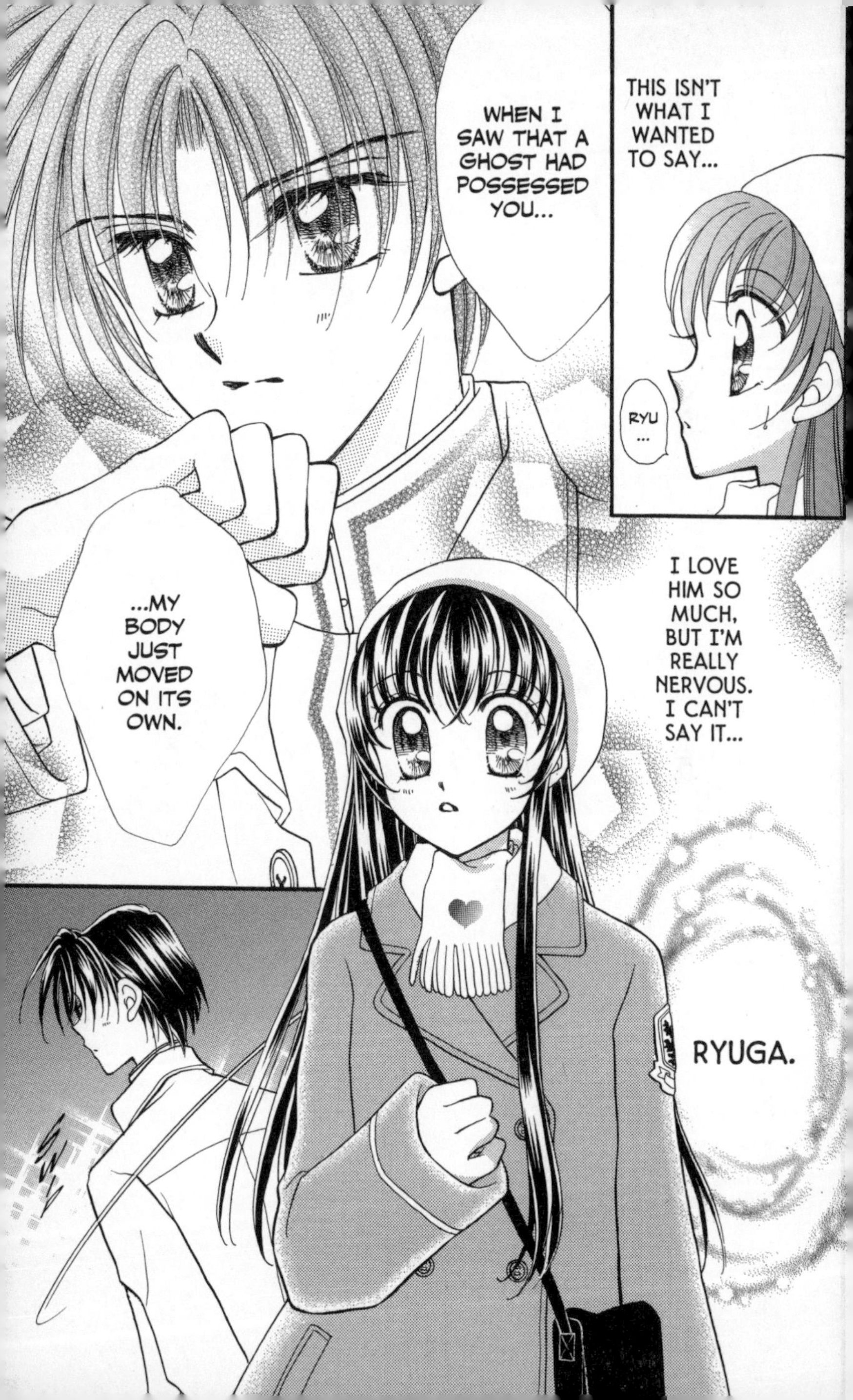
THIS ISN'T WHAT I WANTED TO SAY...
RYU ...
WHEN I SAW THAT A GHOST HAD POSSESSED YOU...
...MY BODY JUST MOVED ON ITS OWN.
I LOVE HIM SO MUCH, BUT I'M REALLY NERVOUS. I CAN'T SAY IT...
RYUGA.

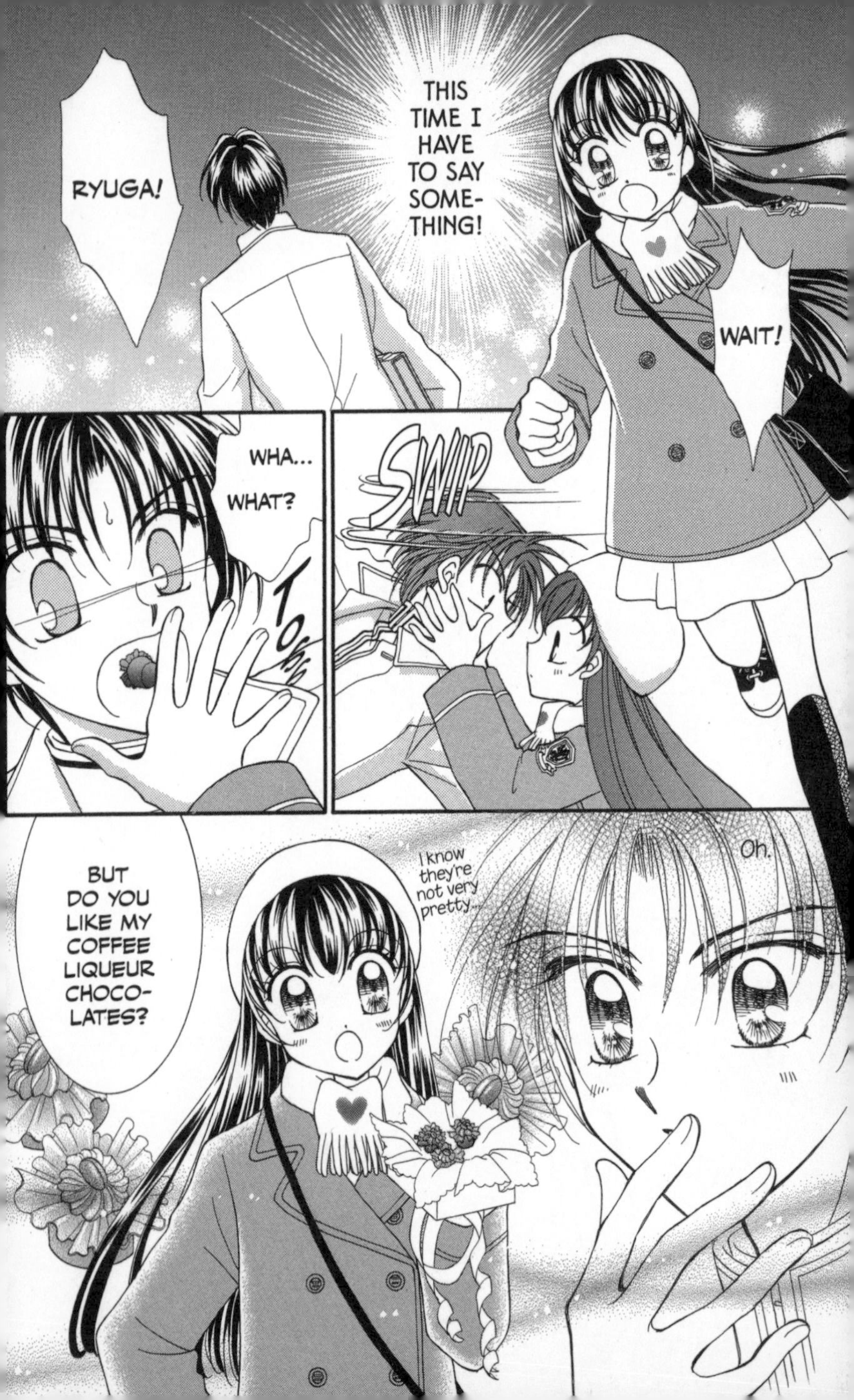
THIS TIME I HAVE TO SAY SOME-THING!
WAIT!
RYUGA!
SWIP
WHA...
WHAT?
TOKK
Oh.
I know they're not very pretty...
BUT DO YOU LIKE MY COFFEE LIQUEUR CHOCO-LATES?

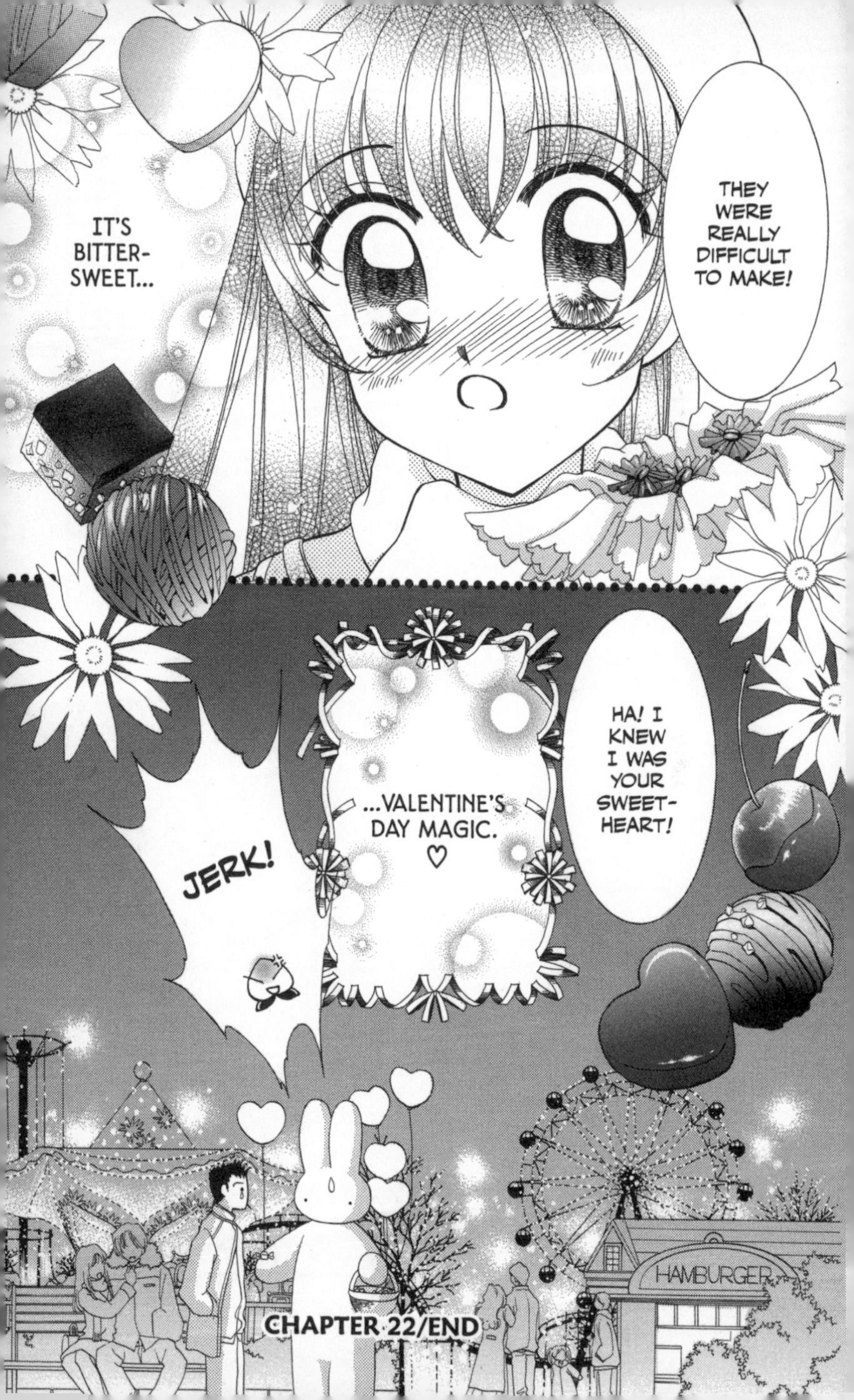
THEY WERE REALLY DIFFICULT TO MAKE!
IT'S BITTER-SWEET...
HA! I KNEW I WAS YOUR SWEET-HEART!
...VALENTINE'S DAY MAGIC. ♡
JERK!
HAMBURGER
CHAPTER 22/END

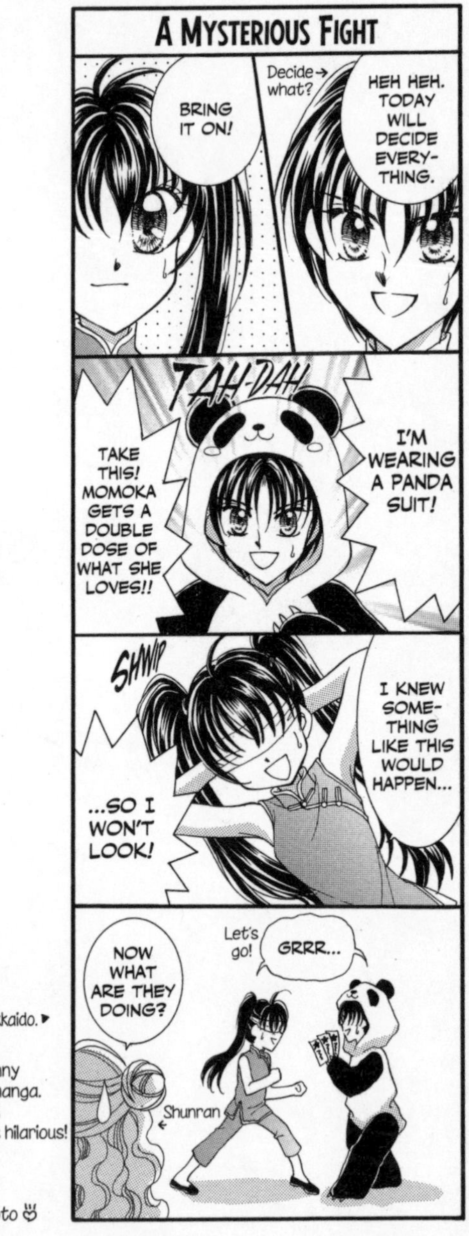
A MYSTERIOUS FIGHT
HEH HEH. TODAY WILL DECIDE EVERYTHING.
Decide→ what?
BRING IT ON!
TAH-DAH
I'M WEARING A PANDA SUIT!
TAKE THIS! MOMOKA GETS A DOUBLE DOSE OF WHAT SHE LOVES!!
SHWIP
I KNEW SOMETHING LIKE THIS WOULD HAPPEN...
...SO I WON'T LOOK!
GRRR...
Let's go!
NOW WHAT ARE THEY DOING?
Shunran

This is a strip written by Marie Yano from Hokkaido. ▸

The comic strips fans send me are so funny that I redrew this and included it in the manga. (These are the same panels and drawings Marie-chan did. Thanks!) Their silly fight is hilarious! As a thank-you gift, I'll send you some *St.♥Dragon Girl* goods!

Matsumoto

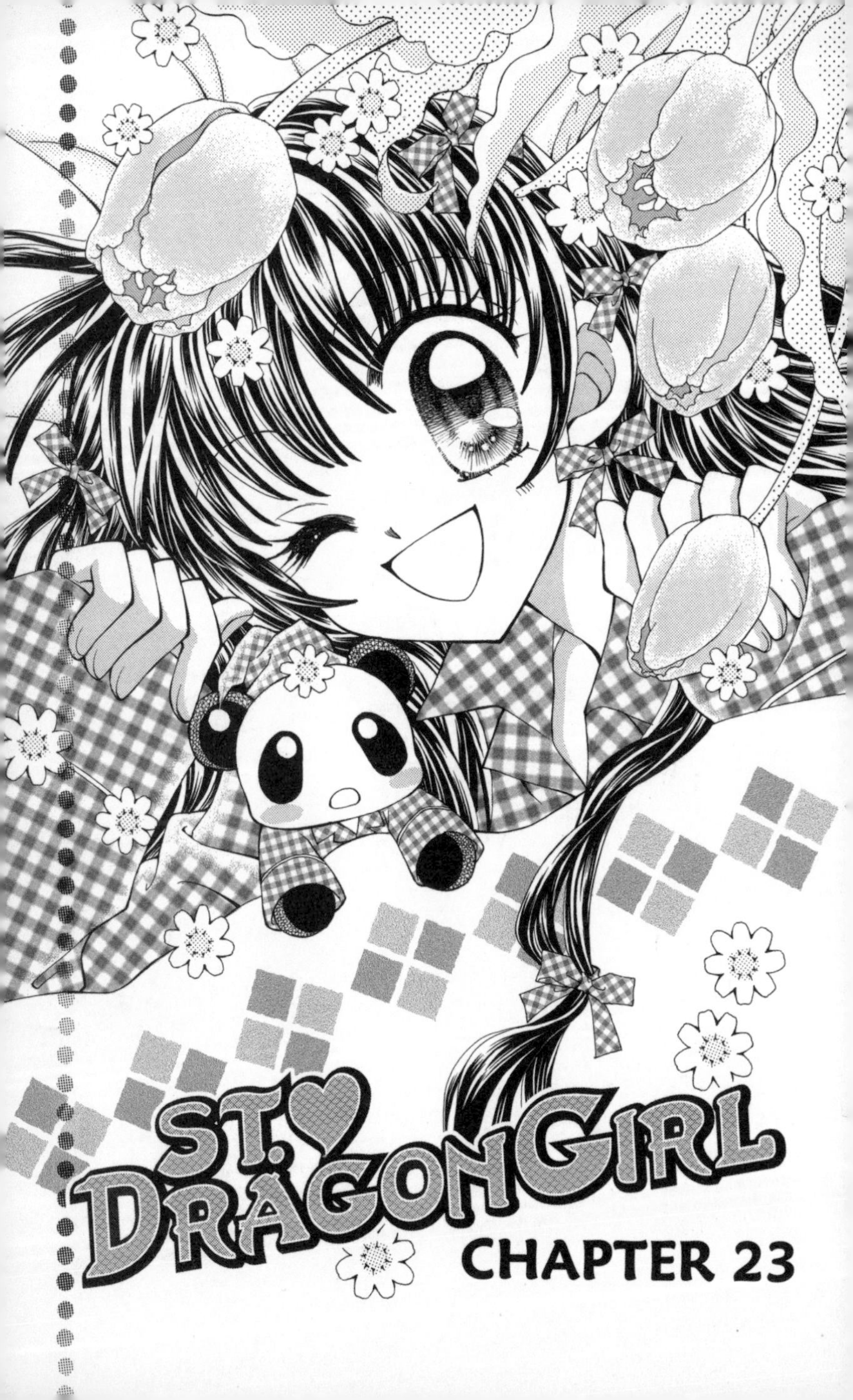
ST. DRAGON GIRL
CHAPTER 23

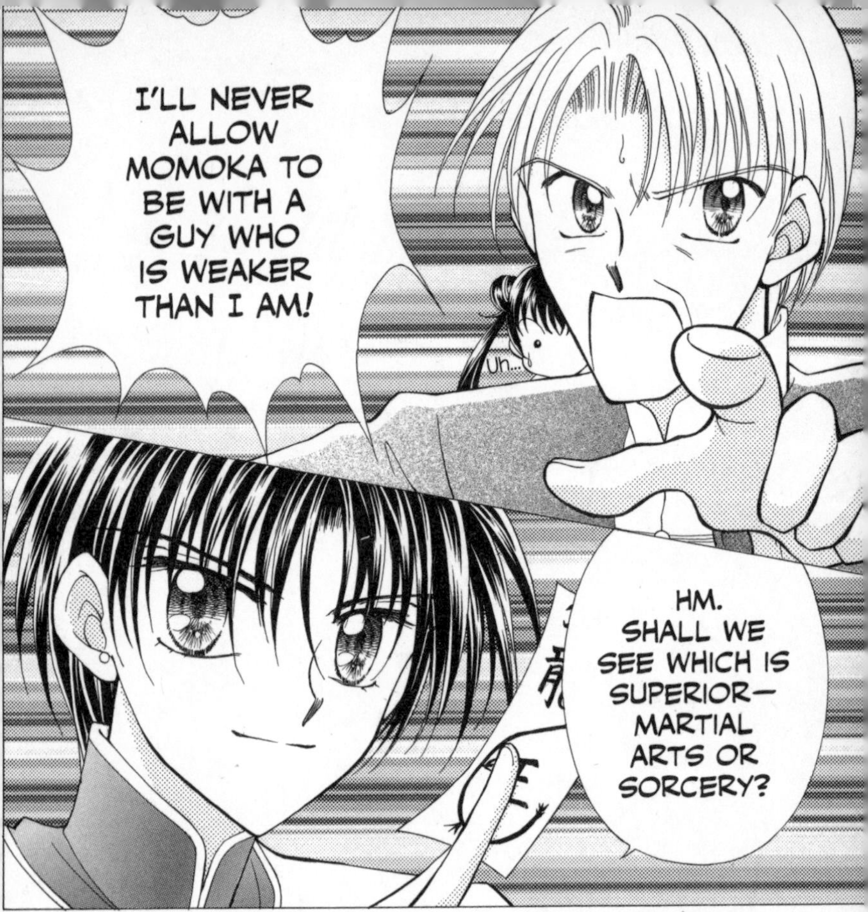
I'LL NEVER ALLOW MOMOKA TO BE WITH A GUY WHO IS WEAKER THAN I AM!
Uh...
HM. SHALL WE SEE WHICH IS SUPERIOR— MARTIAL ARTS OR SORCERY?

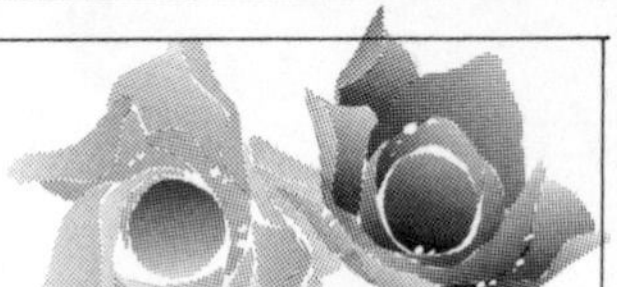

No matter how many times I write the kanji for "rose," I can never remember it. That's why I just write it in katakana. I love that flower. This year I bought some pink roses for my garden. A lot of them bloomed, so I had fun with them and put petals in my bath. A rose petal bath smells so good, and it makes you feel gorgeous! It's a pain to clean up after though! Roses are usually drawn around Ryuga in this manga!

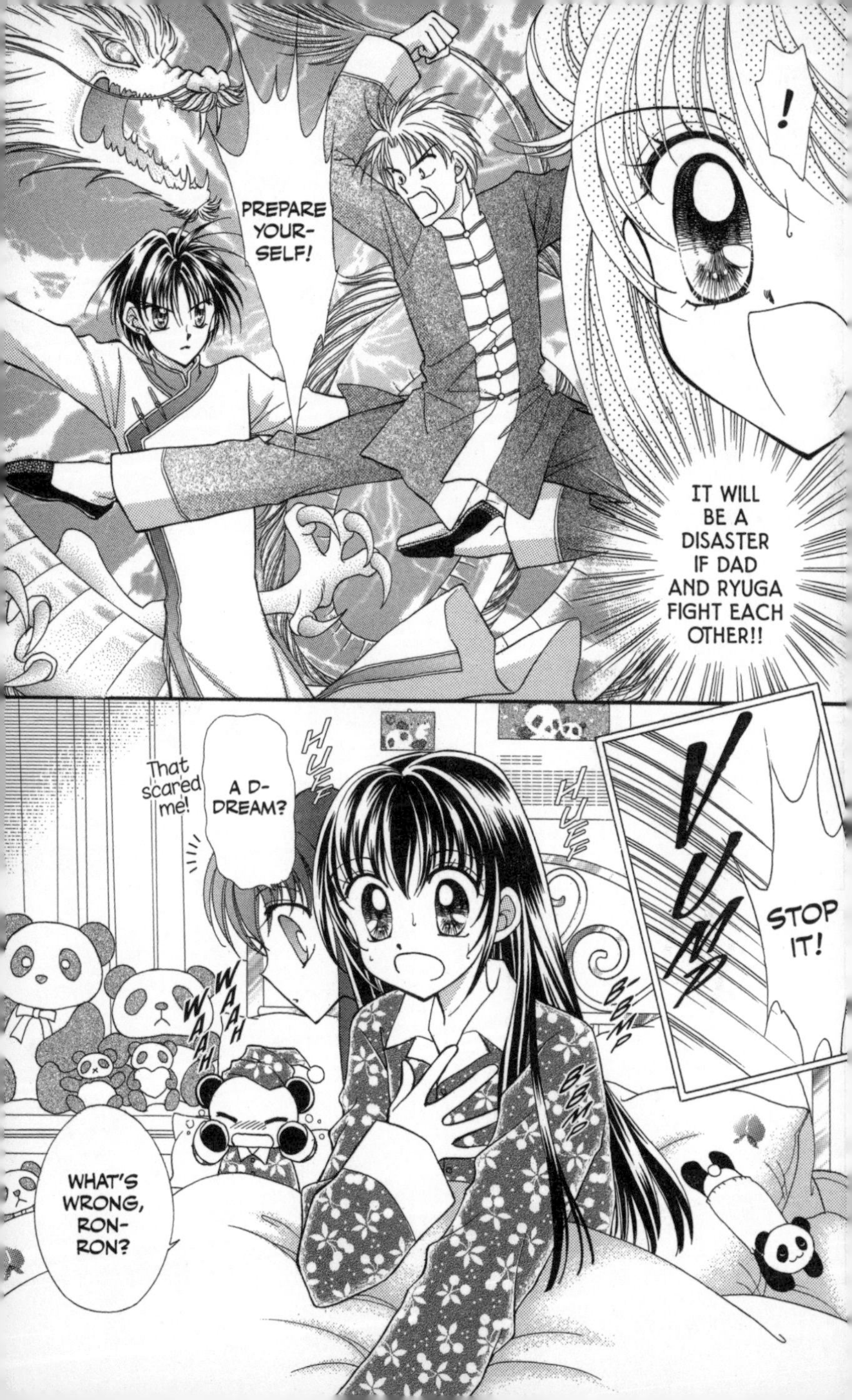
!
PREPARE YOUR-SELF!
IT WILL BE A DISASTER IF DAD AND RYUGA FIGHT EACH OTHER!!
STOP IT!
A D-DREAM?
That scared me!
WHAT'S WRONG, RON-RON?

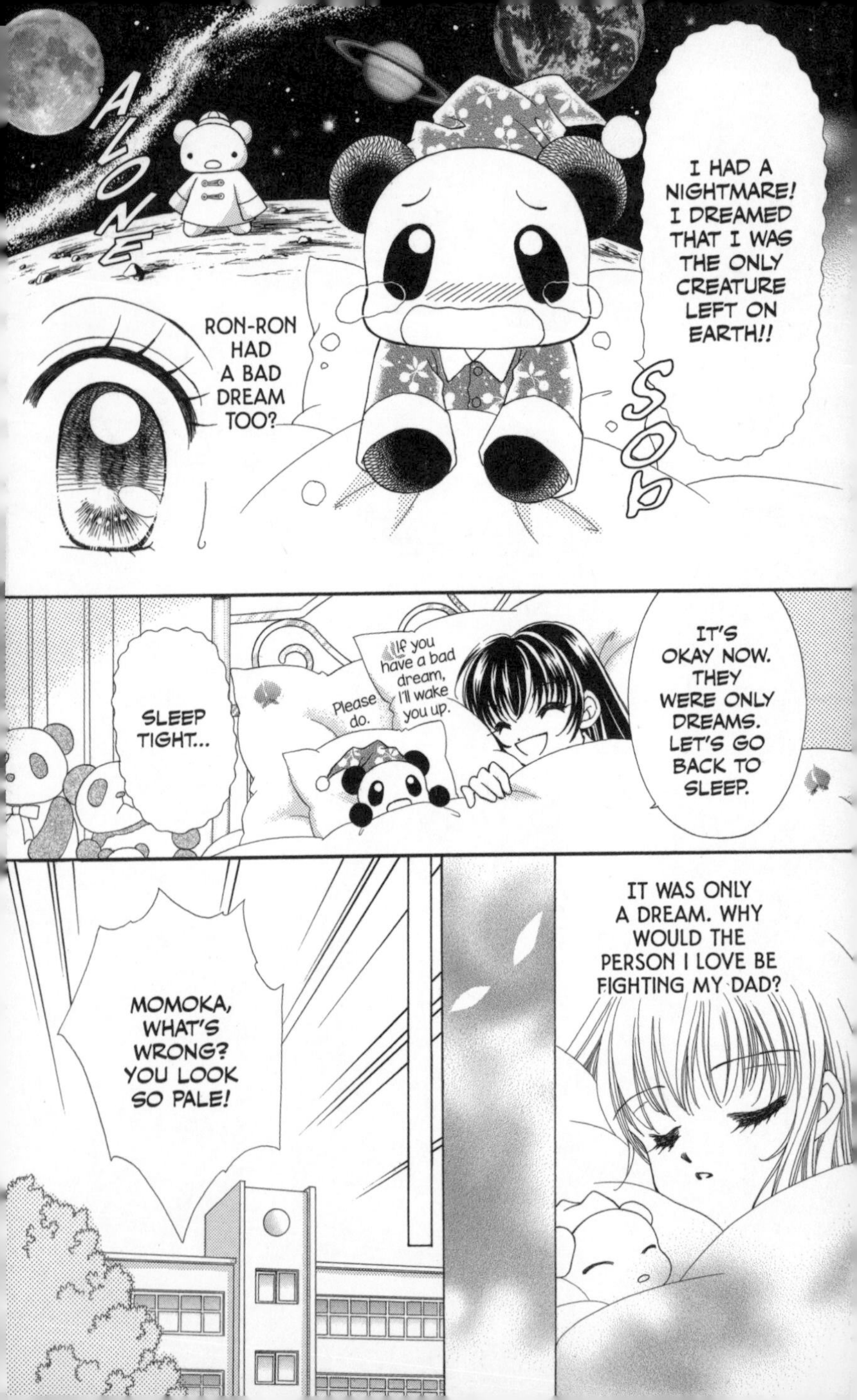
I HAD A NIGHTMARE! I DREAMED THAT I WAS THE ONLY CREATURE LEFT ON EARTH!!
ALONE
SOB
RON-RON HAD A BAD DREAM TOO?
IT'S OKAY NOW. THEY WERE ONLY DREAMS. LET'S GO BACK TO SLEEP.
If you have a bad dream, I'll wake you up.
Please do.
SLEEP TIGHT...
IT WAS ONLY A DREAM. WHY WOULD THE PERSON I LOVE BE FIGHTING MY DAD?
MOMOKA, WHAT'S WRONG? YOU LOOK SO PALE!

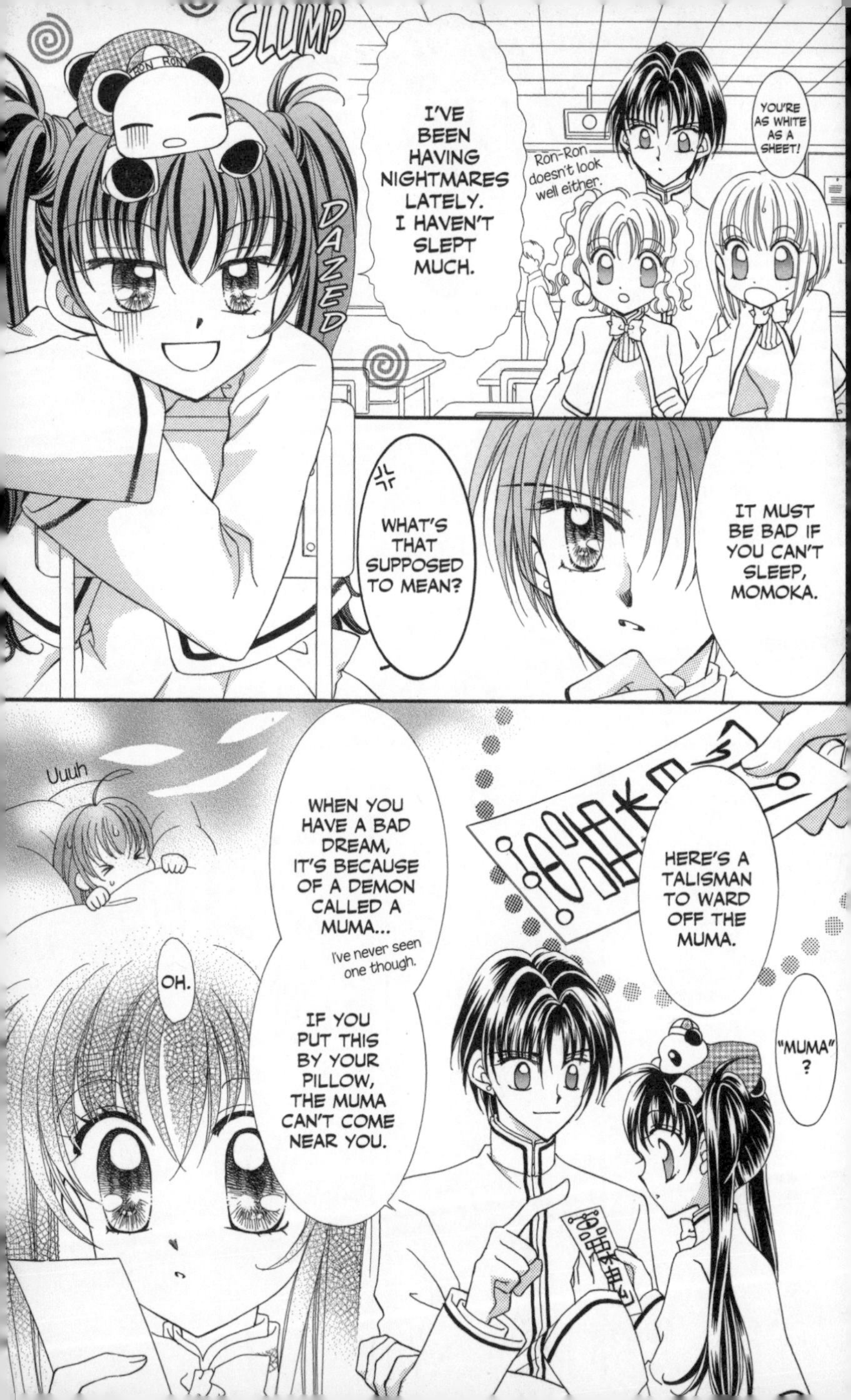
YOU'RE AS WHITE AS A SHEET!
Ron-Ron doesn't look well either.
SLUMP
I'VE BEEN HAVING NIGHTMARES LATELY. I HAVEN'T SLEPT MUCH.
DAZED
IT MUST BE BAD IF YOU CAN'T SLEEP, MOMOKA.
WHAT'S THAT SUPPOSED TO MEAN?
HERE'S A TALISMAN TO WARD OFF THE MUMA.
"MUMA"?
WHEN YOU HAVE A BAD DREAM, IT'S BECAUSE OF A DEMON CALLED A MUMA...
I've never seen one though.
IF YOU PUT THIS BY YOUR PILLOW, THE MUMA CAN'T COME NEAR YOU.
OH.
Uuuh

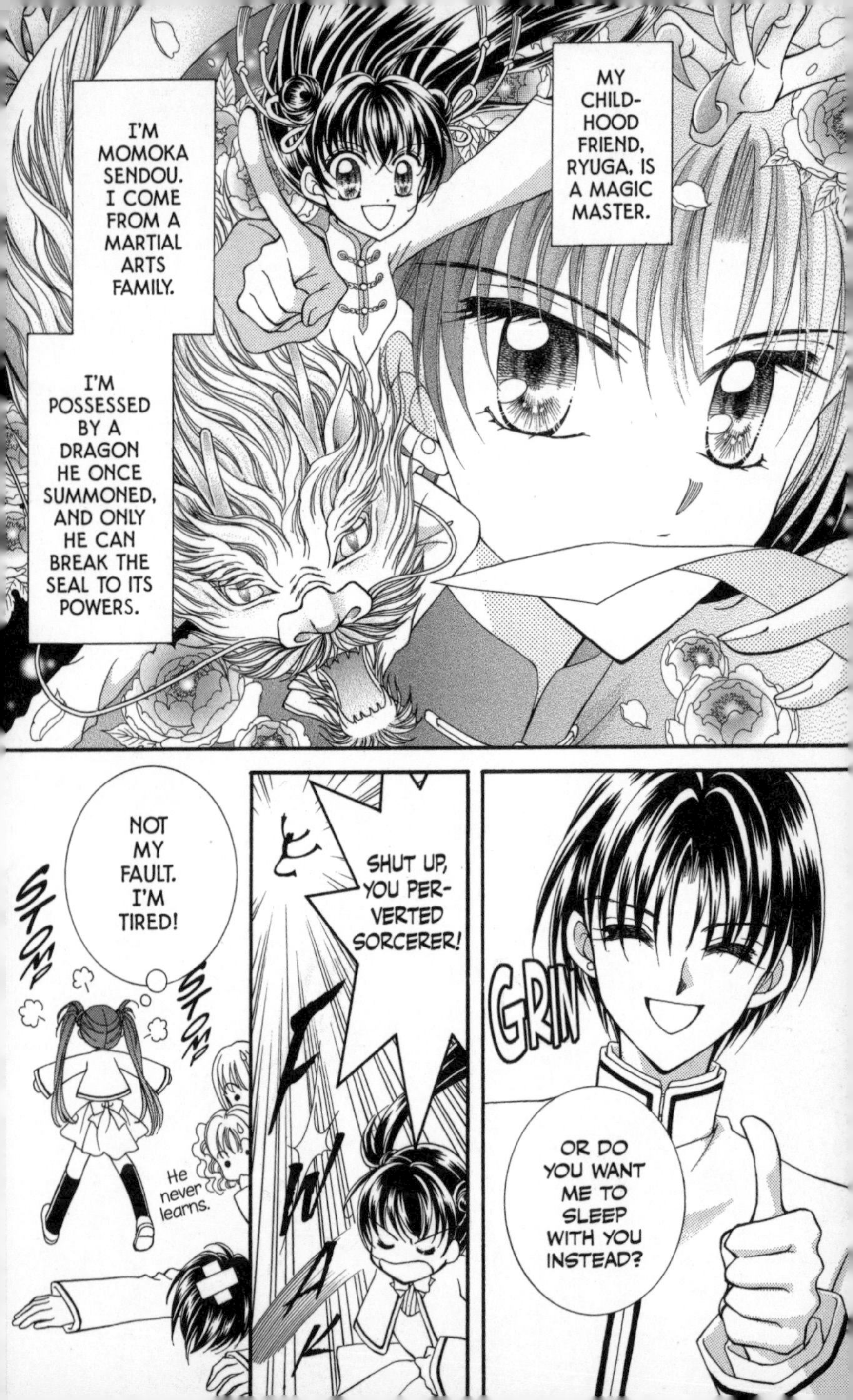
MY CHILD-HOOD FRIEND, RYUGA, IS A MAGIC MASTER.
I'M MOMOKA SENDOU. I COME FROM A MARTIAL ARTS FAMILY.
I'M POSSESSED BY A DRAGON HE ONCE SUMMONED, AND ONLY HE CAN BREAK THE SEAL TO ITS POWERS.
GRIN
OR DO YOU WANT ME TO SLEEP WITH YOU INSTEAD?
SHUT UP, YOU PER-VERTED SORCERER!
FWAK
NOT MY FAULT. I'M TIRED!
STOMP
STOMP
He never learns.

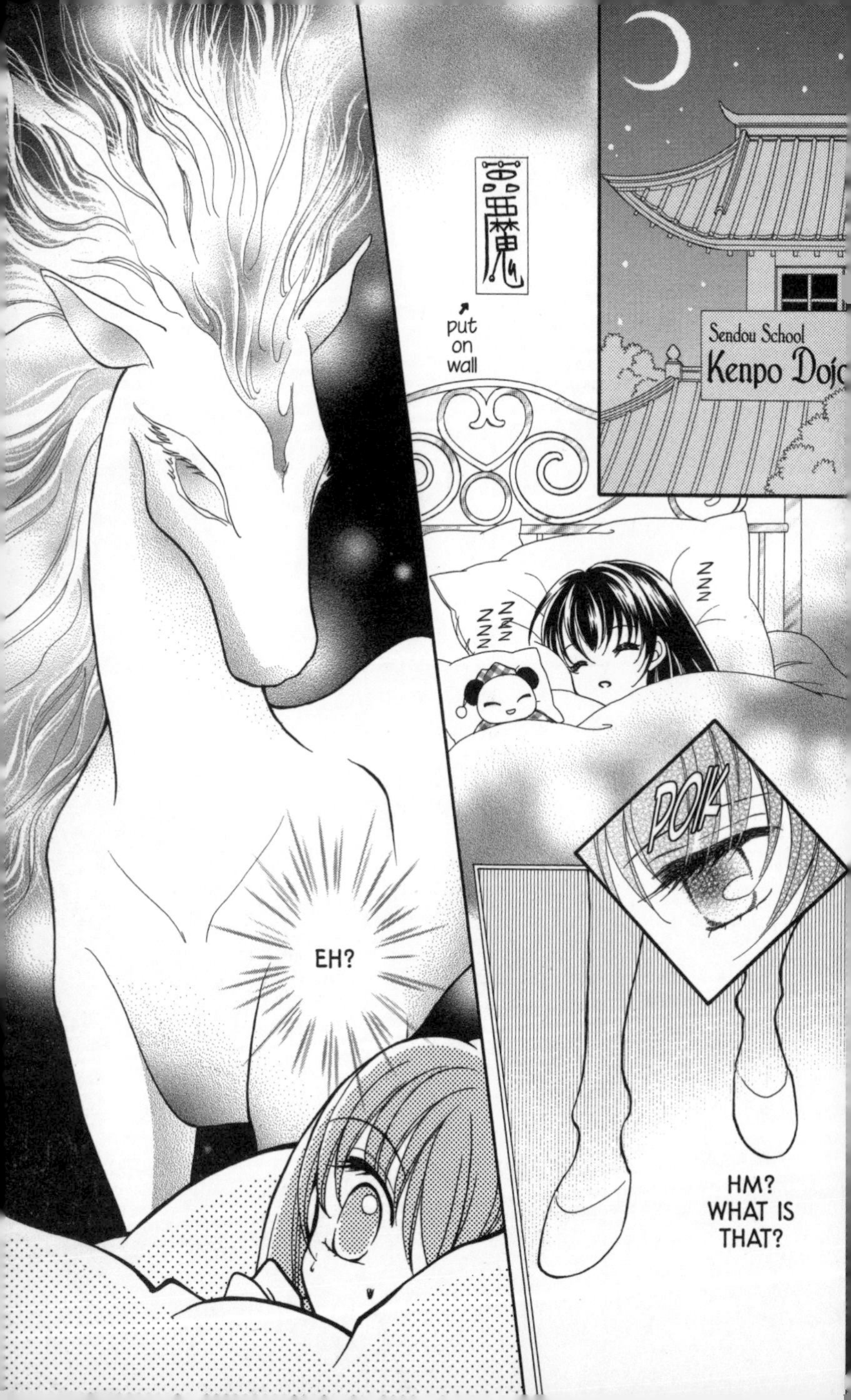
Sendou School
Kenpo Doj
魔
put on wall
ZZZ
ZZZ
ZZZ
POIK
HM? WHAT IS THAT?
EH?

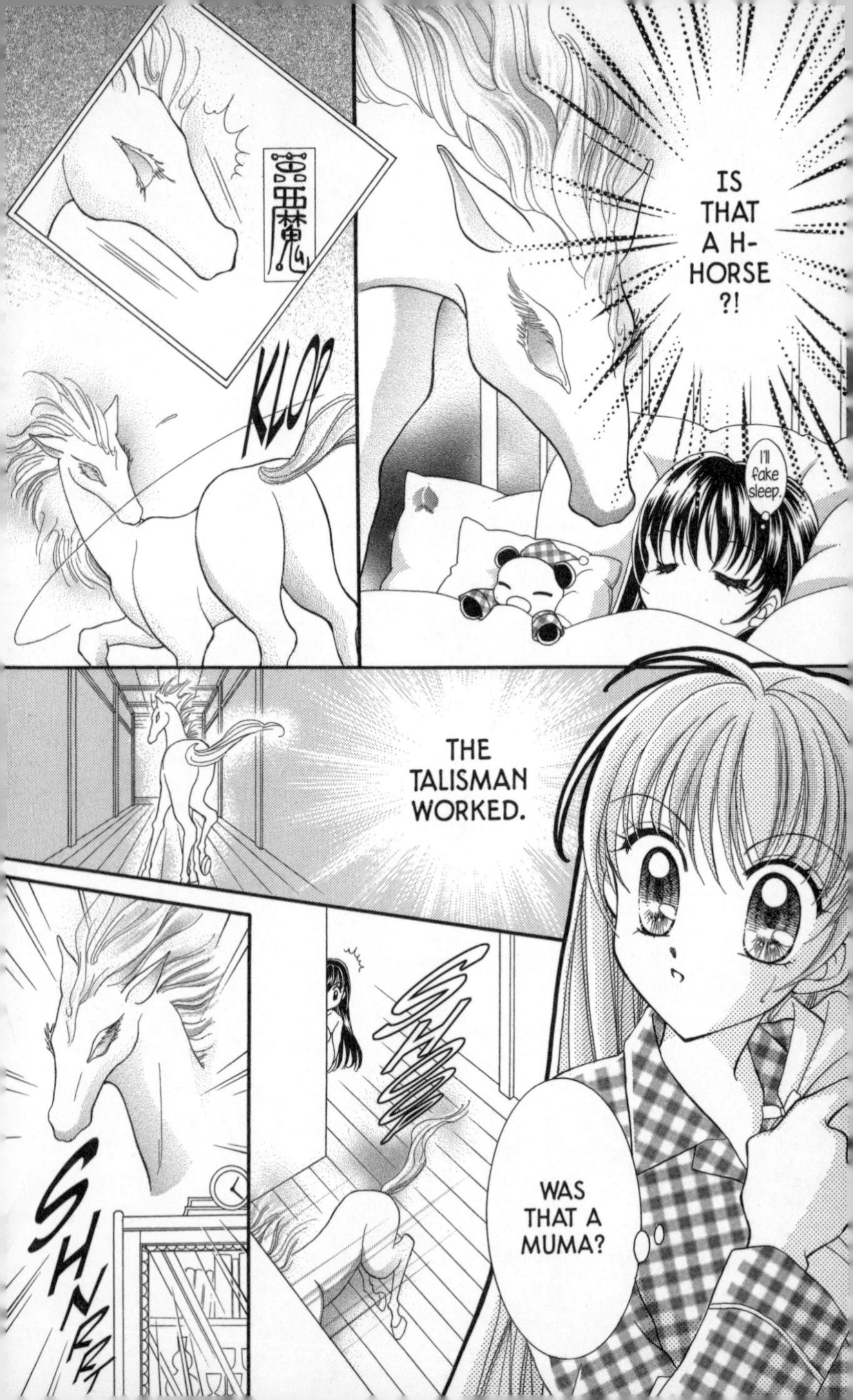
IS THAT A H-HORSE ?!
I'll fake sleep.
KLOP
THE TALISMAN WORKED.
WAS THAT A MUMA?
SHFF

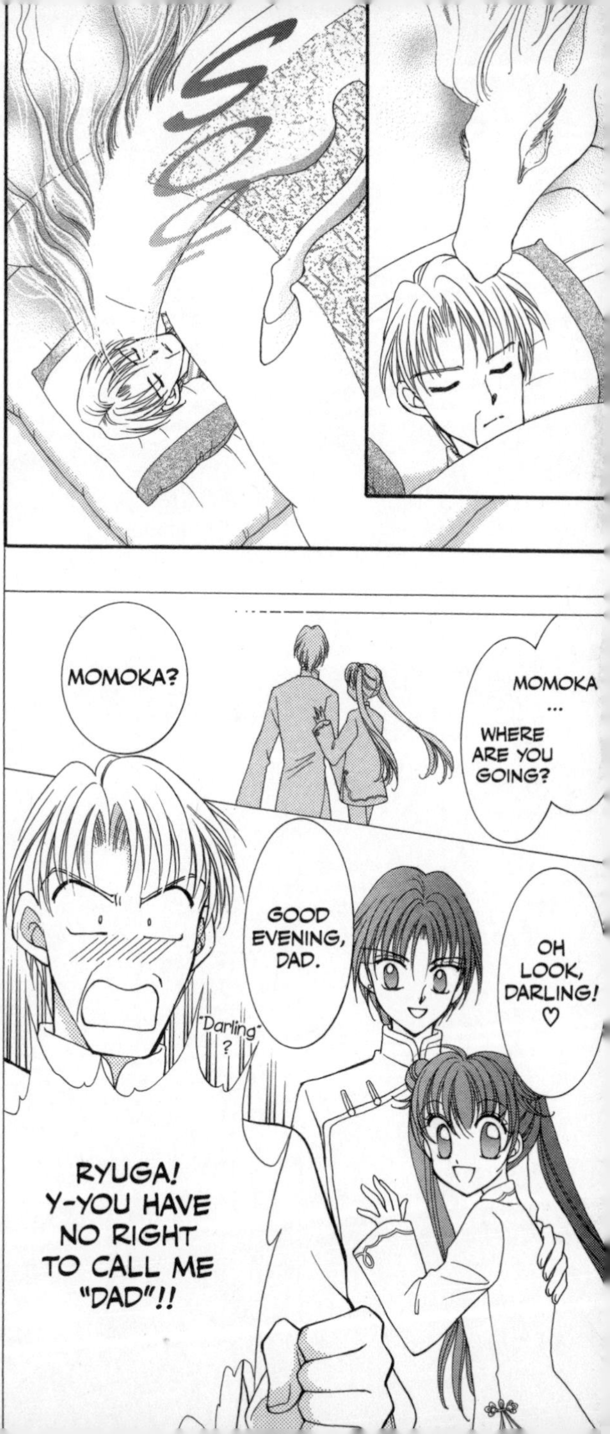
MOMOKA ... WHERE ARE YOU GOING?
MOMOKA?
OH LOOK, DARLING! ♡
GOOD EVENING, DAD.
"Darling"?
RYUGA! Y-YOU HAVE NO RIGHT TO CALL ME "DAD"!!

4

Since I started writing *St.♥Dragon Girl*, I've bought tons of books for research: books on kenpo, sorcery, Chinese architecture... but one-third of them are still untouched.

After I wrote the muma story, the half-read books about sorcery were all around the place, and I saw a page explaining how to get rid of nightmares. It said, "Write your nightmare on a piece of paper, stick it on the wall, and let the sunlight shine on it."

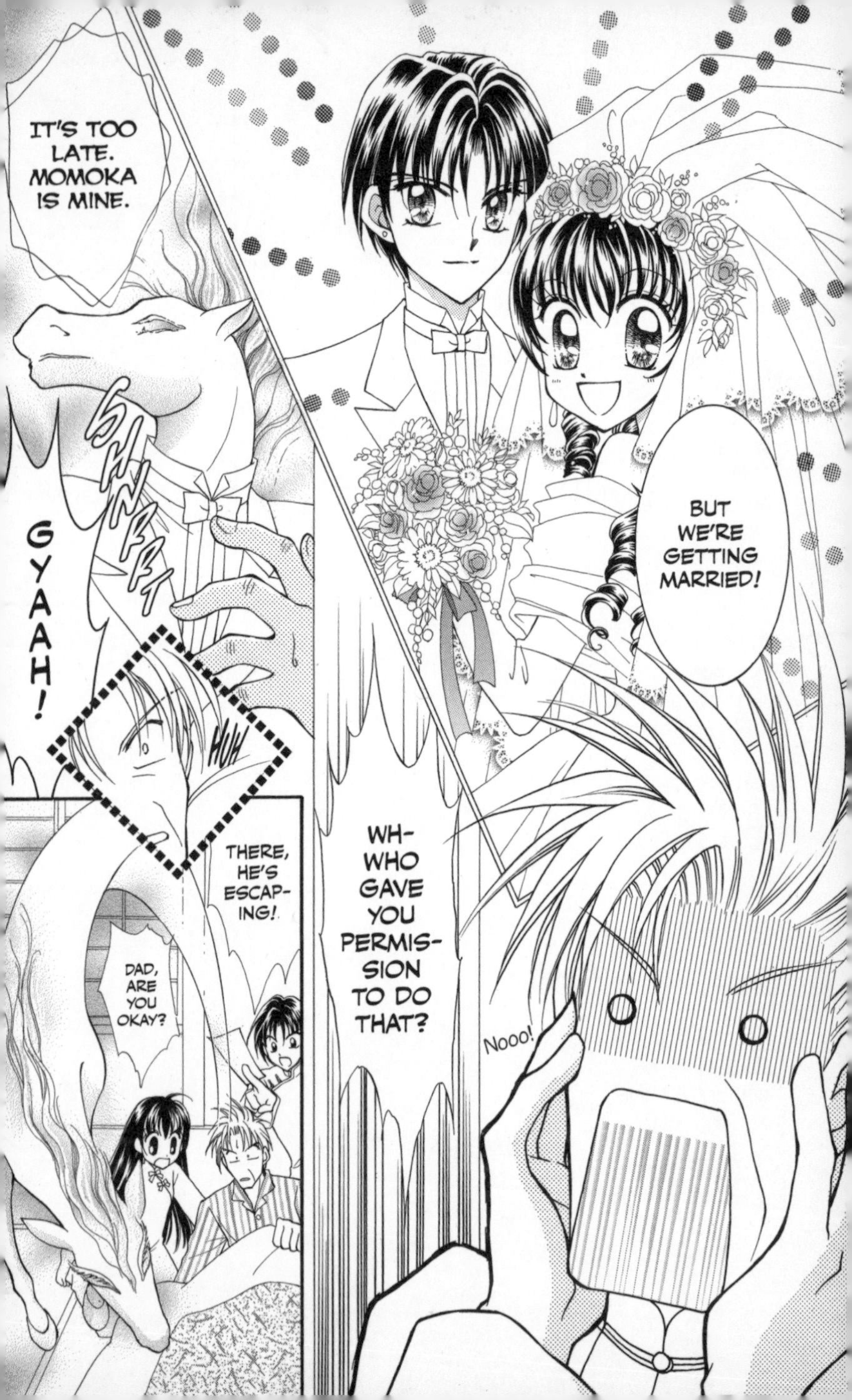
BUT WE'RE GETTING MARRIED!
WH-WHO GAVE YOU PERMISSION TO DO THAT?
Nooo!
IT'S TOO LATE. MOMOKA IS MINE.
SHNFFF
GYAAH!
HUH
THERE, HE'S ESCAPING!
DAD, ARE YOU OKAY?

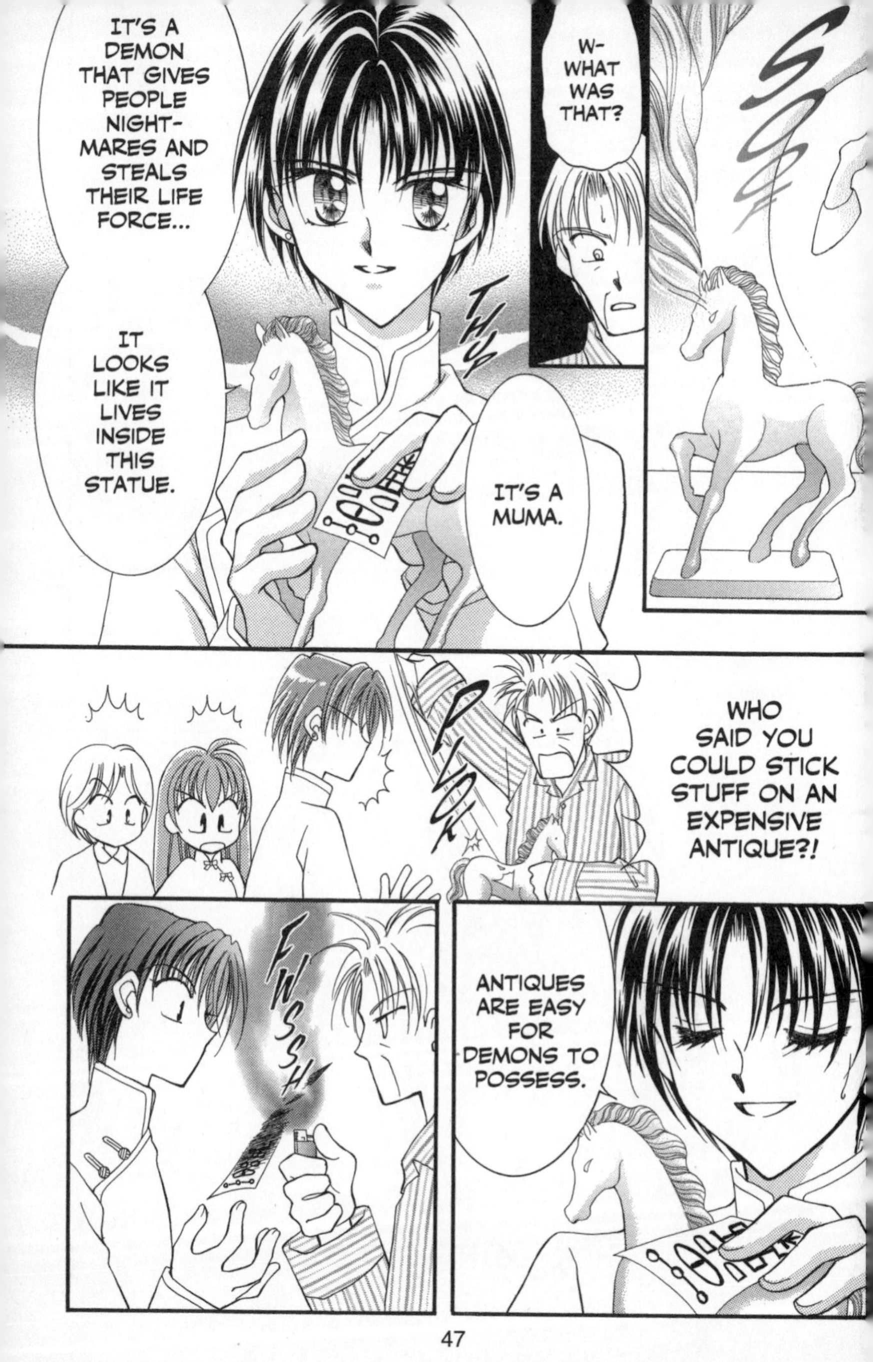
W- WHAT WAS THAT?
IT'S A MUMA.
IT'S A DEMON THAT GIVES PEOPLE NIGHT-MARES AND STEALS THEIR LIFE FORCE...
IT LOOKS LIKE IT LIVES INSIDE THIS STATUE.
WHO SAID YOU COULD STICK STUFF ON AN EXPENSIVE ANTIQUE?!
ANTIQUES ARE EASY FOR DEMONS TO POSSESS.
FWSSH

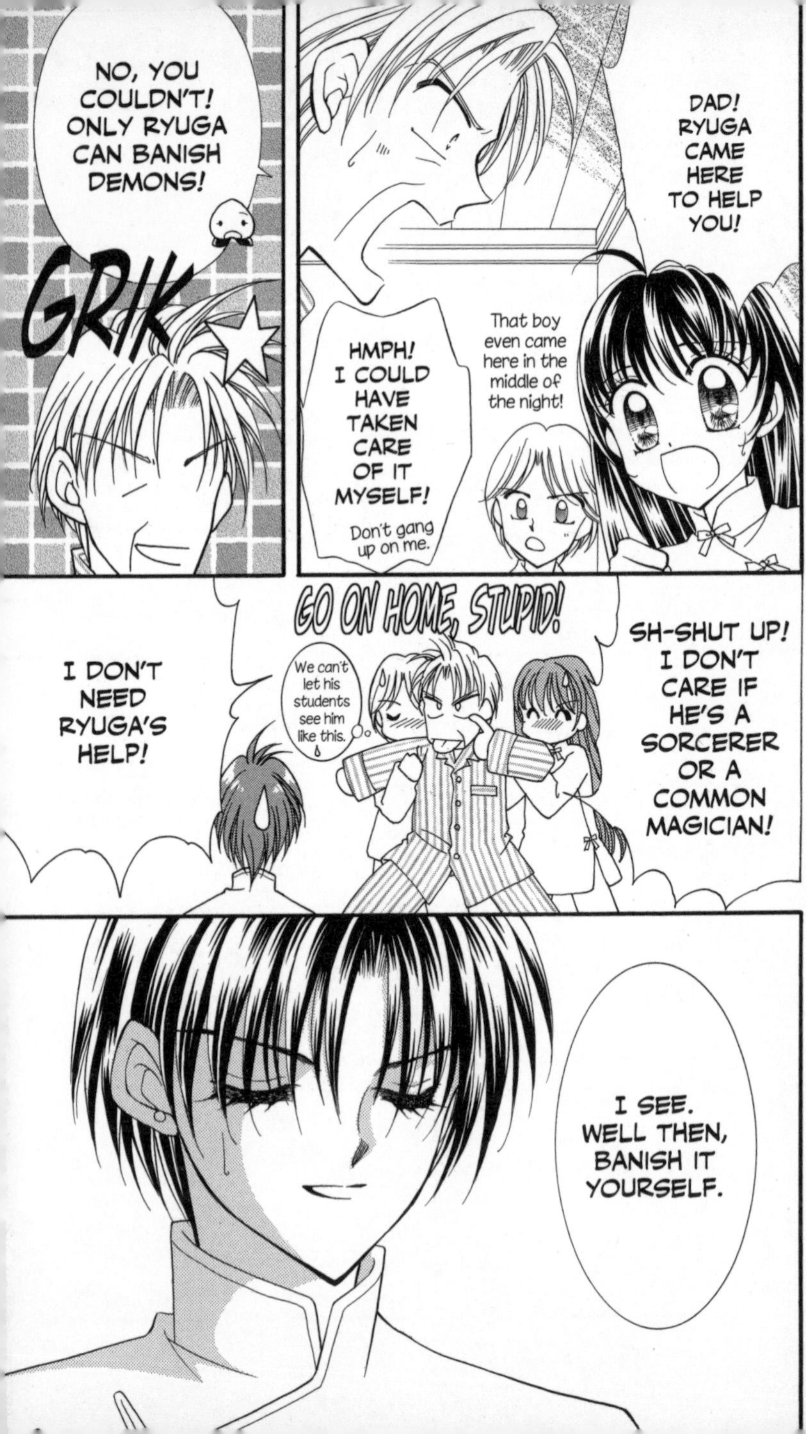
DAD! RYUGA CAME HERE TO HELP YOU!
That boy even came here in the middle of the night!
HMPH! I COULD HAVE TAKEN CARE OF IT MYSELF!
Don't gang up on me.
NO, YOU COULDN'T! ONLY RYUGA CAN BANISH DEMONS!
GRIK
SH-SHUT UP! I DON'T CARE IF HE'S A SORCERER OR A COMMON MAGICIAN!
GO ON HOME, STUPID!
We can't let his students see him like this.
I DON'T NEED RYUGA'S HELP!
I SEE. WELL THEN, BANISH IT YOURSELF.

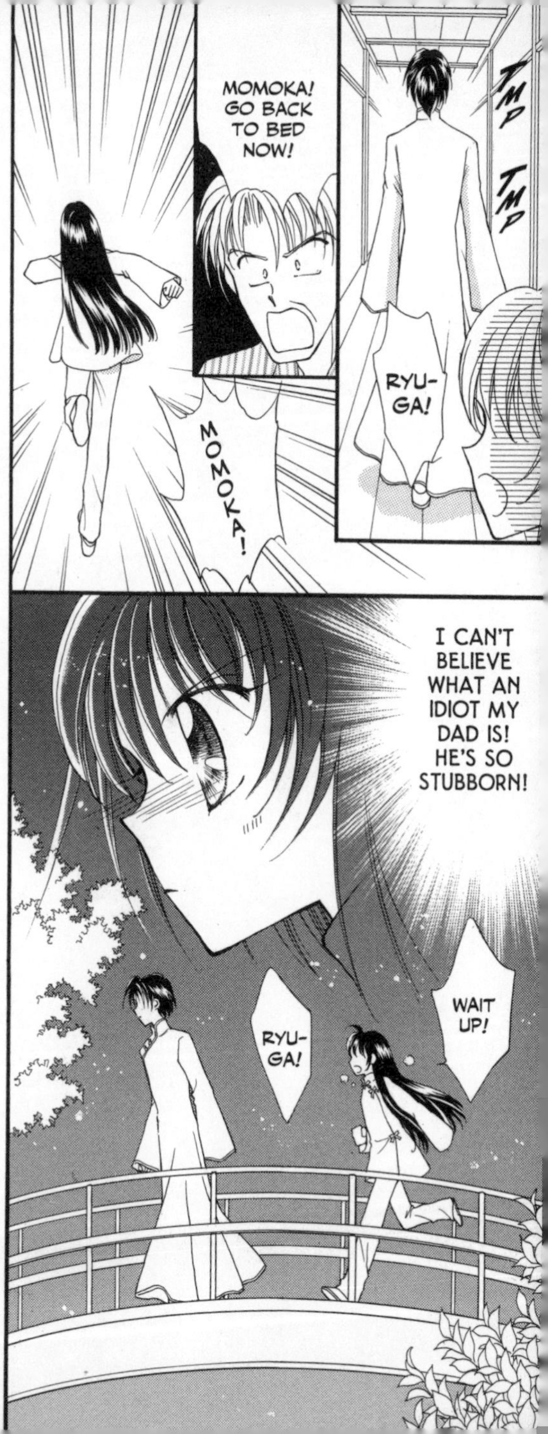
TMP
TMP
RYU-GA!
MOMOKA! GO BACK TO BED NOW!
MOMOKA!
I CAN'T BELIEVE WHAT AN IDIOT MY DAD IS! HE'S SO STUBBORN!
WAIT UP!
RYU-GA!

5

It turns out the way Ryuga banished the muma was kind of similar. The book was pretty timely and interesting, but I wish I had read it before I wrote the story! The book also suggested writing the dream on paper and putting it in a place others could see it. As soon as someone else sees it, it is supposed to leave. When I have another nightmare I might try it, but I think I'll keep my good dreams to myself! Because it's the year of the horse, I decided to draw a Pegasus! I really love horses! ♡

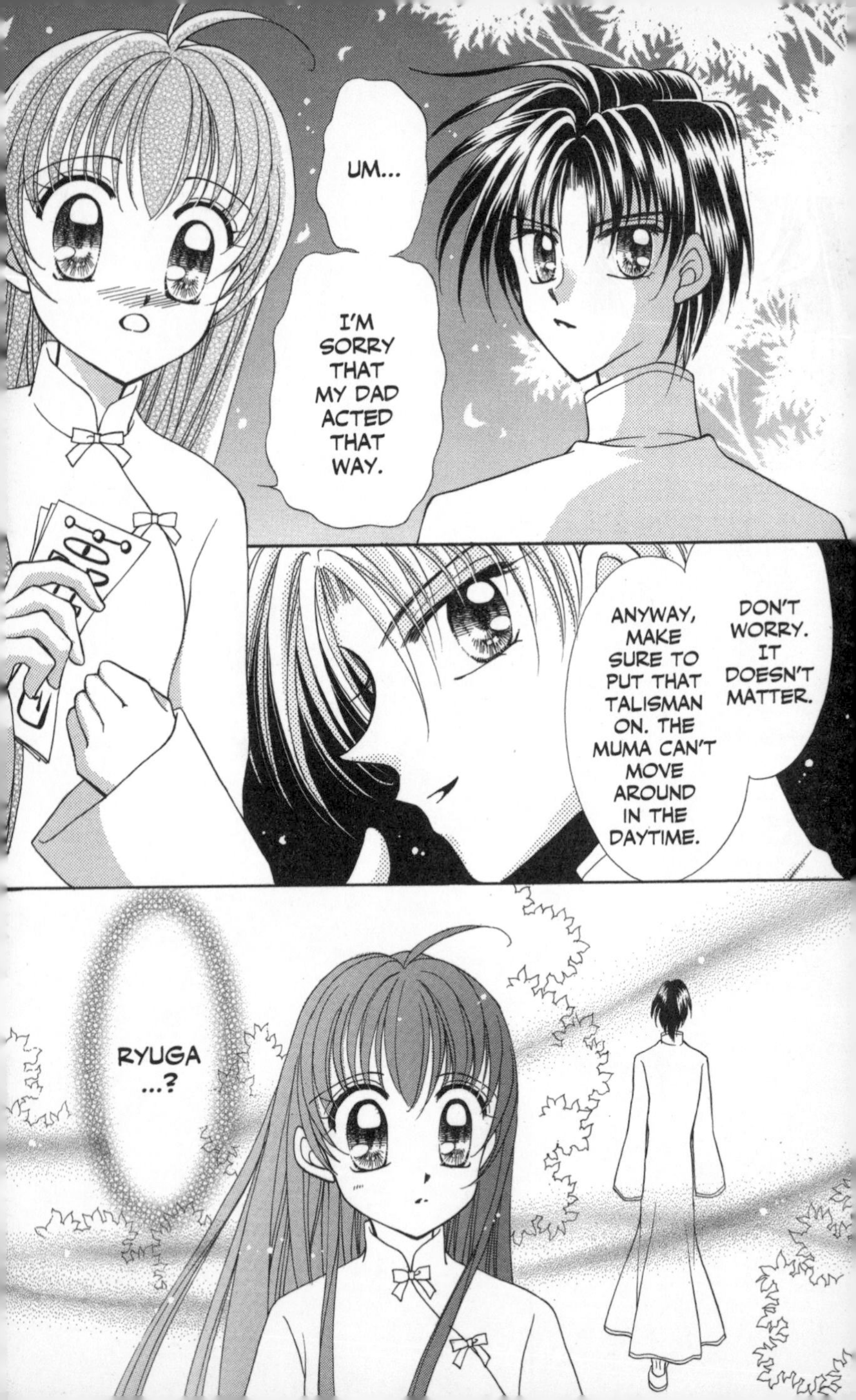
UM...
I'M SORRY THAT MY DAD ACTED THAT WAY.
DON'T WORRY. IT DOESN'T MATTER.
ANYWAY, MAKE SURE TO PUT THAT TALISMAN ON. THE MUMA CAN'T MOVE AROUND IN THE DAYTIME.
RYUGA ...?

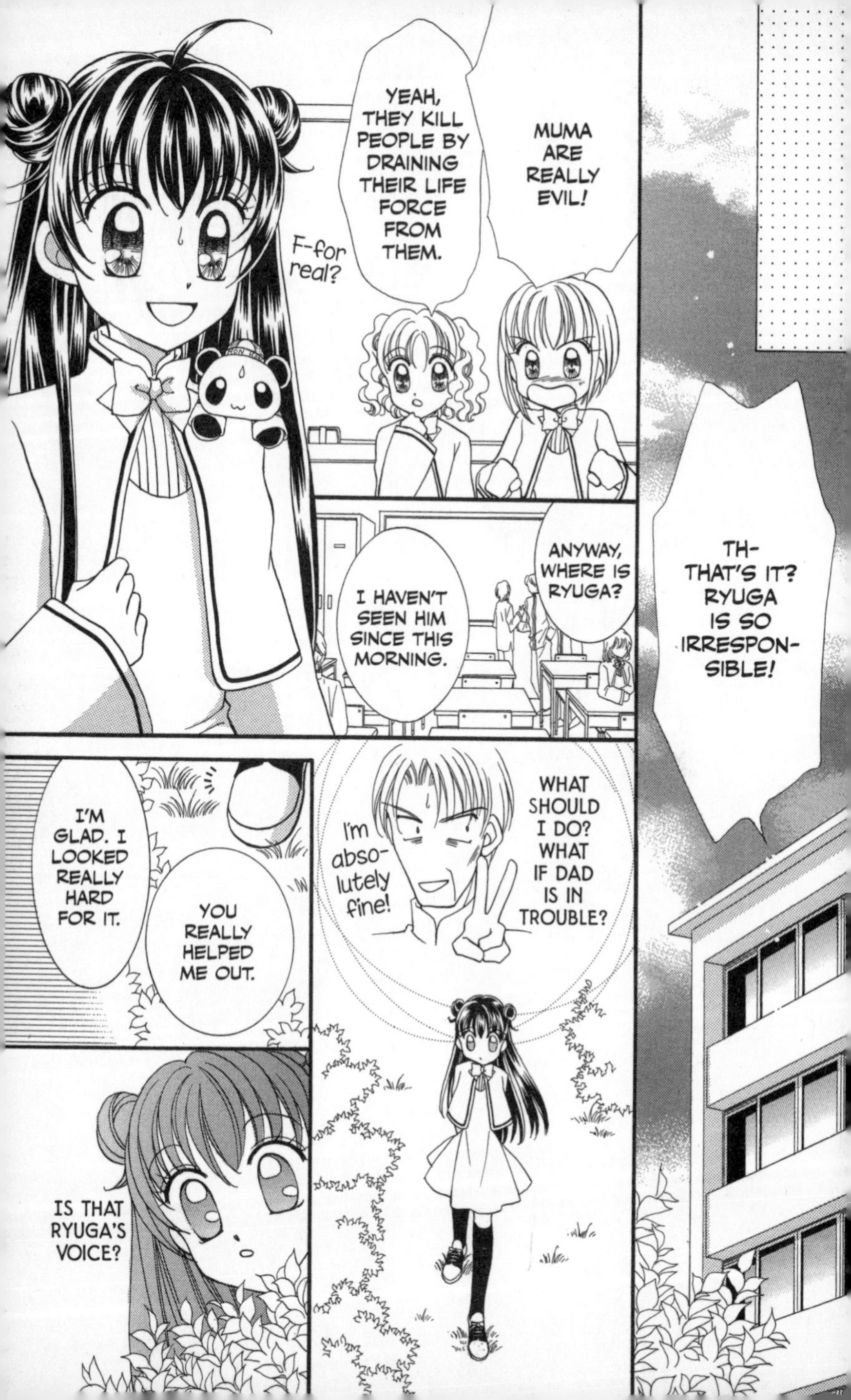
MUMA ARE REALLY EVIL!
YEAH, THEY KILL PEOPLE BY DRAINING THEIR LIFE FORCE FROM THEM.
F-for real?
ANYWAY, WHERE IS RYUGA?
I HAVEN'T SEEN HIM SINCE THIS MORNING.
TH-THAT'S IT? RYUGA IS SO IRRESPONSIBLE!
WHAT SHOULD I DO? WHAT IF DAD IS IN TROUBLE?
I'm absolutely fine!
YOU REALLY HELPED ME OUT.
I'M GLAD. I LOOKED REALLY HARD FOR IT.
IS THAT RYUGA'S VOICE?

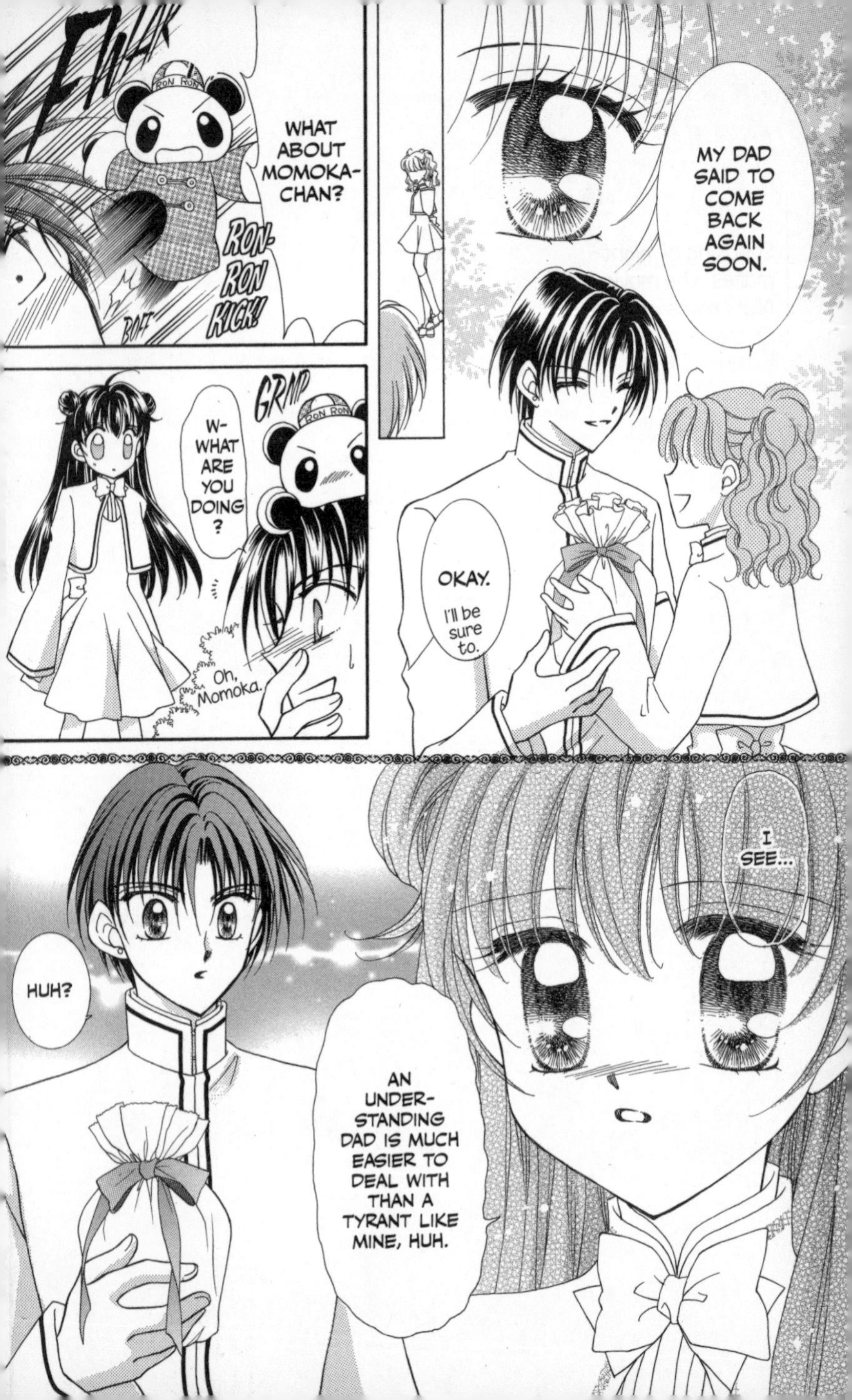

MY DAD SAID TO COME BACK AGAIN SOON.
OKAY.
I'll be sure to.
FWAK
WHAT ABOUT MOMOKA-CHAN?
RON-RON KICK!
BOFF
GRMP
W-WHAT ARE YOU DOING?
Oh, Momoka.
I SEE...
AN UNDER-STANDING DAD IS MUCH EASIER TO DEAL WITH THAN A TYRANT LIKE MINE, HUH.
HUH?

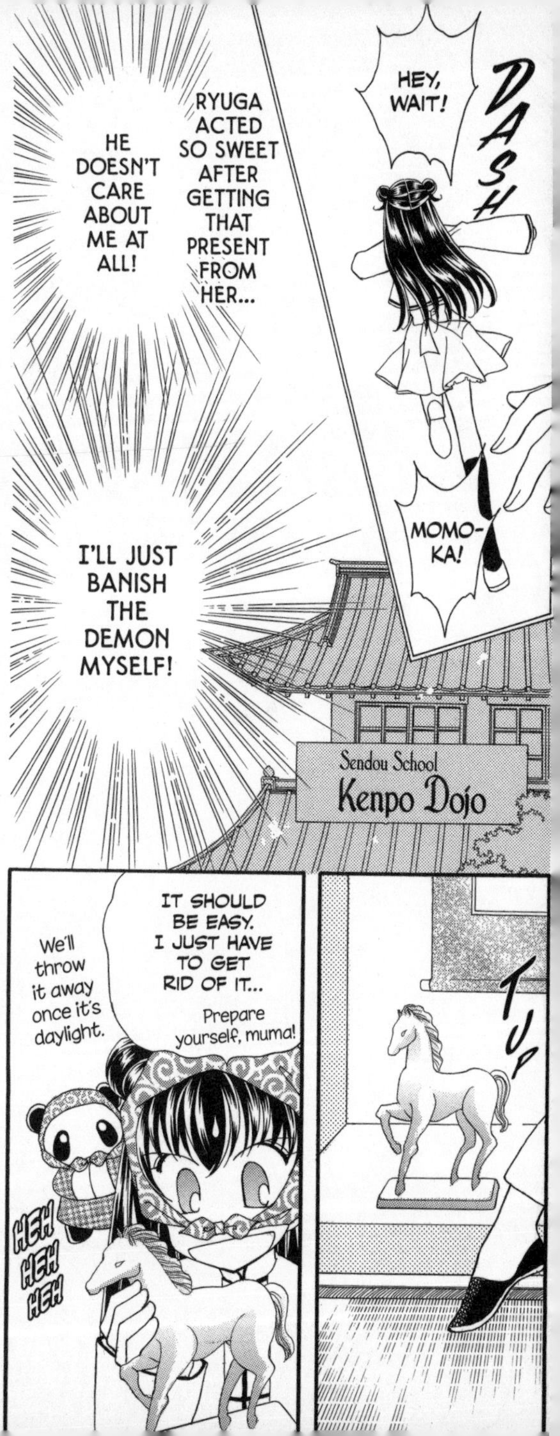
HEY, WAIT!
DASH
MOMO-KA!
RYUGA ACTED SO SWEET AFTER GETTING THAT PRESENT FROM HER...
HE DOESN'T CARE ABOUT ME AT ALL!
I'LL JUST BANISH THE DEMON MYSELF!
Sendou School
Kenpo Dojo
TUP
IT SHOULD BE EASY. I JUST HAVE TO GET RID OF IT...
Prepare yourself, muma!
We'll throw it away once it's daylight.
HEH HEH HEH

6

Speaking of nightmares, the movie *Nightmare on Elm Street* is really good. It starts with students getting attacked by a murderer's spirit, Freddy, in their dreams. When they get injured in their dreams, the same things happen to them in real life. When they get killed, they die in real life too. The protagonists know that if they go to sleep, Freddy will attack them. They try not to fall asleep, but eventually they do. The movie was made into a series, and it's really entertaining. I've rented the series tons of times, and I highly recommend it. However, the movies are really scary (especially the first one). Make sure to watch it with a friend!

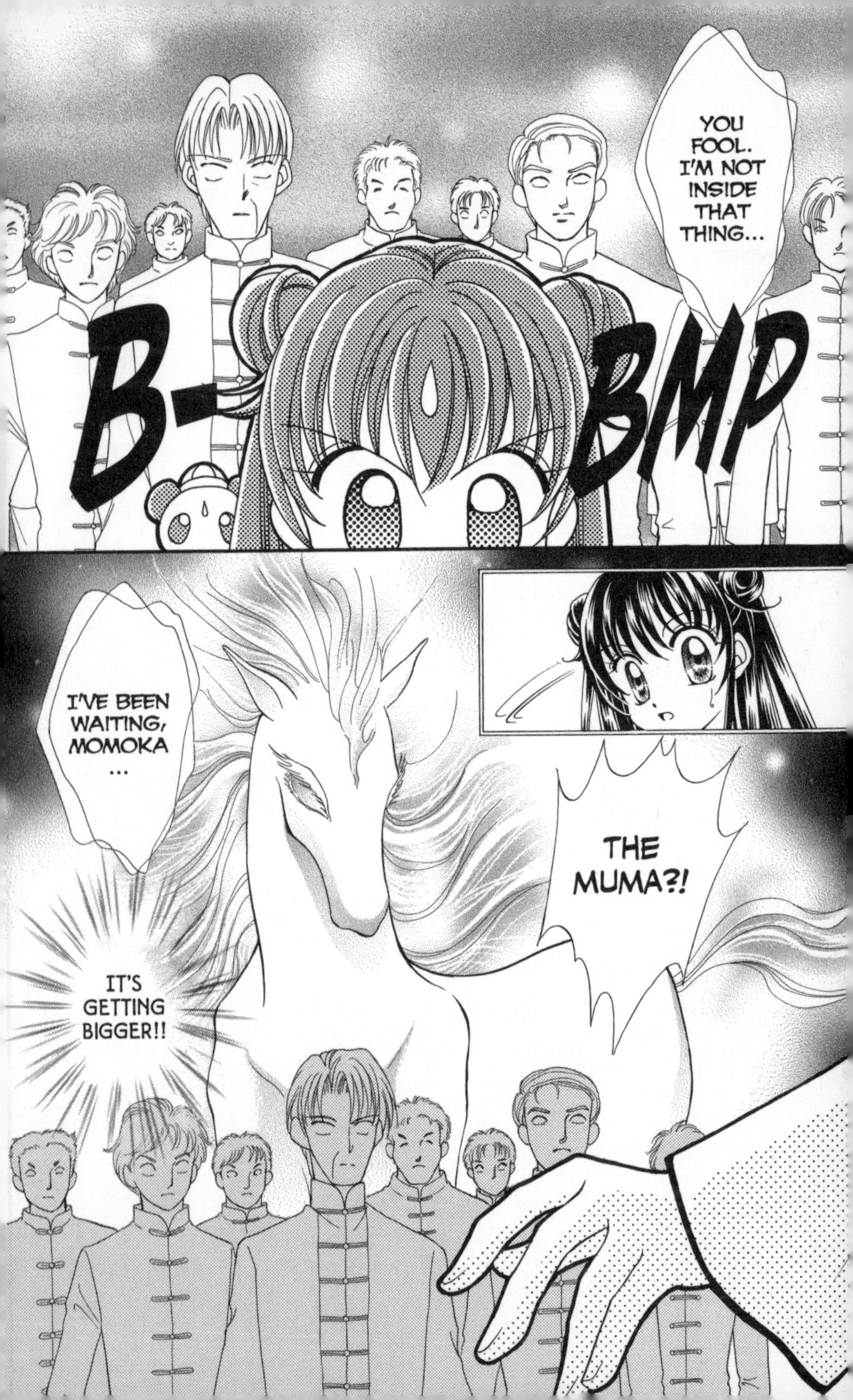
YOU FOOL. I'M NOT INSIDE THAT THING...
B-BMP
THE MUMA?!
I'VE BEEN WAITING, MOMOKA ...
IT'S GETTING BIGGER!!

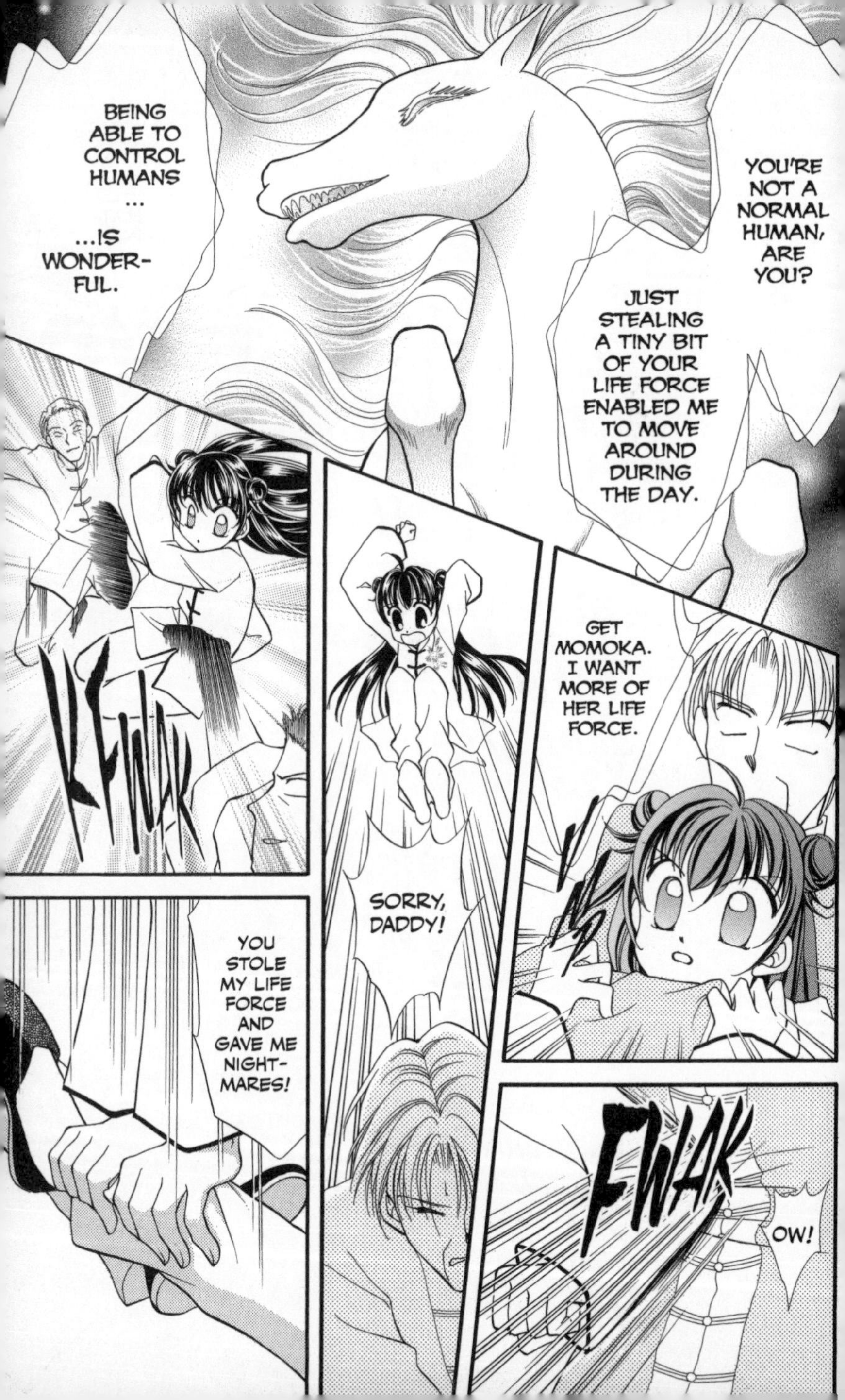
YOU'RE NOT A NORMAL HUMAN, ARE YOU?
JUST STEALING A TINY BIT OF YOUR LIFE FORCE ENABLED ME TO MOVE AROUND DURING THE DAY.
BEING ABLE TO CONTROL HUMANS ...
...IS WONDER-FUL.
GET MOMOKA. I WANT MORE OF HER LIFE FORCE.
FWAK
OW!
SORRY, DADDY!
YOU STOLE MY LIFE FORCE AND GAVE ME NIGHT-MARES!

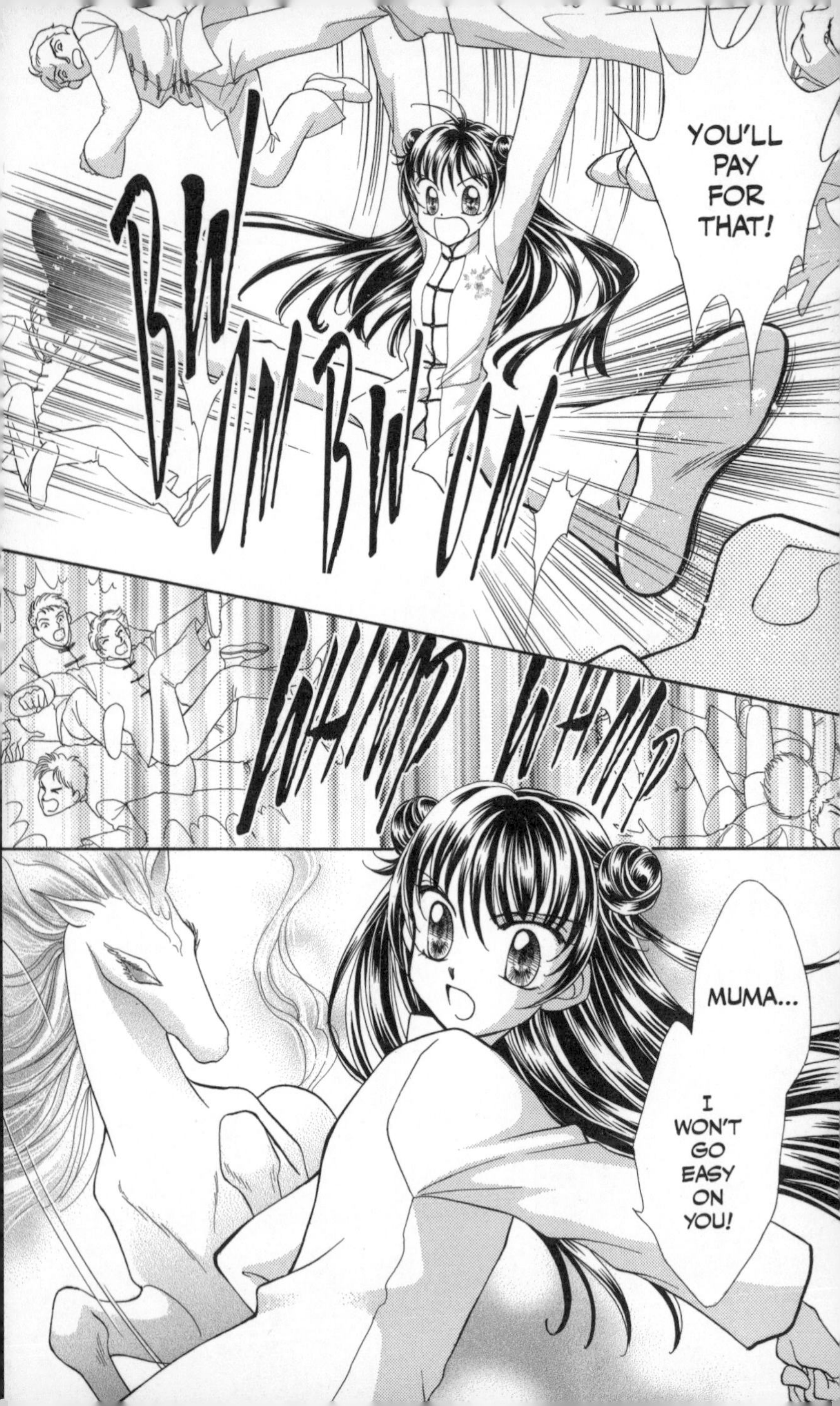
YOU'LL PAY FOR THAT!
BWOM BWOM
THUMP THUMP
MUMA...
I WON'T GO EASY ON YOU!

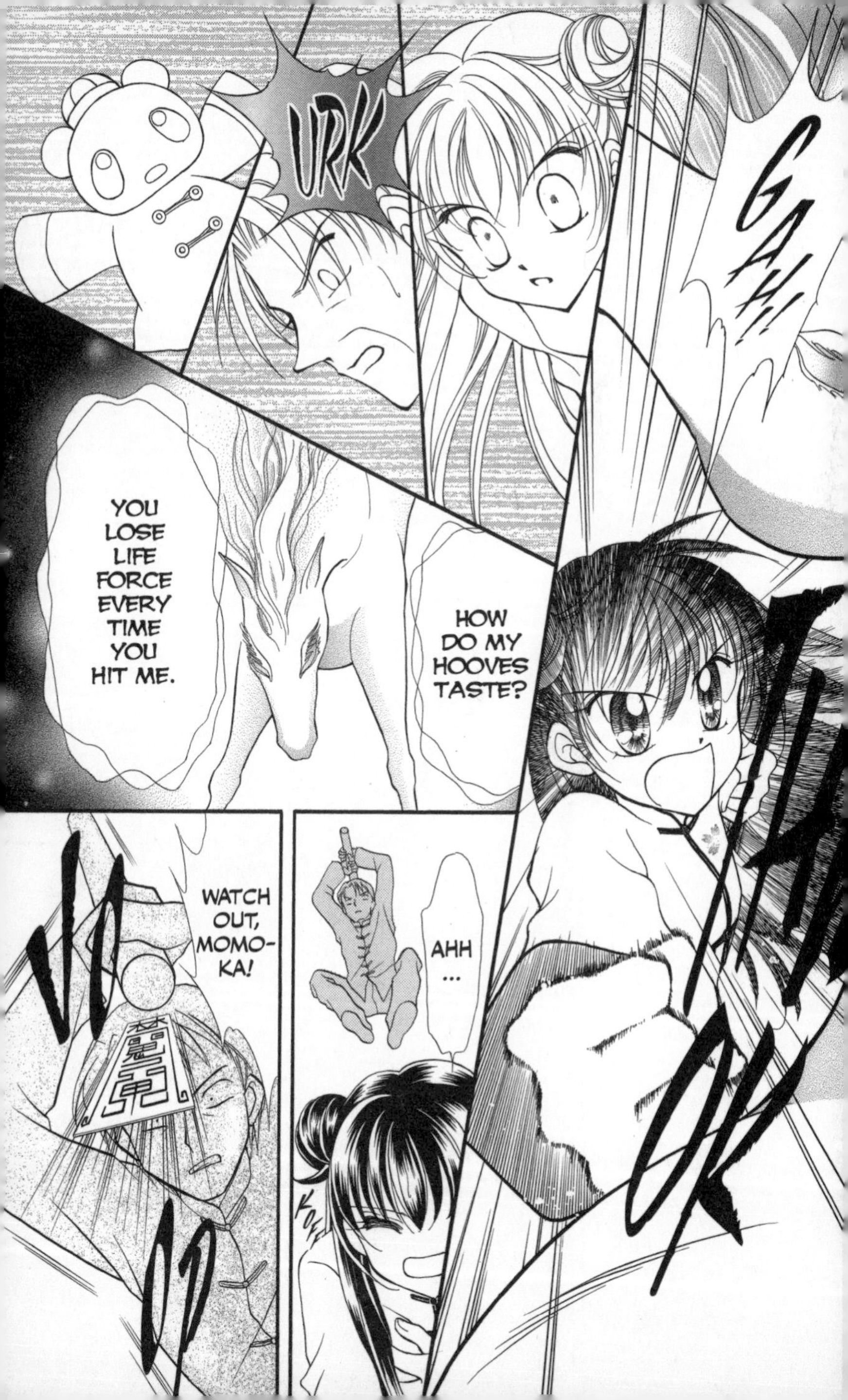
GAAH!
URK
HOW DO MY HOOVES TASTE?
YOU LOSE LIFE FORCE EVERY TIME YOU HIT ME.
AHH ...
KOFF
WATCH OUT, MOMO-KA!

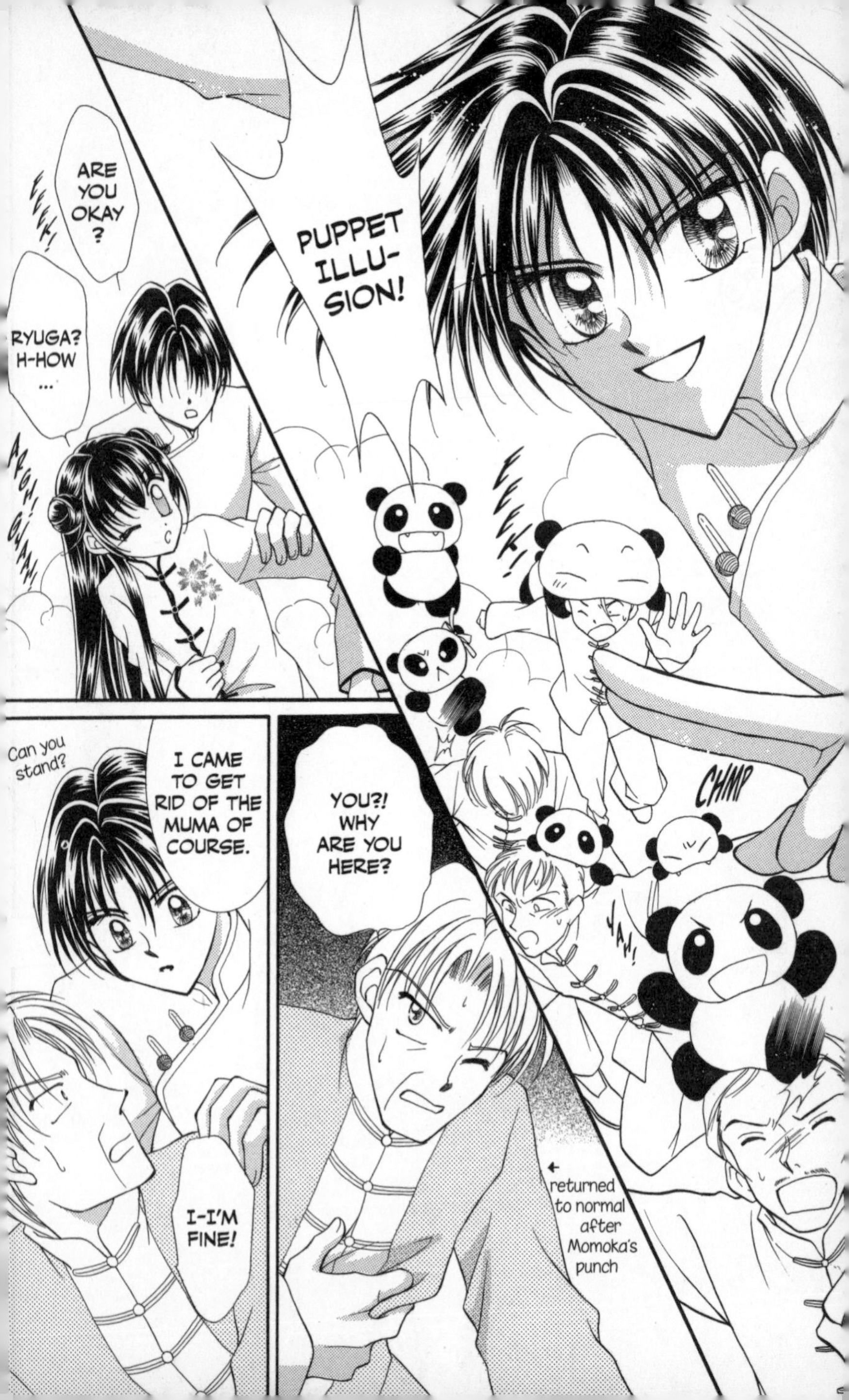
PUPPET ILLUSION!
EEEEK!
CHMP
YAAA!
← returned to normal after Momoka's punch
ARE YOU OKAY?
EEEEK!
RYUGA? H-HOW ...
ARGH! GYAAH!
YOU?! WHY ARE YOU HERE?
I CAME TO GET RID OF THE MUMA OF COURSE.
Can you stand?
I-I'M FINE!

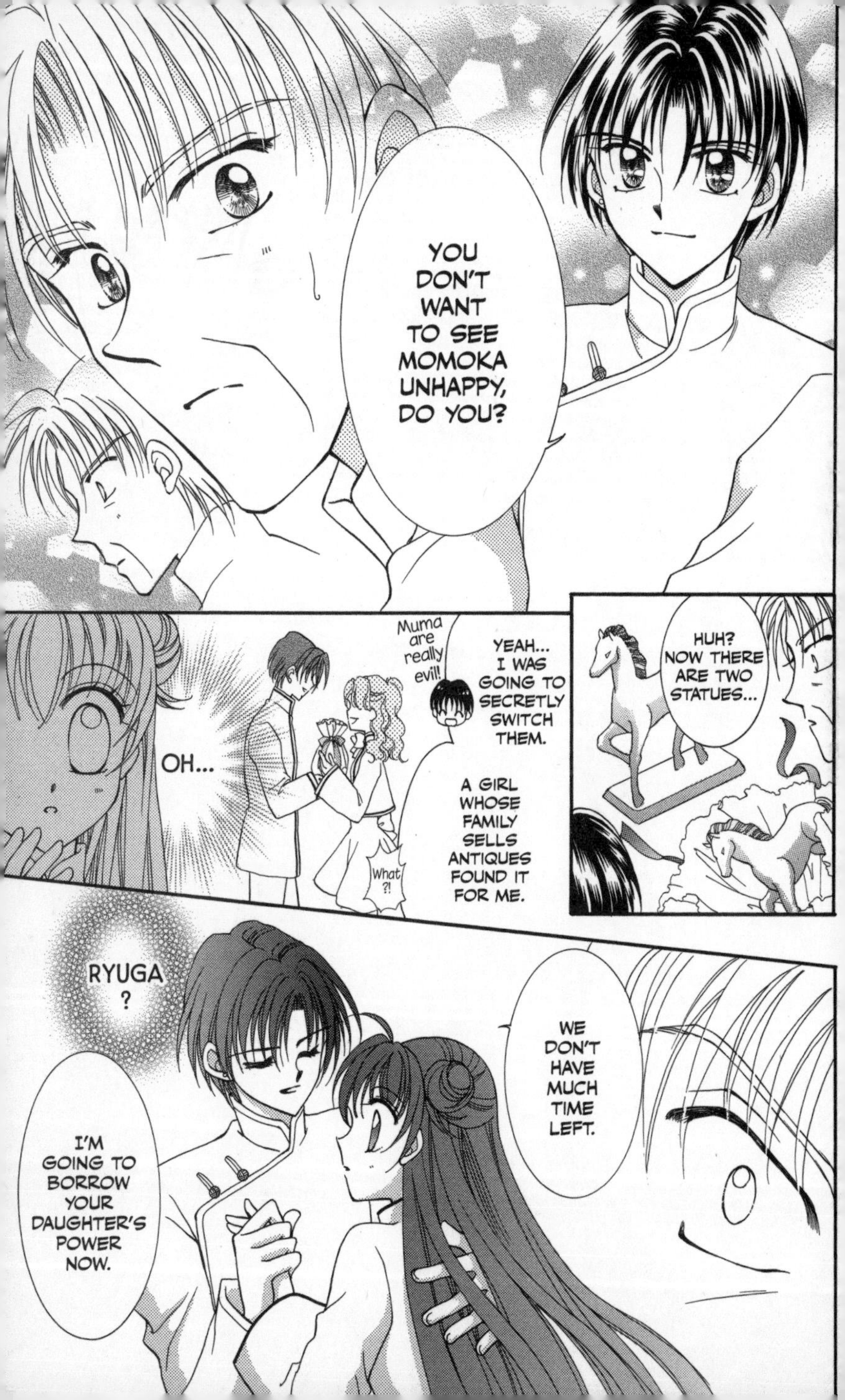
YOU DON'T WANT TO SEE MOMOKA UNHAPPY, DO YOU?
HUH? NOW THERE ARE TWO STATUES...
YEAH... I WAS GOING TO SECRETLY SWITCH THEM.
Muma are really evil!
A GIRL WHOSE FAMILY SELLS ANTIQUES FOUND IT FOR ME.
What?!
OH...
WE DON'T HAVE MUCH TIME LEFT.
RYUGA?
I'M GOING TO BORROW YOUR DAUGHTER'S POWER NOW.

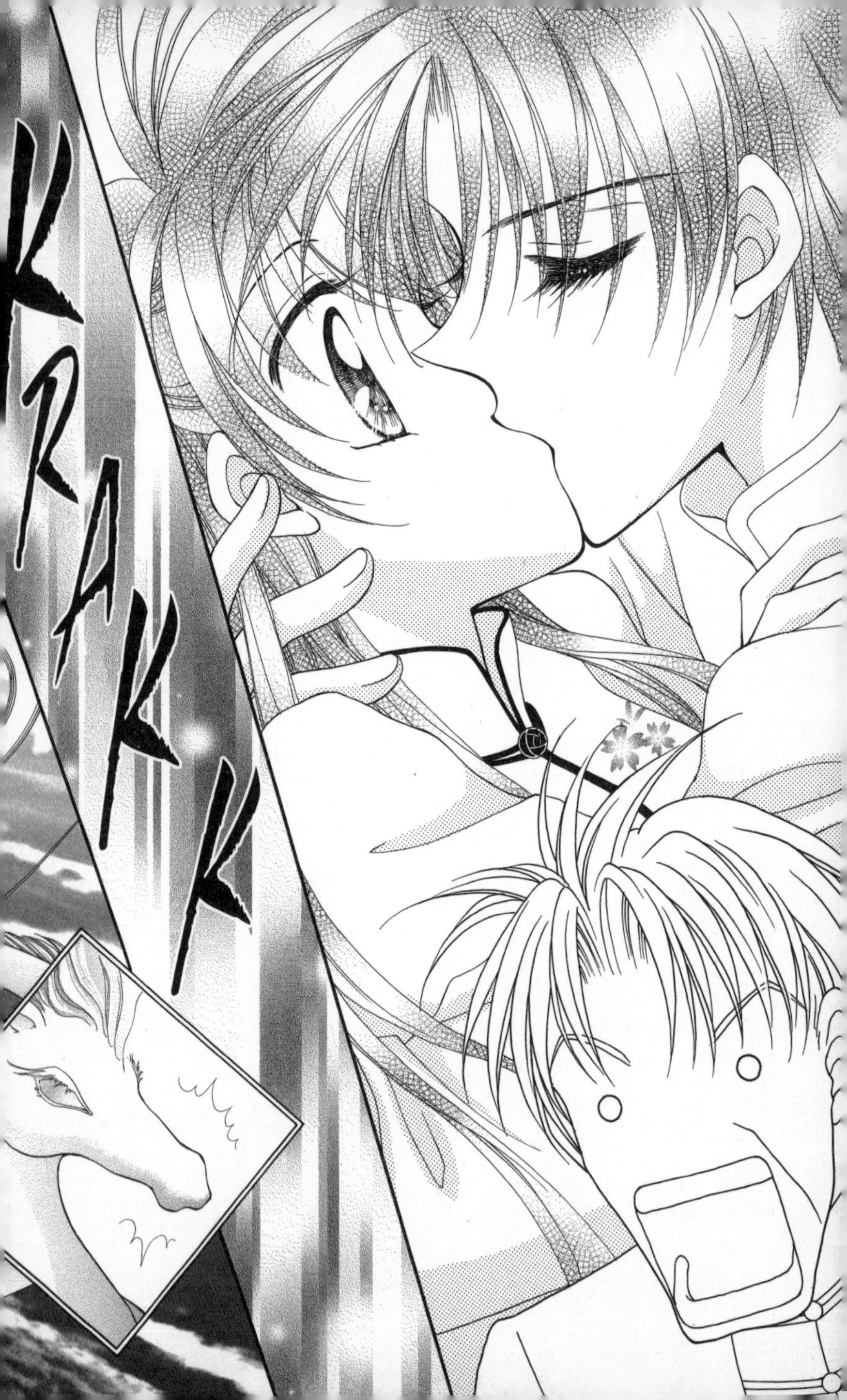
KRAKK

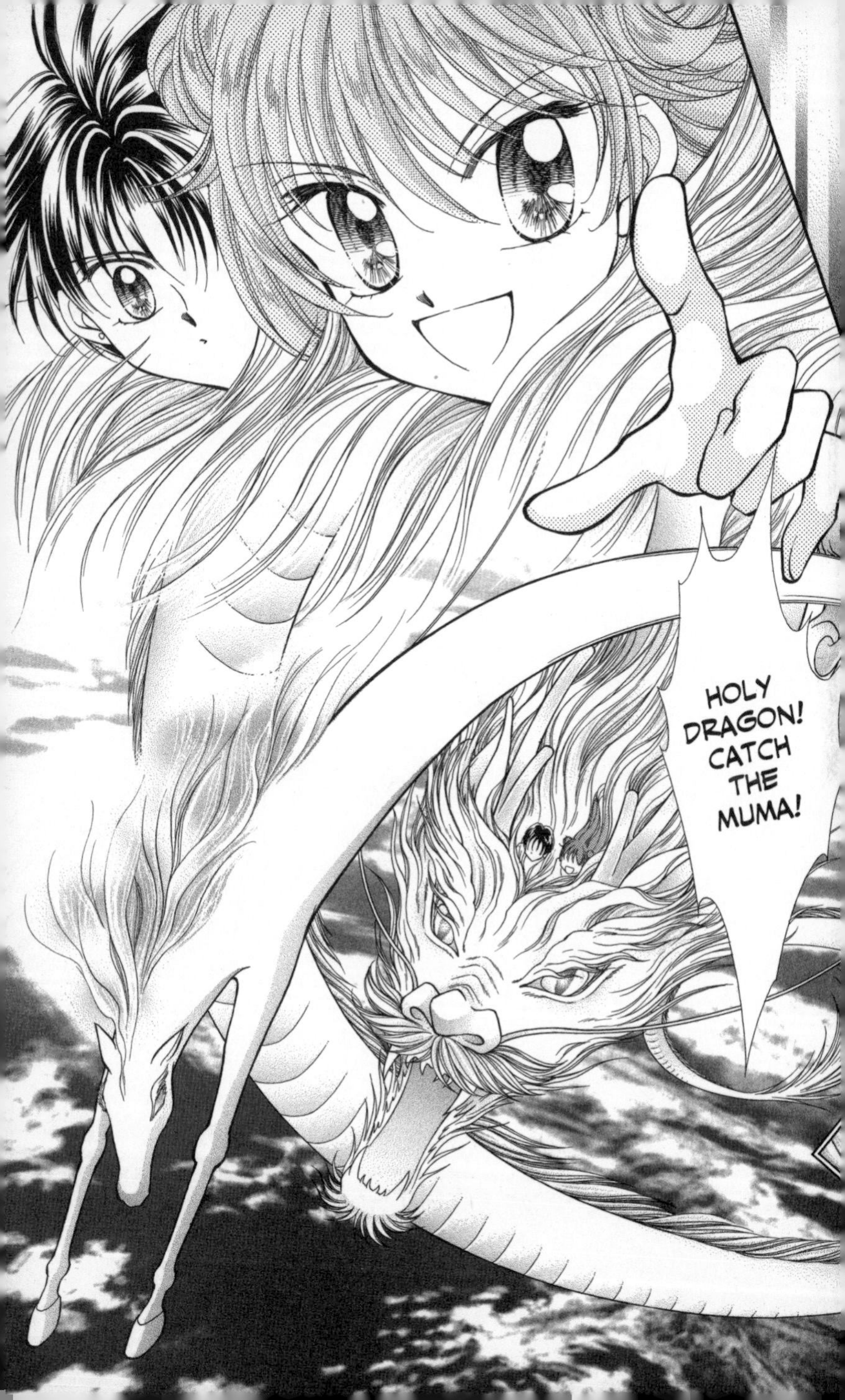
HOLY DRAGON! CATCH THE MUMA!

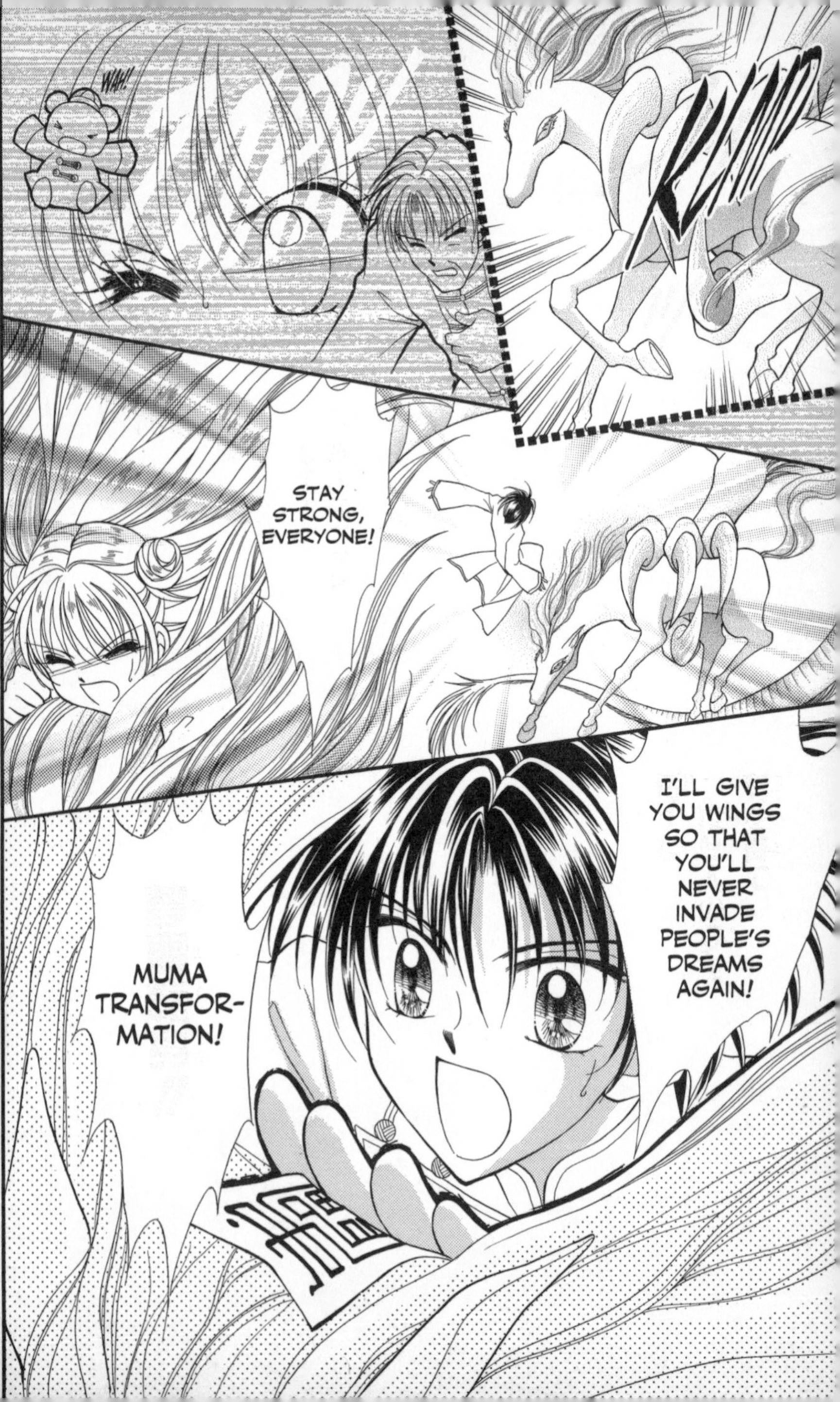
WAH!
STAY STRONG, EVERYONE!
I'LL GIVE YOU WINGS SO THAT YOU'LL NEVER INVADE PEOPLE'S DREAMS AGAIN!
MUMA TRANSFOR-MATION!

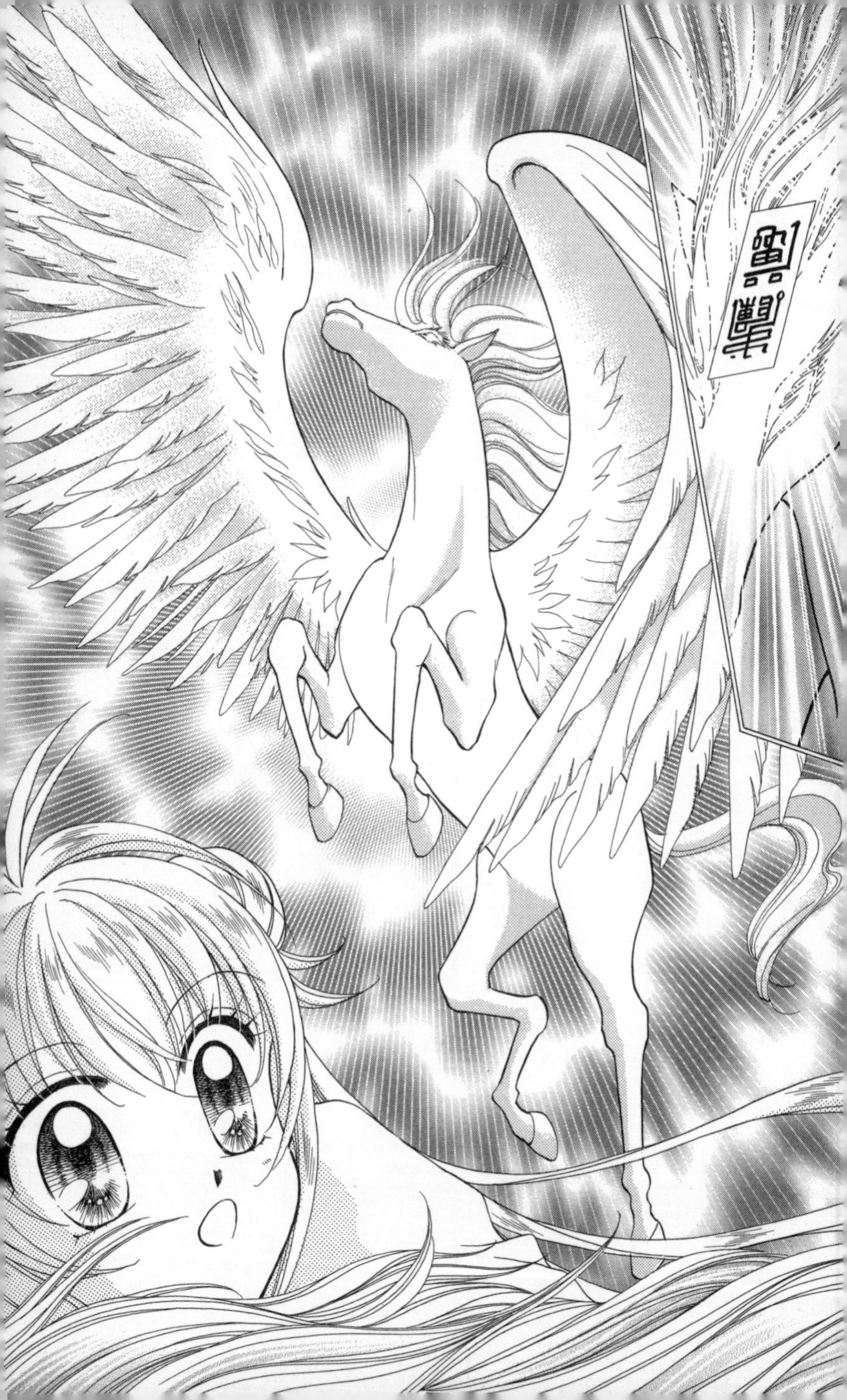

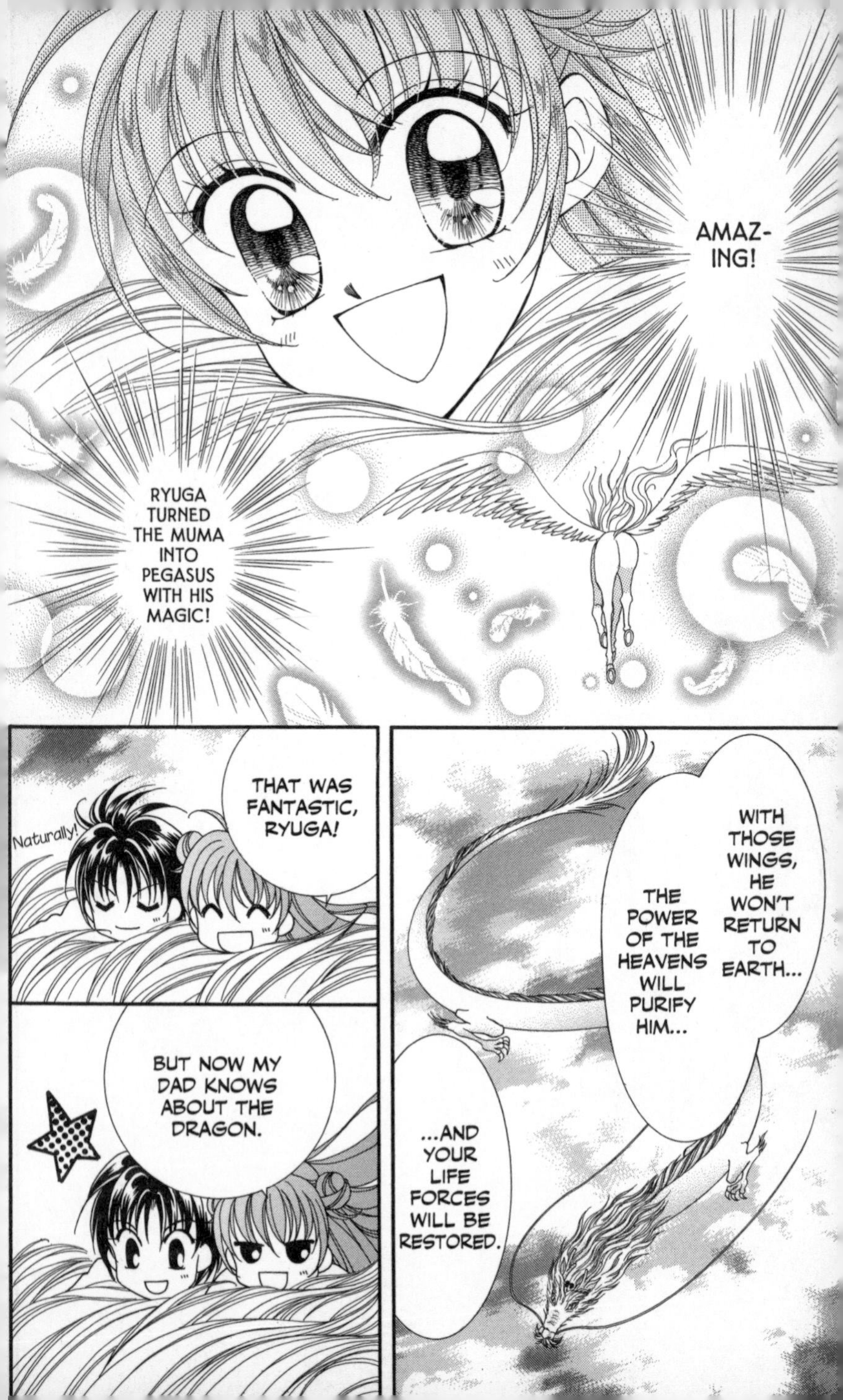
AMAZ-ING!
RYUGA TURNED THE MUMA INTO PEGASUS WITH HIS MAGIC!
WITH THOSE WINGS, HE WON'T RETURN TO EARTH...
THE POWER OF THE HEAVENS WILL PURIFY HIM...
...AND YOUR LIFE FORCES WILL BE RESTORED.
THAT WAS FANTASTIC, RYUGA!
Naturally!
BUT NOW MY DAD KNOWS ABOUT THE DRAGON.

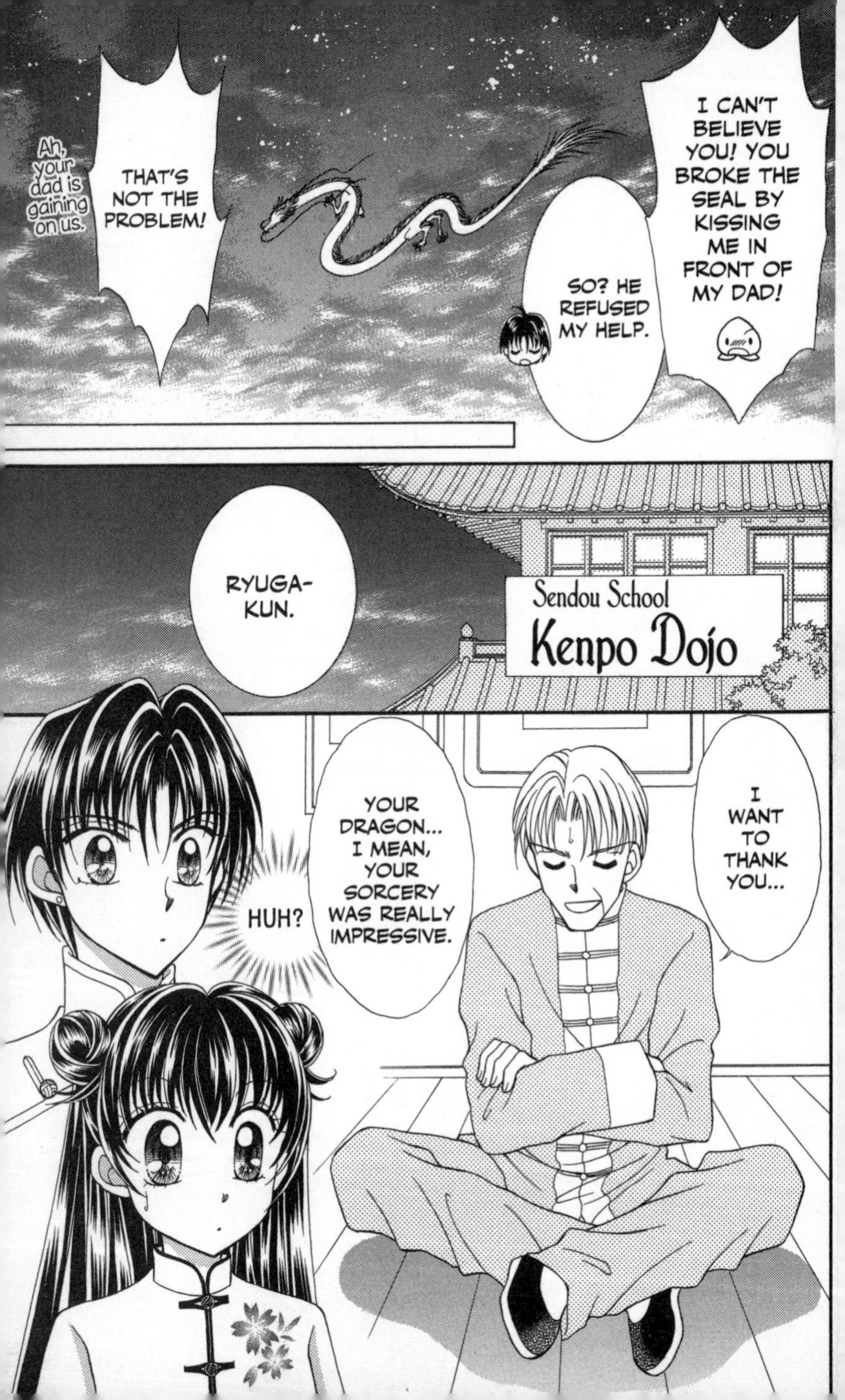
I CAN'T BELIEVE YOU! YOU BROKE THE SEAL BY KISSING ME IN FRONT OF MY DAD!
SO? HE REFUSED MY HELP.
THAT'S NOT THE PROBLEM!
Ah, your dad is gaining on us.
RYUGA-KUN.
Sendou School
Kenpo Dojo
I WANT TO THANK YOU...
YOUR DRAGON... I MEAN, YOUR SORCERY WAS REALLY IMPRESSIVE.
HUH?

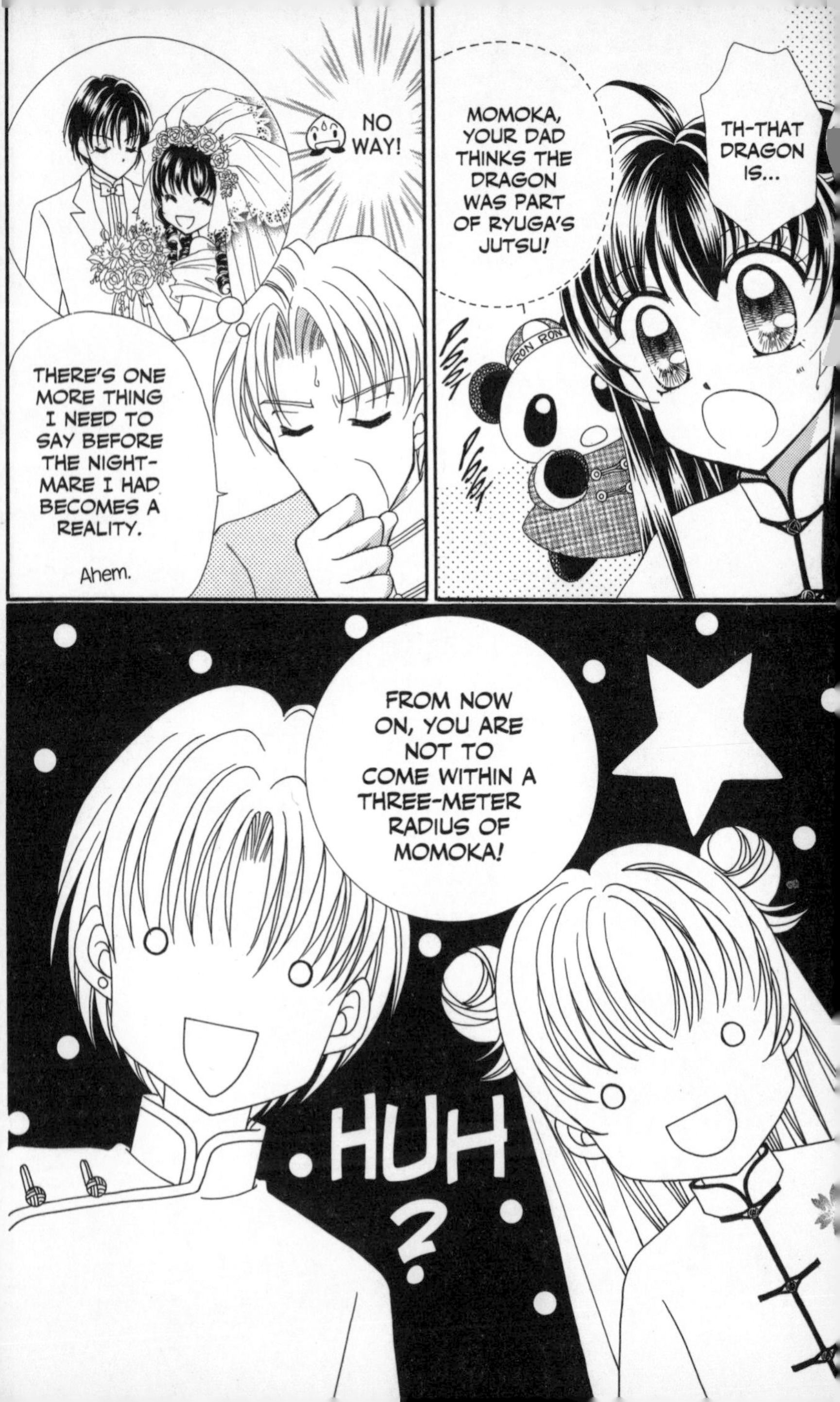
TH-THAT DRAGON IS...
MOMOKA, YOUR DAD THINKS THE DRAGON WAS PART OF RYUGA'S JUTSU!
RON RON
NO WAY!
THERE'S ONE MORE THING I NEED TO SAY BEFORE THE NIGHT-MARE I HAD BECOMES A REALITY.
Ahem.
FROM NOW ON, YOU ARE NOT TO COME WITHIN A THREE-METER RADIUS OF MOMOKA!
HUH?

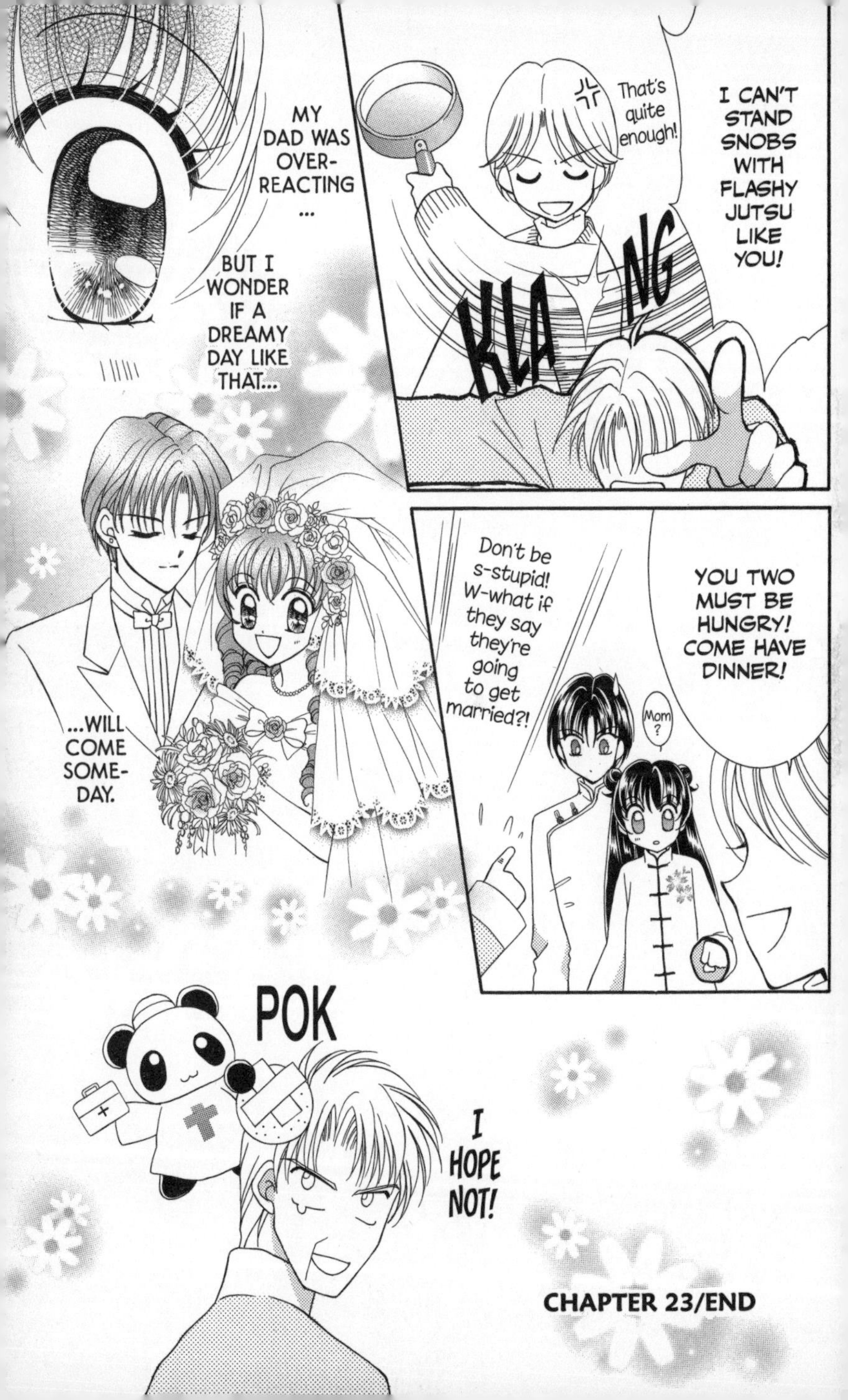
I CAN'T STAND SNOBS WITH FLASHY JUTSU LIKE YOU!
That's quite enough!
KLANG
YOU TWO MUST BE HUNGRY! COME HAVE DINNER!
Mom?
Don't be s-stupid! W-what if they say they're going to get married?!
MY DAD WAS OVER-REACTING...
BUT I WONDER IF A DREAMY DAY LIKE THAT...
...WILL COME SOME-DAY.
POK
I HOPE NOT!

CHAPTER 23/END

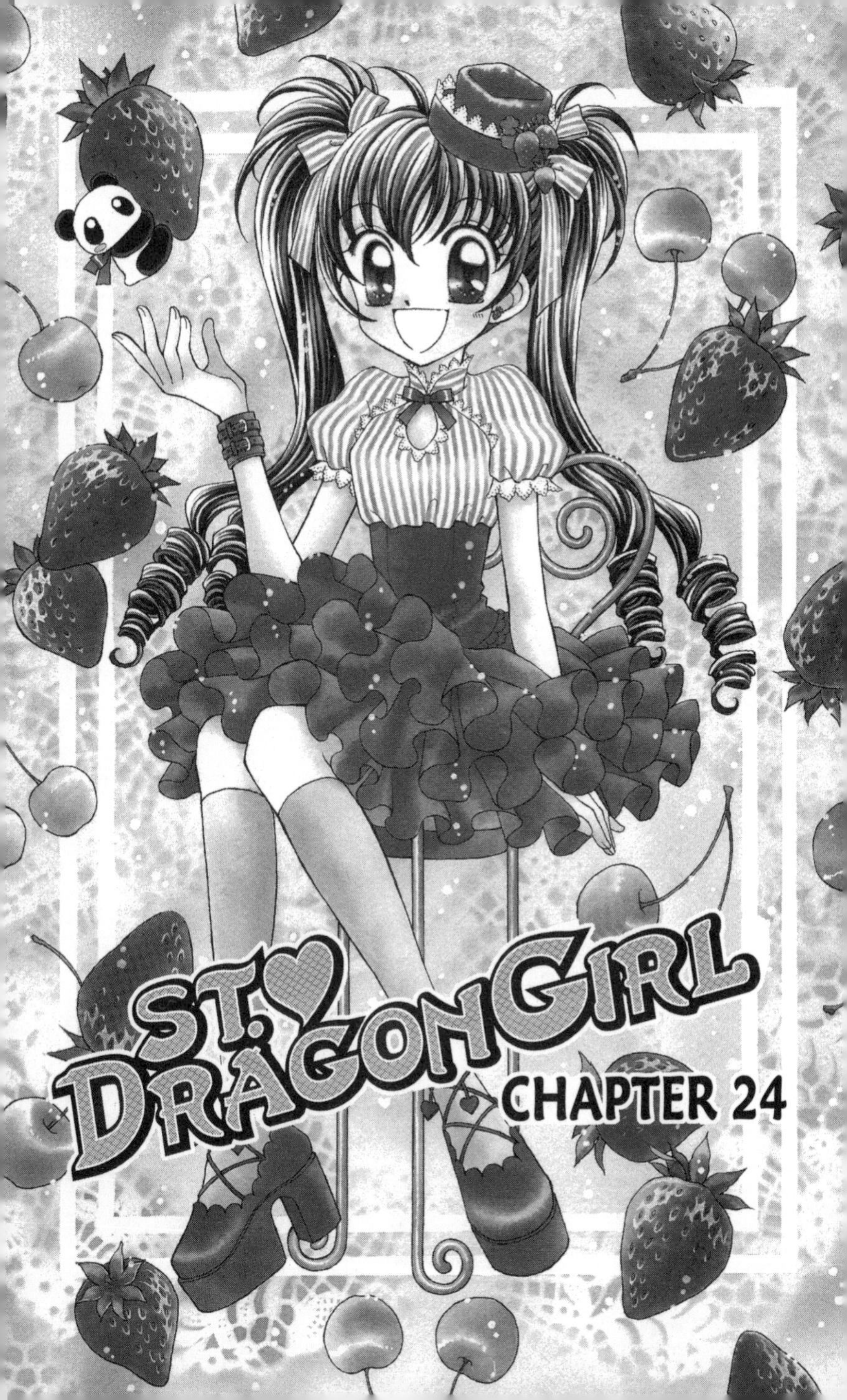
ST.♥ DRAGON GIRL
CHAPTER 24

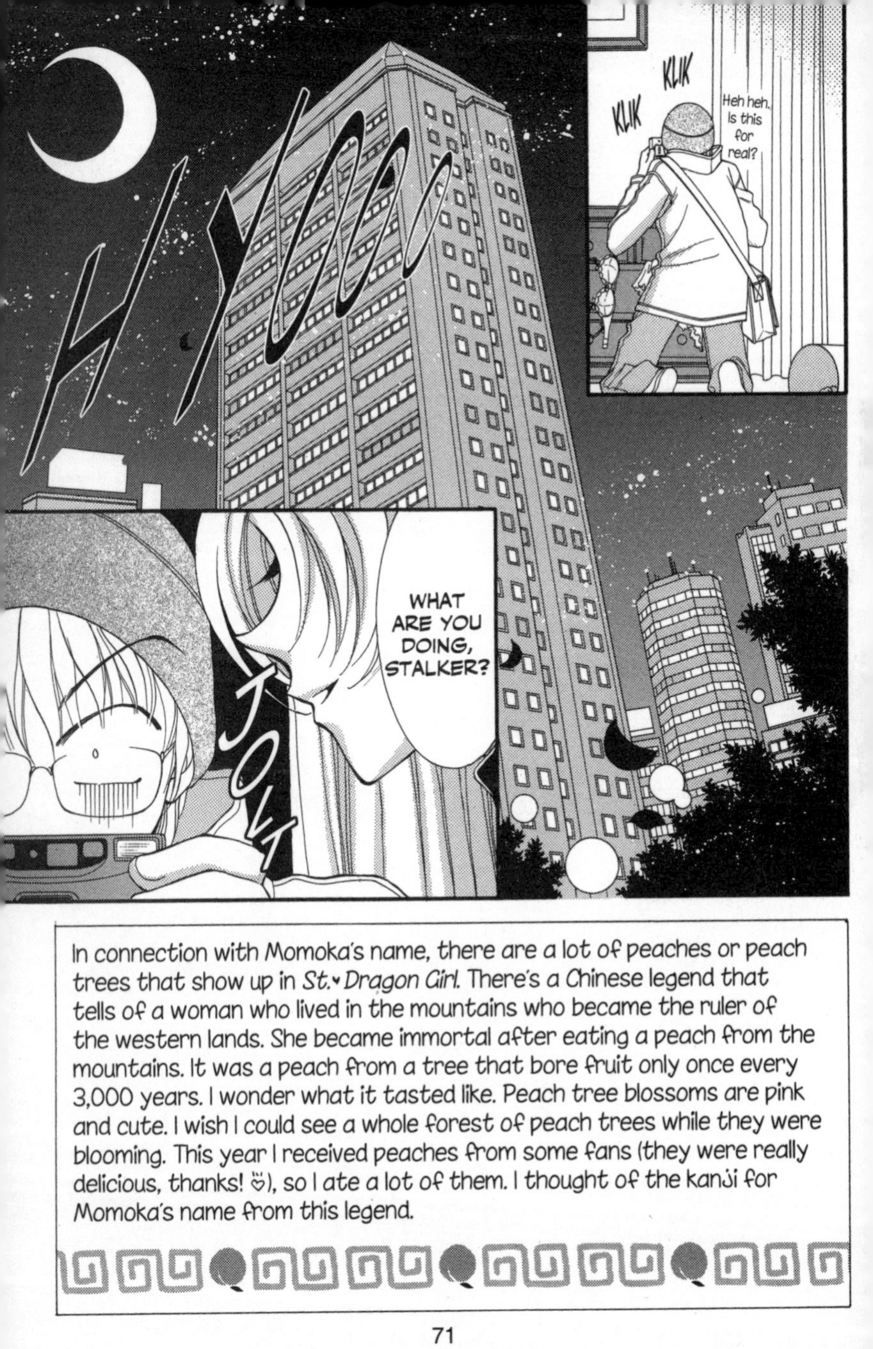
KLIK
KLIK
Heh heh. Is this for real?
WHAT ARE YOU DOING, STALKER?

In connection with Momoka's name, there are a lot of peaches or peach trees that show up in *St.♥Dragon Girl*. There's a Chinese legend that tells of a woman who lived in the mountains who became the ruler of the western lands. She became immortal after eating a peach from the mountains. It was a peach from a tree that bore fruit only once every 3,000 years. I wonder what it tasted like. Peach tree blossoms are pink and cute. I wish I could see a whole forest of peach trees while they were blooming. This year I received peaches from some fans (they were really delicious, thanks! ♡), so I ate a lot of them. I thought of the kanji for Momoka's name from this legend.

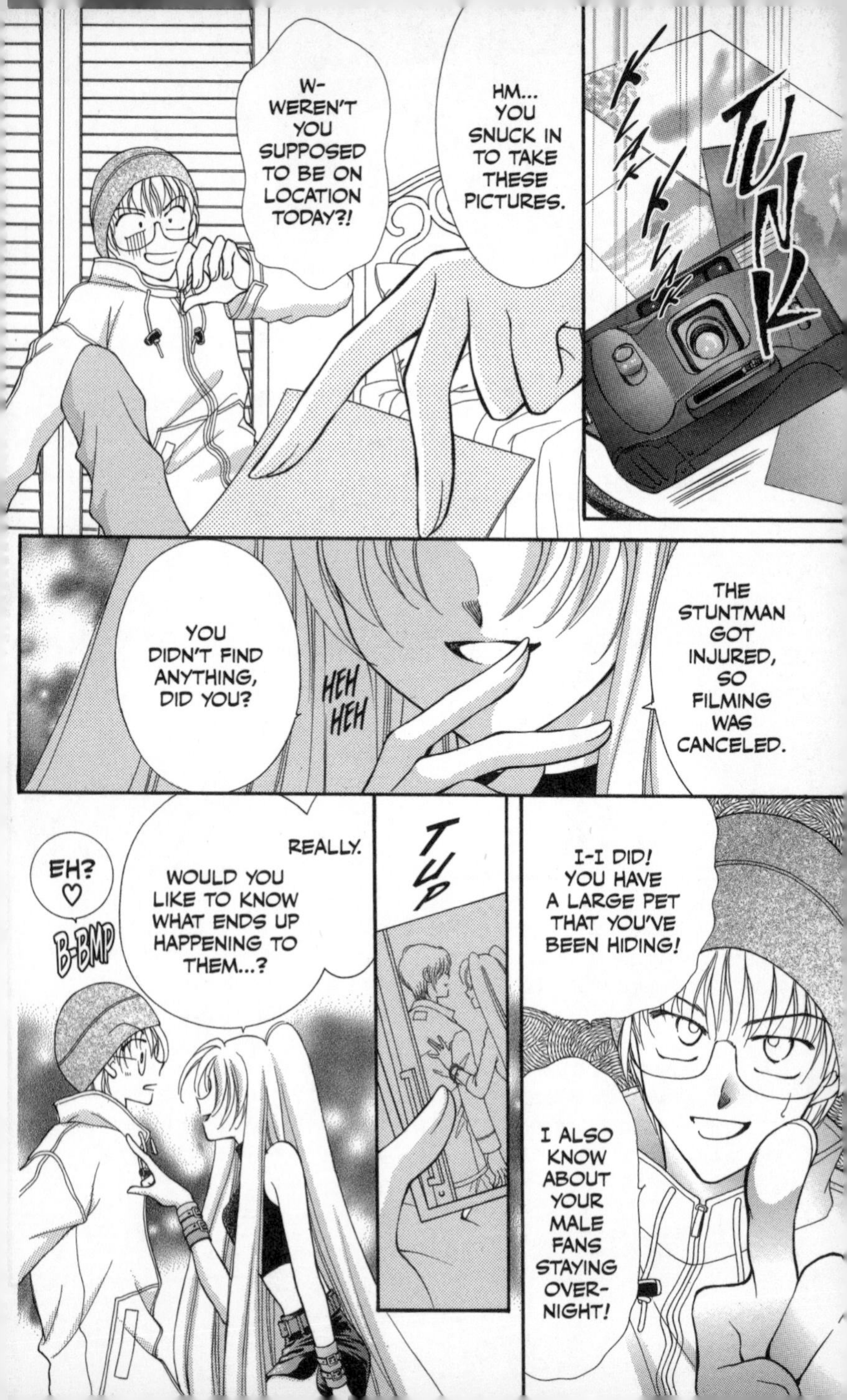
TUNK
KLAK KLAK KLAK
HM... YOU SNUCK IN TO TAKE THESE PICTURES.
W- WEREN'T YOU SUPPOSED TO BE ON LOCATION TODAY?!
THE STUNTMAN GOT INJURED, SO FILMING WAS CANCELED.
HEH HEH
YOU DIDN'T FIND ANYTHING, DID YOU?
I-I DID! YOU HAVE A LARGE PET THAT YOU'VE BEEN HIDING!
I ALSO KNOW ABOUT YOUR MALE FANS STAYING OVER-NIGHT!
TUP
REALLY. WOULD YOU LIKE TO KNOW WHAT ENDS UP HAPPENING TO THEM...?
EH? ♡
B-BMP

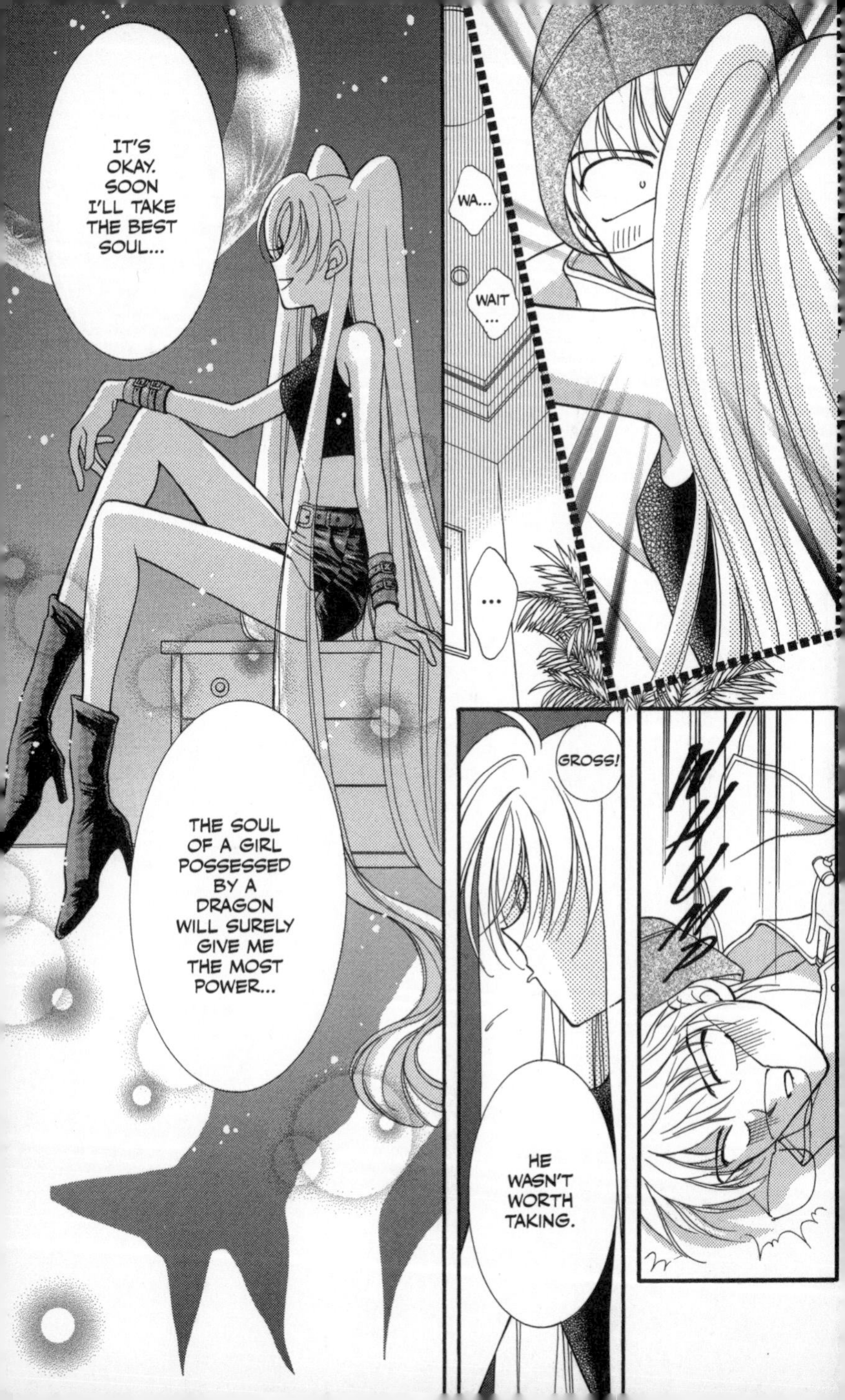
WA...
WAIT...
...
WHUMP
GROSS!
HE WASN'T WORTH TAKING.
IT'S OKAY. SOON I'LL TAKE THE BEST SOUL...
THE SOUL OF A GIRL POSSESSED BY A DRAGON WILL SURELY GIVE ME THE MOST POWER...

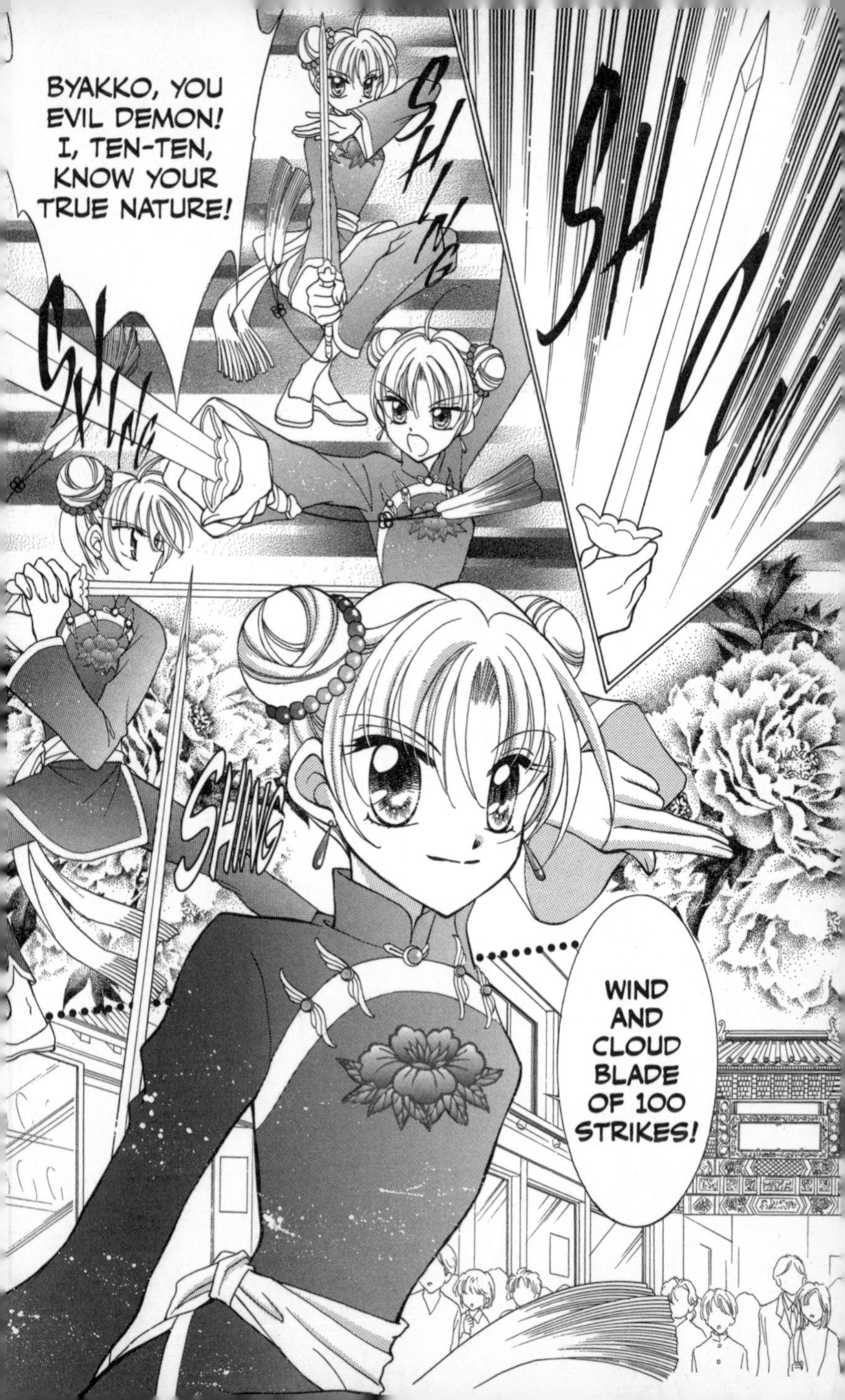
SHOOM
SHING
BYAKKO, YOU EVIL DEMON! I, TEN-TEN, KNOW YOUR TRUE NATURE!
SHING
WIND AND CLOUD BLADE OF 100 STRIKES!
SHING

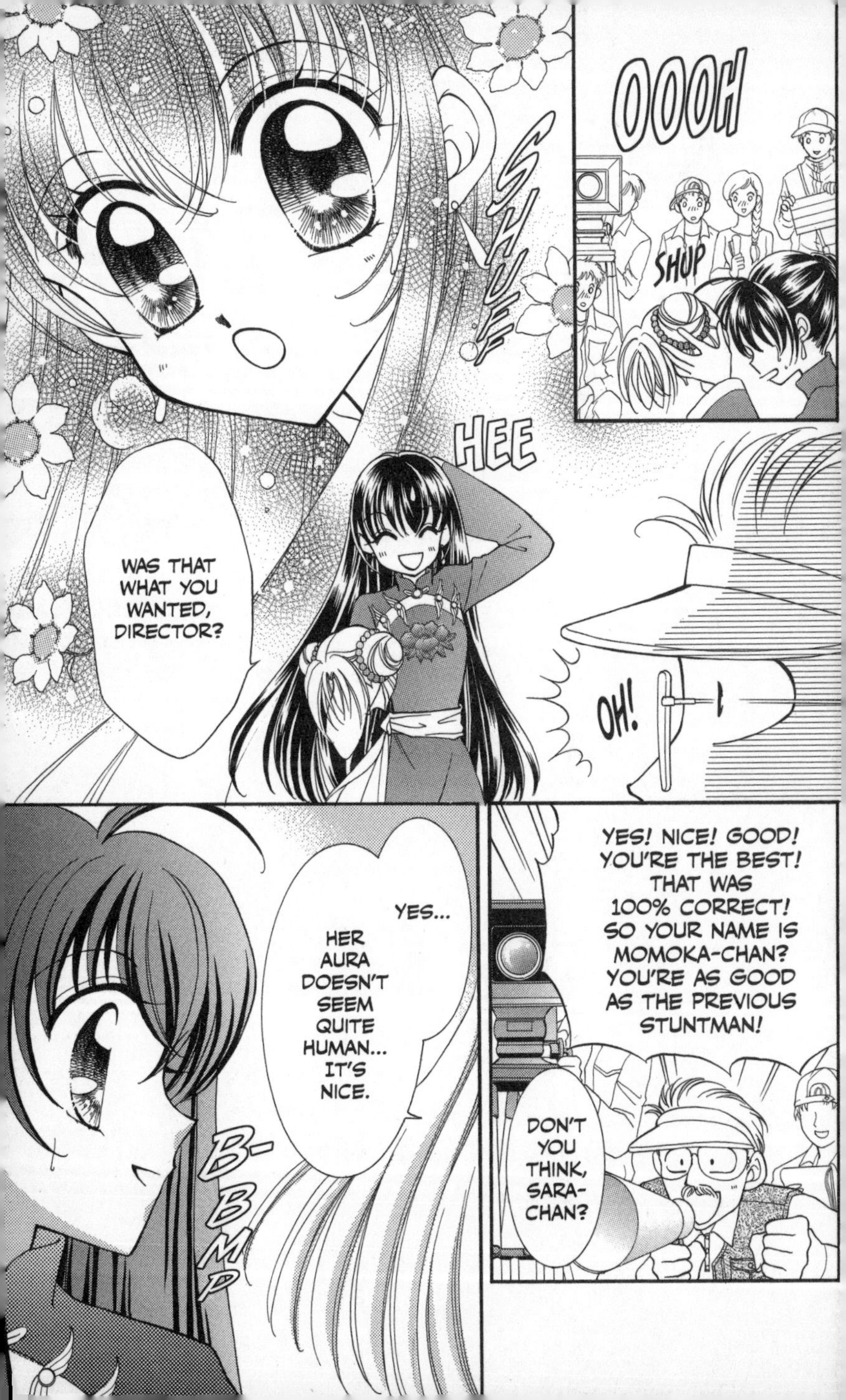
OOOH
SHUP
SHUEE
HEE
OH!
WAS THAT WHAT YOU WANTED, DIRECTOR?
YES! NICE! GOOD! YOU'RE THE BEST! THAT WAS 100% CORRECT! SO YOUR NAME IS MOMOKA-CHAN? YOU'RE AS GOOD AS THE PREVIOUS STUNTMAN!
DON'T YOU THINK, SARA-CHAN?
YES...
HER AURA DOESN'T SEEM QUITE HUMAN... IT'S NICE.
B-BMP

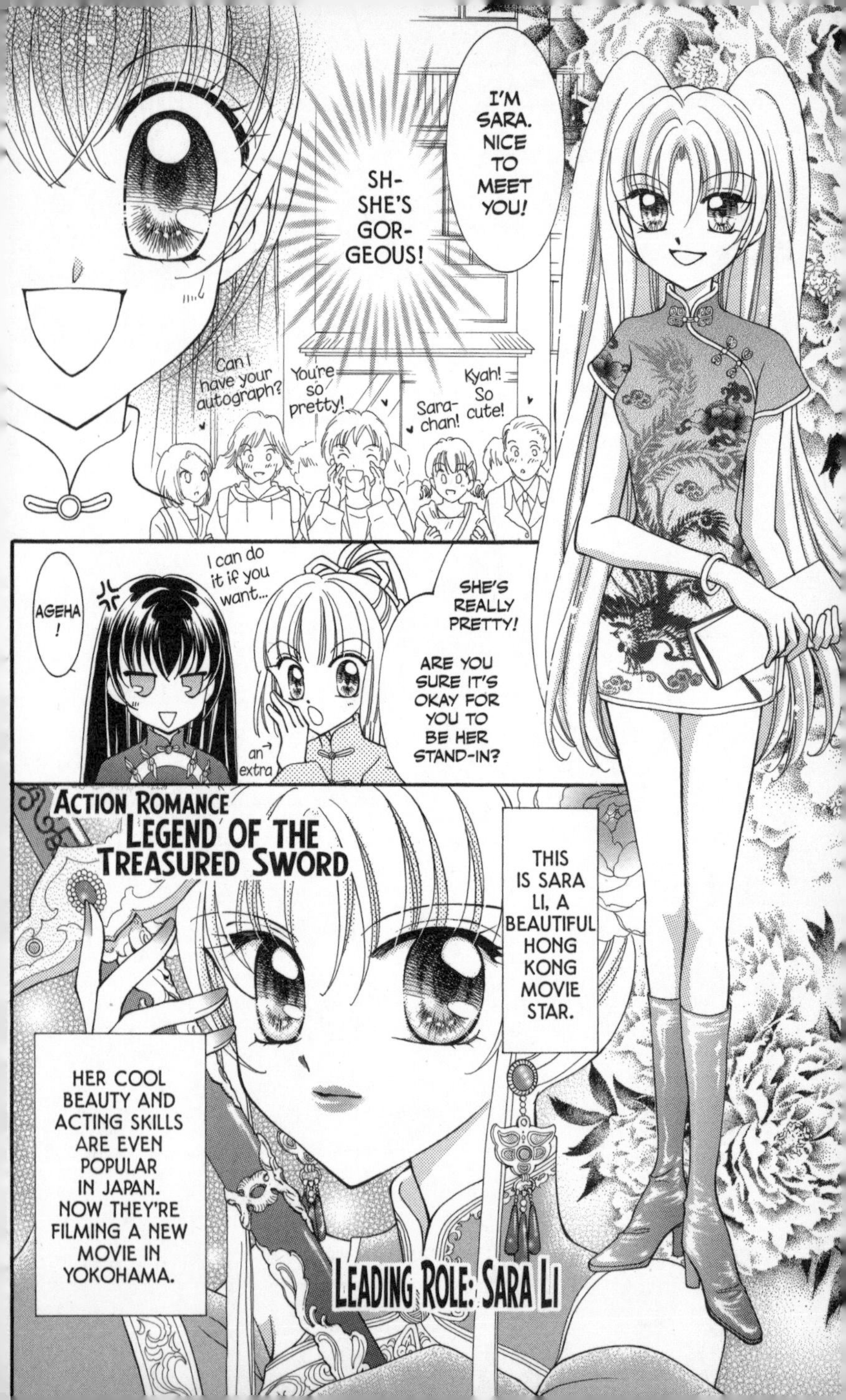
I'M SARA. NICE TO MEET YOU!
SH-SHE'S GORGEOUS!
Kyah! So cute!
Sara-chan!
You're so pretty!
Can I have your autograph?
SHE'S REALLY PRETTY!
ARE YOU SURE IT'S OKAY FOR YOU TO BE HER STAND-IN?
I can do it if you want...
an extra
AGEHA!
THIS IS SARA LI, A BEAUTIFUL HONG KONG MOVIE STAR.
ACTION ROMANCE
LEGEND OF THE TREASURED SWORD
HER COOL BEAUTY AND ACTING SKILLS ARE EVEN POPULAR IN JAPAN. NOW THEY'RE FILMING A NEW MOVIE IN YOKOHAMA.
LEADING ROLE: SARA LI

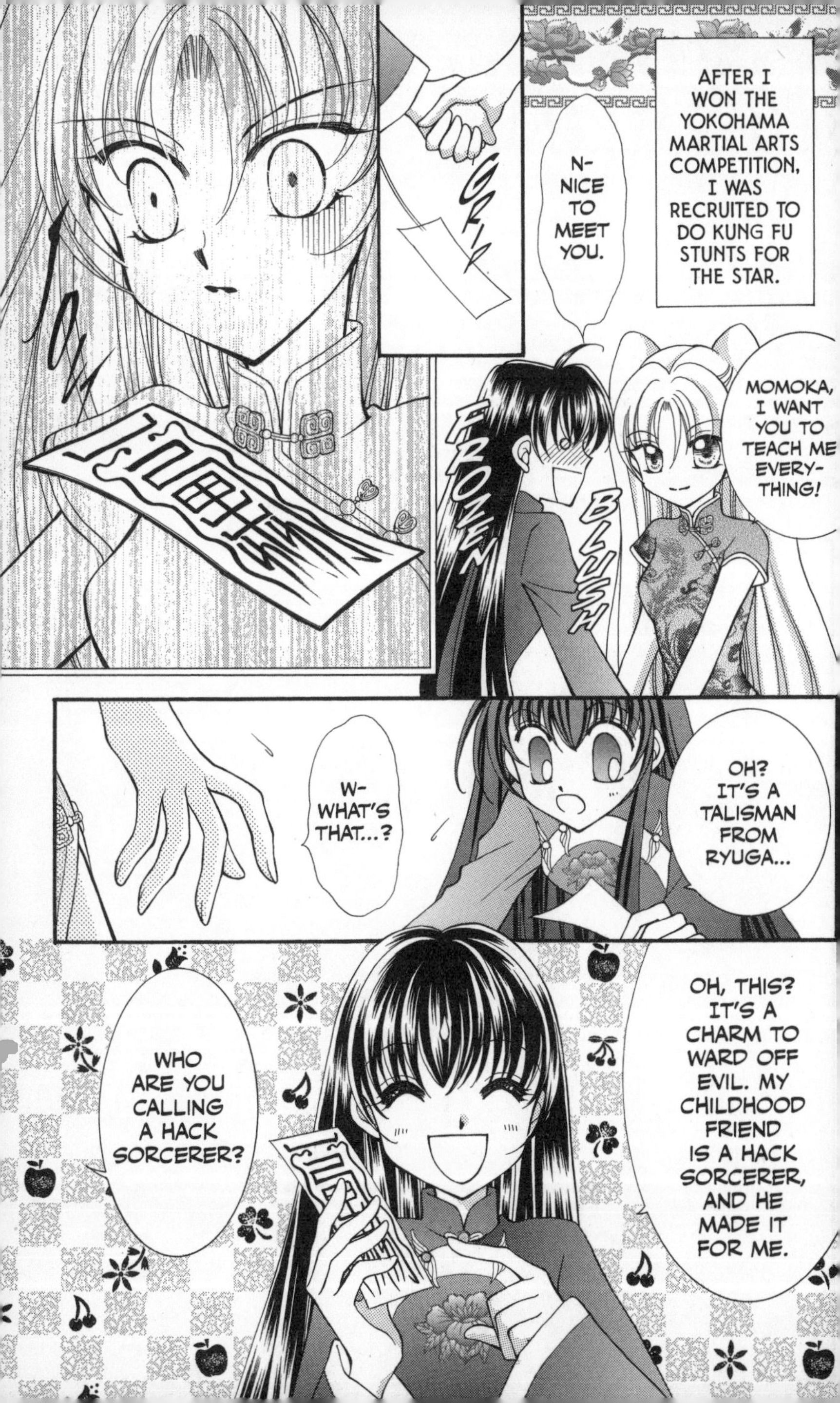
AFTER I WON THE YOKOHAMA MARTIAL ARTS COMPETITION, I WAS RECRUITED TO DO KUNG FU STUNTS FOR THE STAR.
N-NICE TO MEET YOU.
MOMOKA, I WANT YOU TO TEACH ME EVERY-THING!
BLUSH
FROZEN
OH? IT'S A TALISMAN FROM RYUGA...
W-WHAT'S THAT...?
OH, THIS? IT'S A CHARM TO WARD OFF EVIL. MY CHILDHOOD FRIEND IS A HACK SORCERER, AND HE MADE IT FOR ME.
WHO ARE YOU CALLING A HACK SORCERER?

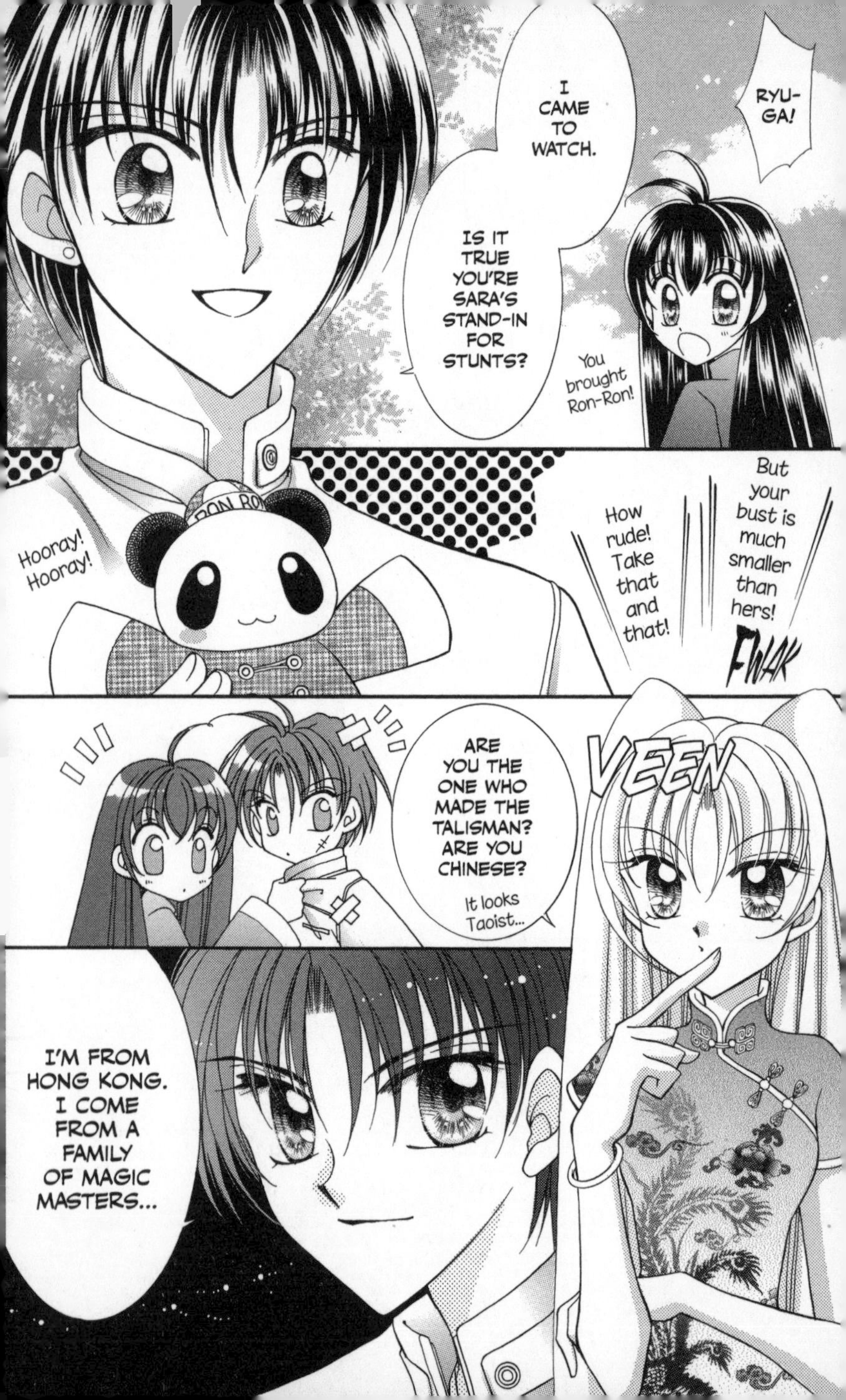
RYU-GA!
I CAME TO WATCH.
IS IT TRUE YOU'RE SARA'S STAND-IN FOR STUNTS?
You brought Ron-Ron!
But your bust is much smaller than hers!
FWAK
How rude! Take that and that!
RON RON
Hooray! Hooray!
VEEN
ARE YOU THE ONE WHO MADE THE TALISMAN? ARE YOU CHINESE?
It looks Taoist...
I'M FROM HONG KONG. I COME FROM A FAMILY OF MAGIC MASTERS...

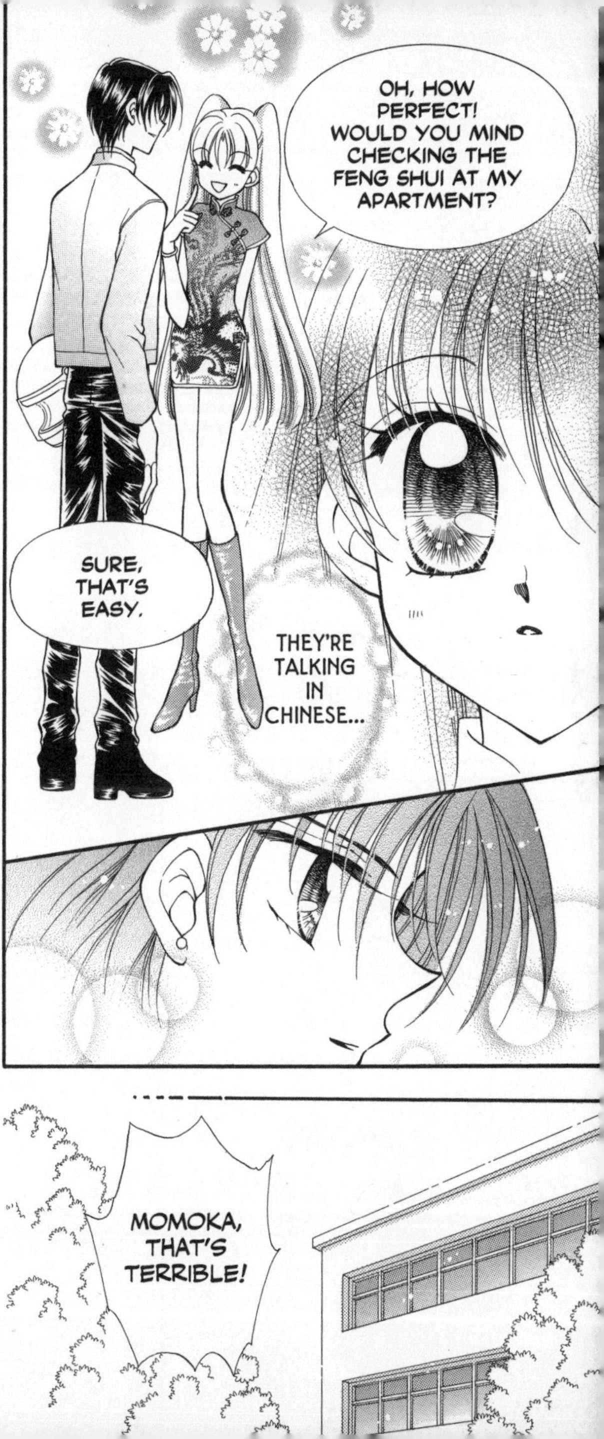
OH, HOW PERFECT! WOULD YOU MIND CHECKING THE FENG SHUI AT MY APARTMENT?
SURE, THAT'S EASY.
THEY'RE TALKING IN CHINESE...
MOMOKA, THAT'S TERRIBLE!

7

The story with Sara is the first ongoing story I've done in a while. I always knew I wanted to write a story about foxes.

After all, foxes are the most powerful of all spirits, aren't they?

I've heard a lot of stories about people being harassed by foxes. I thought those people probably had been drunk or something, until this year when my sister went grocery shopping. She left her 3-year-old daughter in the car, and when she came back about 15 minutes later...

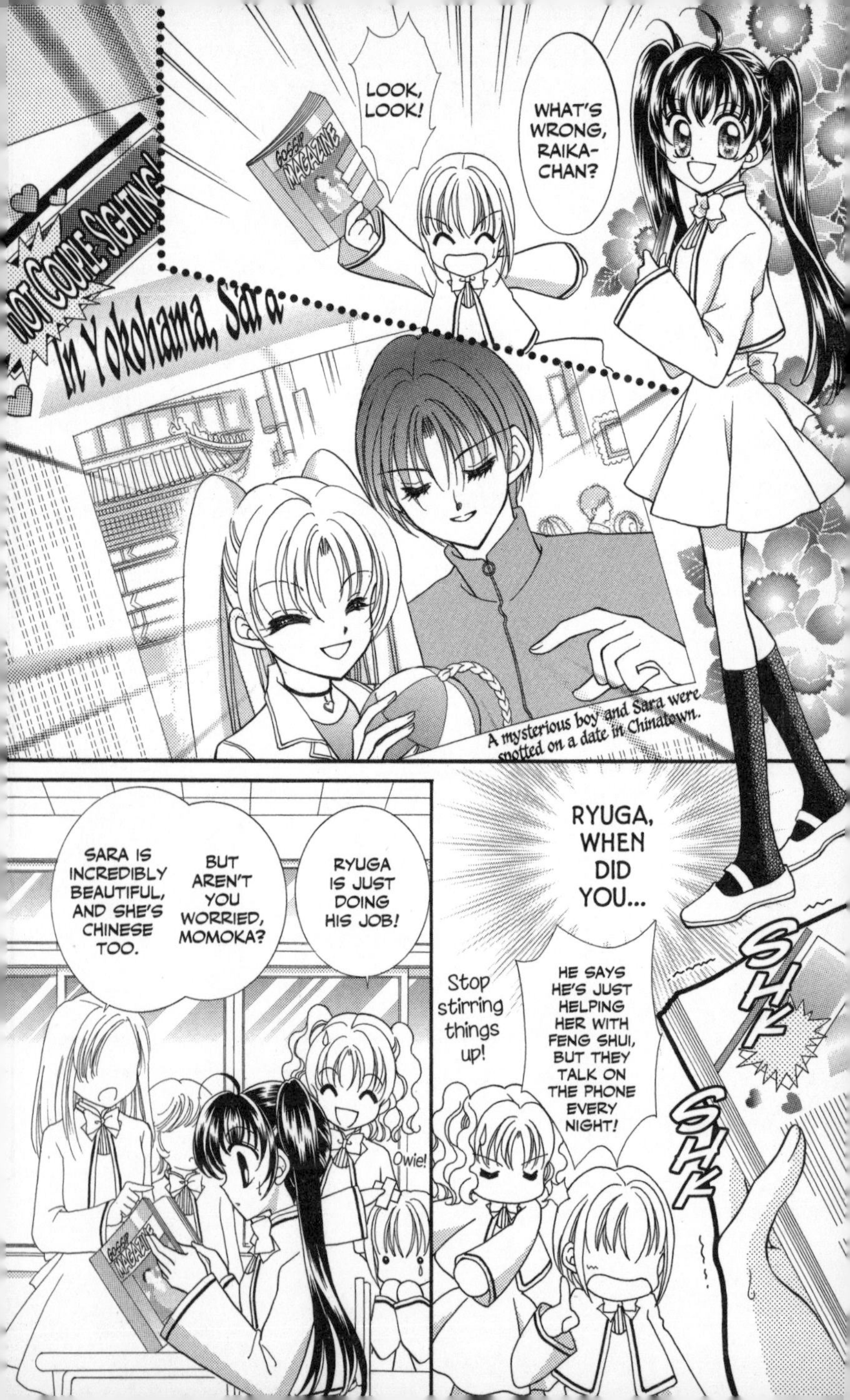
WHAT'S WRONG, RAIKA-CHAN?
LOOK, LOOK!
GOSSIP MAGAZINE
HOT COUPLE SIGHTING!
In Yokohama, Sara
A mysterious boy and Sara were spotted on a date in Chinatown.
RYUGA, WHEN DID YOU...
SHH
SHH
HE SAYS HE'S JUST HELPING HER WITH FENG SHUI, BUT THEY TALK ON THE PHONE EVERY NIGHT!
Stop stirring things up!
RYUGA IS JUST DOING HIS JOB!
BUT AREN'T YOU WORRIED, MOMOKA?
SARA IS INCREDIBLY BEAUTIFUL, AND SHE'S CHINESE TOO.
Owie!

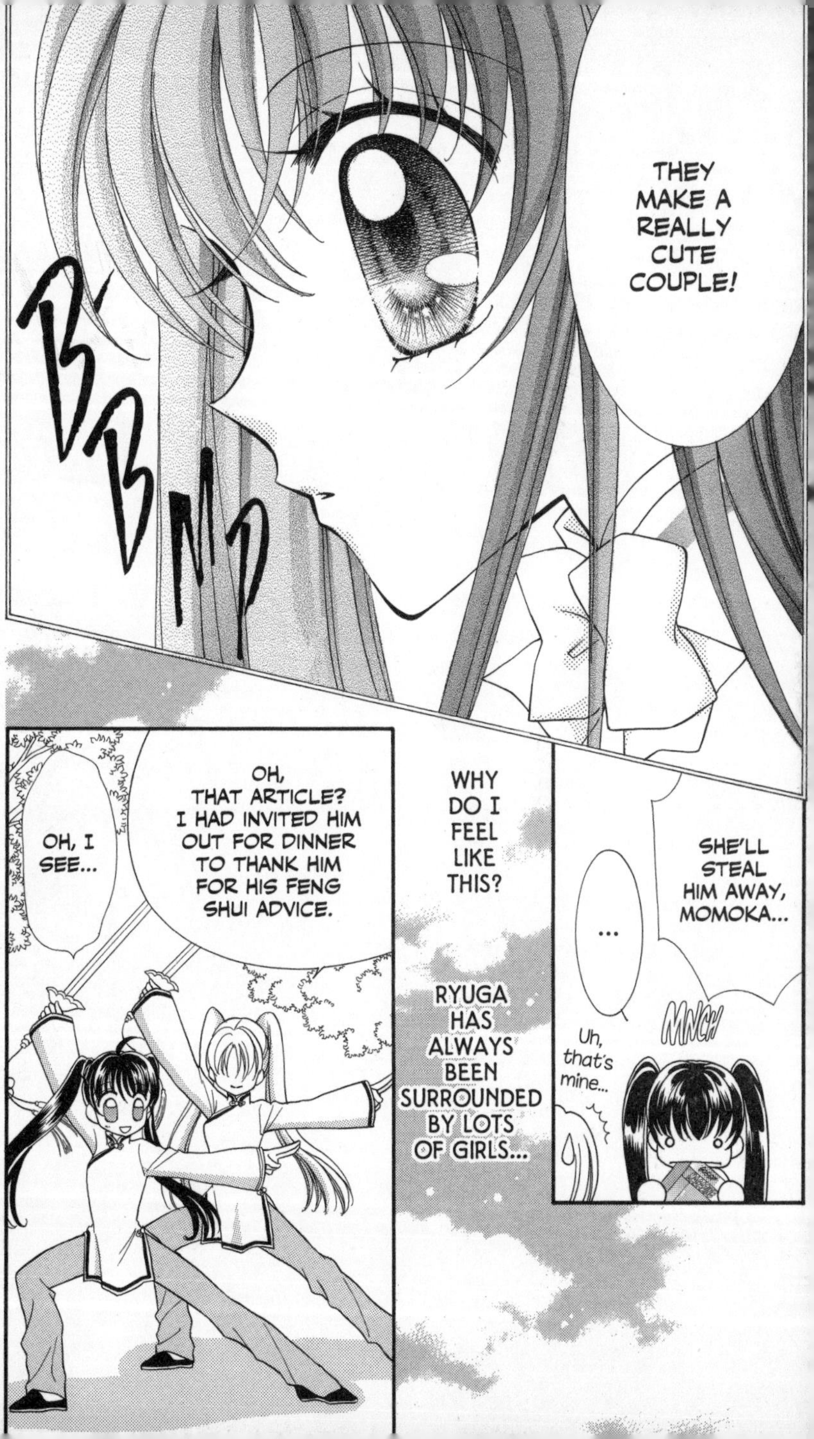

THEY MAKE A REALLY CUTE COUPLE!
BBMP
SHE'LL STEAL HIM AWAY, MOMOKA...
...
MNCH
Uh, that's mine...
WHY DO I FEEL LIKE THIS?
RYUGA HAS ALWAYS BEEN SURROUNDED BY LOTS OF GIRLS...
OH, THAT ARTICLE? I HAD INVITED HIM OUT FOR DINNER TO THANK HIM FOR HIS FENG SHUI ADVICE.
OH, I SEE...

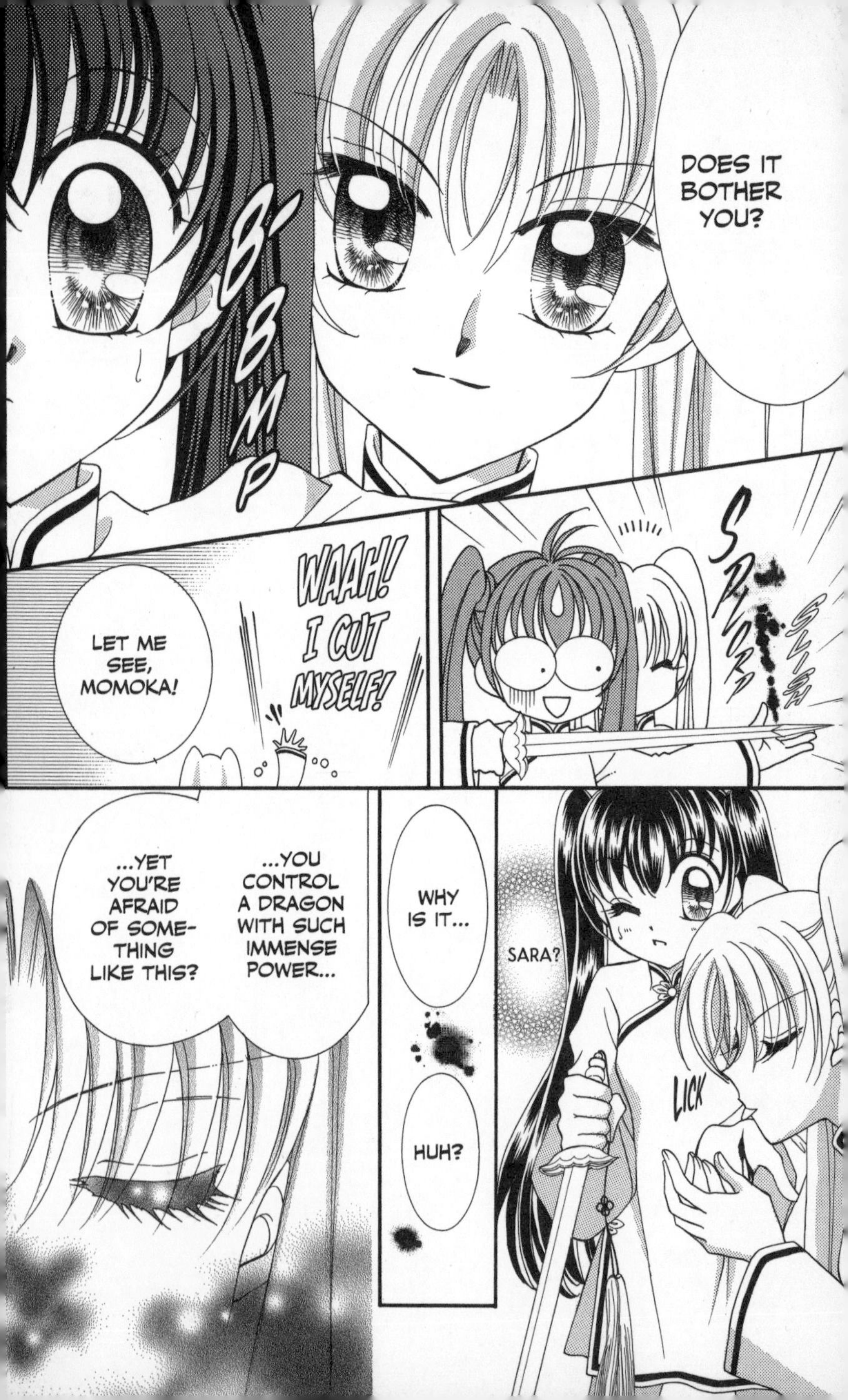
DOES IT BOTHER YOU?
B-BUMP
WAAH! I CUT MYSELF!
LET ME SEE, MOMOKA!
SARA?
LICK
WHY IS IT...
HUH?
...YOU CONTROL A DRAGON WITH SUCH IMMENSE POWER...
...YET YOU'RE AFRAID OF SOME-THING LIKE THIS?

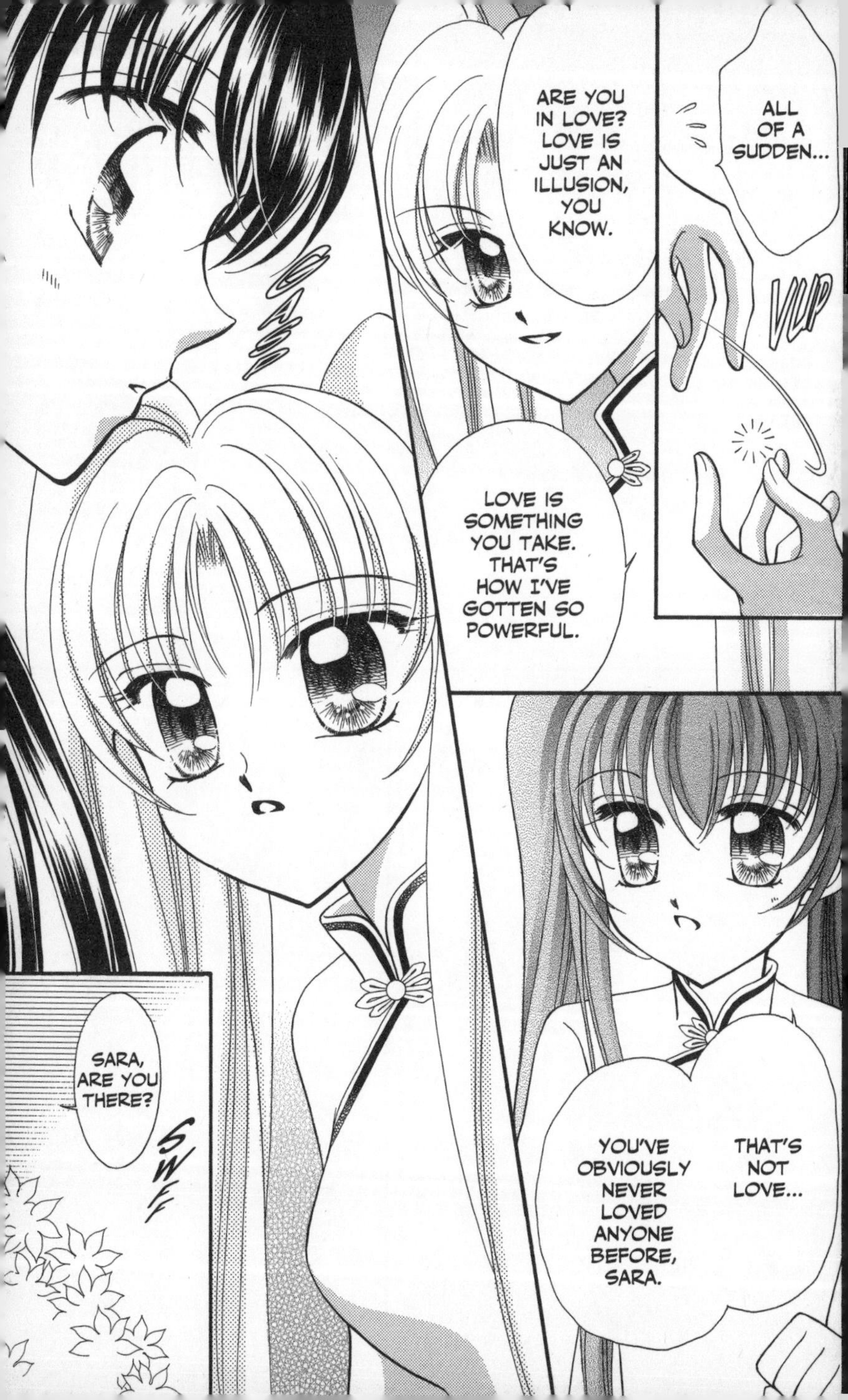
ALL OF A SUDDEN...
VUP
ARE YOU IN LOVE? LOVE IS JUST AN ILLUSION, YOU KNOW.
LOVE IS SOMETHING YOU TAKE. THAT'S HOW I'VE GOTTEN SO POWERFUL.
THAT'S NOT LOVE...
YOU'VE OBVIOUSLY NEVER LOVED ANYONE BEFORE, SARA.
SARA, ARE YOU THERE?

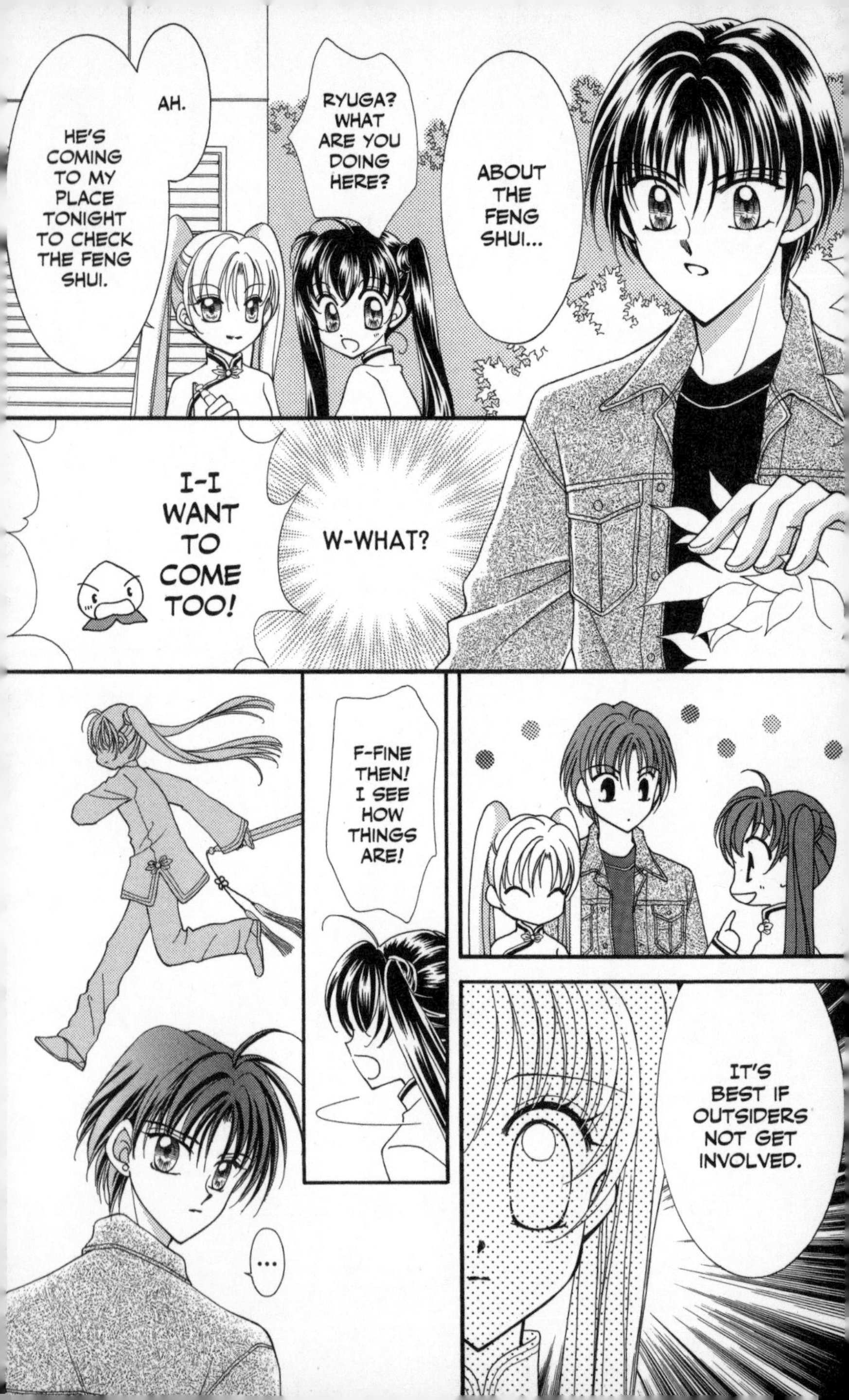
ABOUT THE FENG SHUI...
RYUGA? WHAT ARE YOU DOING HERE?
AH.
HE'S COMING TO MY PLACE TONIGHT TO CHECK THE FENG SHUI.
W-WHAT?
I-I WANT TO COME TOO!
IT'S BEST IF OUTSIDERS NOT GET INVOLVED.
F-FINE THEN! I SEE HOW THINGS ARE!
...

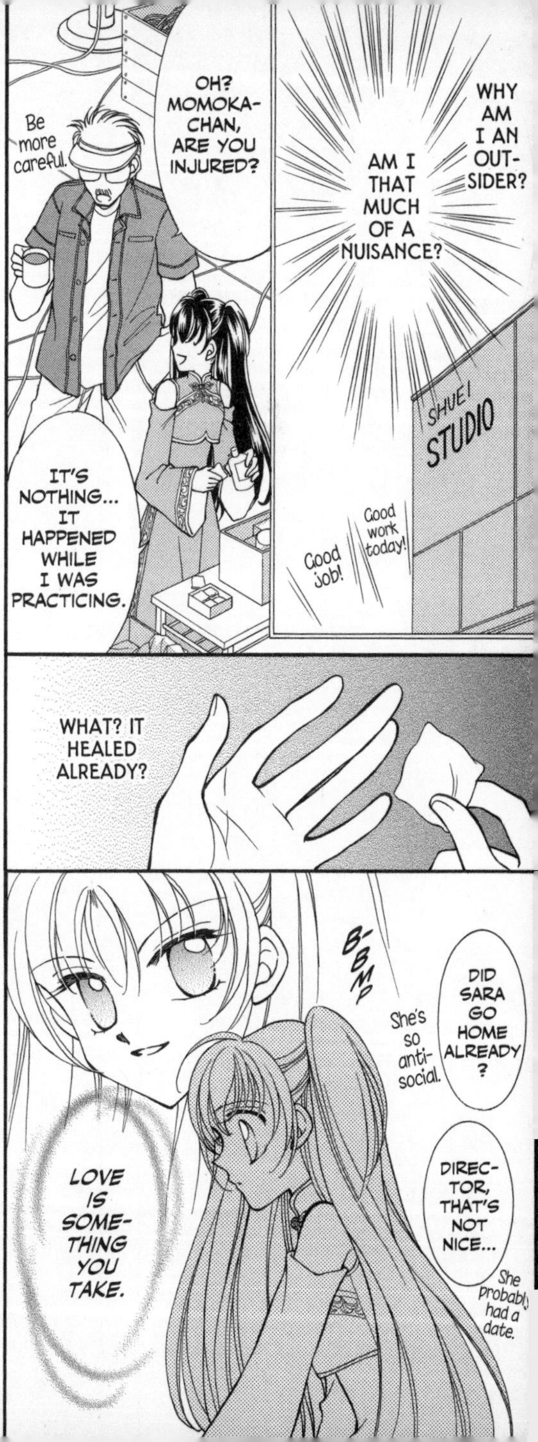

WHY AM I AN OUTSIDER?
AM I THAT MUCH OF A NUISANCE?
SHUEI STUDIO
Good work today!
Good job!
OH? MOMOKA-CHAN, ARE YOU INJURED?
Be more careful.
IT'S NOTHING... IT HAPPENED WHILE I WAS PRACTICING.
WHAT? IT HEALED ALREADY?
B-BMP
DID SARA GO HOME ALREADY?
She's so anti-social.
DIRECTOR, THAT'S NOT NICE...
She probably had a date.
LOVE IS SOMETHING YOU TAKE.

8

Her daughter was pressed up against the window. My sister said, "I'm sorry I'm late. What's wrong? What did you see out the window?" My niece answered, "A fox just played with me! When you came back, it went up that tree!"

My sister said to herself, "A fox? There's no way a fox would be in a place like this! She probably just confused it with a dog. But wouldn't she know it was a dog?"

My sister went over to the tree my niece was pointing to, and she was shocked. It was an Inari shrine with a fox on it! (Foxes are said to be messengers of Inari, the god of harvest.)

So a 3-year-old really saw it!

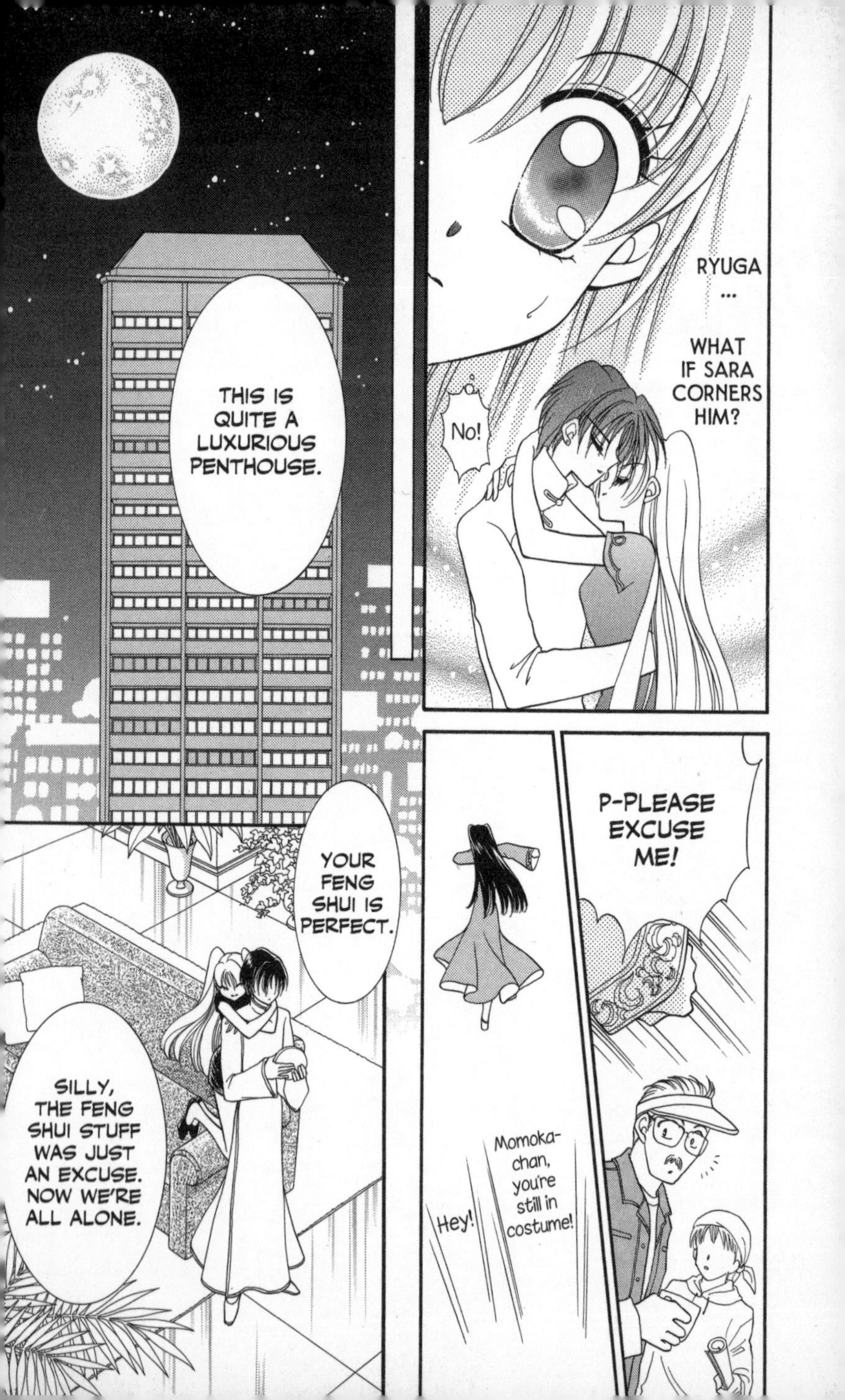
RYUGA ...
WHAT IF SARA CORNERS HIM?
No!
THIS IS QUITE A LUXURIOUS PENTHOUSE.
P-PLEASE EXCUSE ME!
Hey!
Momoka-chan, you're still in costume!
YOUR FENG SHUI IS PERFECT.
SILLY, THE FENG SHUI STUFF WAS JUST AN EXCUSE. NOW WE'RE ALL ALONE.

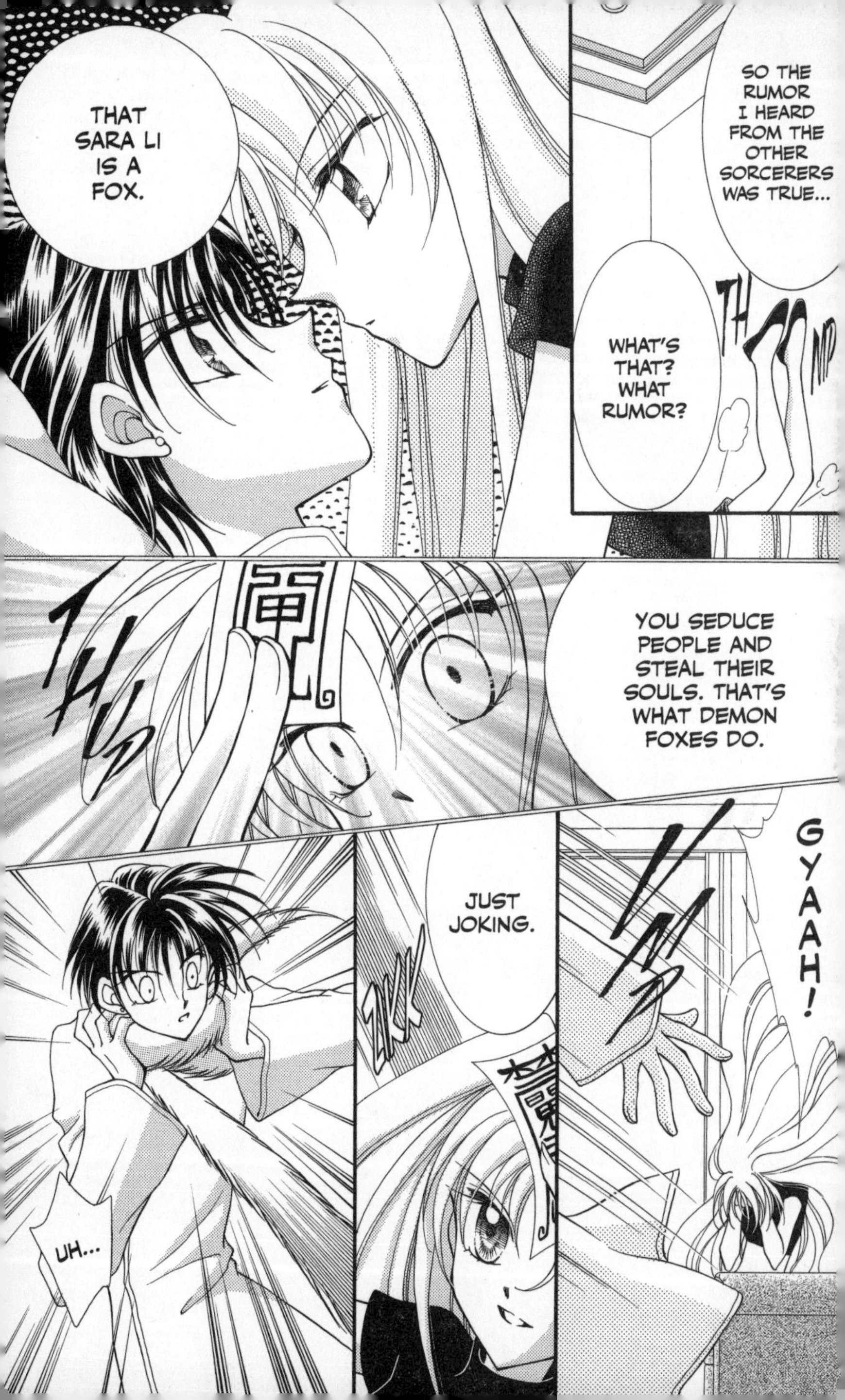
SO THE RUMOR I HEARD FROM THE OTHER SORCERERS WAS TRUE...
WHAT'S THAT? WHAT RUMOR?
THAT SARA LI IS A FOX.
YOU SEDUCE PEOPLE AND STEAL THEIR SOULS. THAT'S WHAT DEMON FOXES DO.
GYAAH!
JUST JOKING.
UH...

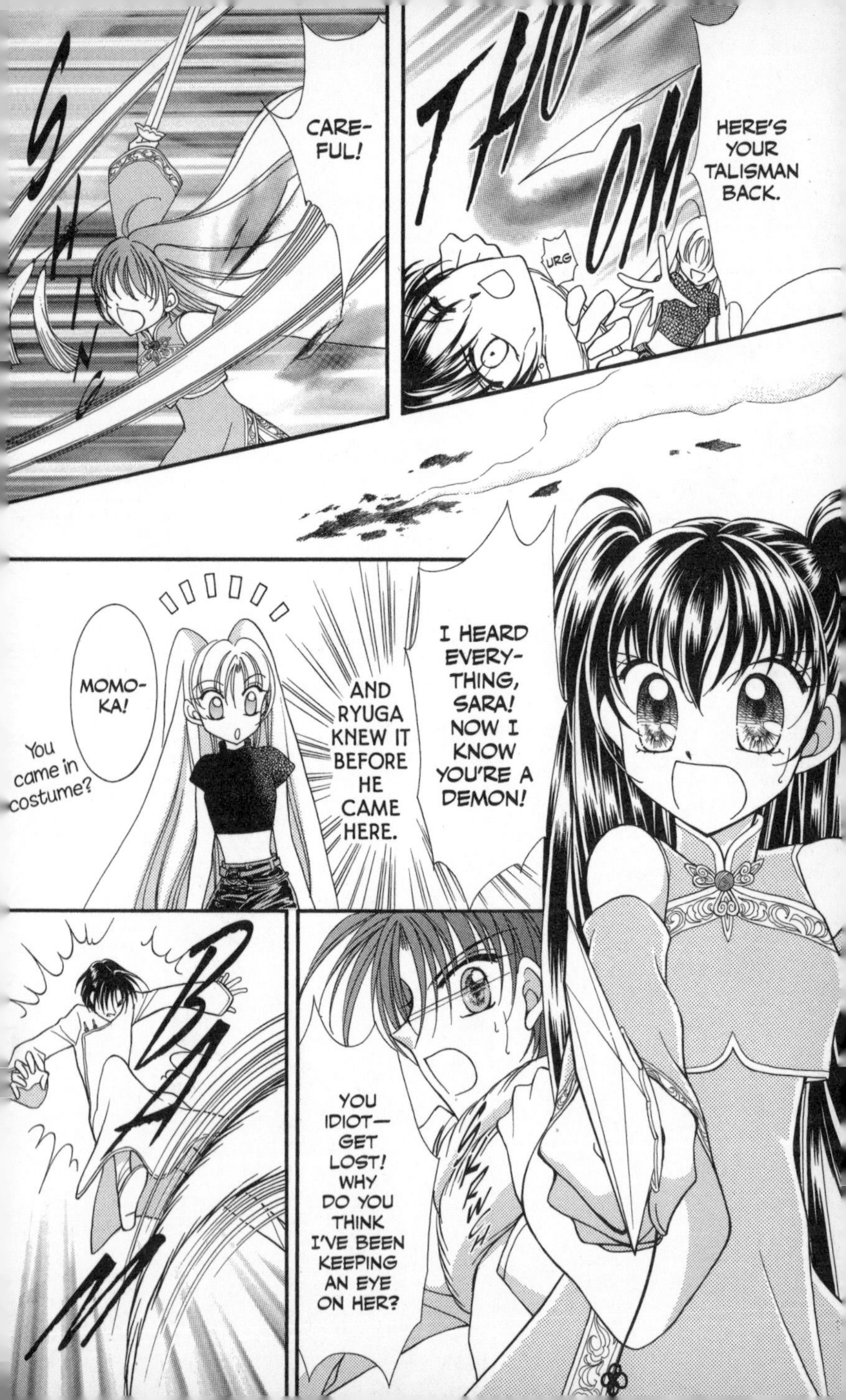
THOOM
URG
HERE'S YOUR TALISMAN BACK.
SHING
CARE-FUL!
I HEARD EVERY-THING, SARA! NOW I KNOW YOU'RE A DEMON!
AND RYUGA KNEW IT BEFORE HE CAME HERE.
MOMO-KA!
You came in costume?
YOU IDIOT— GET LOST! WHY DO YOU THINK I'VE BEEN KEEPING AN EYE ON HER?
BAM

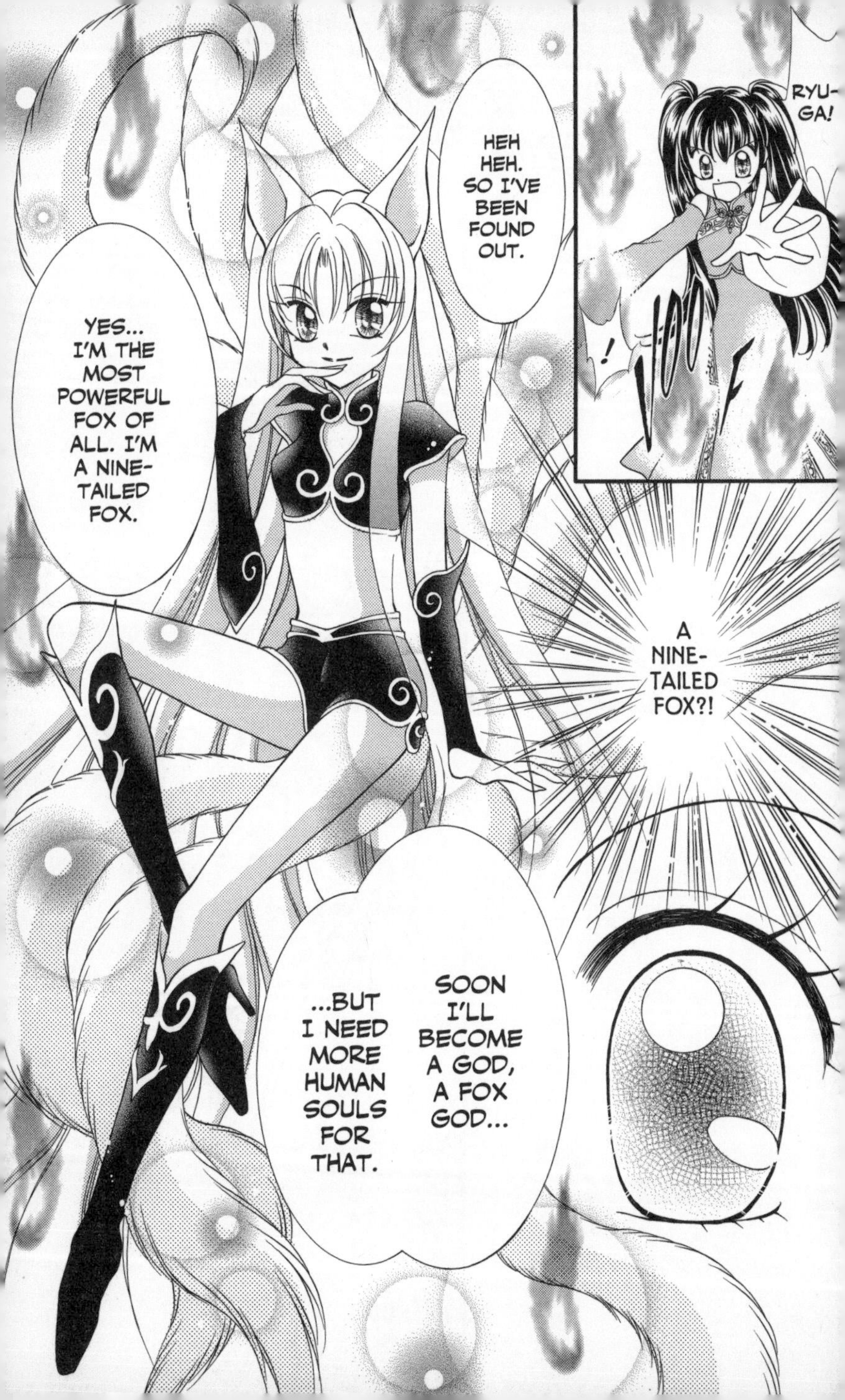

RYU-GA!
!
VOOF
HEH HEH. SO I'VE BEEN FOUND OUT.
YES... I'M THE MOST POWERFUL FOX OF ALL. I'M A NINE-TAILED FOX.
A NINE-TAILED FOX?!
SOON I'LL BECOME A GOD, A FOX GOD...
...BUT I NEED MORE HUMAN SOULS FOR THAT.

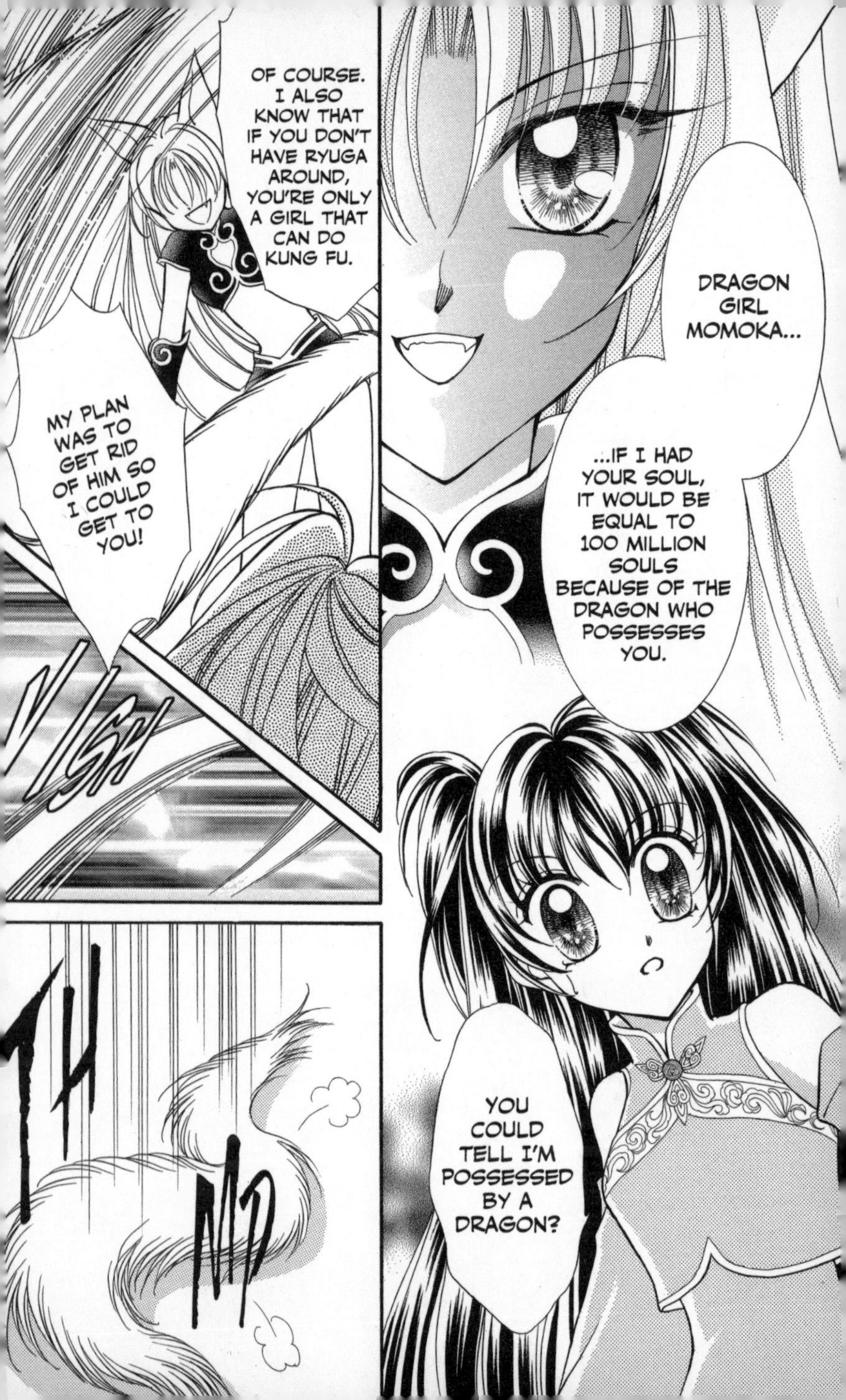
DRAGON GIRL MOMOKA...
...IF I HAD YOUR SOUL, IT WOULD BE EQUAL TO 100 MILLION SOULS BECAUSE OF THE DRAGON WHO POSSESSES YOU.
YOU COULD TELL I'M POSSESSED BY A DRAGON?
OF COURSE. I ALSO KNOW THAT IF YOU DON'T HAVE RYUGA AROUND, YOU'RE ONLY A GIRL THAT CAN DO KUNG FU.
MY PLAN WAS TO GET RID OF HIM SO I COULD GET TO YOU!
THMP

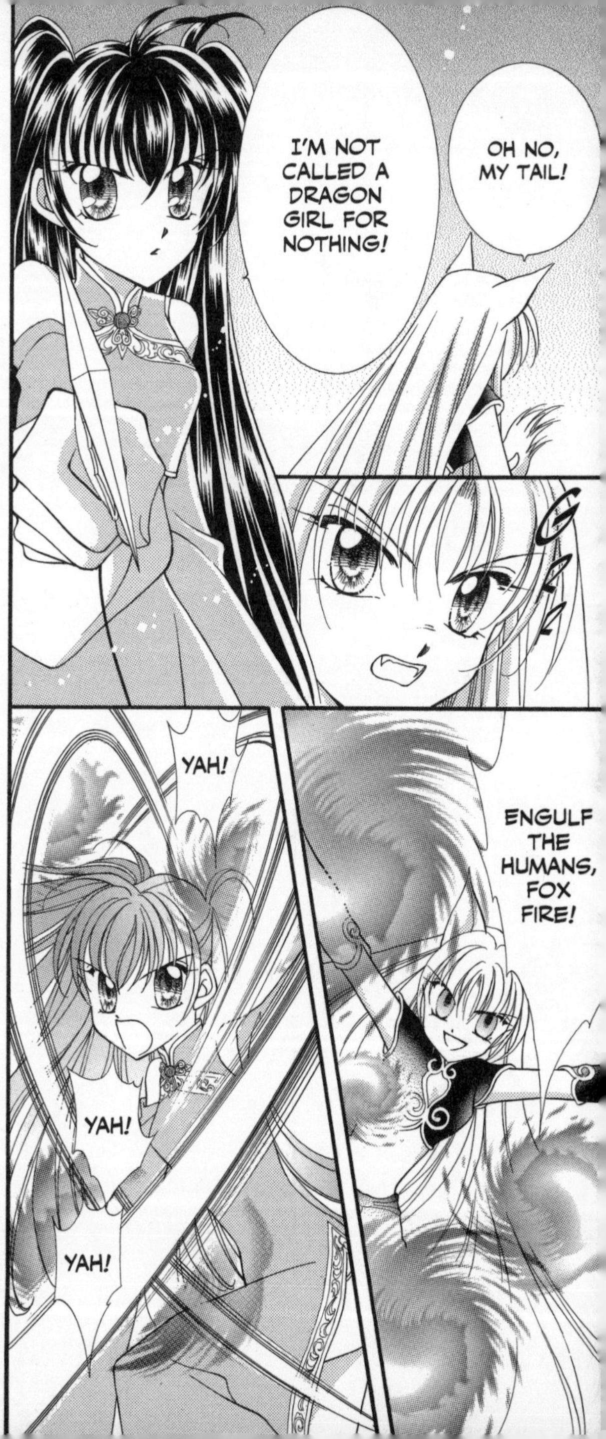
OH NO, MY TAIL!
I'M NOT CALLED A DRAGON GIRL FOR NOTHING!
ENGULF THE HUMANS, FOX FIRE!
YAH!
YAH!
YAH!

9

Ever since I heard that, I've started to believe in fox spirits. I'd like to see one. I believe there is a turtle god too! There was a show on TV about some village people who saw an image of a turtle god by a dam. It seems the town's guardian deity is a turtle god.

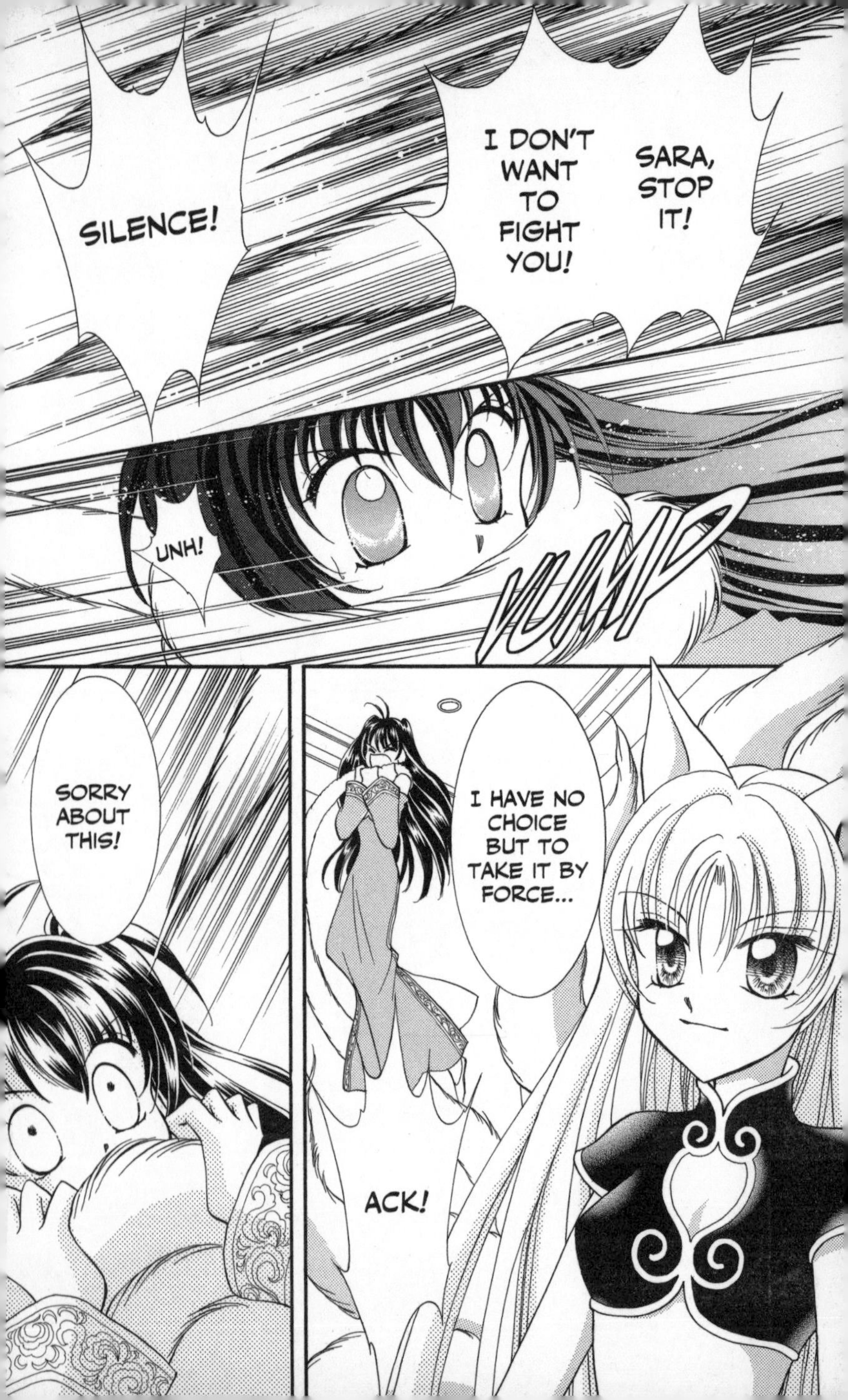
SARA, STOP IT!
I DON'T WANT TO FIGHT YOU!
SILENCE!
VUMP
UNH!
I HAVE NO CHOICE BUT TO TAKE IT BY FORCE...
ACK!
SORRY ABOUT THIS!

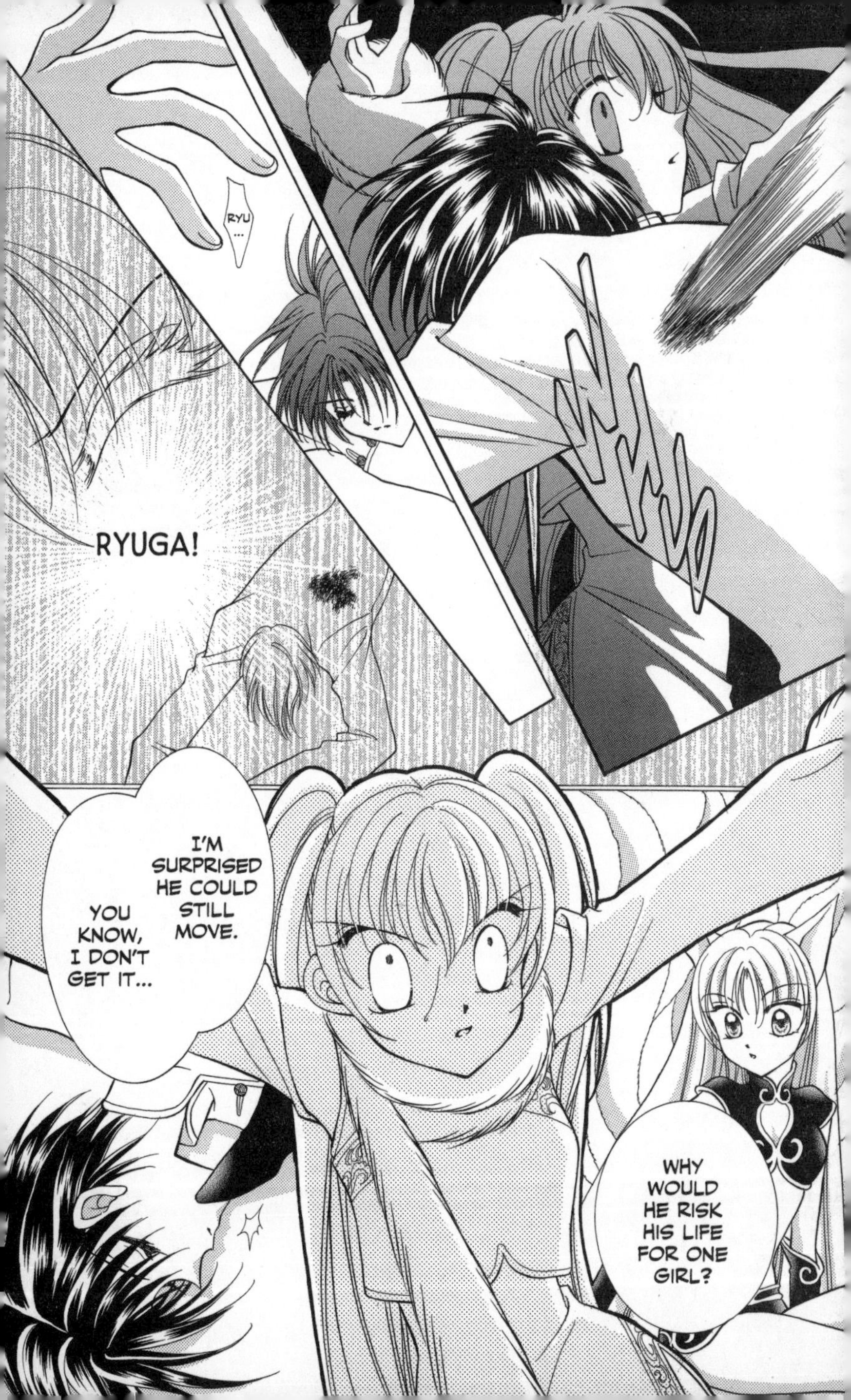
RYU ...
RYUGA!
I'M SURPRISED HE COULD STILL MOVE.
YOU KNOW, I DON'T GET IT...
WHY WOULD HE RISK HIS LIFE FOR ONE GIRL?

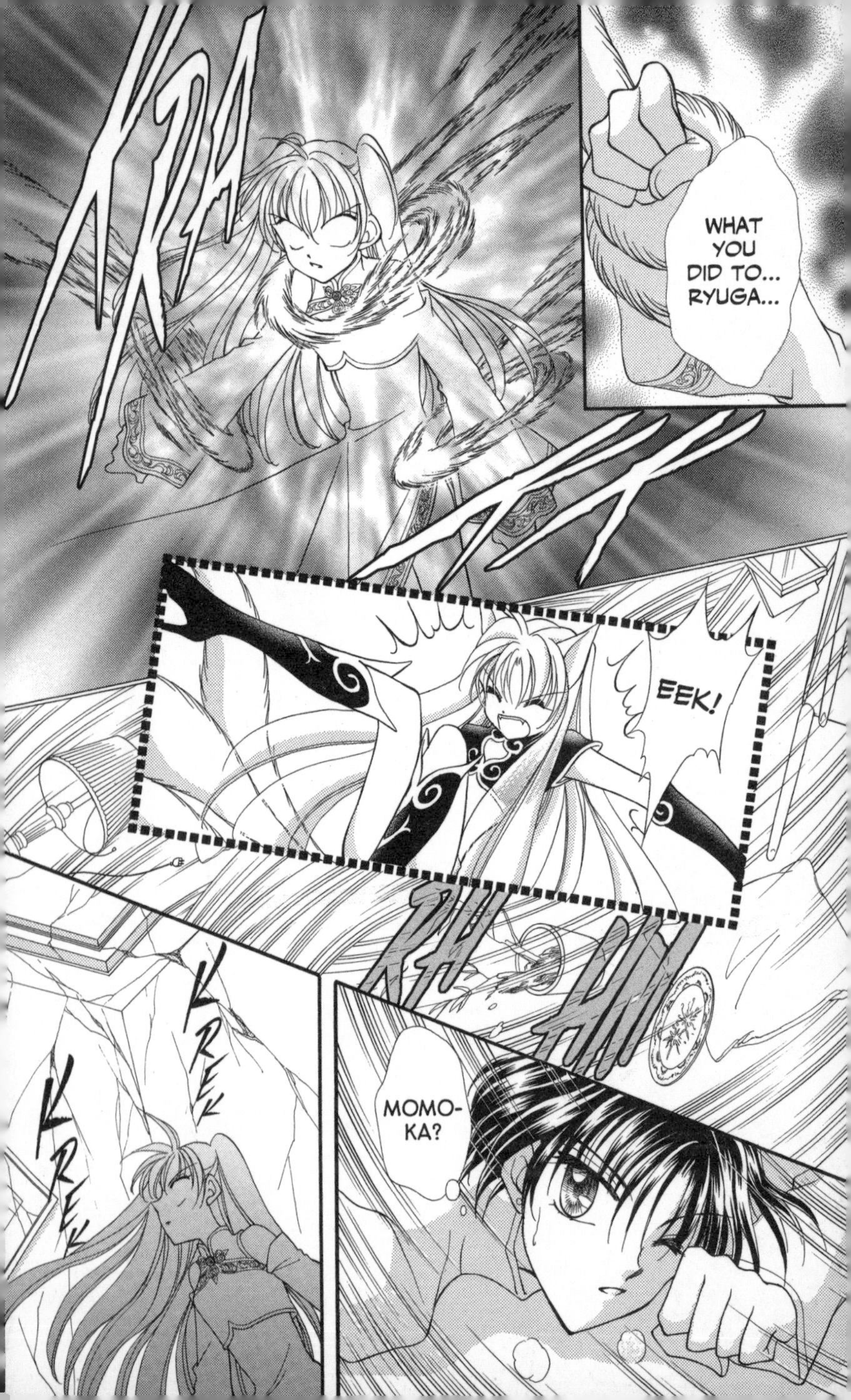
WHAT YOU DID TO... RYUGA...
EEK!
MOMO-KA?

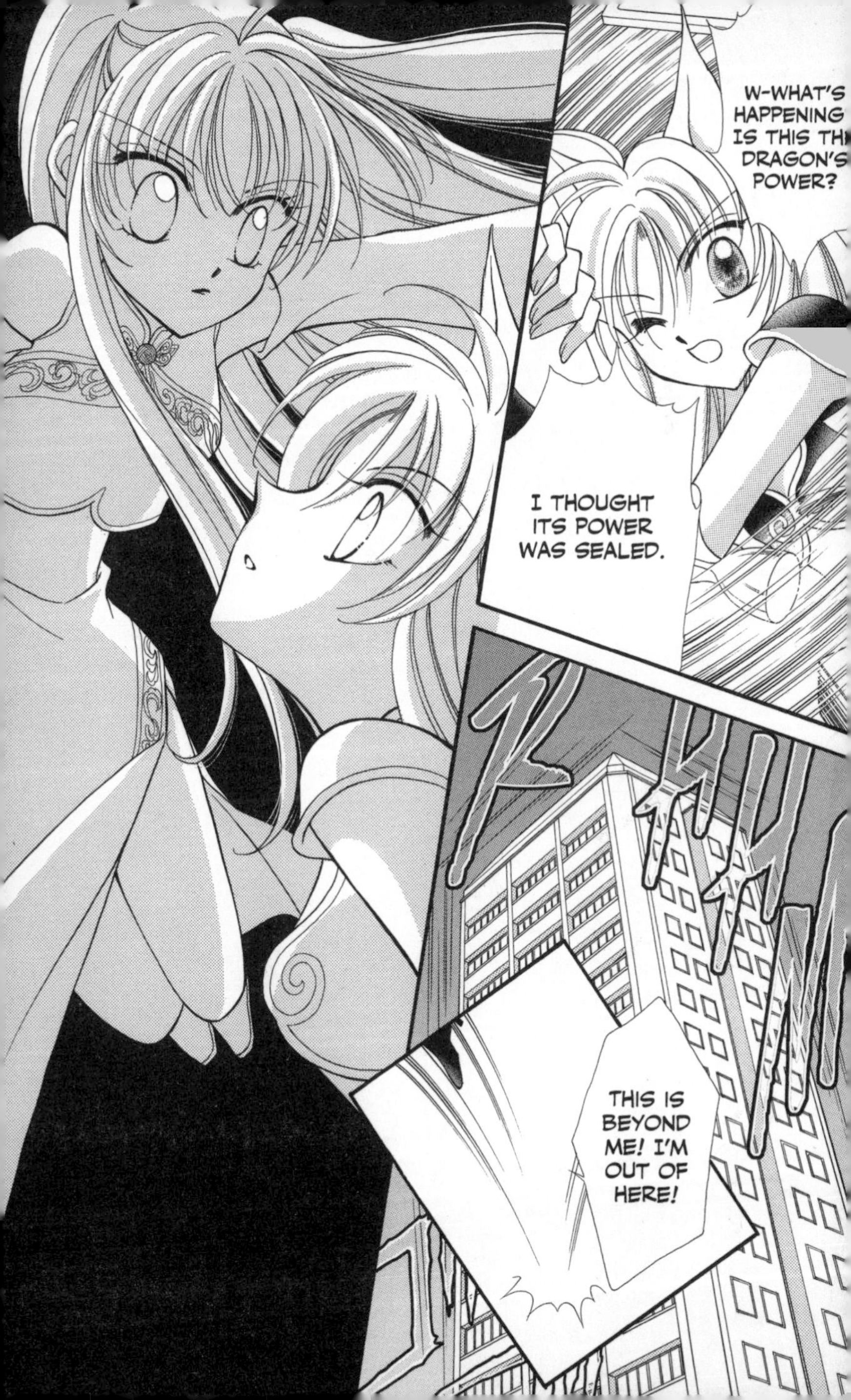
W-WHAT'S HAPPENING IS THIS TH DRAGON'S POWER?
I THOUGHT ITS POWER WAS SEALED.
THIS IS BEYOND ME! I'M OUT OF HERE!

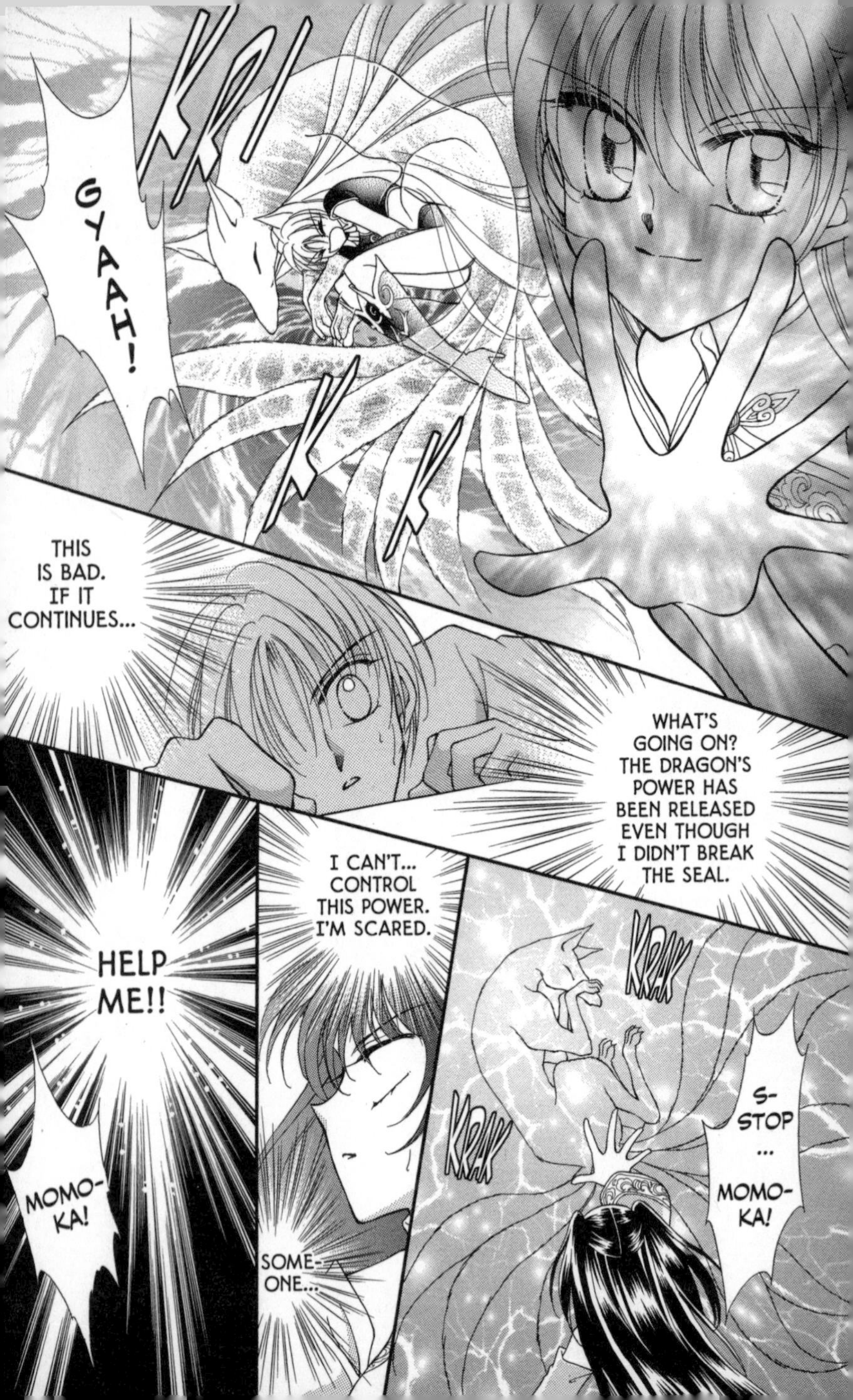
KRI
GYAAH!
KK
KK
WHAT'S GOING ON? THE DRAGON'S POWER HAS BEEN RELEASED EVEN THOUGH I DIDN'T BREAK THE SEAL.
THIS IS BAD. IF IT CONTINUES...
KRAK
S-STOP... MOMO-KA!
KRAK
I CAN'T... CONTROL THIS POWER. I'M SCARED.
SOME-ONE...
HELP ME!!
MOMO-KA!

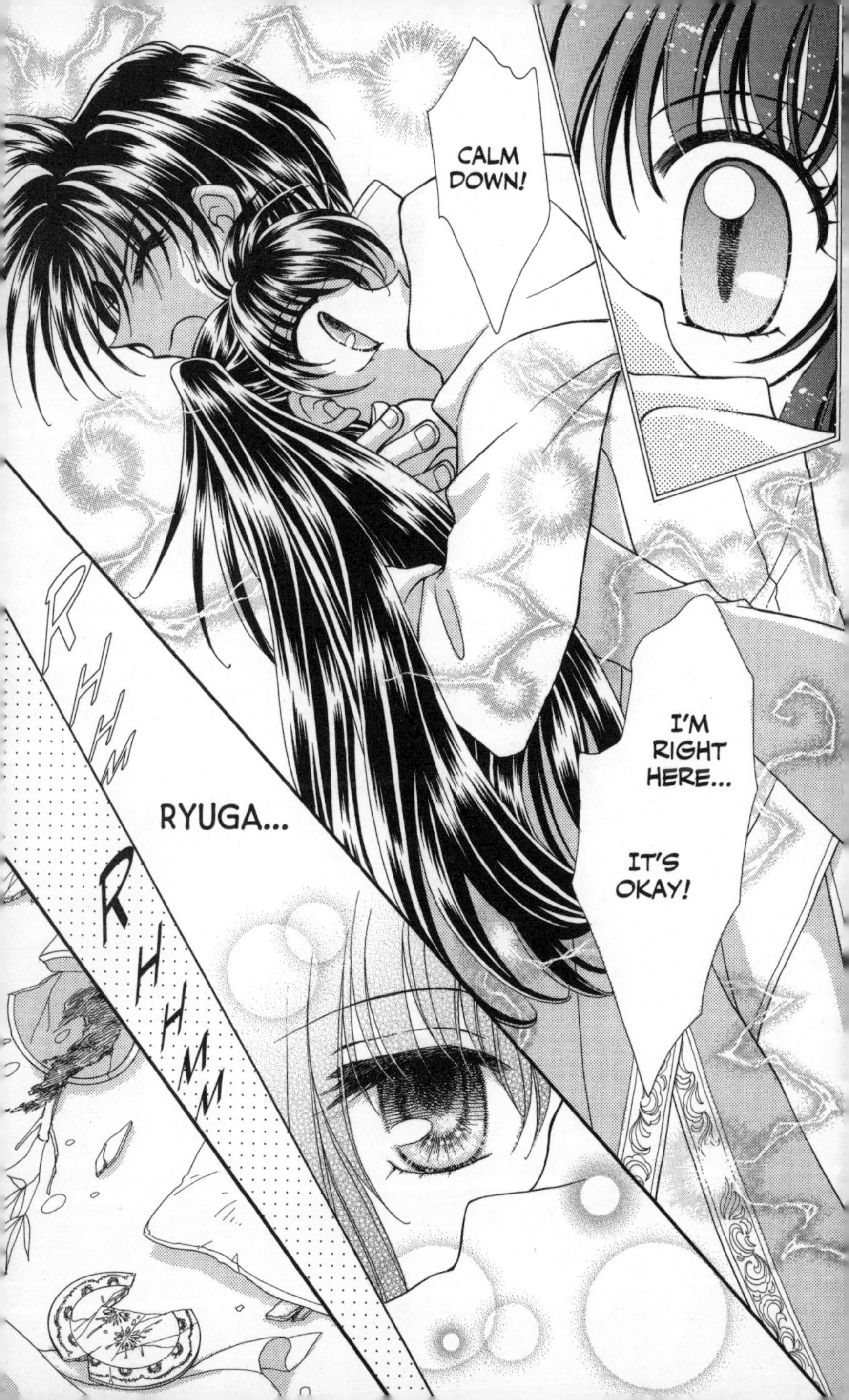
CALM DOWN!
I'M RIGHT HERE...
IT'S OKAY!
RYUGA...
RHHMM
RHHMM

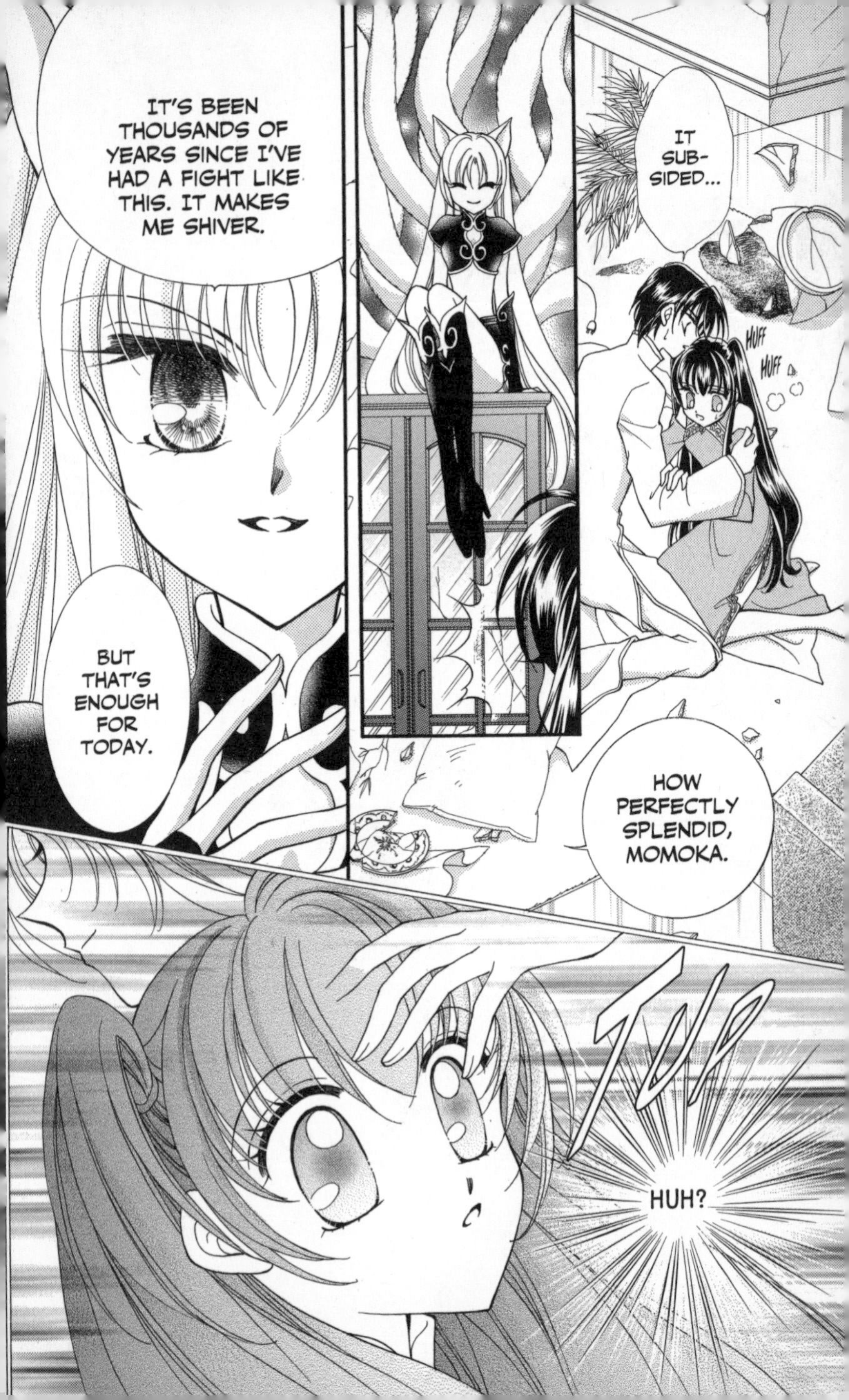
IT SUB-SIDED...
HUFF
HUFF
HOW PERFECTLY SPLENDID, MOMOKA.
IT'S BEEN THOUSANDS OF YEARS SINCE I'VE HAD A FIGHT LIKE THIS. IT MAKES ME SHIVER.
BUT THAT'S ENOUGH FOR TODAY.
TUP
HUH?

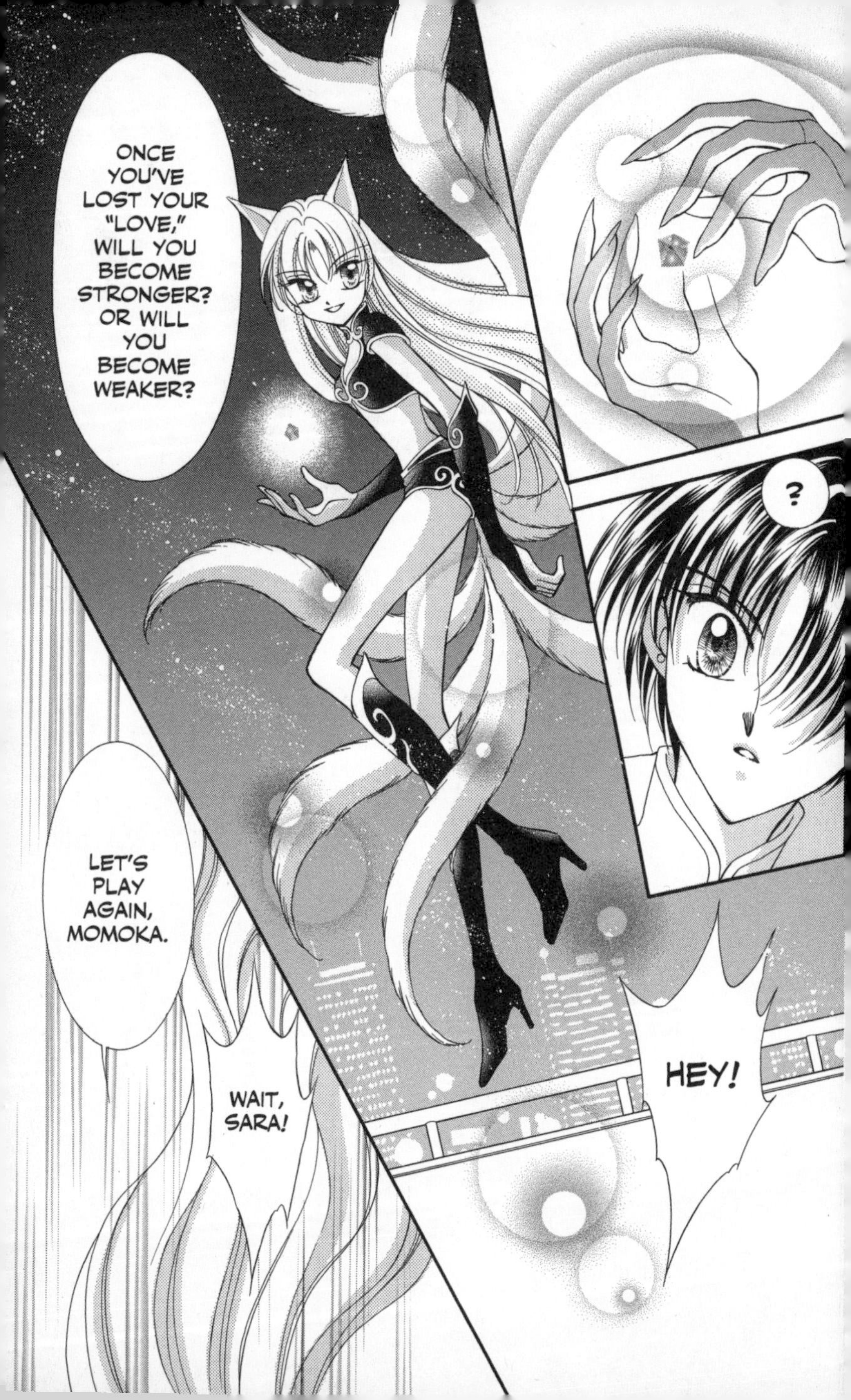
?
ONCE YOU'VE LOST YOUR "LOVE," WILL YOU BECOME STRONGER? OR WILL YOU BECOME WEAKER?
LET'S PLAY AGAIN, MOMOKA.
HEY!
WAIT, SARA!

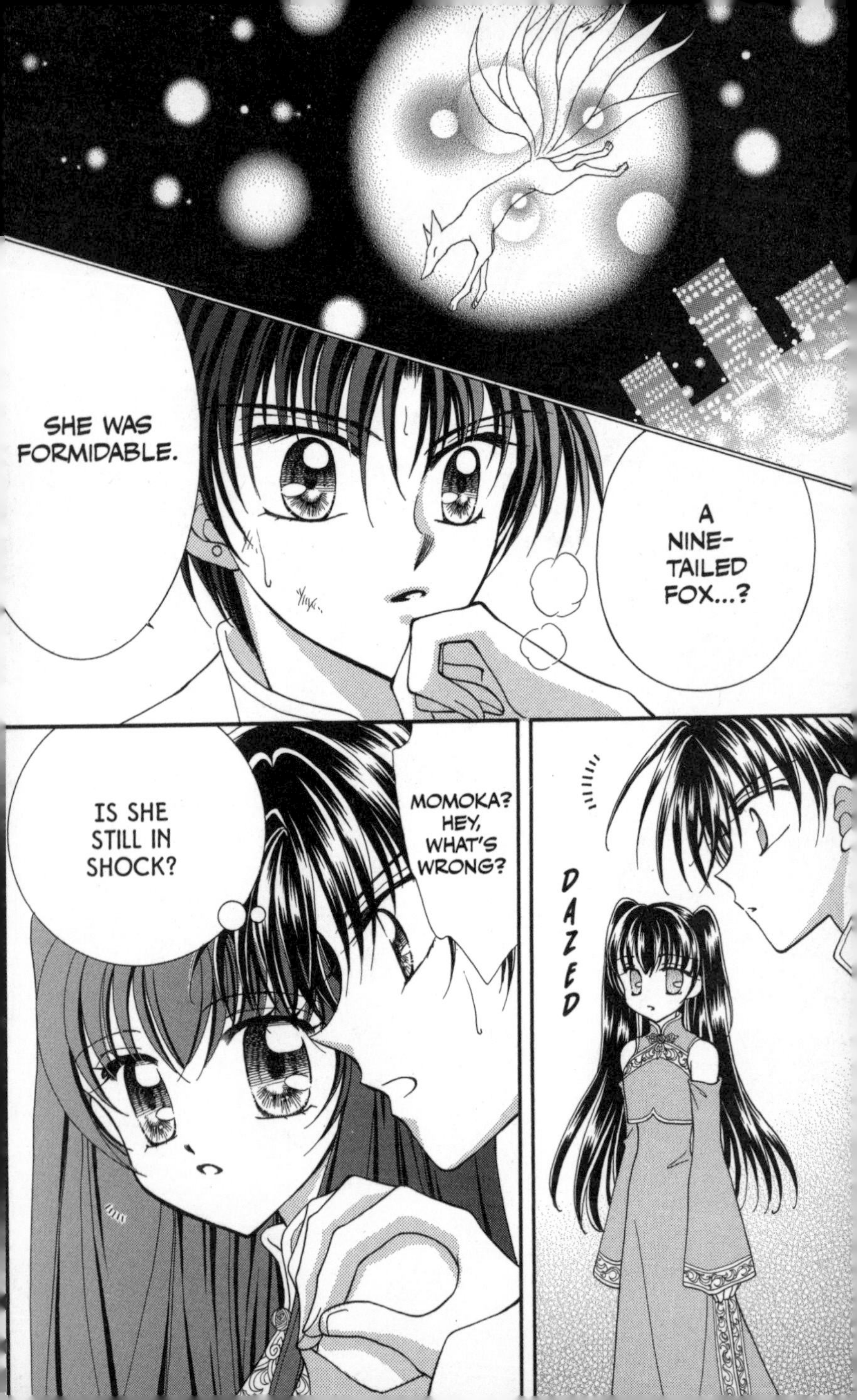
A NINE-TAILED FOX...?
SHE WAS FORMIDABLE.
DAZED
MOMOKA? HEY, WHAT'S WRONG?
IS SHE STILL IN SHOCK?

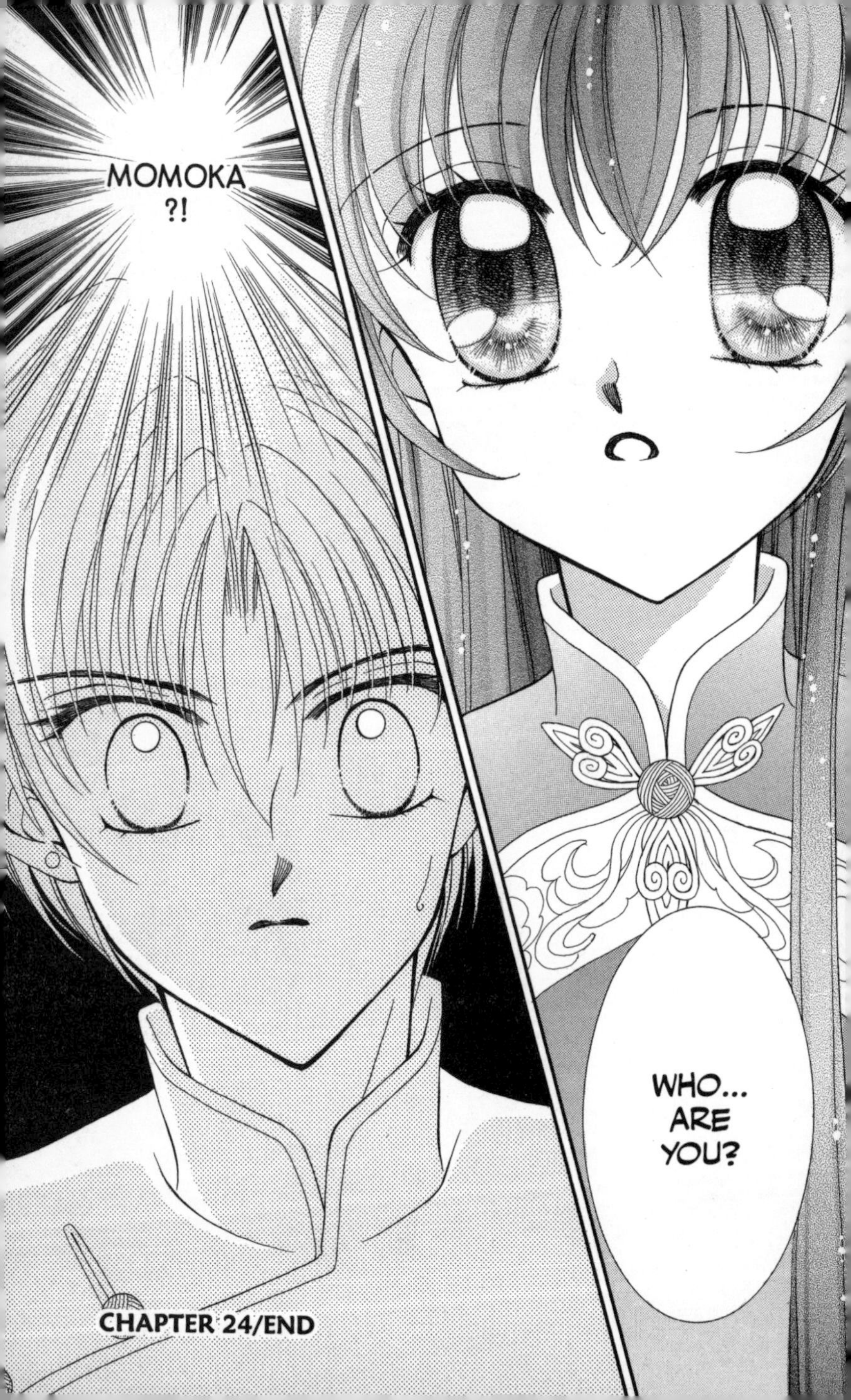
WHO... ARE YOU?
MOMOKA ?!
CHAPTER 24/END

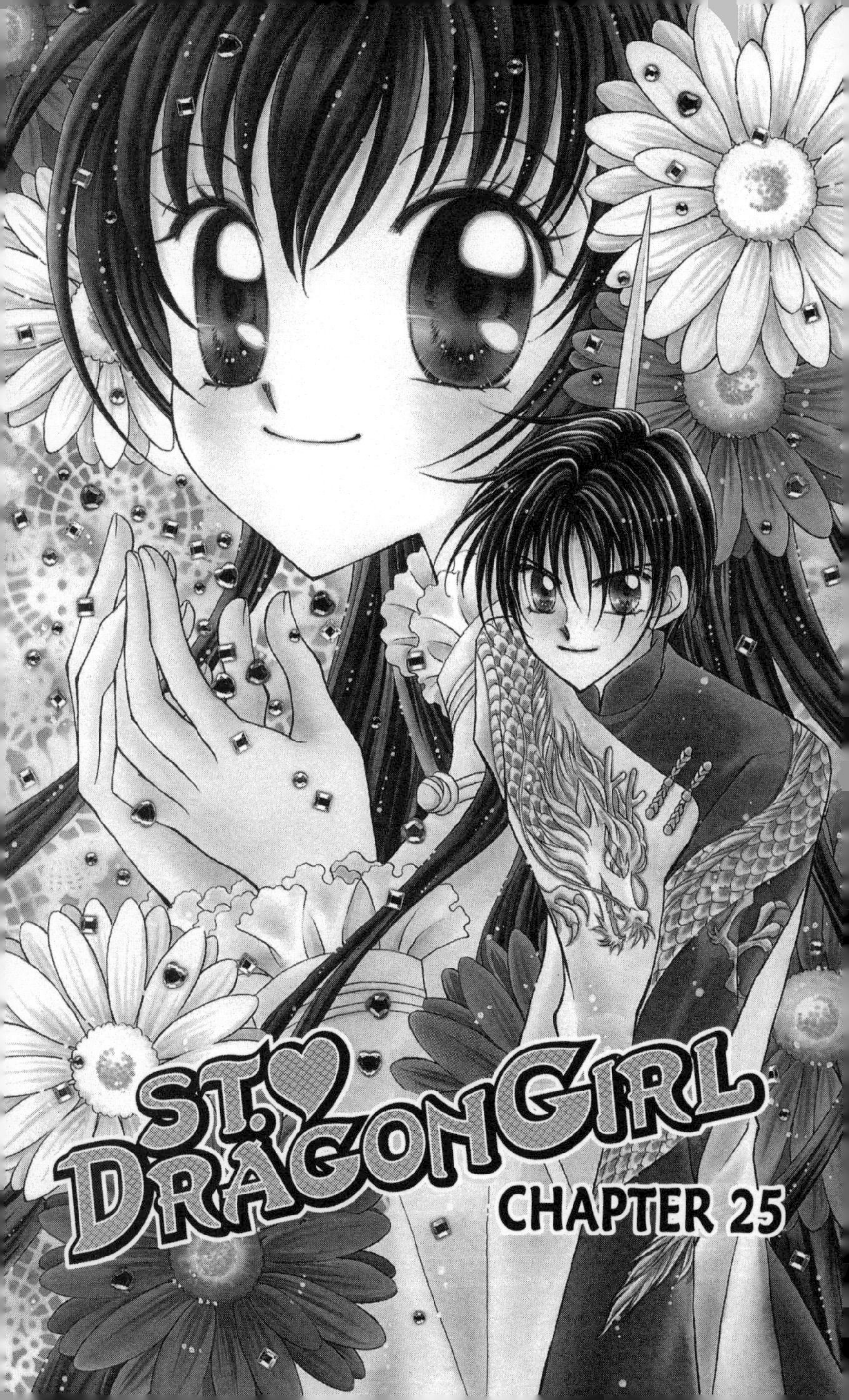
ST.♥DRAGON GIRL
CHAPTER 25

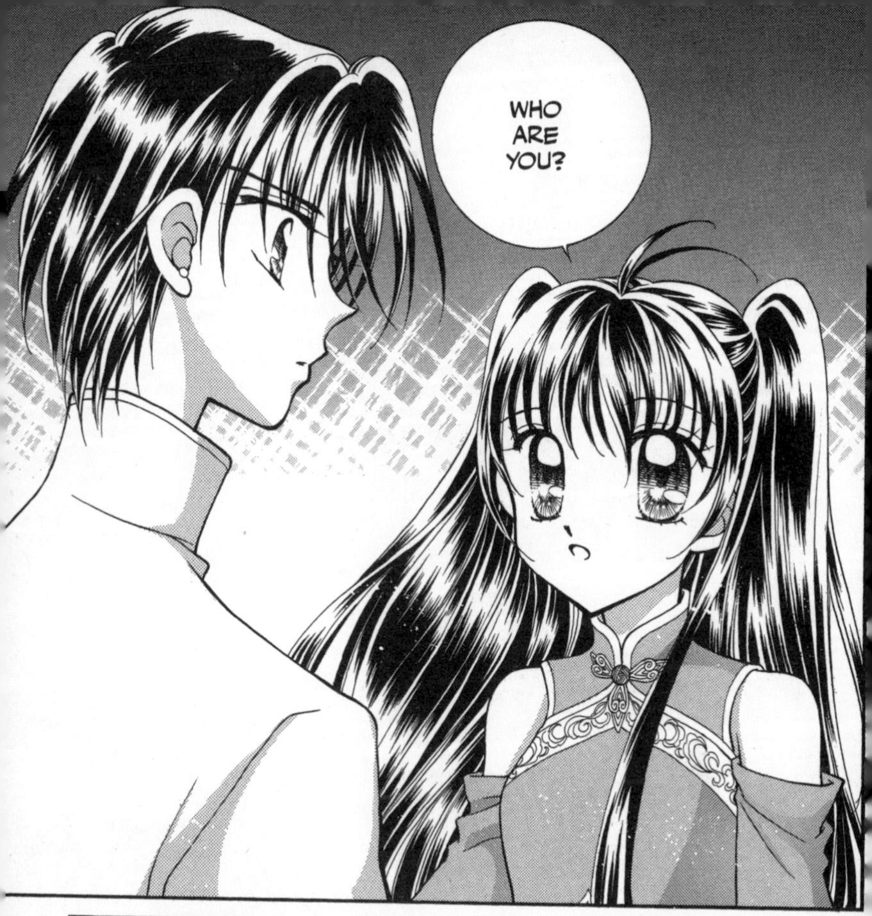
WHO ARE YOU?

I love tall sunflowers. I planted tons of seeds in my garden this year. The small sprouts grew really fast. In August, there were tons of sunflowers everywhere! When I see sunflowers, it puts me in a cheerful mood. I draw those flowers a lot in color illustrations. I'm writing this now at the end of August. Sparrows seem to have eaten all the sunflower seeds! I guess I'll plant more next year.

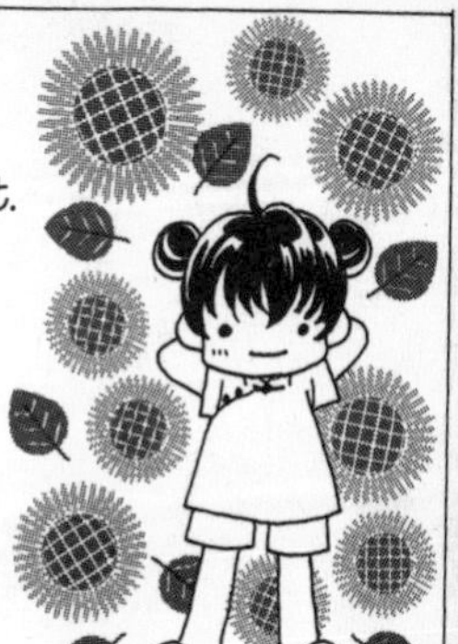

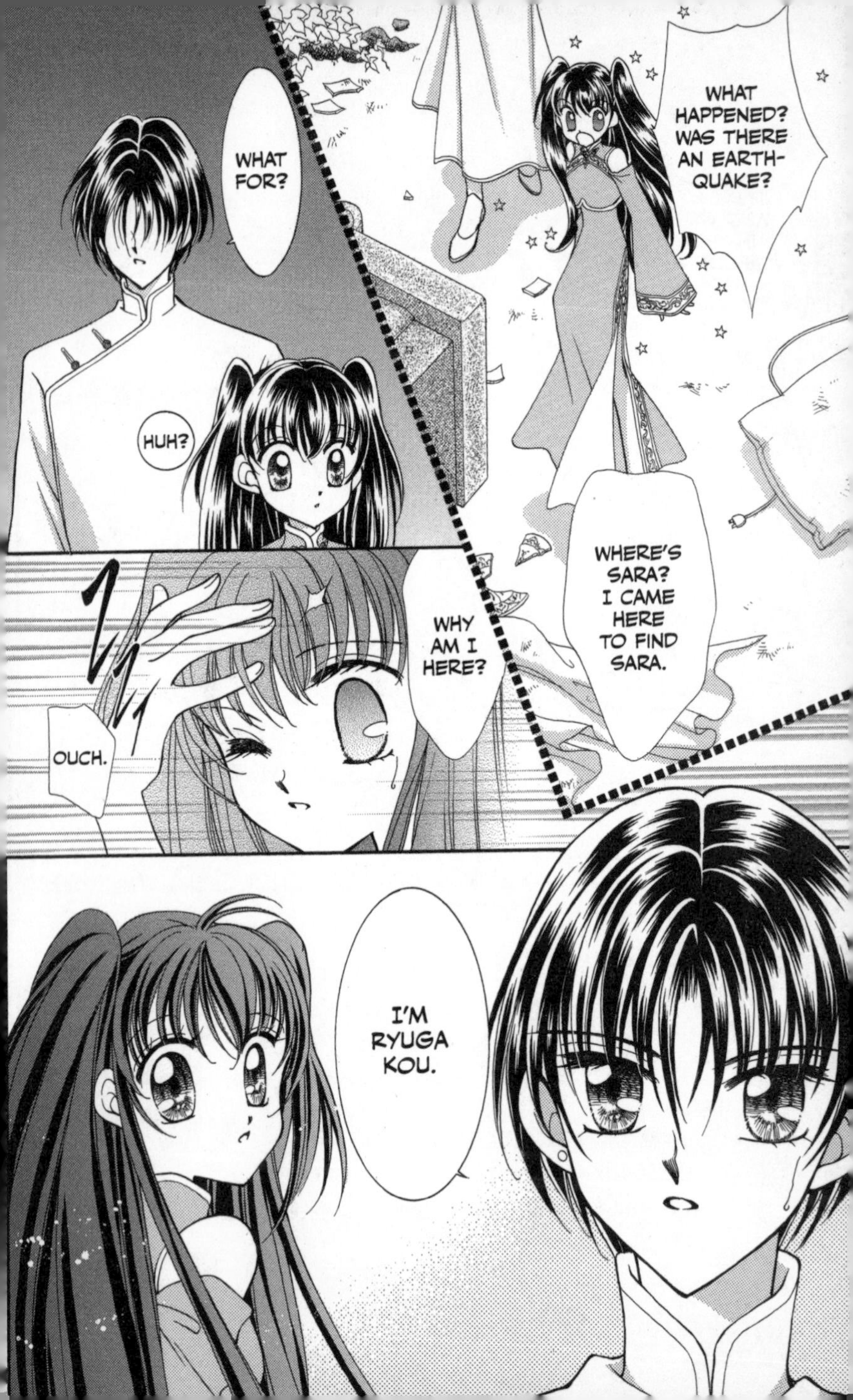
WHAT HAPPENED? WAS THERE AN EARTH-QUAKE?
WHERE'S SARA? I CAME HERE TO FIND SARA.
WHAT FOR?
HUH?
WHY AM I HERE?
OUCH.
I'M RYUGA KOU.

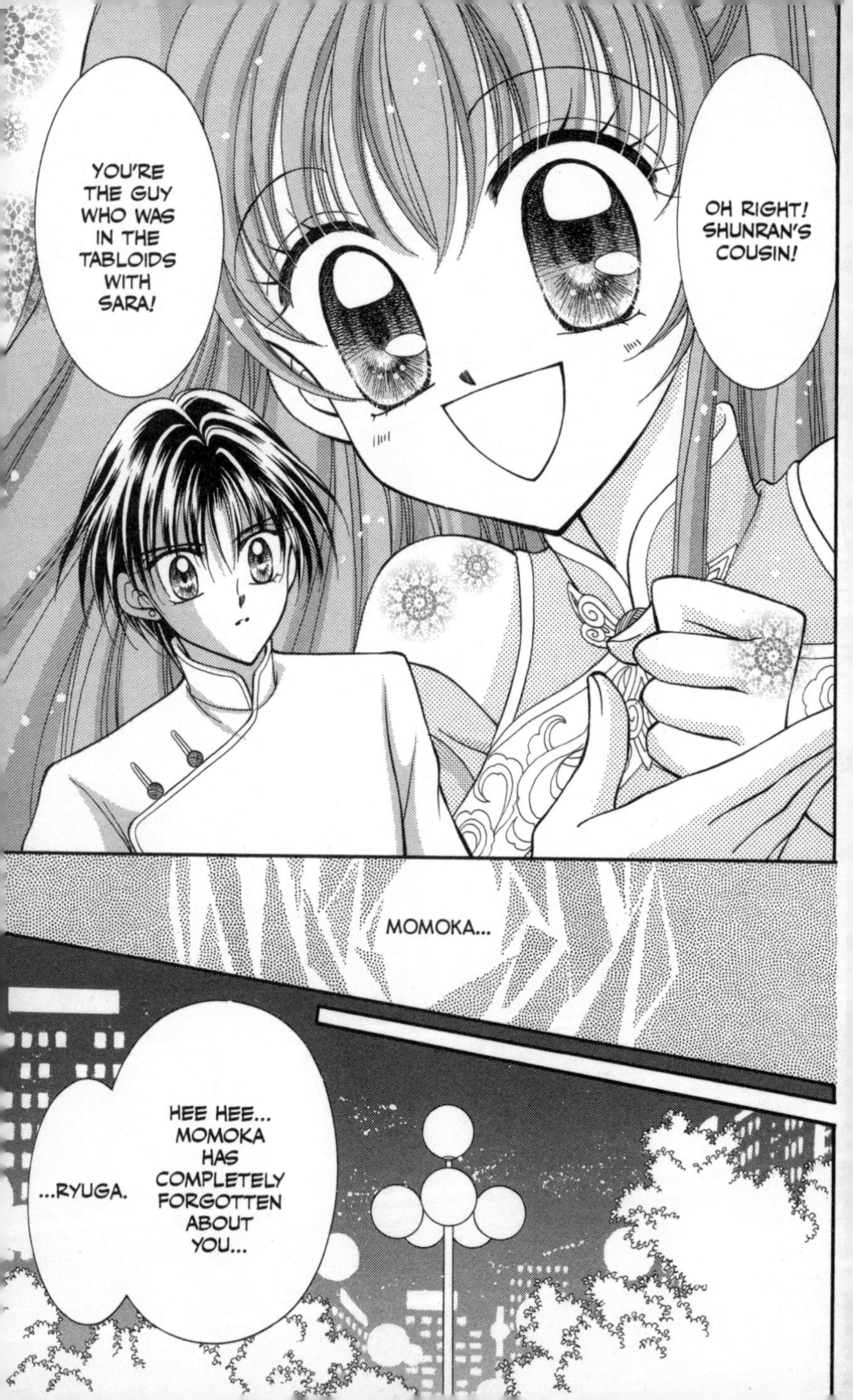
OH RIGHT! SHUNRAN'S COUSIN!
YOU'RE THE GUY WHO WAS IN THE TABLOIDS WITH SARA!
MOMOKA...
HEE HEE... MOMOKA HAS COMPLETELY FORGOTTEN ABOUT YOU...
...RYUGA.

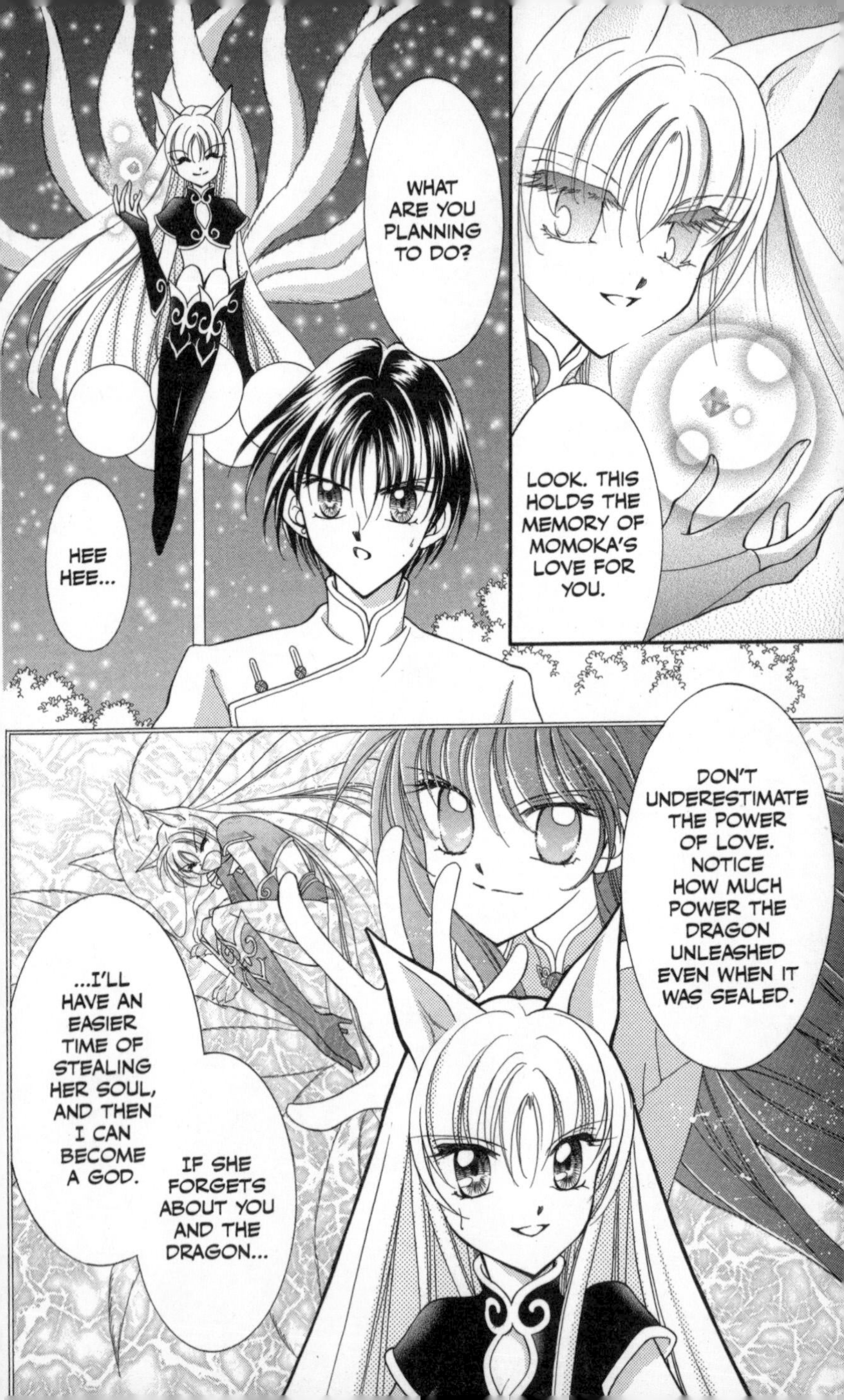
LOOK. THIS HOLDS THE MEMORY OF MOMOKA'S LOVE FOR YOU.
WHAT ARE YOU PLANNING TO DO?
HEE HEE...
DON'T UNDERESTIMATE THE POWER OF LOVE. NOTICE HOW MUCH POWER THE DRAGON UNLEASHED EVEN WHEN IT WAS SEALED.
IF SHE FORGETS ABOUT YOU AND THE DRAGON...
...I'LL HAVE AN EASIER TIME OF STEALING HER SOUL, AND THEN I CAN BECOME A GOD.

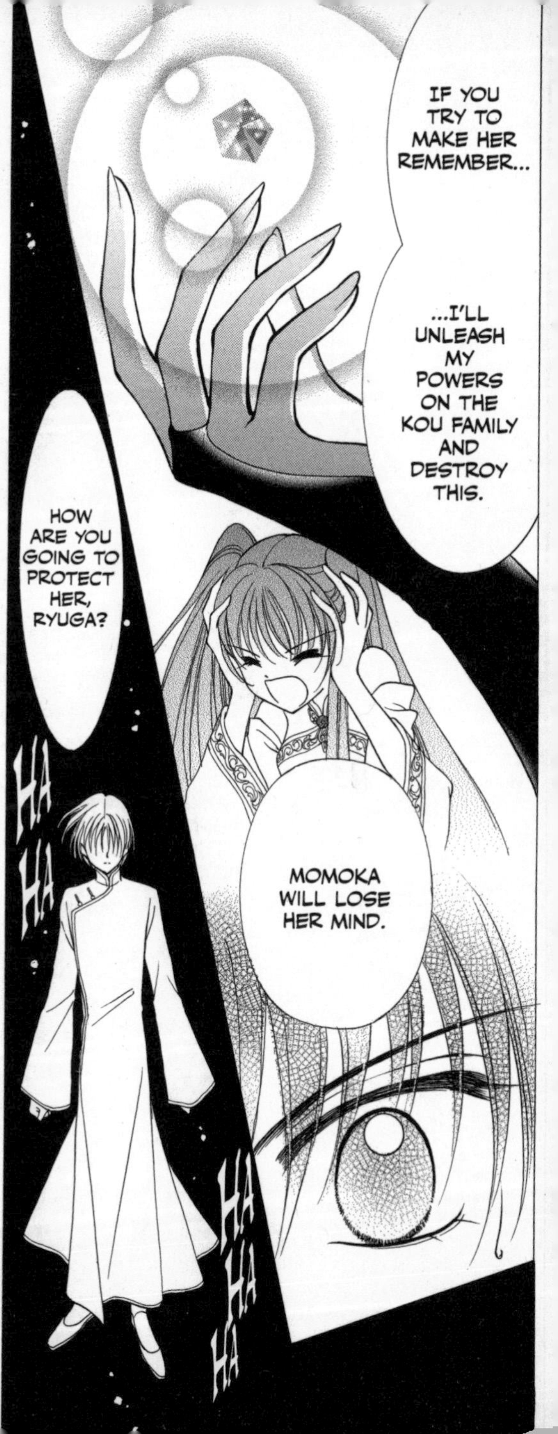
IF YOU TRY TO MAKE HER REMEMBER...
...I'LL UNLEASH MY POWERS ON THE KOU FAMILY AND DESTROY THIS.
MOMOKA WILL LOSE HER MIND.
HOW ARE YOU GOING TO PROTECT HER, RYUGA?
HA HA HA HA
HA HA HA

10

I'm going to change the subject now. I had my first autograph session this year, and I was really nervous about it. Even though I had participated in the *Ribon* festival in Osaka, there was no autograph session at that one. This year, we held discussions and did autograph sessions in pairs. I was paired with Akasuga-sensei! Our birthdays are on the same day–May 2! However, that's the only thing we have in common... Takasuga-sensei is really thin, stylish, and cute. I had dieted for that day, but...

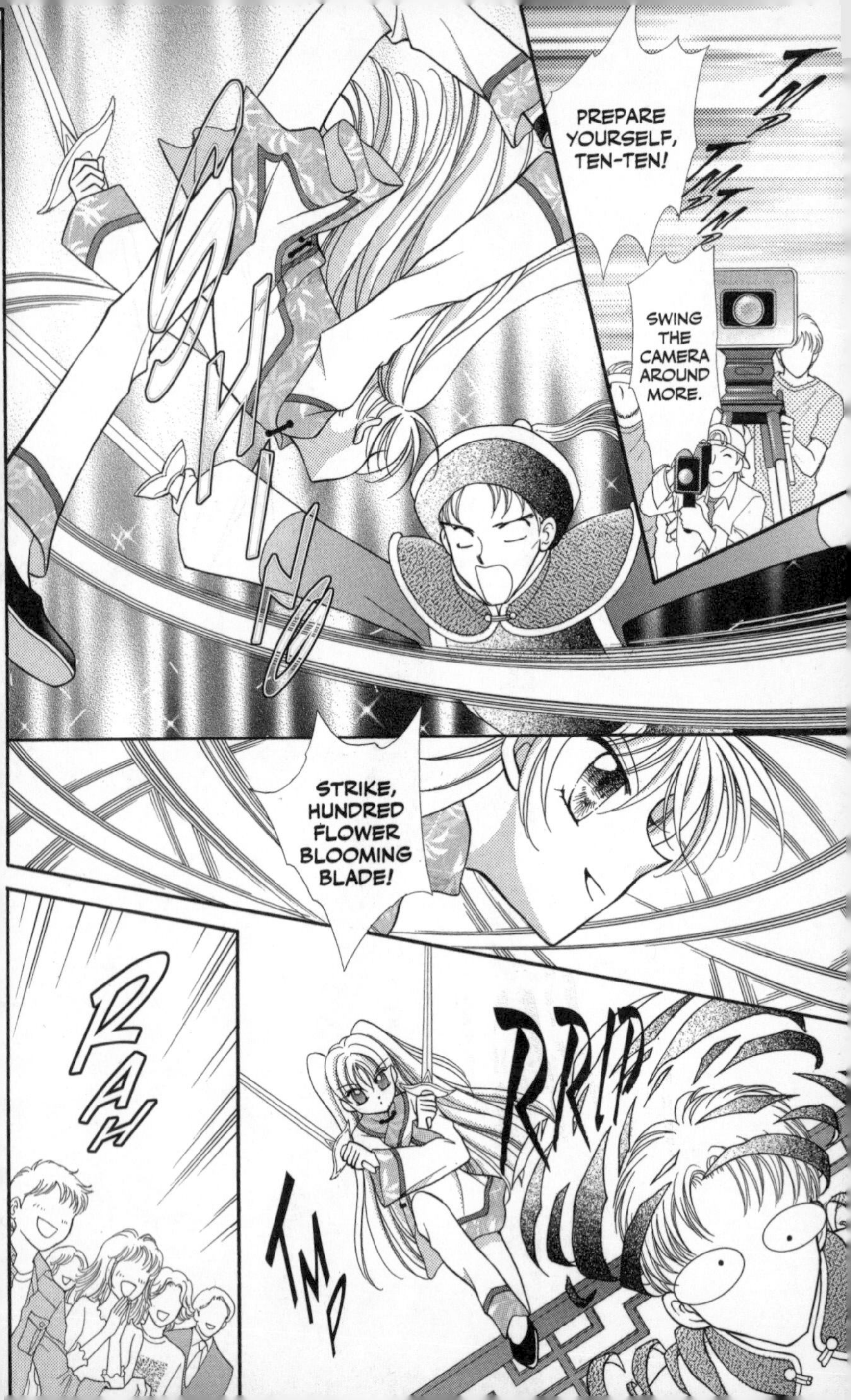
TMP TMP
PREPARE YOURSELF, TEN-TEN!
SWING THE CAMERA AROUND MORE.
STRIKE, HUNDRED FLOWER BLOOMING BLADE!
RRIP
TMP
RAH

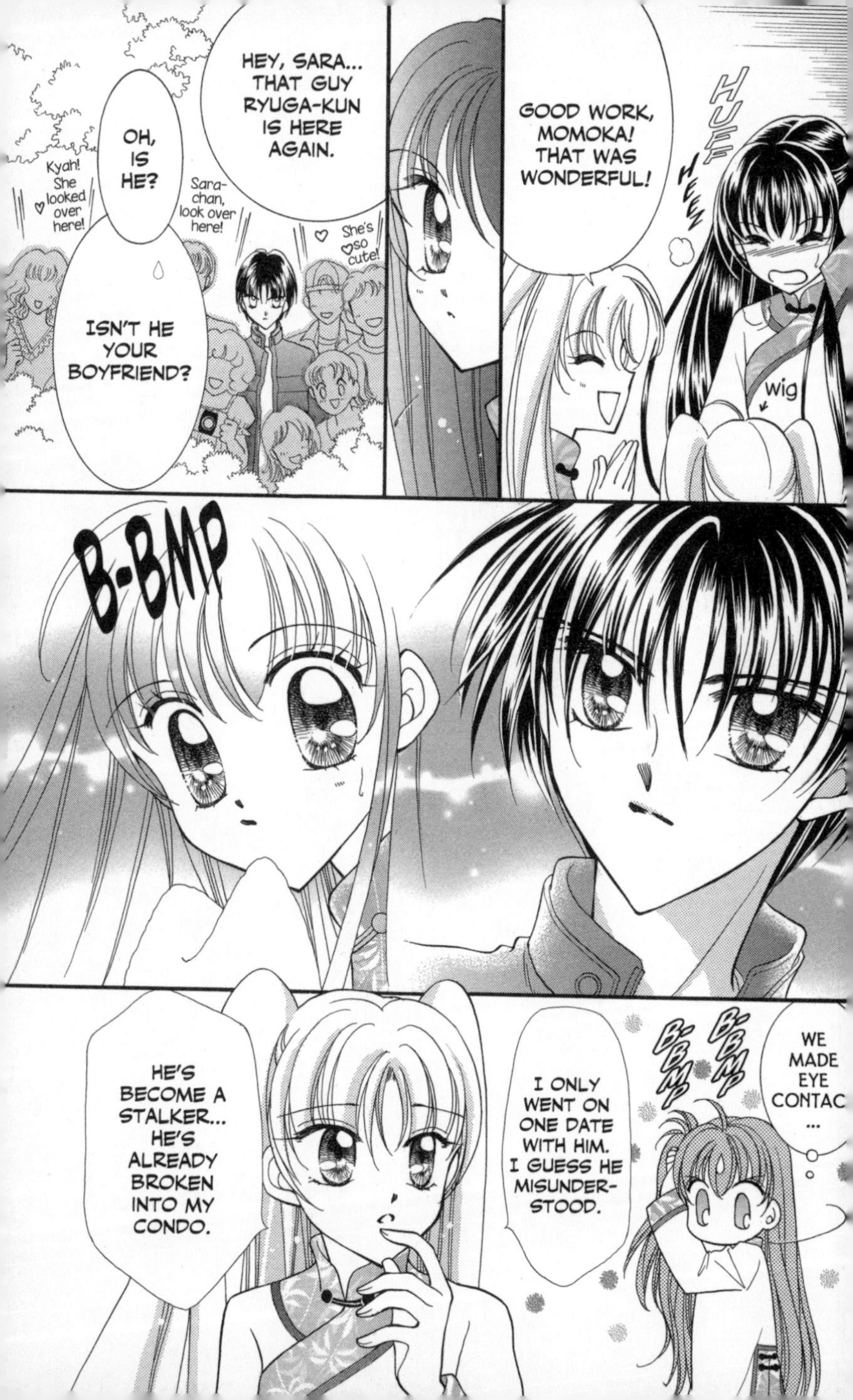
HUFF
HEEE
Wig
GOOD WORK, MOMOKA! THAT WAS WONDERFUL!
HEY, SARA... THAT GUY RYUGA-KUN IS HERE AGAIN.
OH, IS HE?
She's so cute!
Sara-chan, look over here!
Kyah! She looked over here!
ISN'T HE YOUR BOYFRIEND?
B-BMP
WE MADE EYE CONTAC...
B-BMP
B-BMP
I ONLY WENT ON ONE DATE WITH HIM. I GUESS HE MISUNDER-STOOD.
HE'S BECOME A STALKER... HE'S ALREADY BROKEN INTO MY CONDO.

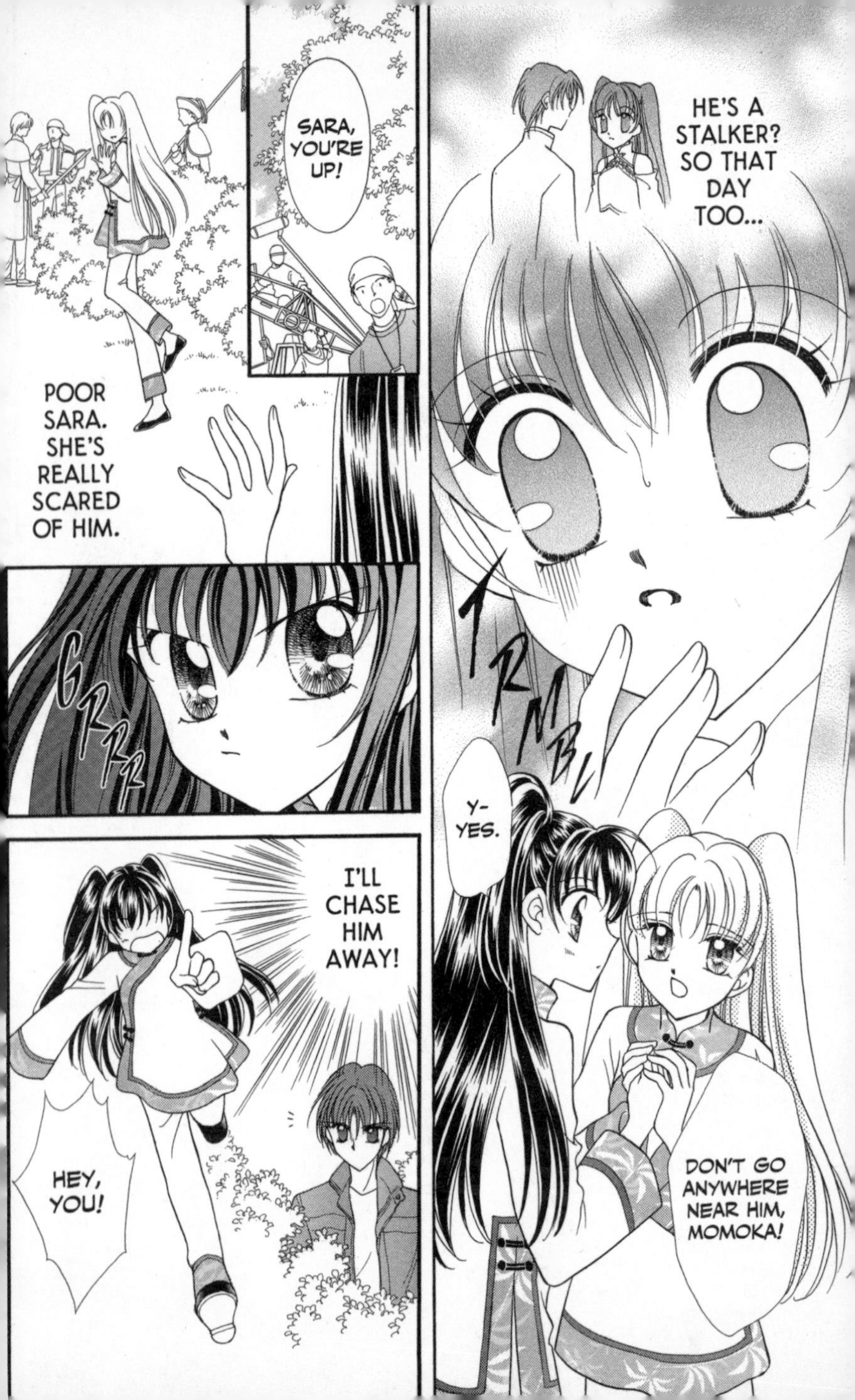
HE'S A STALKER? SO THAT DAY TOO...
TRMBL
DON'T GO ANYWHERE NEAR HIM, MOMOKA!
Y-YES.
SARA, YOU'RE UP!
POOR SARA. SHE'S REALLY SCARED OF HIM.
GRRR
I'LL CHASE HIM AWAY!
HEY, YOU!

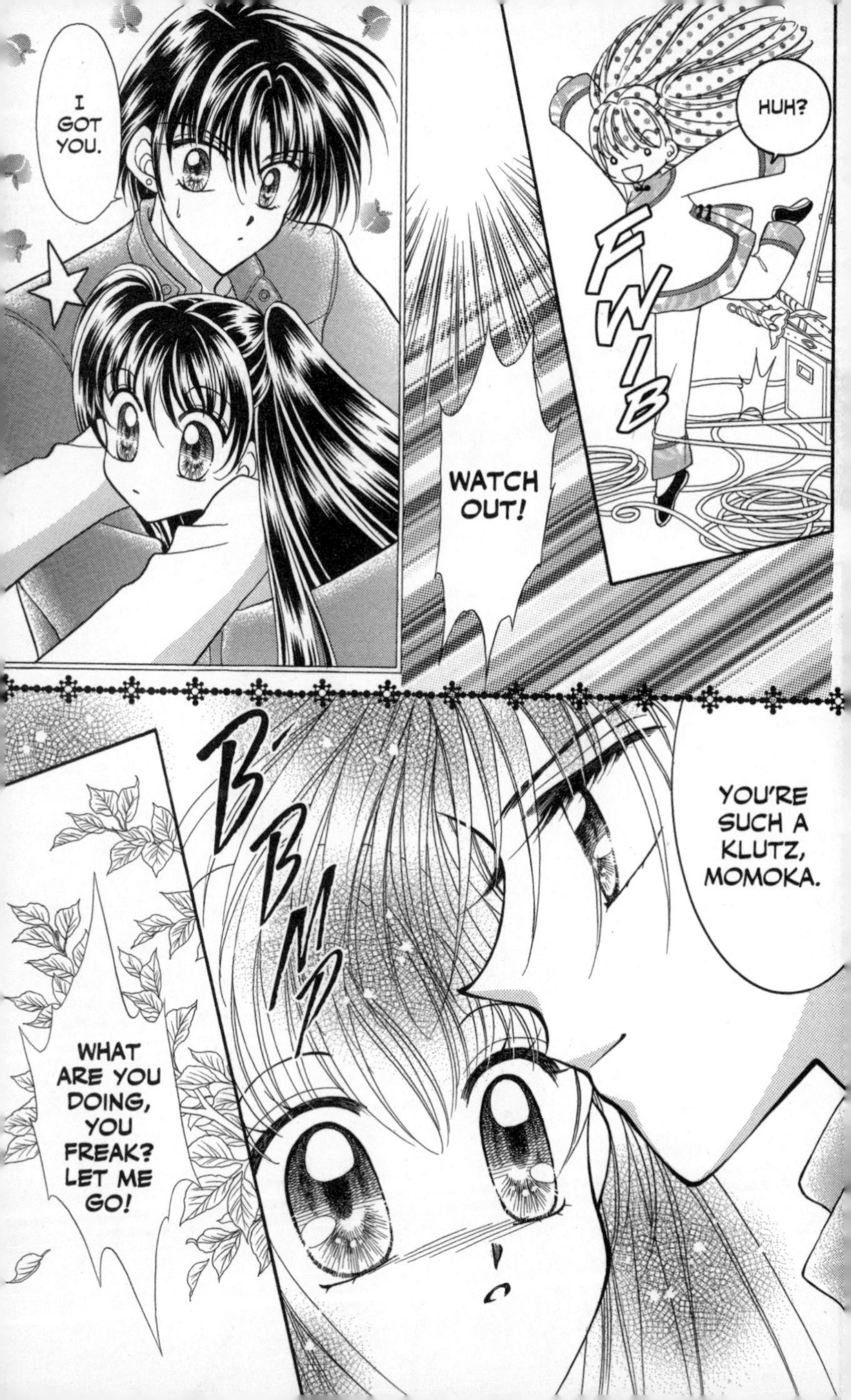
HUH?
FWIB
WATCH OUT!
I GOT YOU.
YOU'RE SUCH A KLUTZ, MOMOKA.
B-BMP
WHAT ARE YOU DOING, YOU FREAK? LET ME GO!

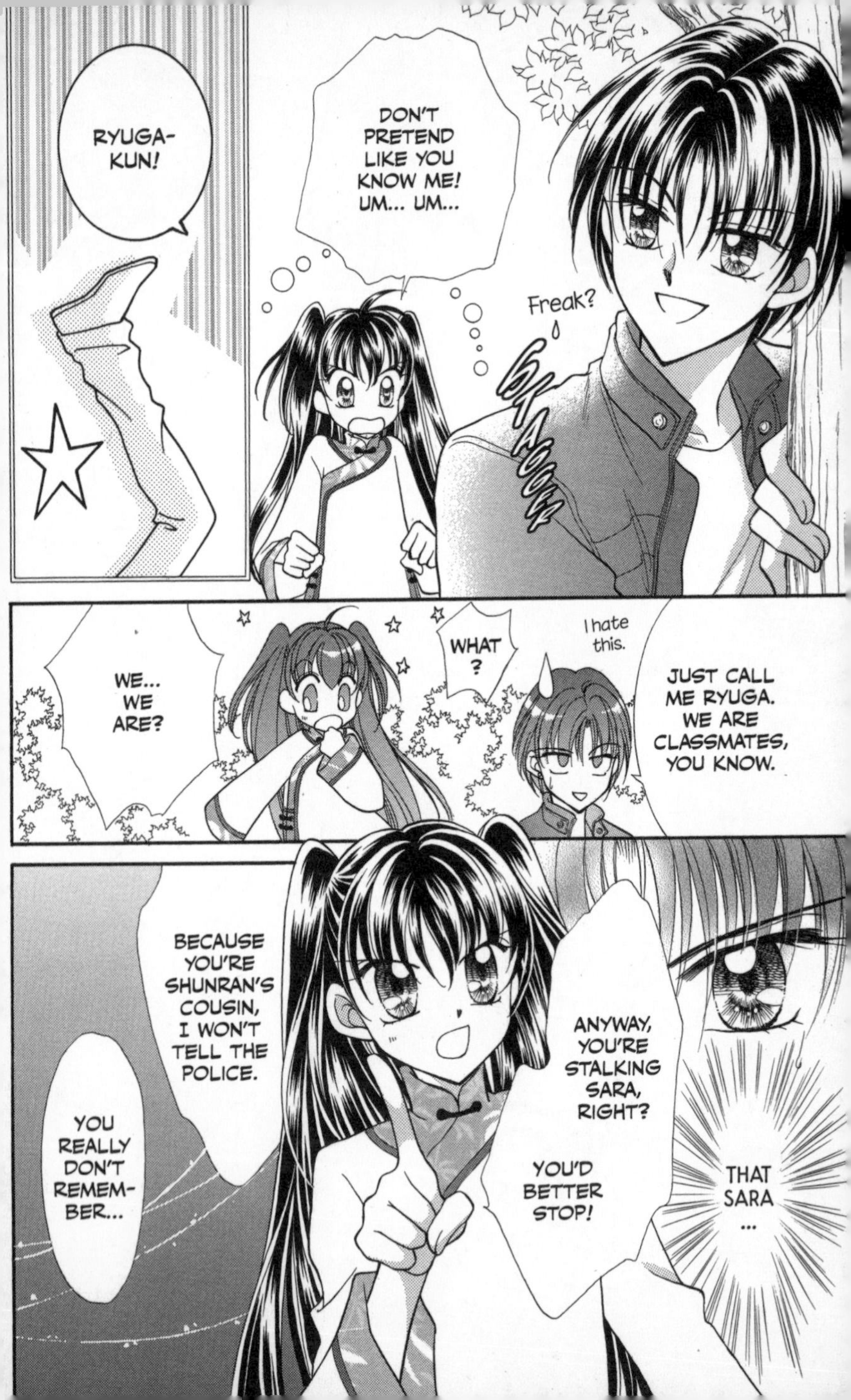
DON'T PRETEND LIKE YOU KNOW ME! UM... UM...
Freak?
RYUGA-KUN!
JUST CALL ME RYUGA. WE ARE CLASSMATES, YOU KNOW.
I hate this.
WHAT?
WE... WE ARE?
THAT SARA ...
ANYWAY, YOU'RE STALKING SARA, RIGHT?
YOU'D BETTER STOP!
BECAUSE YOU'RE SHUNRAN'S COUSIN, I WON'T TELL THE POLICE.
YOU REALLY DON'T REMEMBER...

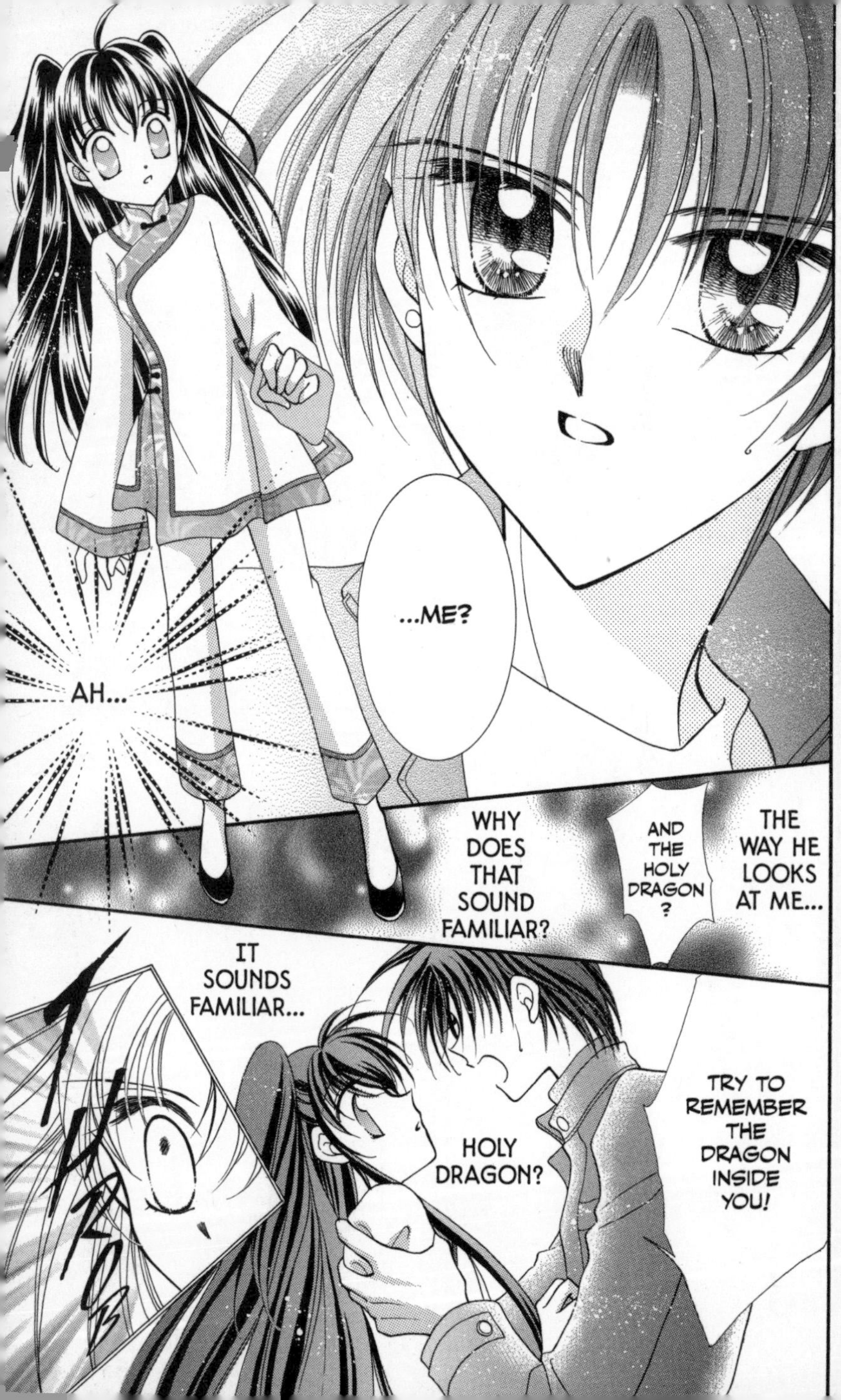
...ME?
AH...
THE WAY HE LOOKS AT ME...
AND THE HOLY DRAGON?
WHY DOES THAT SOUND FAMILIAR?
TRY TO REMEMBER THE DRAGON INSIDE YOU!
HOLY DRAGON?
IT SOUNDS FAMILIAR...

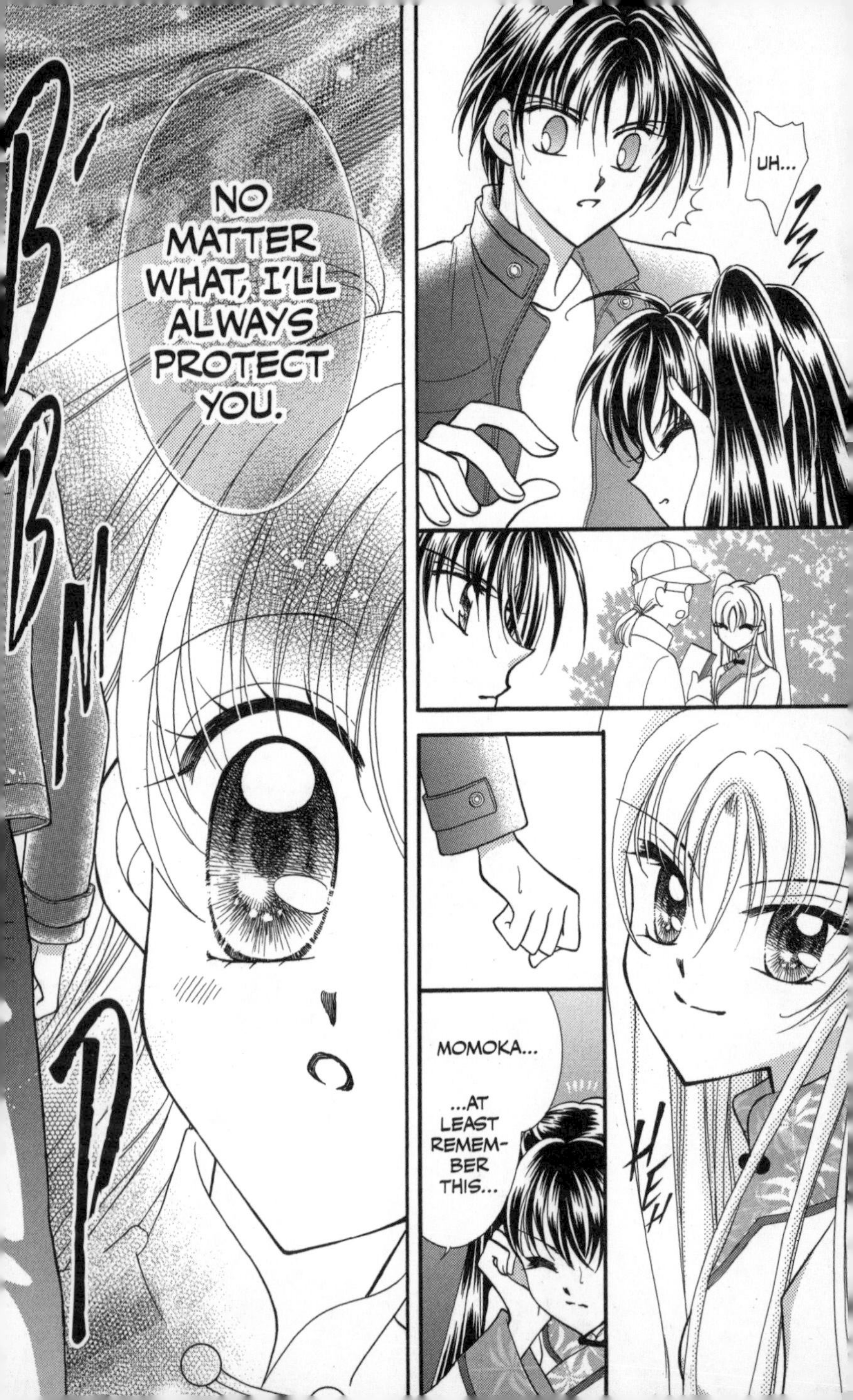
UH...
HEH
MOMOKA...
...AT LEAST REMEMBER THIS...
NO MATTER WHAT, I'LL ALWAYS PROTECT YOU.

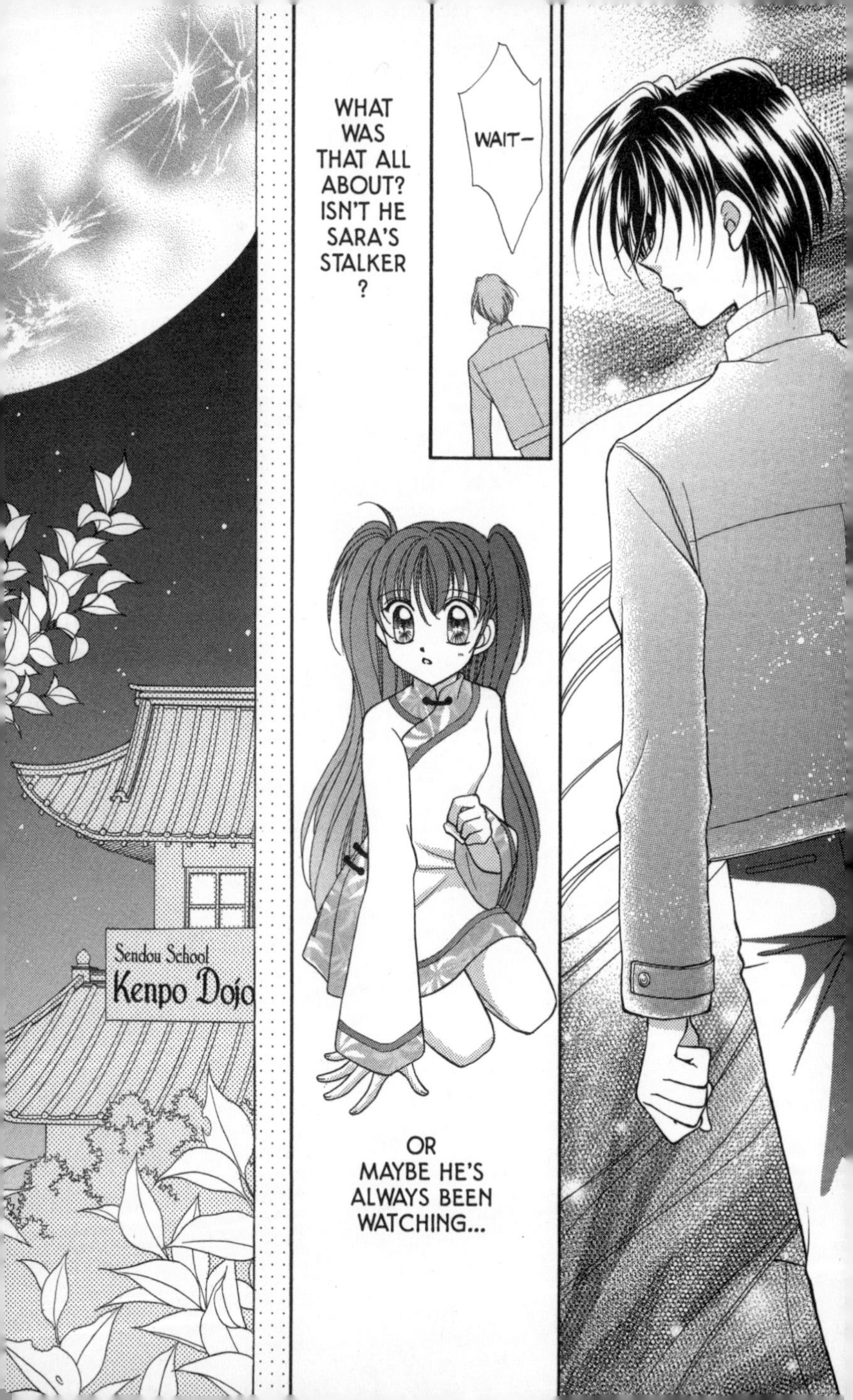
WAIT—
WHAT WAS THAT ALL ABOUT? ISN'T HE SARA'S STALKER?
OR MAYBE HE'S ALWAYS BEEN WATCHING...
Sendou School Kenpo Dojo

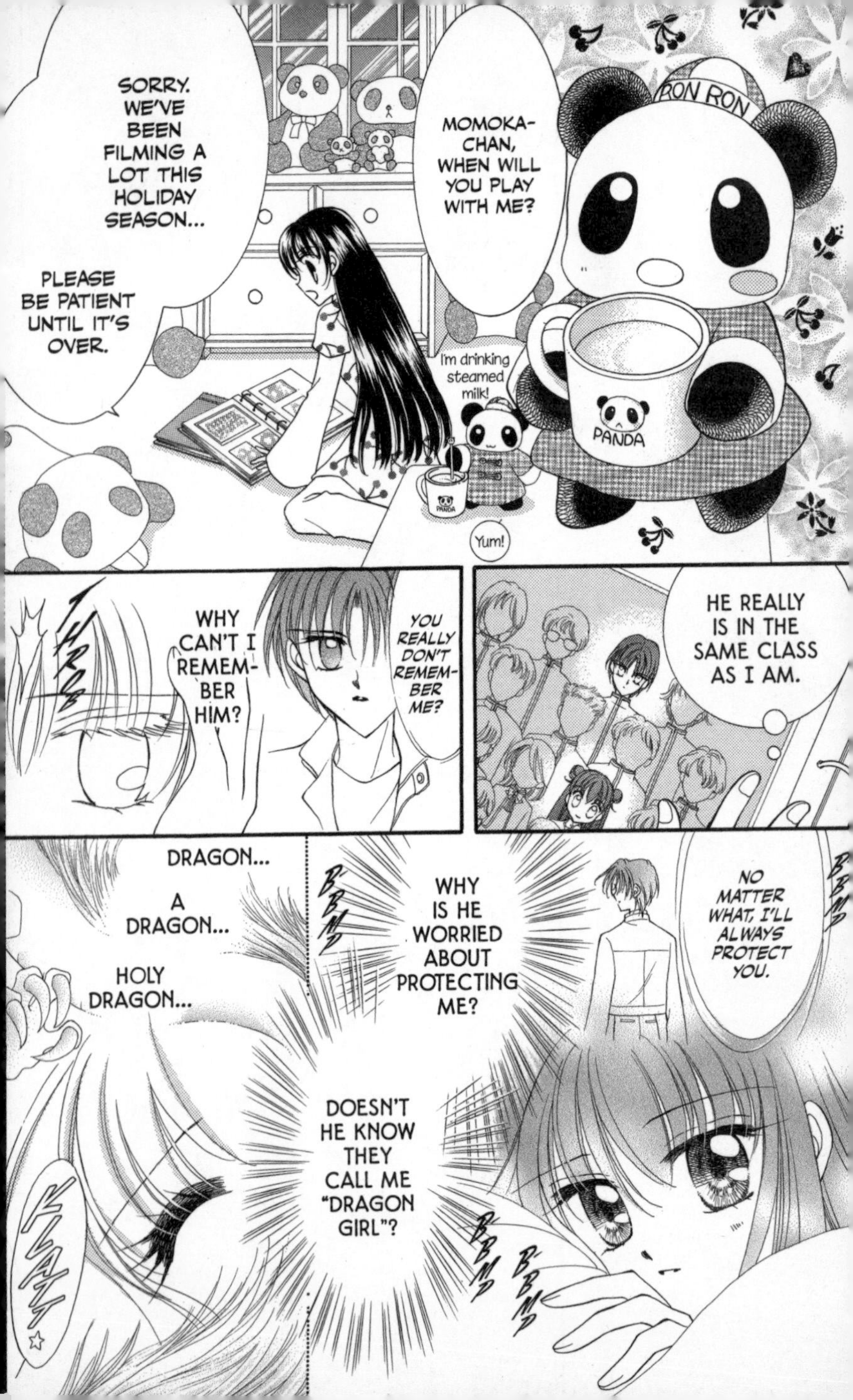
RON RON
MOMOKA-CHAN, WHEN WILL YOU PLAY WITH ME?
I'm drinking steamed milk!
PANDA
PANDA
Yum!
SORRY. WE'VE BEEN FILMING A LOT THIS HOLIDAY SEASON...
PLEASE BE PATIENT UNTIL IT'S OVER.
HE REALLY IS IN THE SAME CLASS AS I AM.
YOU REALLY DON'T REMEMBER ME?
WHY CAN'T I REMEMBER HIM?
THROB
NO MATTER WHAT, I'LL ALWAYS PROTECT YOU.
BBMP
WHY IS HE WORRIED ABOUT PROTECTING ME?
BBMP
DOESN'T HE KNOW THEY CALL ME "DRAGON GIRL"?
BBMP
BBMP
DRAGON...
A DRAGON...
HOLY DRAGON...

11

I had been dieting since New Year's, and I lost only 11 pounds. (I gained 24 pounds in two years.) When we made our speeches, the lights were hot and bright, and I couldn't quite remember what I was going to say. Speaking in front of everyone helped ease my nerves for the autograph session, but I wish I could have talked with my fans more. It really made me happy to hear people encouraging me in person. I got fan letters and presents too! Thank you, everyone! ♡

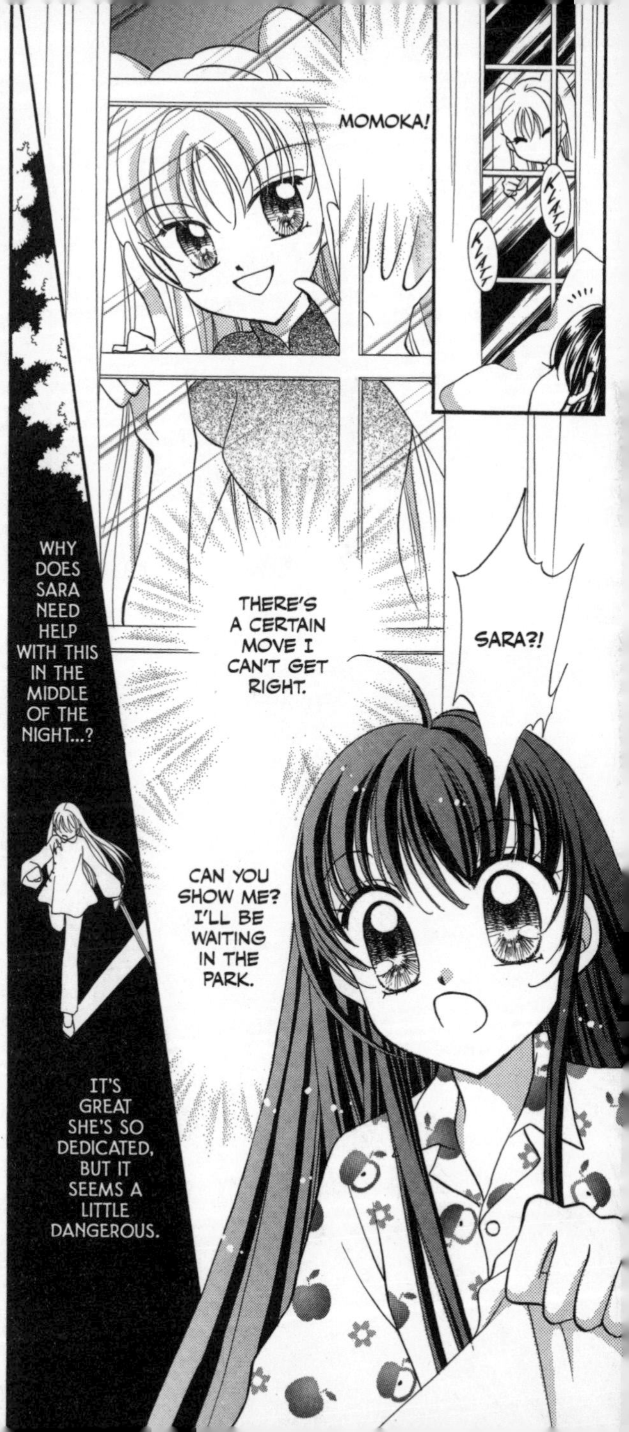

MOMOKA!
SARA?!
THERE'S A CERTAIN MOVE I CAN'T GET RIGHT.
CAN YOU SHOW ME? I'LL BE WAITING IN THE PARK.
WHY DOES SARA NEED HELP WITH THIS IN THE MIDDLE OF THE NIGHT...?
IT'S GREAT SHE'S SO DEDICATED, BUT IT SEEMS A LITTLE DANGEROUS.

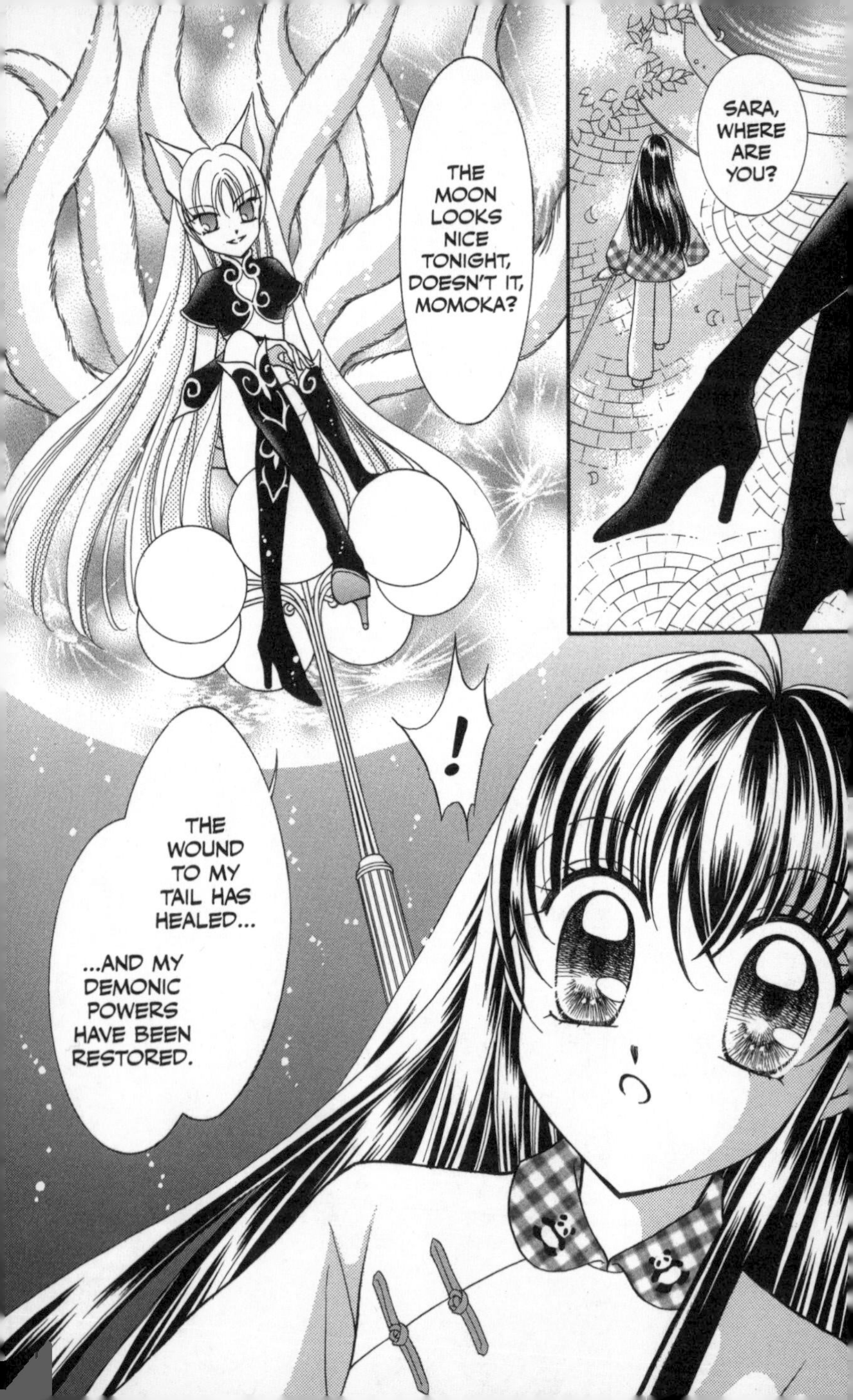
SARA, WHERE ARE YOU?
THE MOON LOOKS NICE TONIGHT, DOESN'T IT, MOMOKA?
!
THE WOUND TO MY TAIL HAS HEALED...
...AND MY DEMONIC POWERS HAVE BEEN RESTORED.

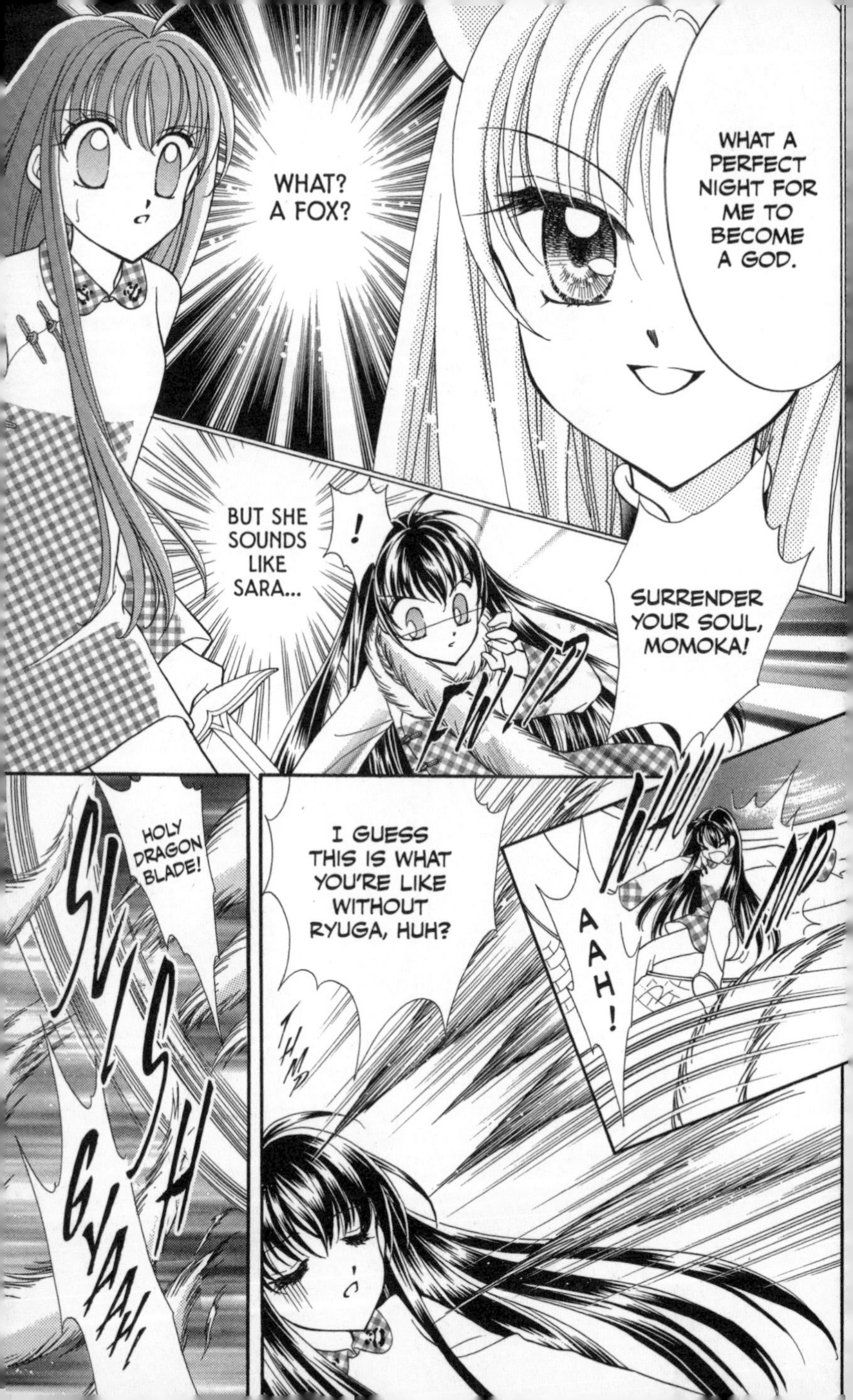
WHAT A PERFECT NIGHT FOR ME TO BECOME A GOD.
WHAT? A FOX?
SURRENDER YOUR SOUL, MOMOKA!
!
BUT SHE SOUNDS LIKE SARA...
AAH!
I GUESS THIS IS WHAT YOU'RE LIKE WITHOUT RYUGA, HUH?
HOLY DRAGON BLADE!
SLISH
GYAAH!

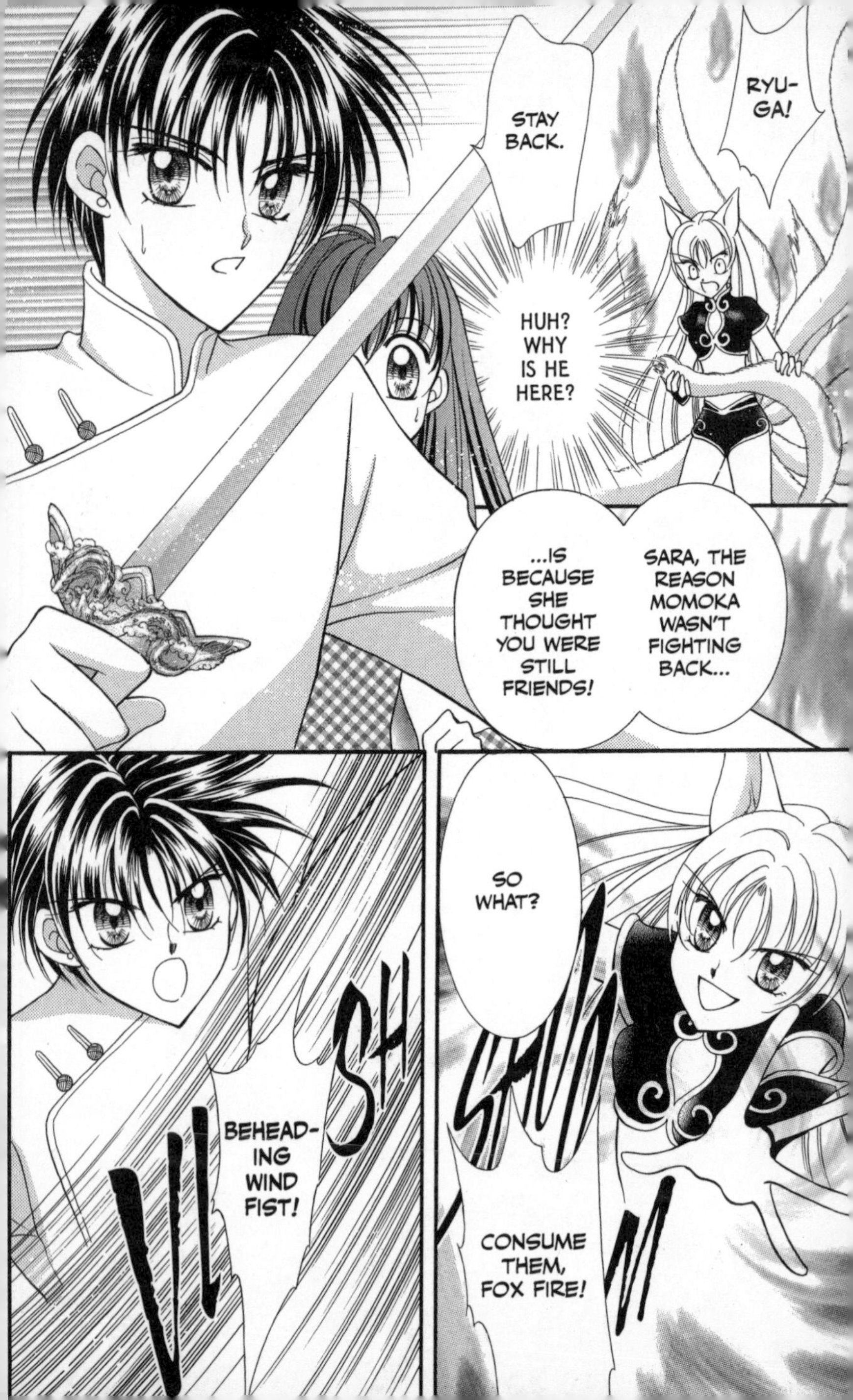
RYU-GA!
STAY BACK.
HUH? WHY IS HE HERE?
SARA, THE REASON MOMOKA WASN'T FIGHTING BACK...
...IS BECAUSE SHE THOUGHT YOU WERE STILL FRIENDS!
SO WHAT?
CONSUME THEM, FOX FIRE!
BEHEAD-ING WIND FIST!

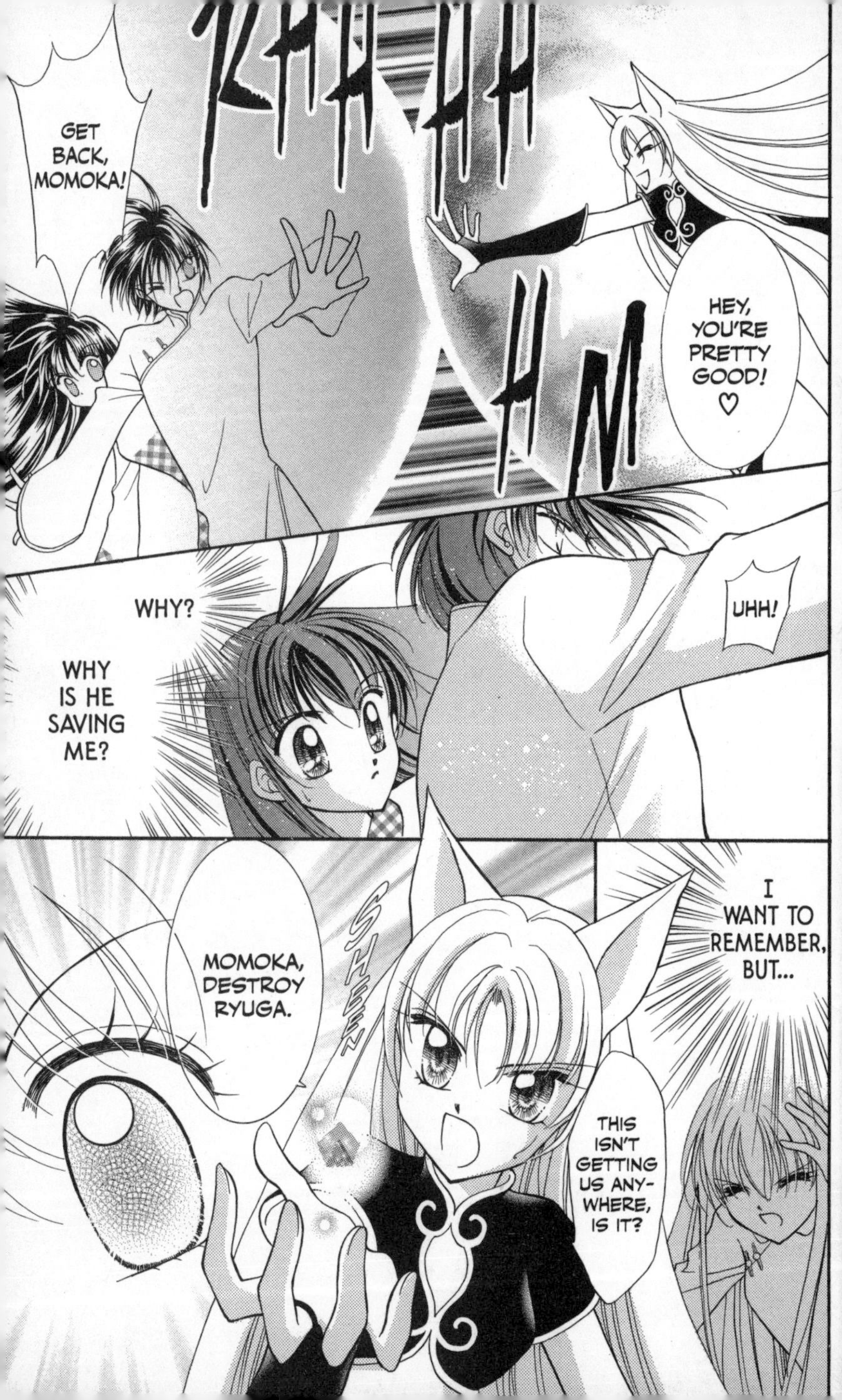
HEY, YOU'RE PRETTY GOOD! ♡
GET BACK, MOMOKA!
UHH!
WHY?
WHY IS HE SAVING ME?
I WANT TO REMEMBER, BUT...
THIS ISN'T GETTING US ANY-WHERE, IS IT?
SHHEEN
MOMOKA, DESTROY RYUGA.

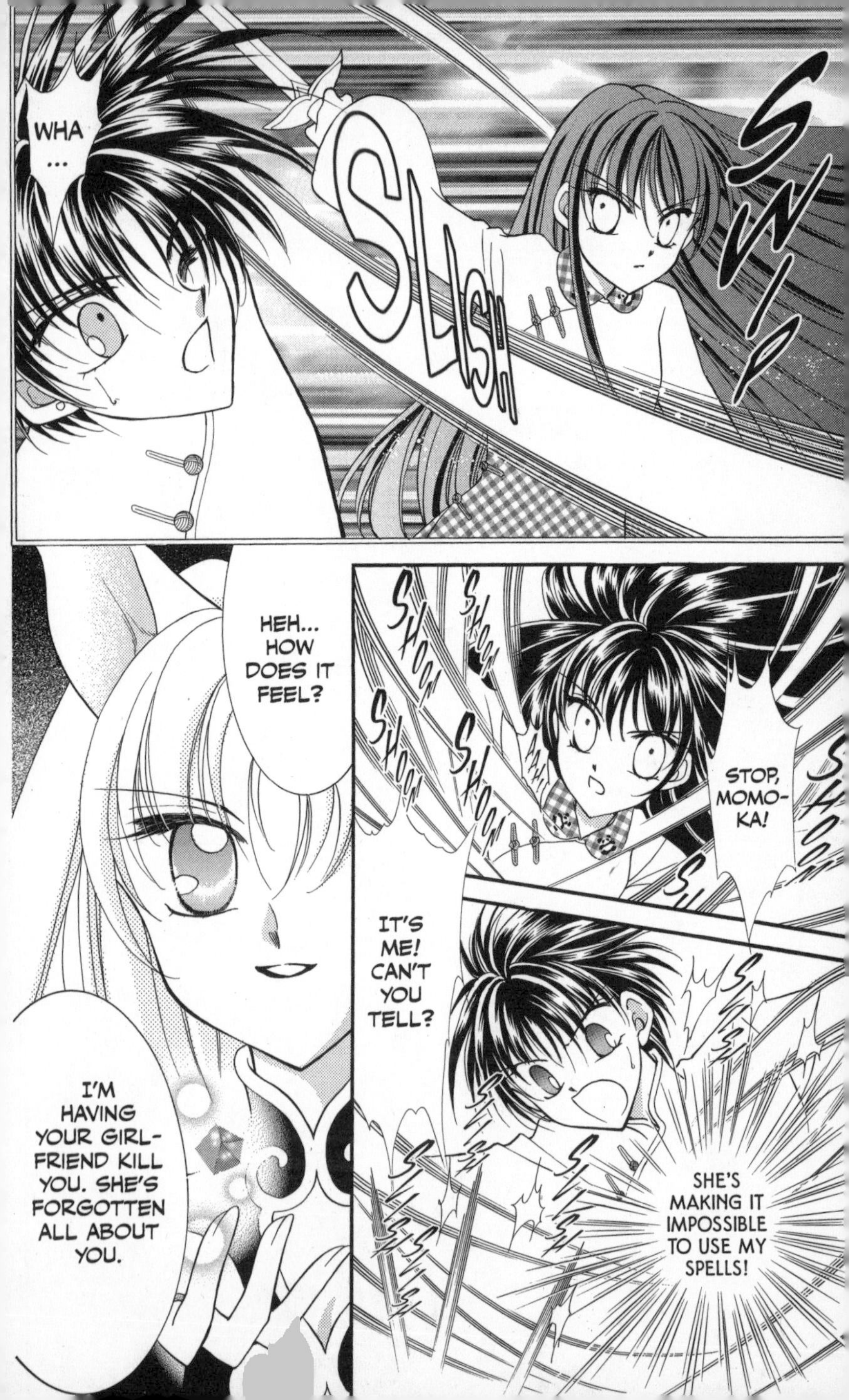
SLISH
WHA ...
STOP, MOMO-KA!
IT'S ME! CAN'T YOU TELL?
SHE'S MAKING IT IMPOSSIBLE TO USE MY SPELLS!
HEH... HOW DOES IT FEEL?
I'M HAVING YOUR GIRL-FRIEND KILL YOU. SHE'S FORGOTTEN ALL ABOUT YOU.

12

After the autograph session, I went around to look at the exhibitions. Many mangaka had color illustrations and drafts of their manga on display. It was really fun. Everyone had different ways of using color, which really changed the final product. I learned a lot. All the young artists at *Ribon* were so enthusiastic! They'll have big debuts someday in the future. This year it was held in Tokyo, but next year I hope it's somewhere different!

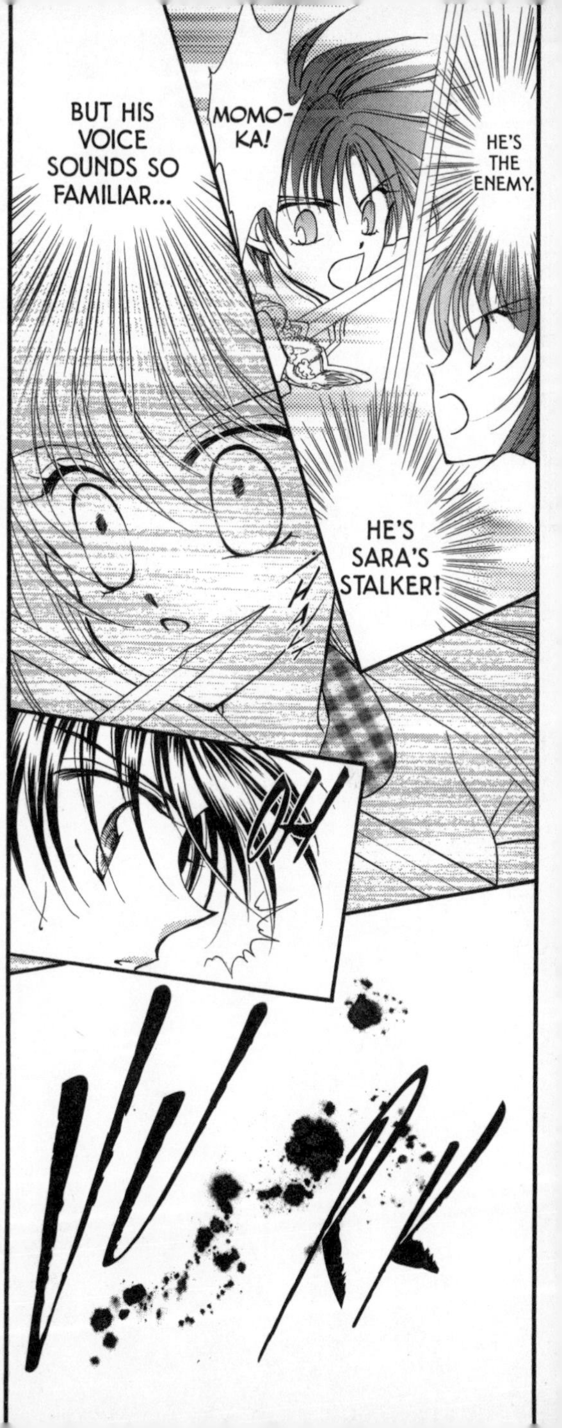
HE'S THE ENEMY.
MOMO-KA!
HE'S SARA'S STALKER!
BUT HIS VOICE SOUNDS SO FAMILIAR...
OH

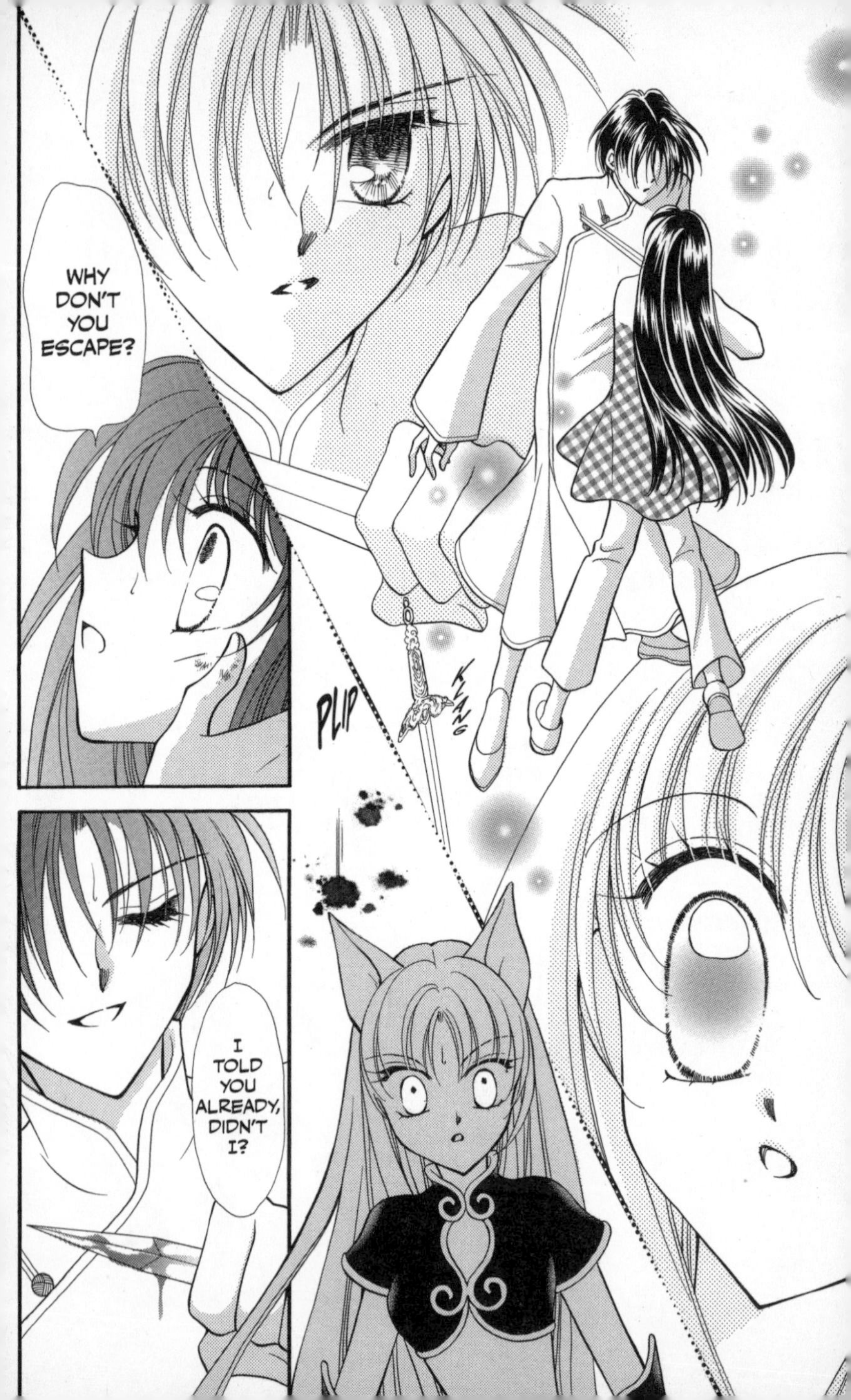
KLANG
PLIP
WHY DON'T YOU ESCAPE?
I TOLD YOU ALREADY, DIDN'T I?

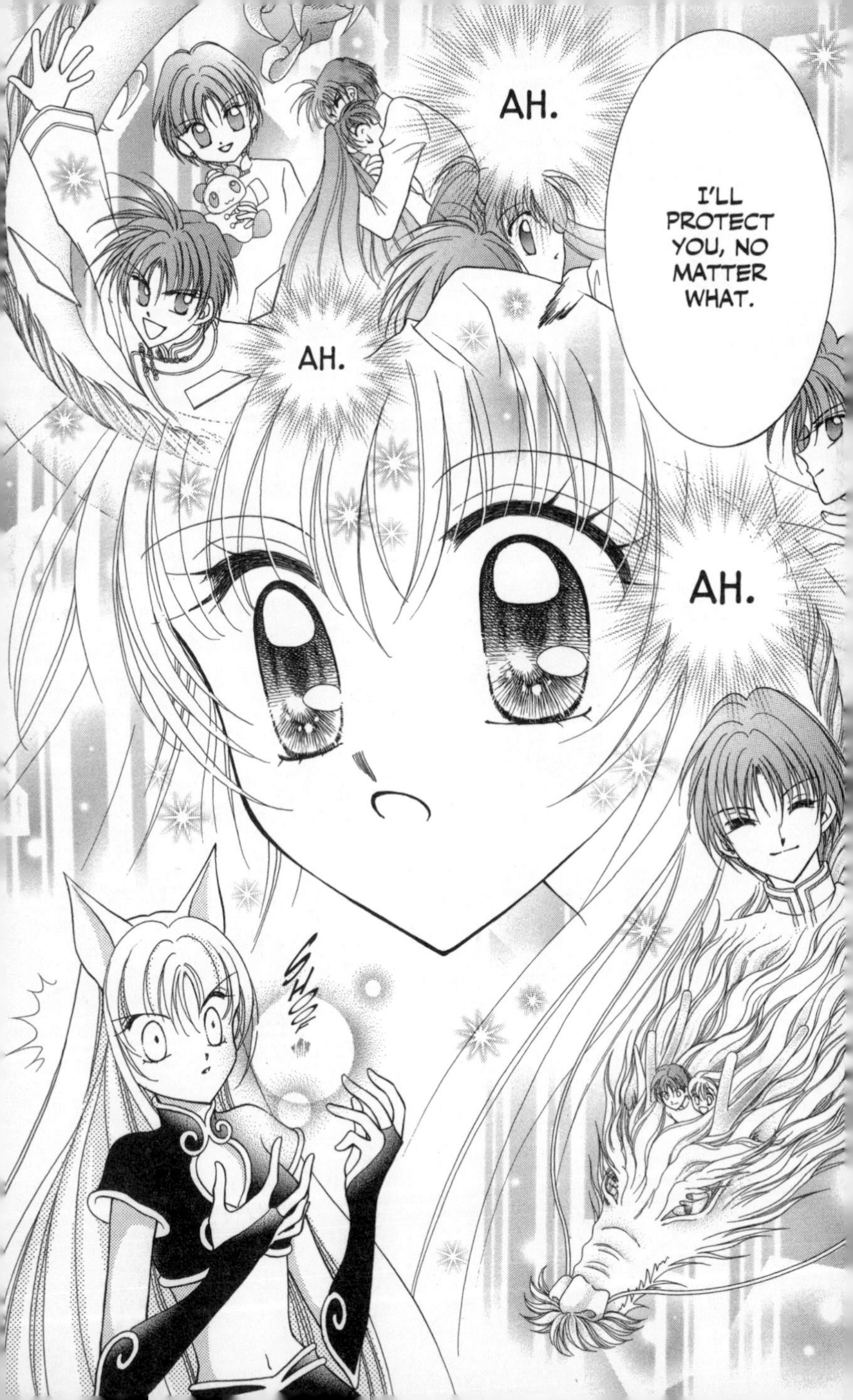
I'LL PROTECT YOU, NO MATTER WHAT.
AH.
AH.
AH.

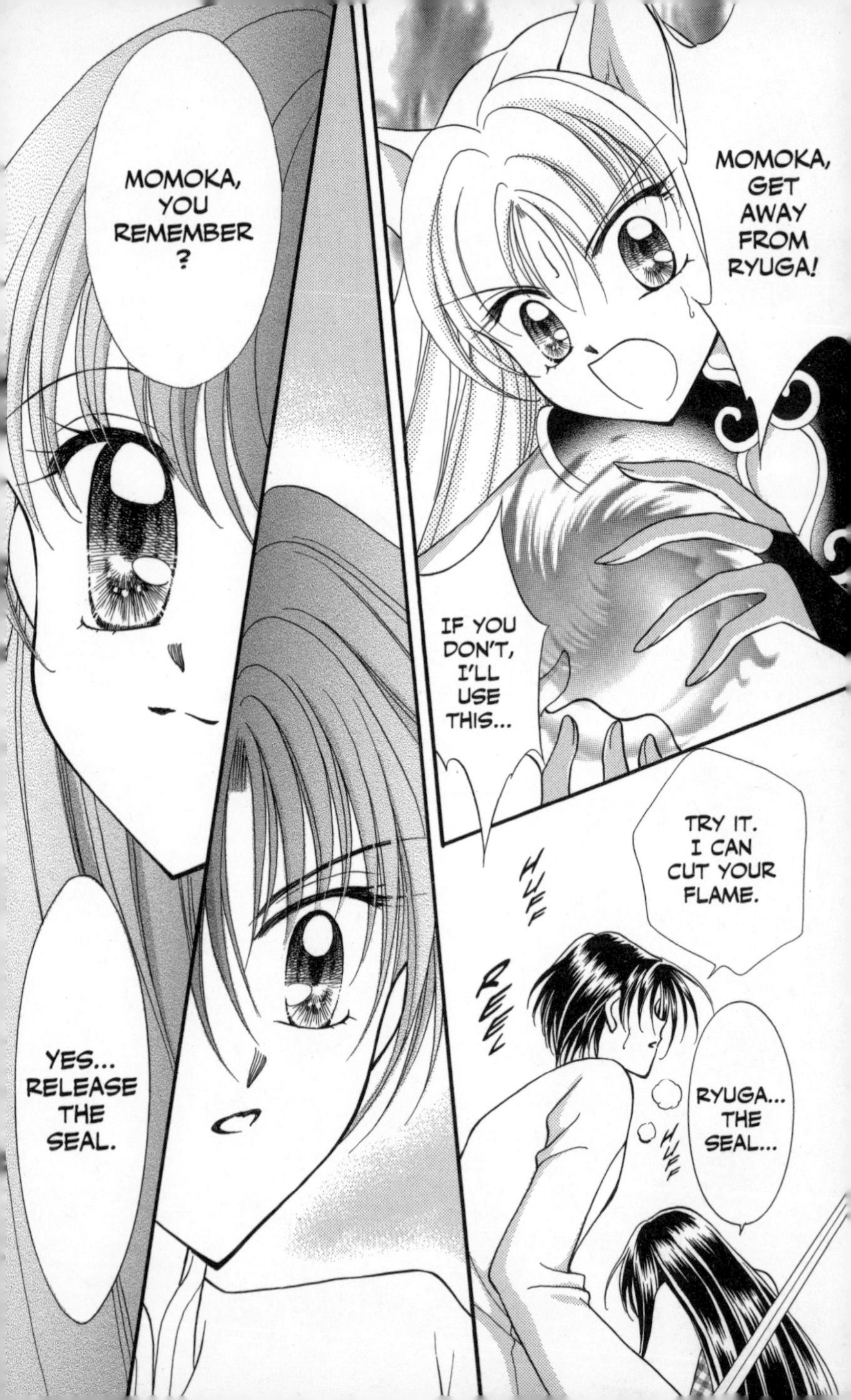
MOMOKA, GET AWAY FROM RYUGA!
IF YOU DON'T, I'LL USE THIS...
TRY IT. I CAN CUT YOUR FLAME.
HUFF
REEL
RYUGA... THE SEAL...
HUFF
MOMOKA, YOU REMEMBER?
YES... RELEASE THE SEAL.

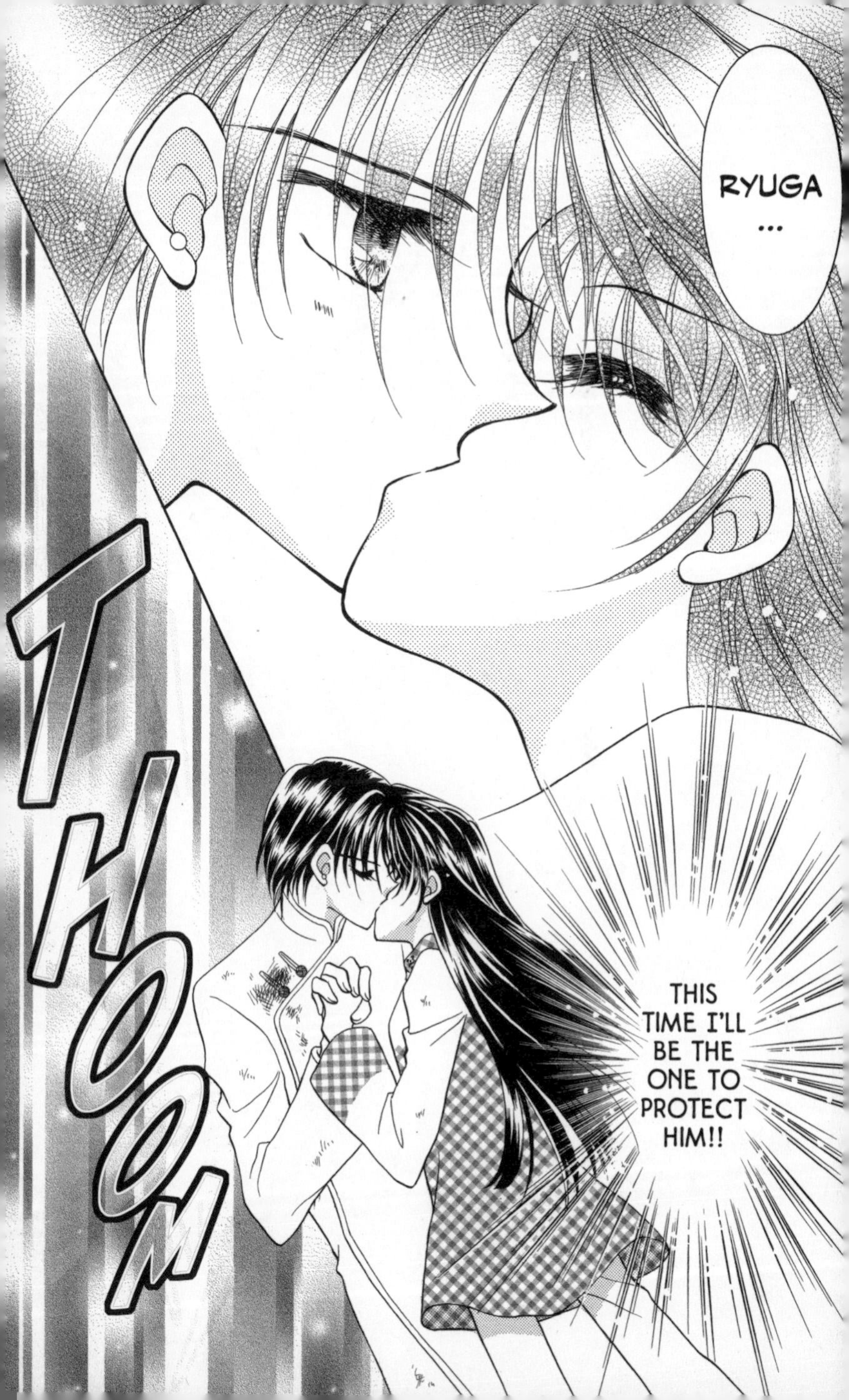
RYUGA ...
THOOM
THIS TIME I'LL BE THE ONE TO PROTECT HIM!!

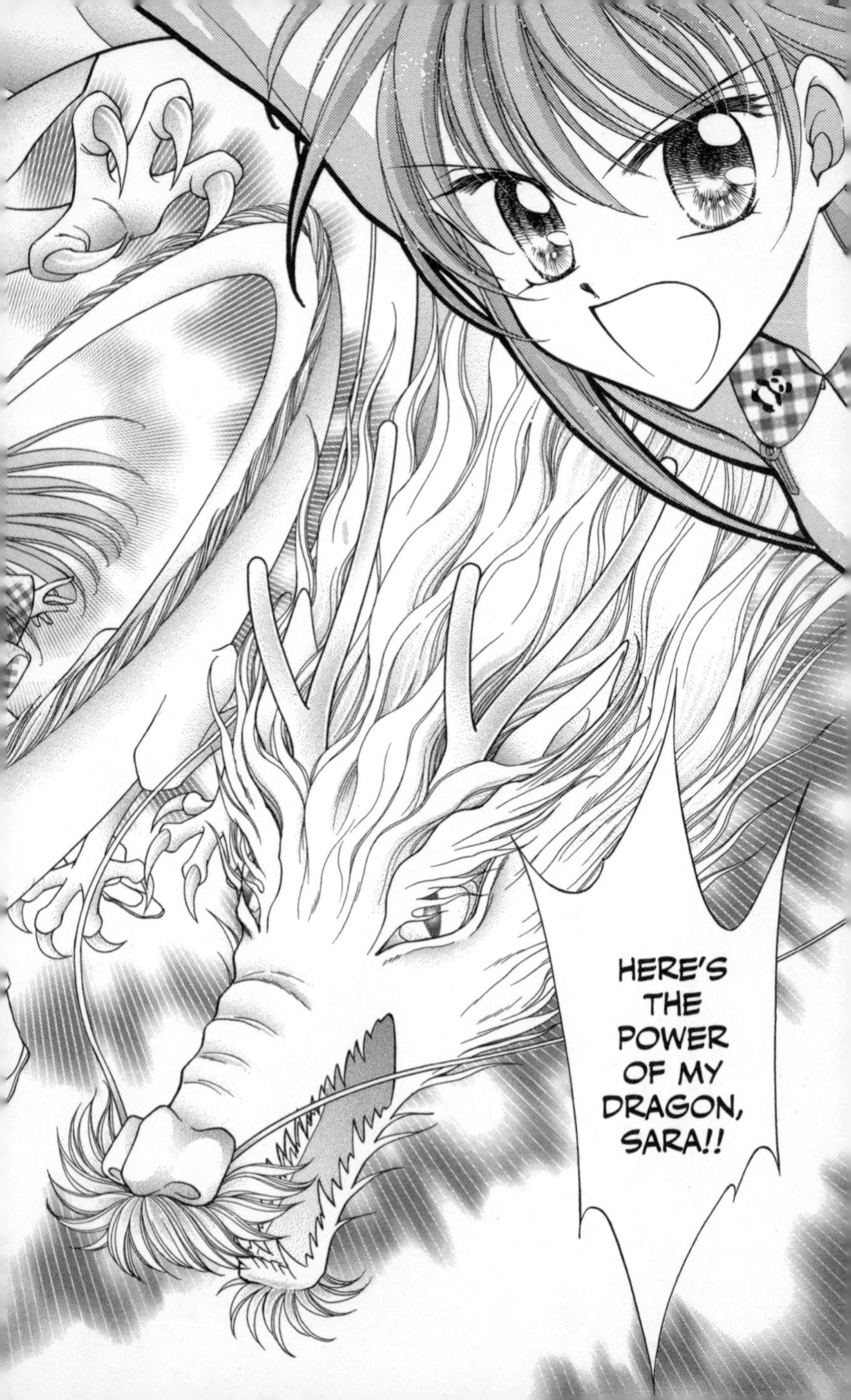
HERE'S THE POWER OF MY DRAGON, SARA!!

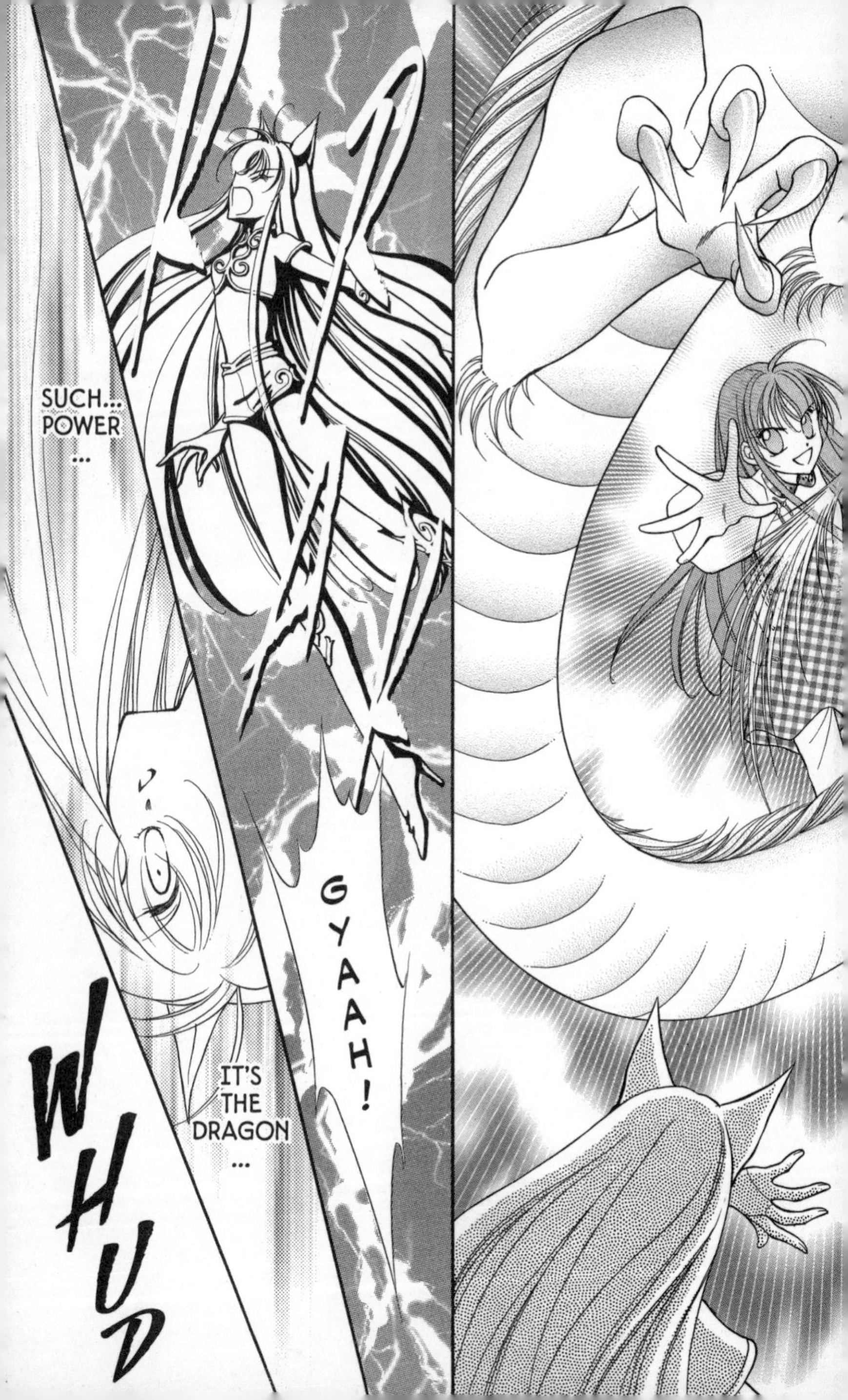

SUCH... POWER ...
GYAAH!
IT'S THE DRAGON ...
WHUD

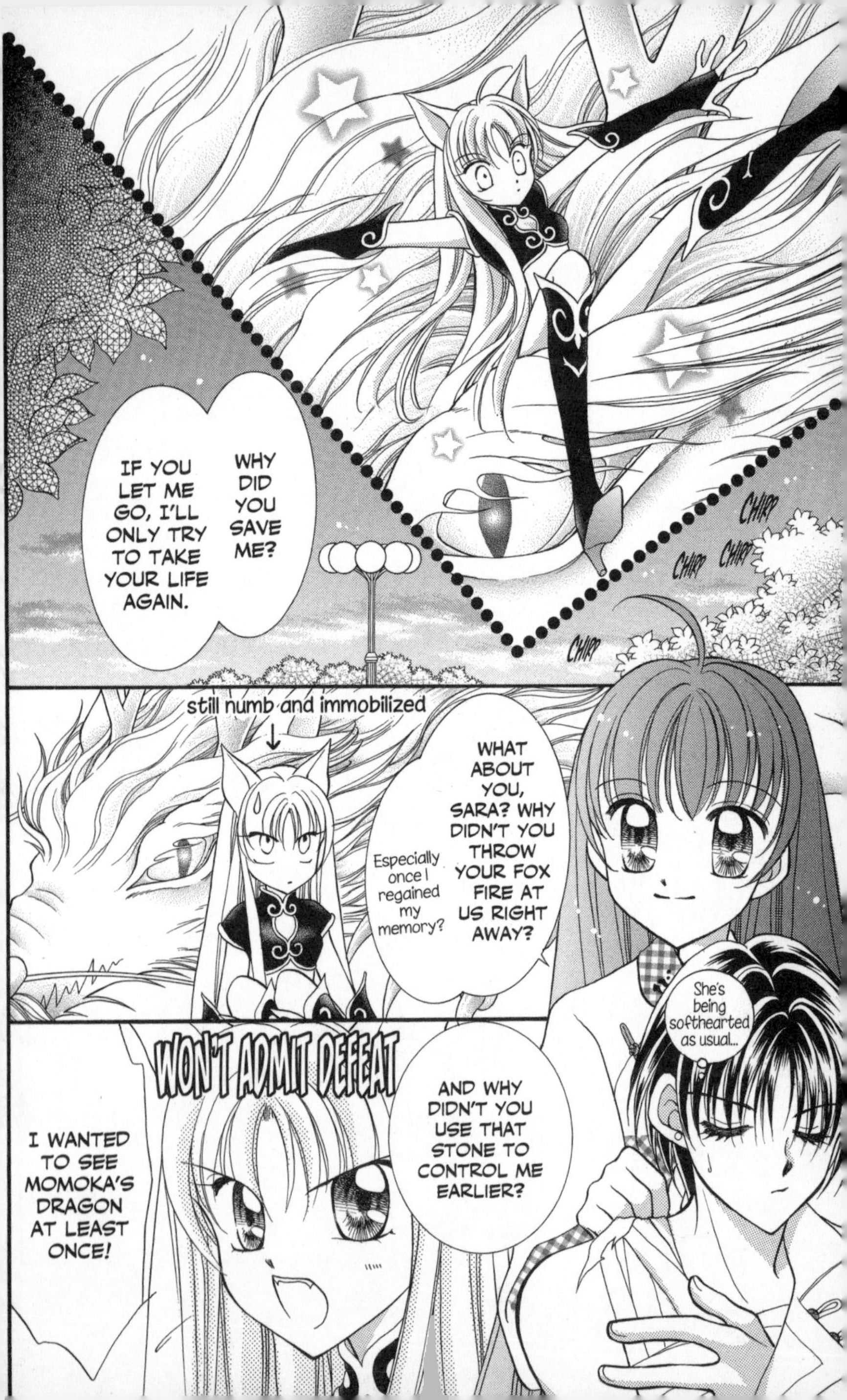
CHIRP
CHIRP
CHIRP
CHIRP
WHY DID YOU SAVE ME?
IF YOU LET ME GO, I'LL ONLY TRY TO TAKE YOUR LIFE AGAIN.
WHAT ABOUT YOU, SARA? WHY DIDN'T YOU THROW YOUR FOX FIRE AT US RIGHT AWAY?
Especially once I regained my memory?
She's being softhearted as usual...
AND WHY DIDN'T YOU USE THAT STONE TO CONTROL ME EARLIER?
still numb and immobilized
WON'T ADMIT DEFEAT
I WANTED TO SEE MOMOKA'S DRAGON AT LEAST ONCE!

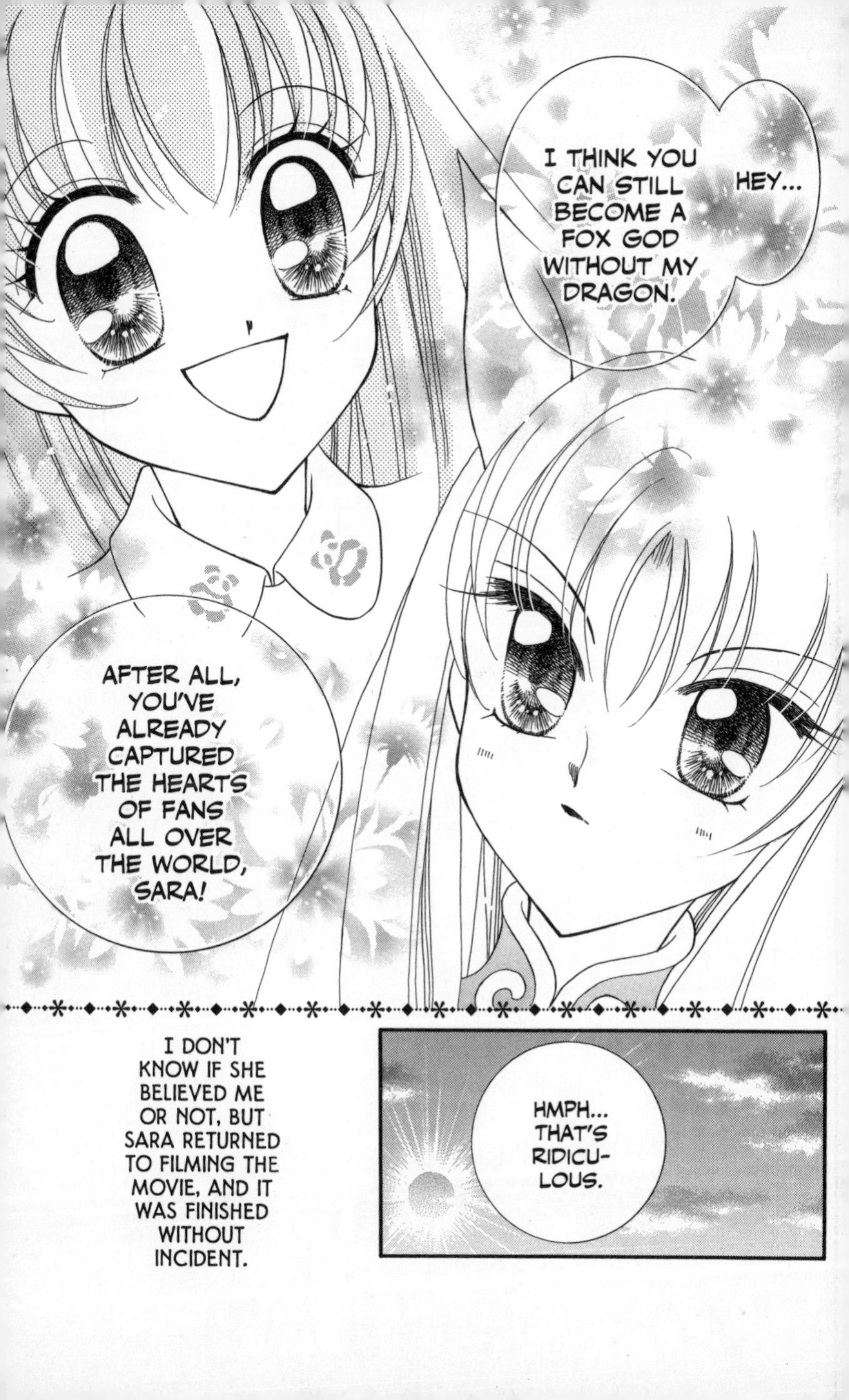
HEY...
I THINK YOU CAN STILL BECOME A FOX GOD WITHOUT MY DRAGON.
AFTER ALL, YOU'VE ALREADY CAPTURED THE HEARTS OF FANS ALL OVER THE WORLD, SARA!
HMPH... THAT'S RIDICU-LOUS.
I DON'T KNOW IF SHE BELIEVED ME OR NOT, BUT SARA RETURNED TO FILMING THE MOVIE, AND IT WAS FINISHED WITHOUT INCIDENT.

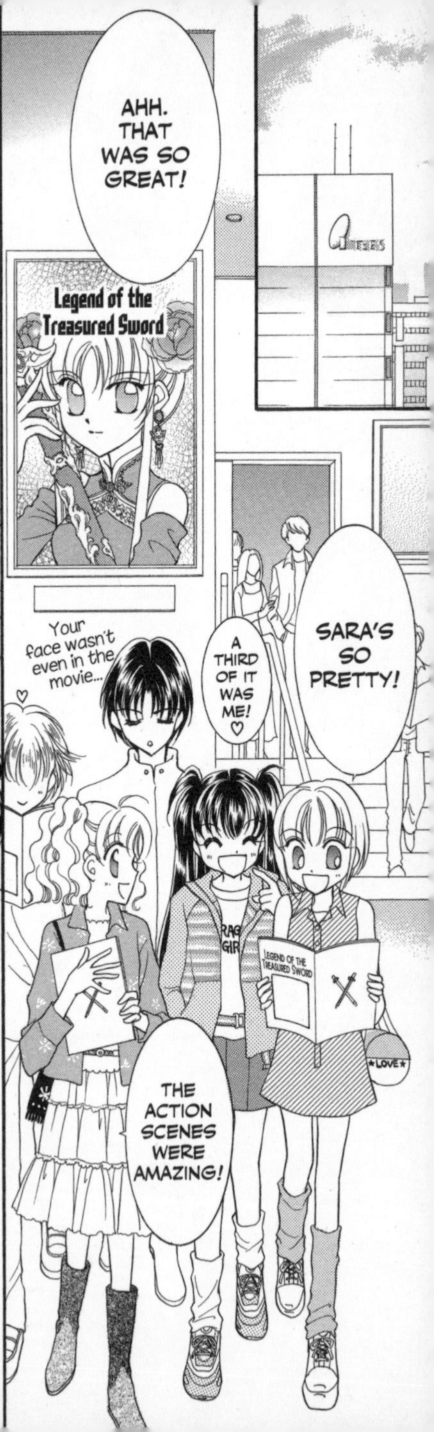
AHH. THAT WAS SO GREAT!
Legend of the Treasured Sword
SARA'S SO PRETTY!
A THIRD OF IT WAS ME! ♡
Your face wasn't even in the movie...
LEGEND OF THE TREASURED SWORD
LOVE
THE ACTION SCENES WERE AMAZING!
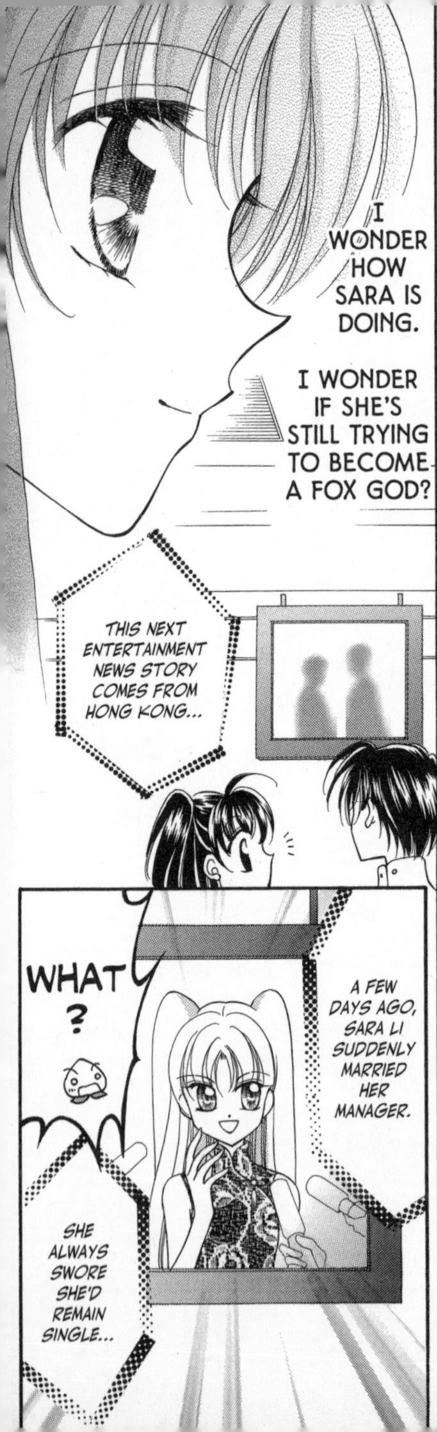
I WONDER HOW SARA IS DOING.
I WONDER IF SHE'S STILL TRYING TO BECOME A FOX GOD?
THIS NEXT ENTERTAINMENT NEWS STORY COMES FROM HONG KONG...
A FEW DAYS AGO, SARA LI SUDDENLY MARRIED HER MANAGER.
WHAT?
SHE ALWAYS SWORE SHE'D REMAIN SINGLE...

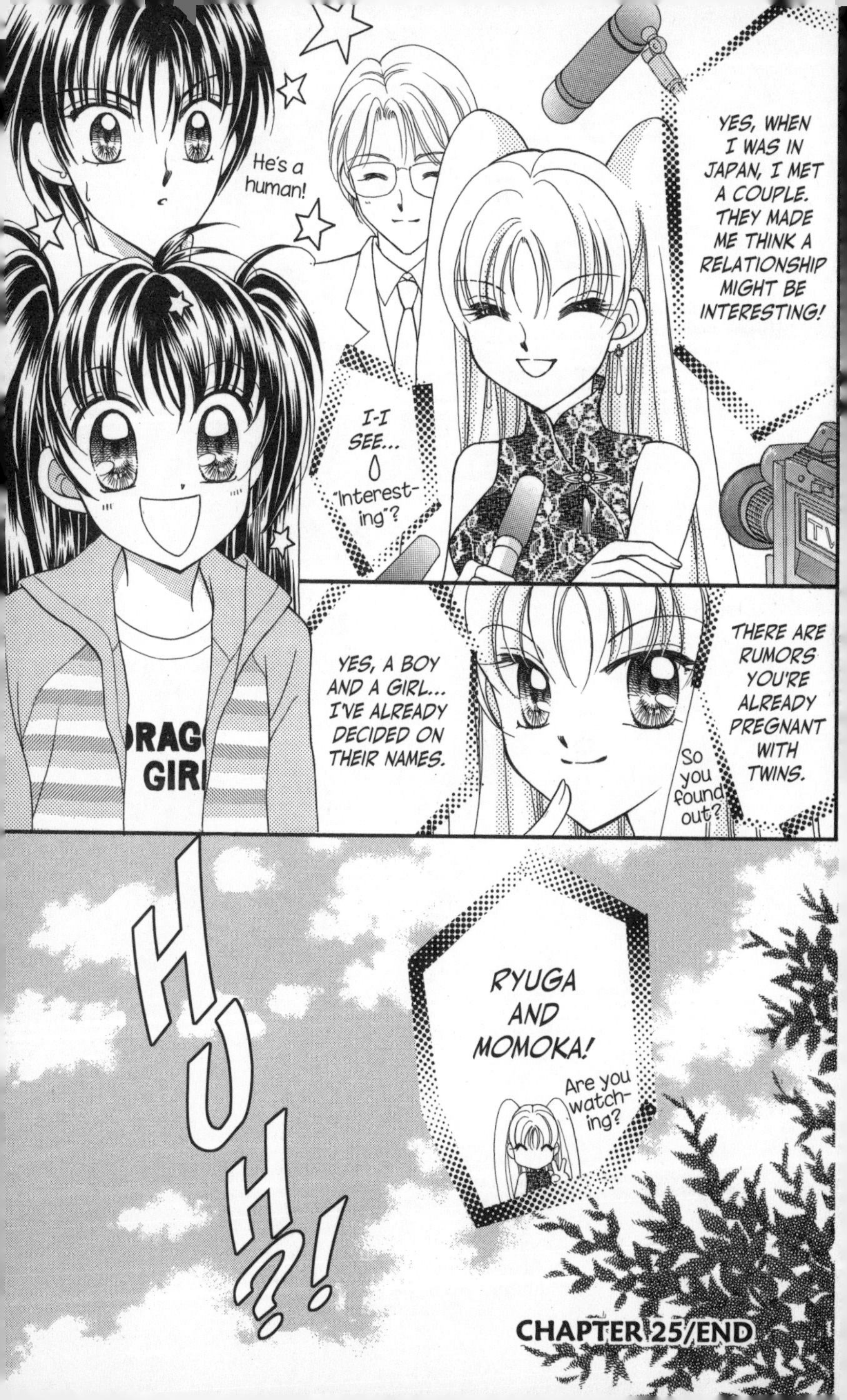
YES, WHEN I WAS IN JAPAN, I MET A COUPLE. THEY MADE ME THINK A RELATIONSHIP MIGHT BE INTERESTING!
THERE ARE RUMORS YOU'RE ALREADY PREGNANT WITH TWINS.
So you found out?
YES, A BOY AND A GIRL... I'VE ALREADY DECIDED ON THEIR NAMES.
He's a human!
I-I SEE...
"Interesting"?
DRAG GIRL
TV
RYUGA AND MOMOKA!
Are you watching?
HUH?!
CHAPTER 25/END

St. Dragon Girl
Fan Art

Alexandra Lockhart

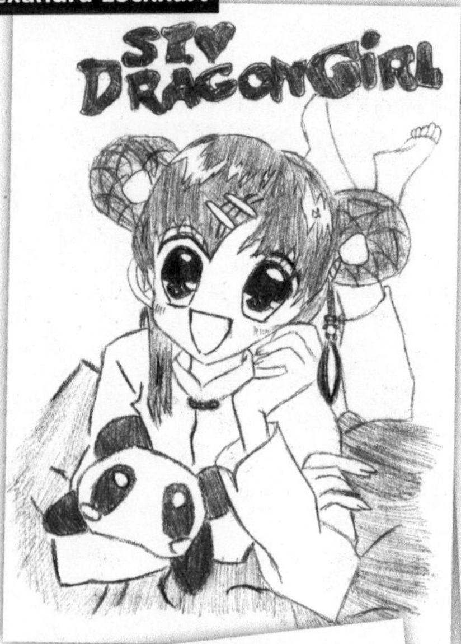
ST
DRAGONGIRL

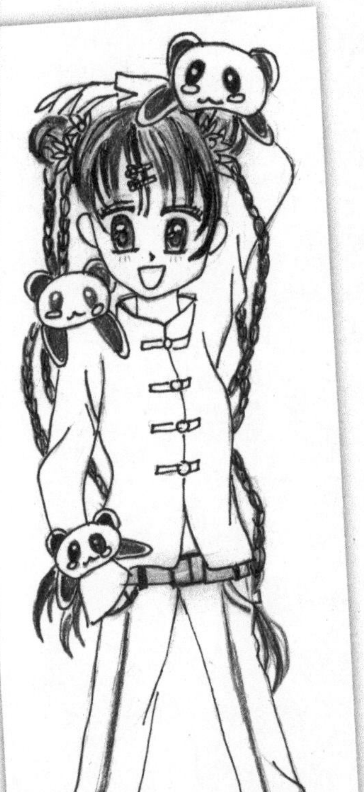

Eunice Kim

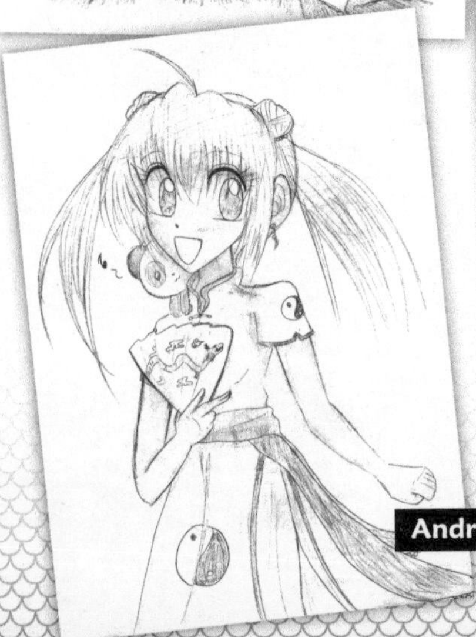

Andrea Velador

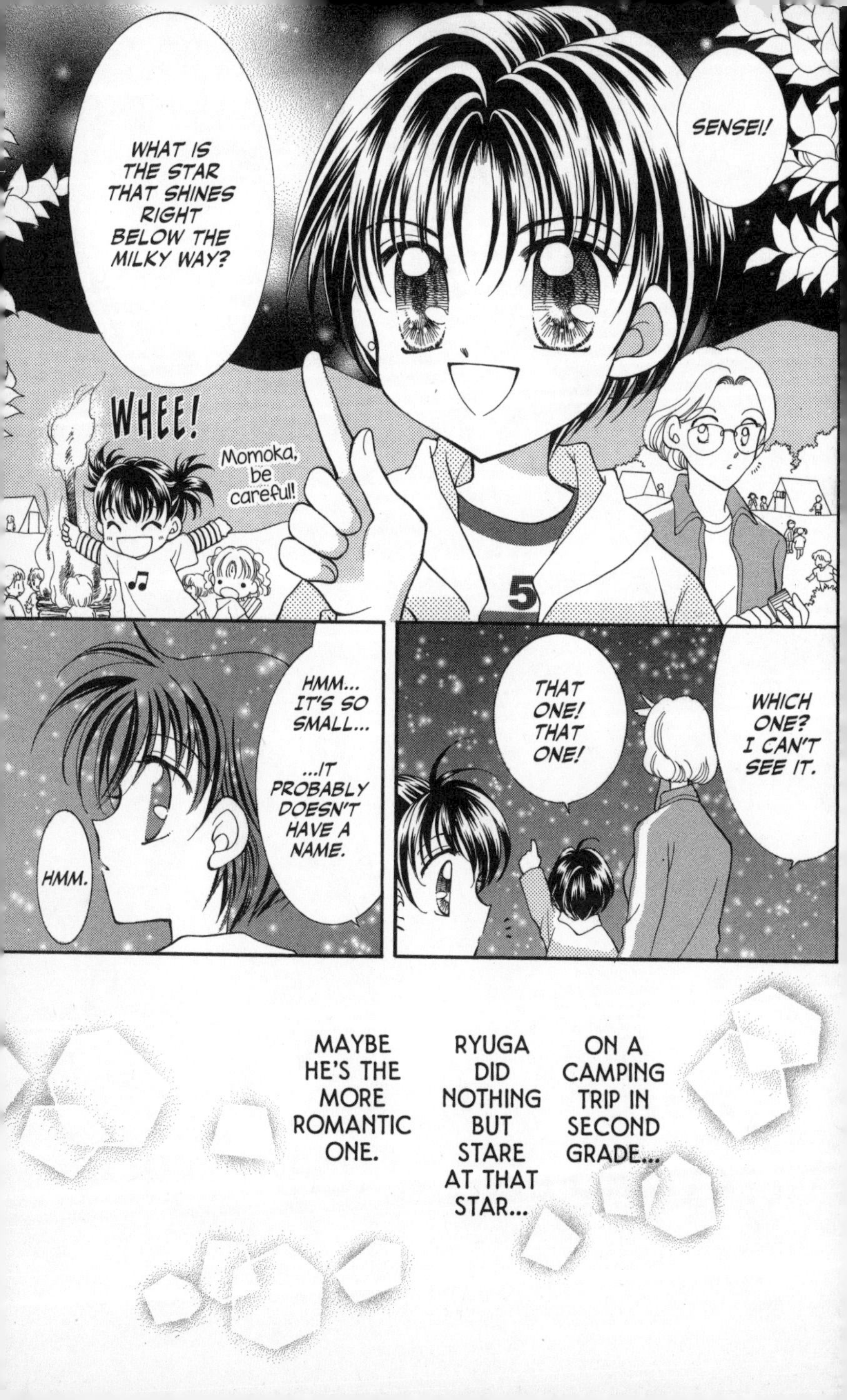
SENSEI!
WHAT IS THE STAR THAT SHINES RIGHT BELOW THE MILKY WAY?
WHEE!
Momoka, be careful!
WHICH ONE? I CAN'T SEE IT.
THAT ONE! THAT ONE!
HMM... IT'S SO SMALL...
...IT PROBABLY DOESN'T HAVE A NAME.
HMM.
ON A CAMPING TRIP IN SECOND GRADE...
RYUGA DID NOTHING BUT STARE AT THAT STAR...
MAYBE HE'S THE MORE ROMANTIC ONE.

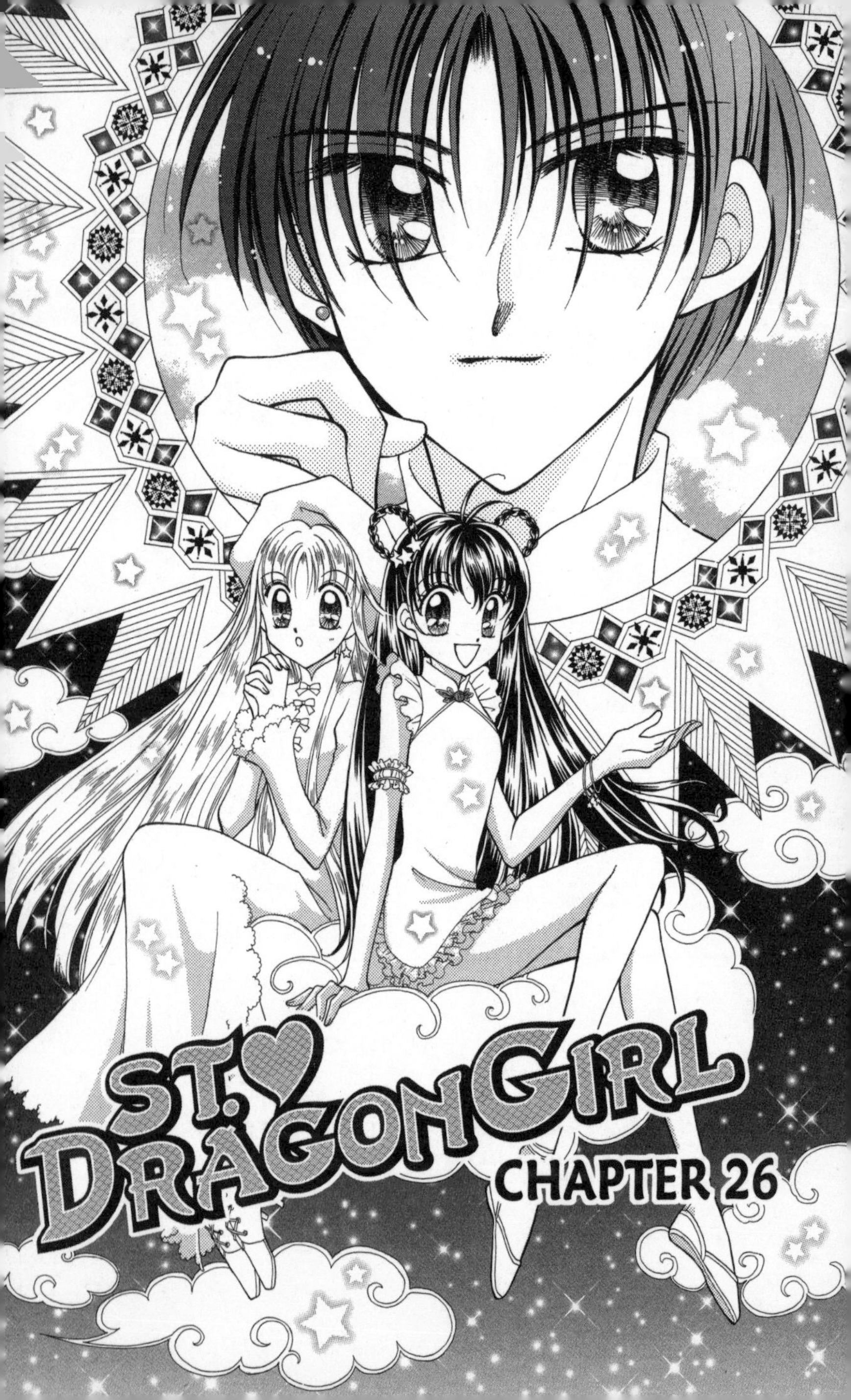
ST. DRAGON GIRL
CHAPTER 26

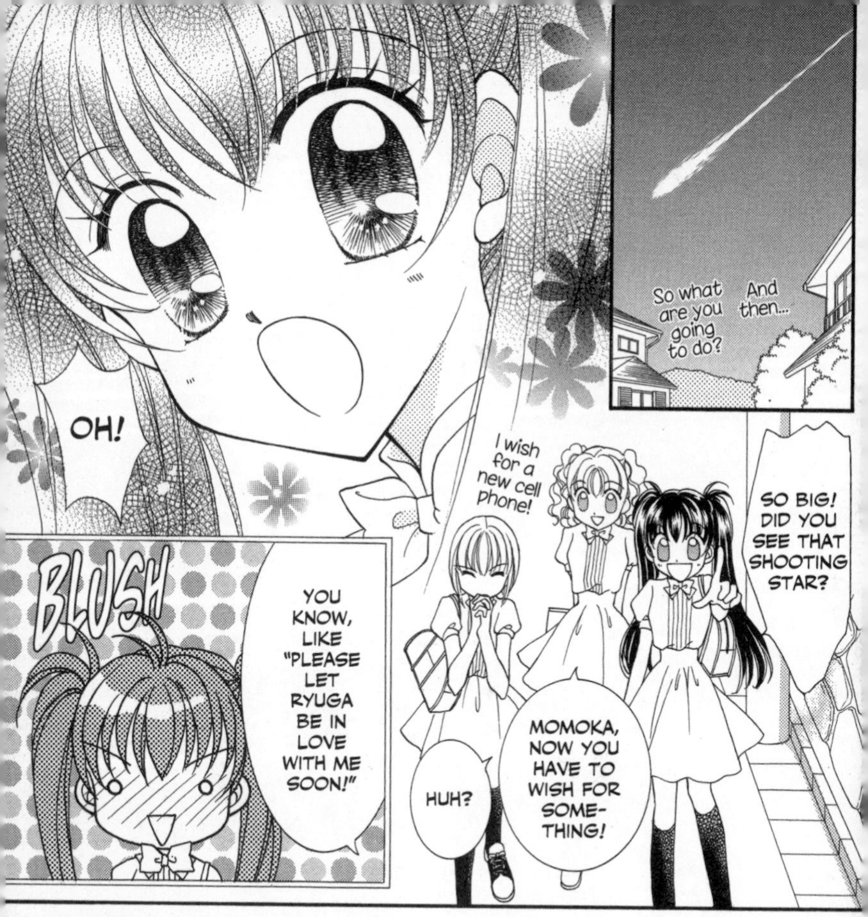
And then...
So what are you going to do?
SO BIG! DID YOU SEE THAT SHOOTING STAR?
I wish for a new cell phone!
MOMOKA, NOW YOU HAVE TO WISH FOR SOME-THING!
HUH?
YOU KNOW, LIKE "PLEASE LET RYUGA BE IN LOVE WITH ME SOON!"
BLUSH
OH!

This isn't a flower,
but I've always loved star motifs.
☆I use all kinds of star motifs in my manga. It's said that some stars protect against evil power.
When I was in elementary school, we had a superstition that if we drew a star on the back of our tests we'd get good grades! Of course I drew them too! (laugh) One day the teacher found out and made us stop, but I can't remember if we still got good grades or not!

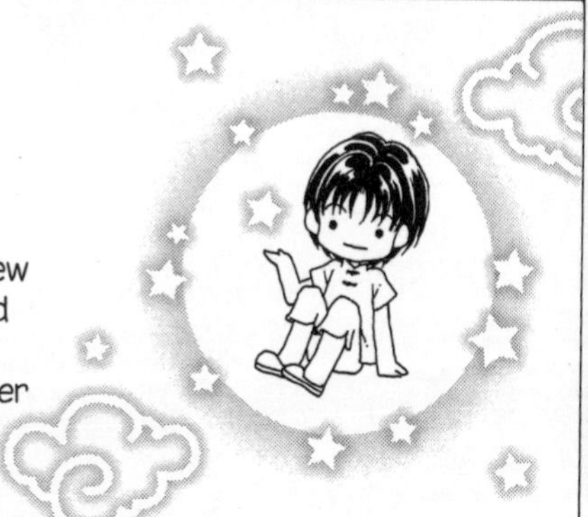

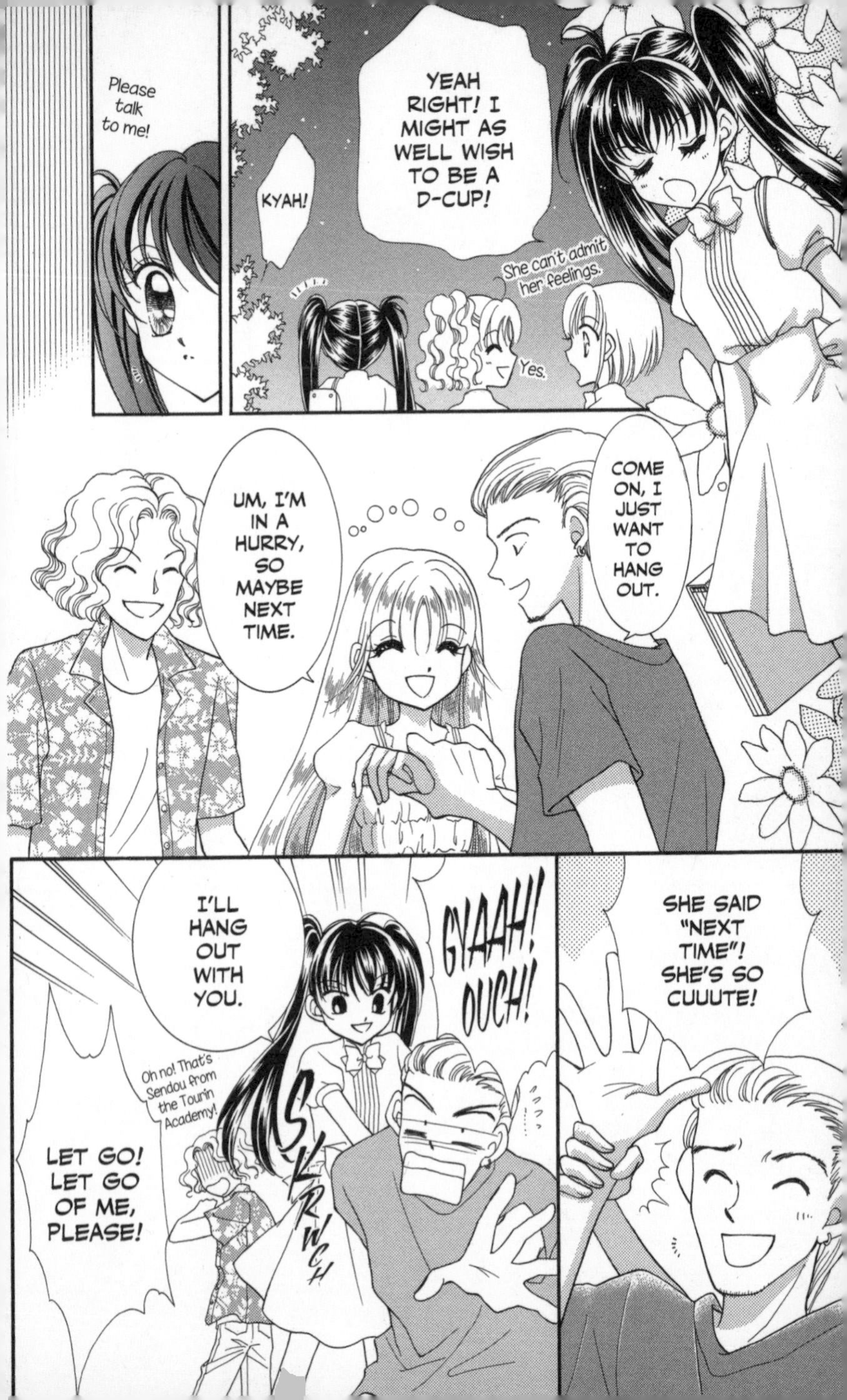
YEAH RIGHT! I MIGHT AS WELL WISH TO BE A D-CUP!
KYAH!
She can't admit her feelings.
Yes.
Please talk to me!
COME ON, I JUST WANT TO HANG OUT.
UM, I'M IN A HURRY, SO MAYBE NEXT TIME.
SHE SAID "NEXT TIME"! SHE'S SO CUUUTE!
GYAAH! OUCH!
I'LL HANG OUT WITH YOU.
Oh no! That's Sendou from the Tourin Academy!
SKRWCH
LET GO! LET GO OF ME, PLEASE!

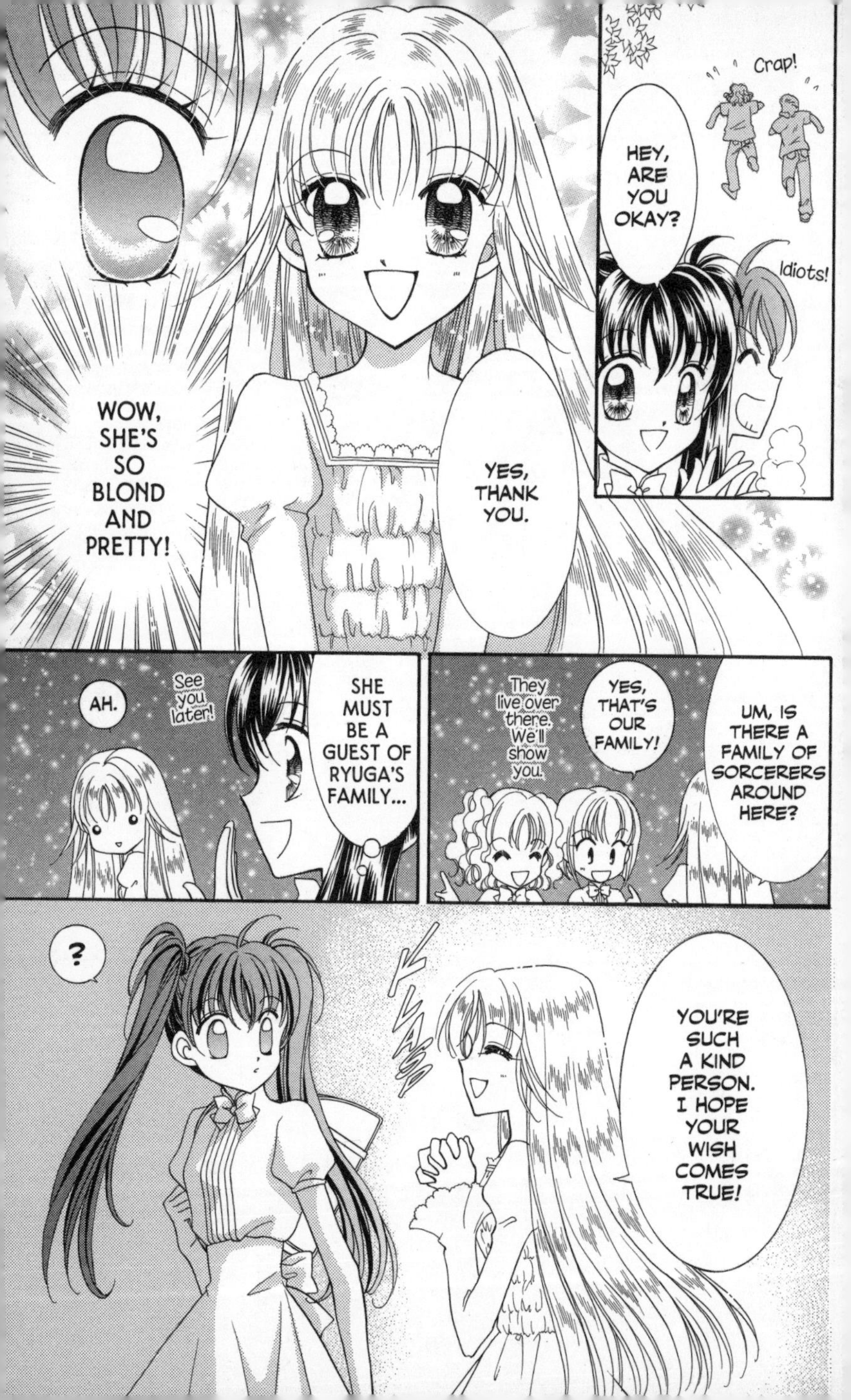
Crap!
HEY, ARE YOU OKAY?
Idiots!
YES, THANK YOU.
WOW, SHE'S SO BLOND AND PRETTY!
UM, IS THERE A FAMILY OF SORCERERS AROUND HERE?
YES, THAT'S OUR FAMILY!
They live over there. We'll show you.
SHE MUST BE A GUEST OF RYUGA'S FAMILY...
See you later!
AH.
YOU'RE SUCH A KIND PERSON. I HOPE YOUR WISH COMES TRUE!
?

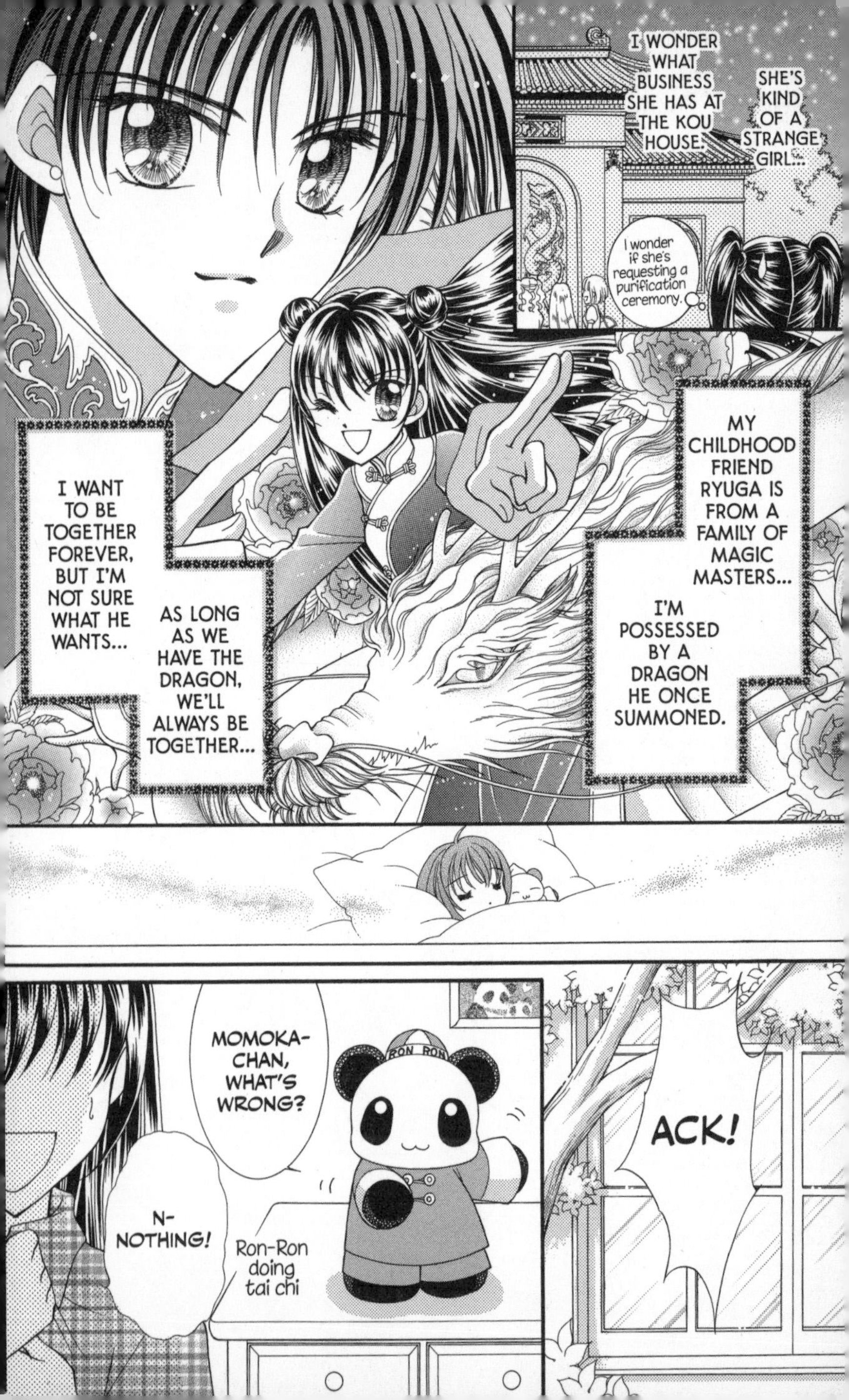
SHE'S KIND OF A STRANGE GIRL...
I WONDER WHAT BUSINESS SHE HAS AT THE KOU HOUSE.
I wonder if she's requesting a purification ceremony.
MY CHILDHOOD FRIEND RYUGA IS FROM A FAMILY OF MAGIC MASTERS...
I'M POSSESSED BY A DRAGON HE ONCE SUMMONED.
AS LONG AS WE HAVE THE DRAGON, WE'LL ALWAYS BE TOGETHER...
I WANT TO BE TOGETHER FOREVER, BUT I'M NOT SURE WHAT HE WANTS...
ACK!
MOMOKA-CHAN, WHAT'S WRONG?
N-NOTHING!
Ron-Ron doing tai chi
RON RON

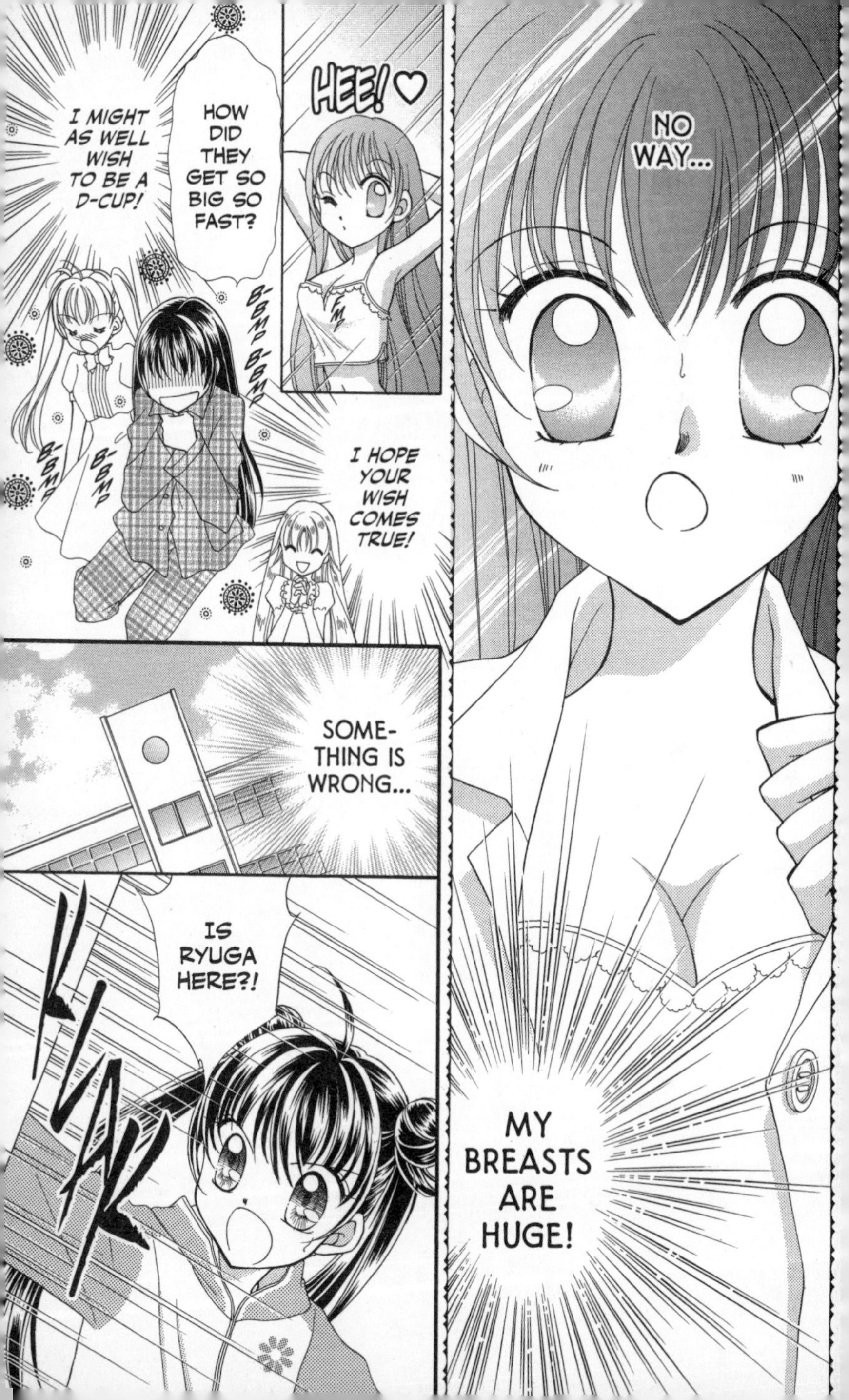
NO WAY...
MY BREASTS ARE HUGE!
HEE! ♥
HOW DID THEY GET SO BIG SO FAST?
I MIGHT AS WELL WISH TO BE A D-CUP!
I HOPE YOUR WISH COMES TRUE!
SOME-THING IS WRONG...
IS RYUGA HERE?!

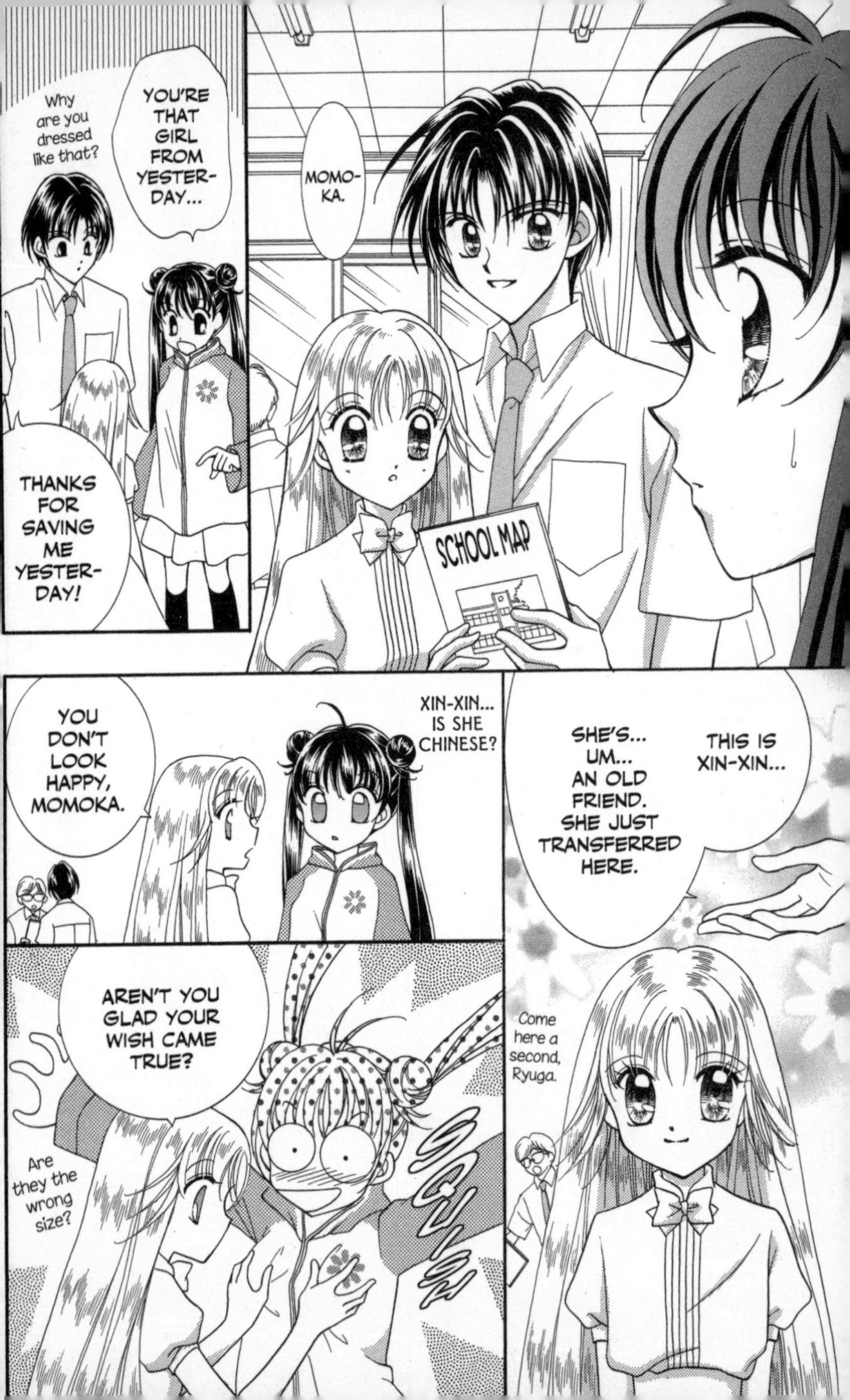
MOMO-KA.
YOU'RE THAT GIRL FROM YESTER-DAY...
Why are you dressed like that?
THANKS FOR SAVING ME YESTER-DAY!
THIS IS XIN-XIN...
SHE'S... UM... AN OLD FRIEND. SHE JUST TRANSFERRED HERE.
Come here a second, Ryuga.
XIN-XIN... IS SHE CHINESE?
YOU DON'T LOOK HAPPY, MOMOKA.
AREN'T YOU GLAD YOUR WISH CAME TRUE?
Are they the wrong size?

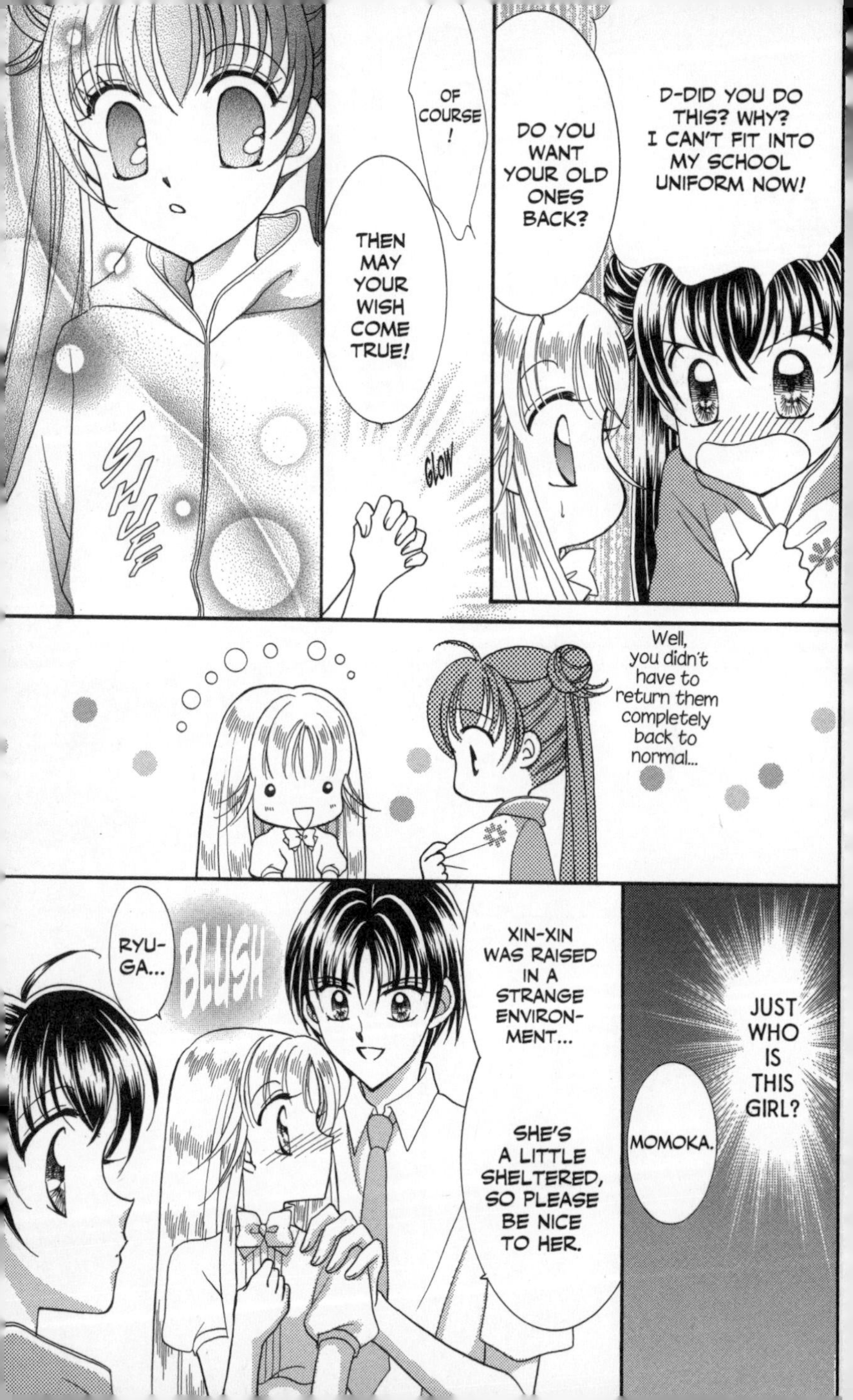
D-DID YOU DO THIS? WHY? I CAN'T FIT INTO MY SCHOOL UNIFORM NOW!
DO YOU WANT YOUR OLD ONES BACK?
OF COURSE!
THEN MAY YOUR WISH COME TRUE!
GLOW
SHUFF
Well, you didn't have to return them completely back to normal...
JUST WHO IS THIS GIRL?
MOMOKA.
XIN-XIN WAS RAISED IN A STRANGE ENVIRONMENT...
SHE'S A LITTLE SHELTERED, SO PLEASE BE NICE TO HER.
BLUSH
RYU-GA...

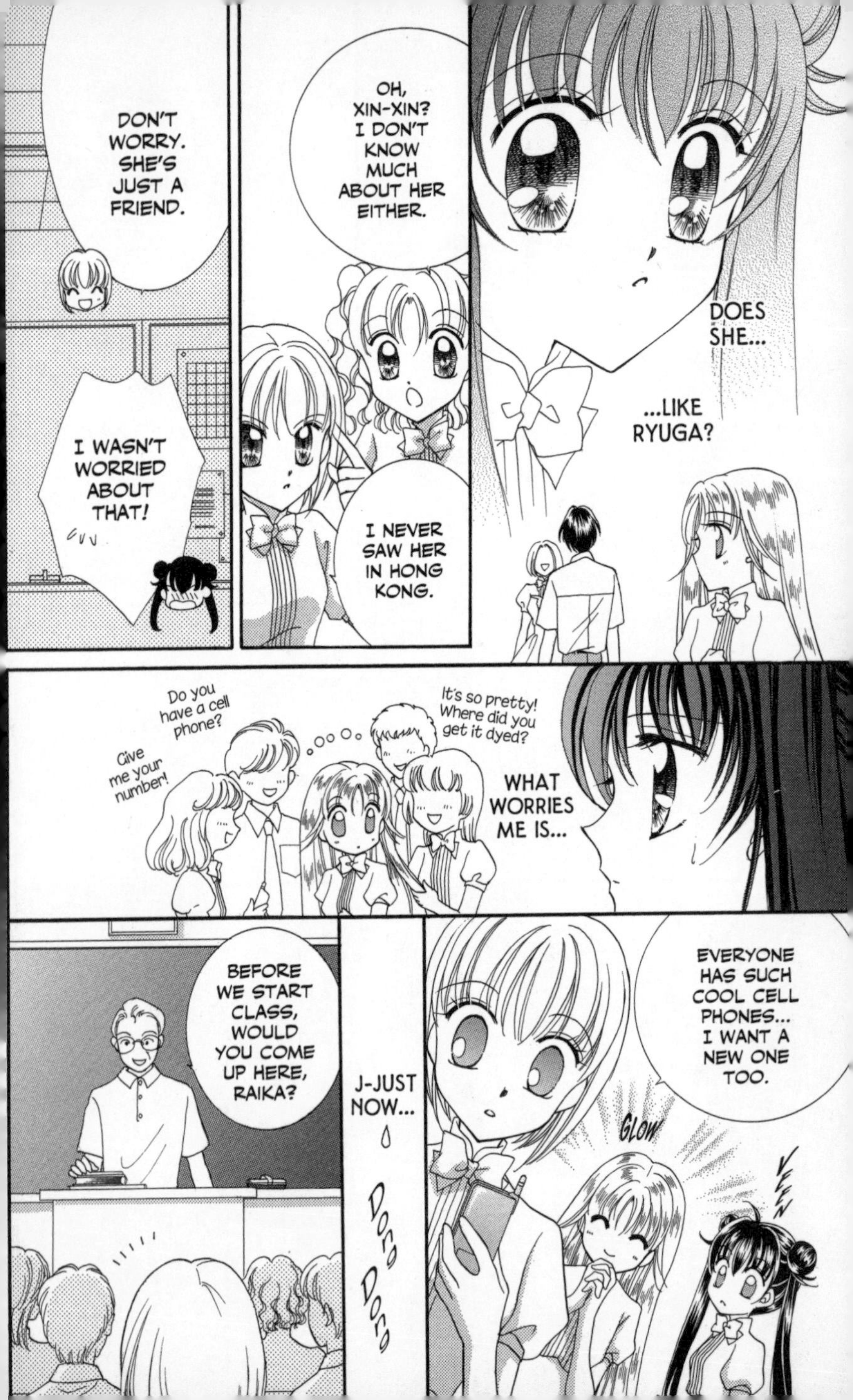
DOES SHE...
...LIKE RYUGA?
OH, XIN-XIN? I DON'T KNOW MUCH ABOUT HER EITHER.
I NEVER SAW HER IN HONG KONG.
DON'T WORRY. SHE'S JUST A FRIEND.
I WASN'T WORRIED ABOUT THAT!
WHAT WORRIES ME IS...
It's so pretty! Where did you get it dyed?
Do you have a cell phone?
Give me your number!
EVERYONE HAS SUCH COOL CELL PHONES... I WANT A NEW ONE TOO.
VEEN
GLOW
J-JUST NOW...
Doro Doro
BEFORE WE START CLASS, WOULD YOU COME UP HERE, RAIKA?

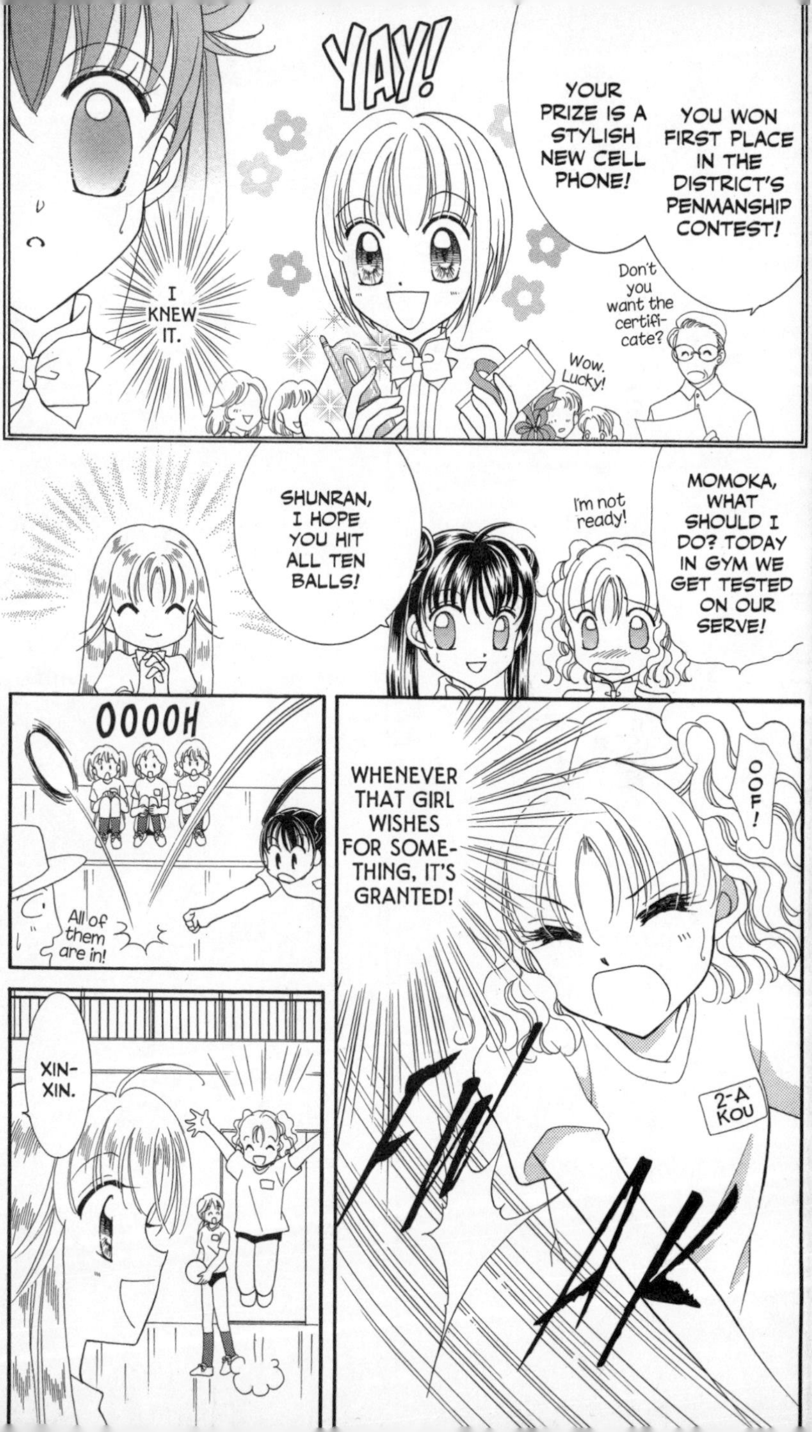
YOU WON FIRST PLACE IN THE DISTRICT'S PENMANSHIP CONTEST!
YOUR PRIZE IS A STYLISH NEW CELL PHONE!
Don't you want the certifi-cate?
Wow. Lucky!
YAY!
I KNEW IT.
MOMOKA, WHAT SHOULD I DO? TODAY IN GYM WE GET TESTED ON OUR SERVE!
I'm not ready!
SHUNRAN, I HOPE YOU HIT ALL TEN BALLS!
OOF!
WHENEVER THAT GIRL WISHES FOR SOME-THING, IT'S GRANTED!
OOOOH
All of them are in!
XIN-XIN.

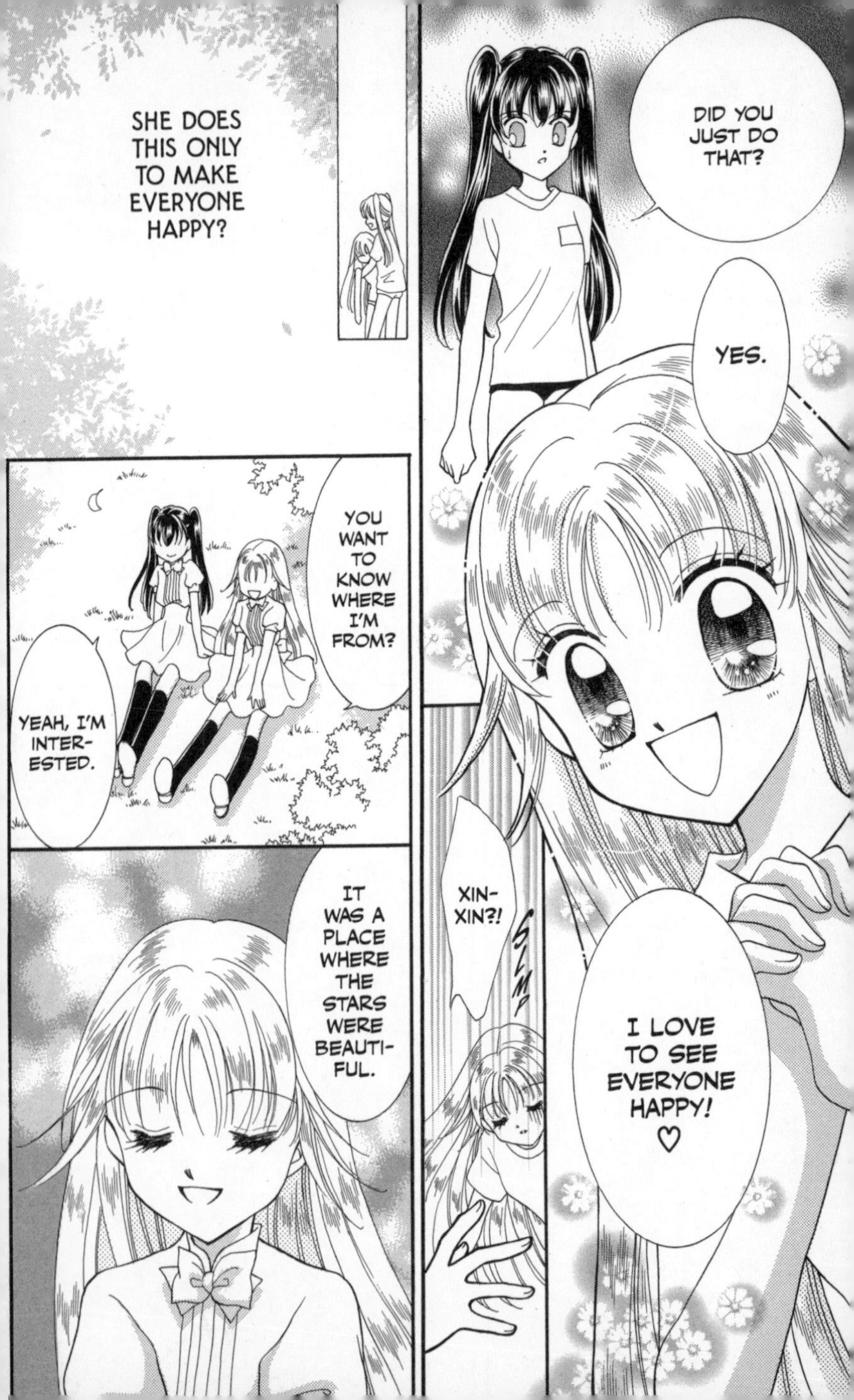
DID YOU JUST DO THAT?
YES.
I LOVE TO SEE EVERYONE HAPPY! ♡
XIN-XIN?!
SHE DOES THIS ONLY TO MAKE EVERYONE HAPPY?
YOU WANT TO KNOW WHERE I'M FROM?
YEAH, I'M INTER-ESTED.
IT WAS A PLACE WHERE THE STARS WERE BEAUTI-FUL.

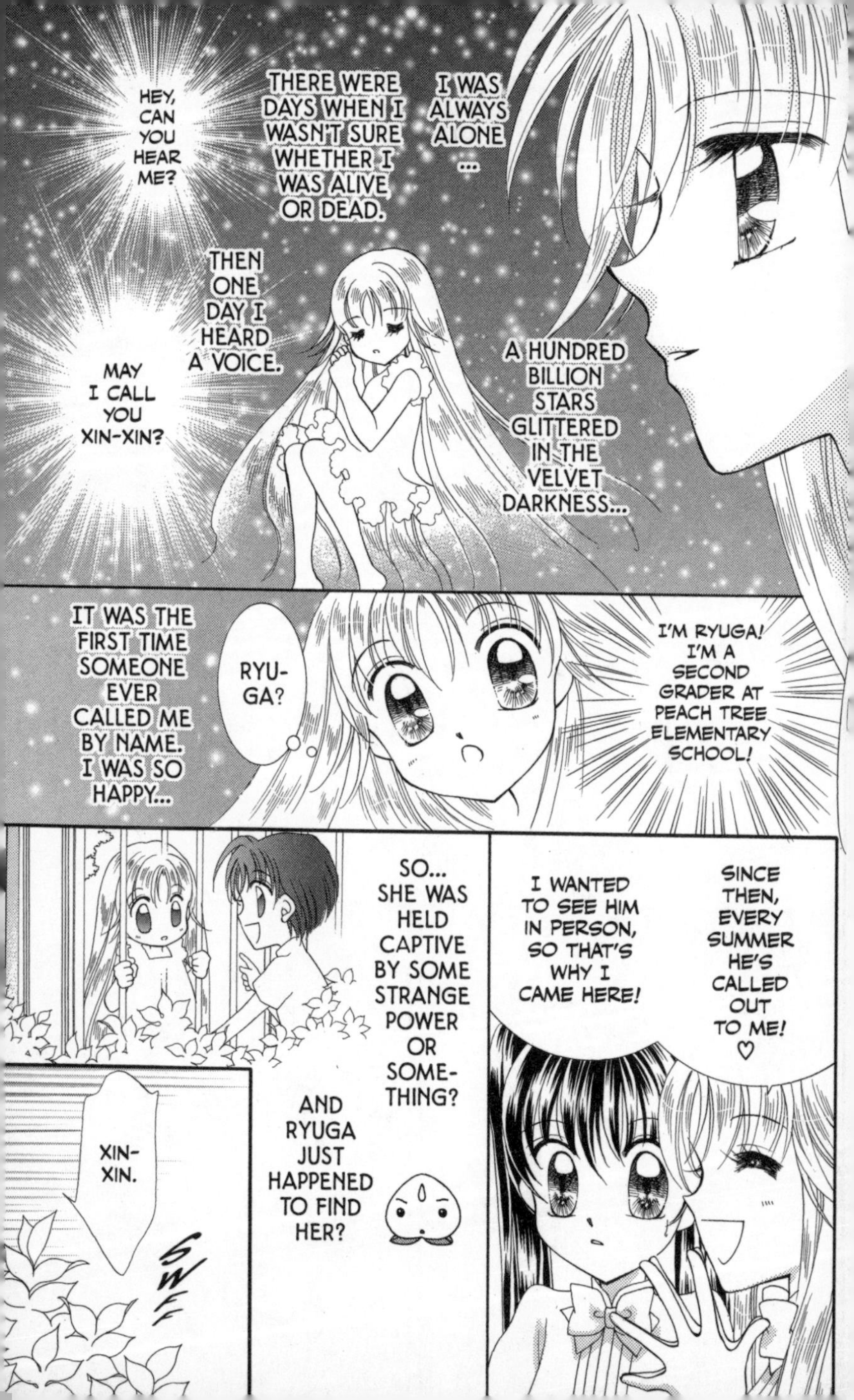

I WAS ALWAYS ALONE...
THERE WERE DAYS WHEN I WASN'T SURE WHETHER I WAS ALIVE OR DEAD.
HEY, CAN YOU HEAR ME?
A HUNDRED BILLION STARS GLITTERED IN THE VELVET DARKNESS...
THEN ONE DAY I HEARD A VOICE.
MAY I CALL YOU XIN-XIN?
I'M RYUGA! I'M A SECOND GRADER AT PEACH TREE ELEMENTARY SCHOOL!
RYU-GA?
IT WAS THE FIRST TIME SOMEONE EVER CALLED ME BY NAME. I WAS SO HAPPY...
SINCE THEN, EVERY SUMMER HE'S CALLED OUT TO ME! ♡
I WANTED TO SEE HIM IN PERSON, SO THAT'S WHY I CAME HERE!
SO... SHE WAS HELD CAPTIVE BY SOME STRANGE POWER OR SOME-THING?
AND RYUGA JUST HAPPENED TO FIND HER?
XIN-XIN.
SWFF

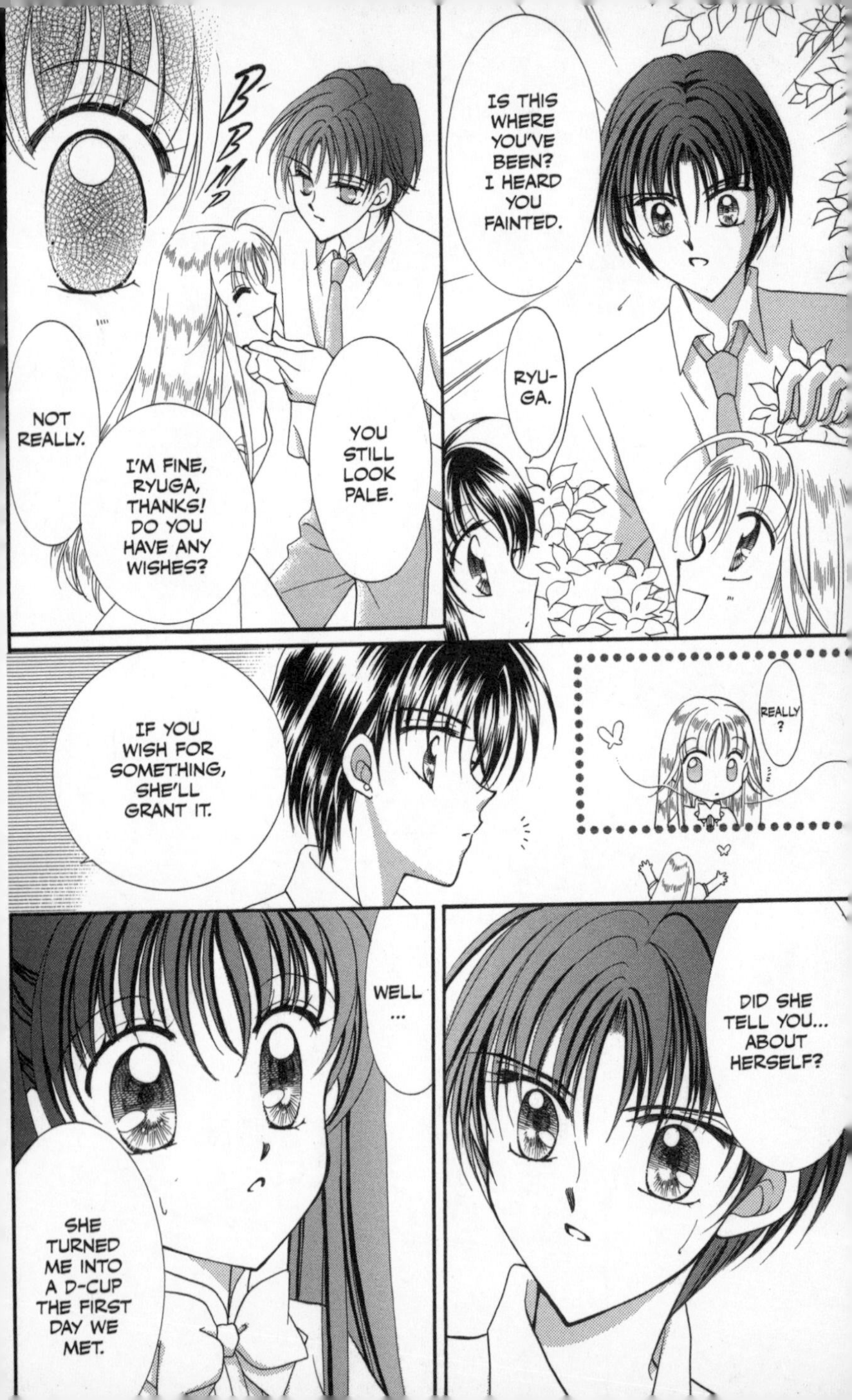
IS THIS WHERE YOU'VE BEEN? I HEARD YOU FAINTED.
RYU-GA.
B-BBMP
YOU STILL LOOK PALE.
I'M FINE, RYUGA, THANKS! DO YOU HAVE ANY WISHES?
NOT REALLY.
REALLY?
IF YOU WISH FOR SOMETHING, SHE'LL GRANT IT.
DID SHE TELL YOU... ABOUT HERSELF?
WELL ...
SHE TURNED ME INTO A D-CUP THE FIRST DAY WE MET.

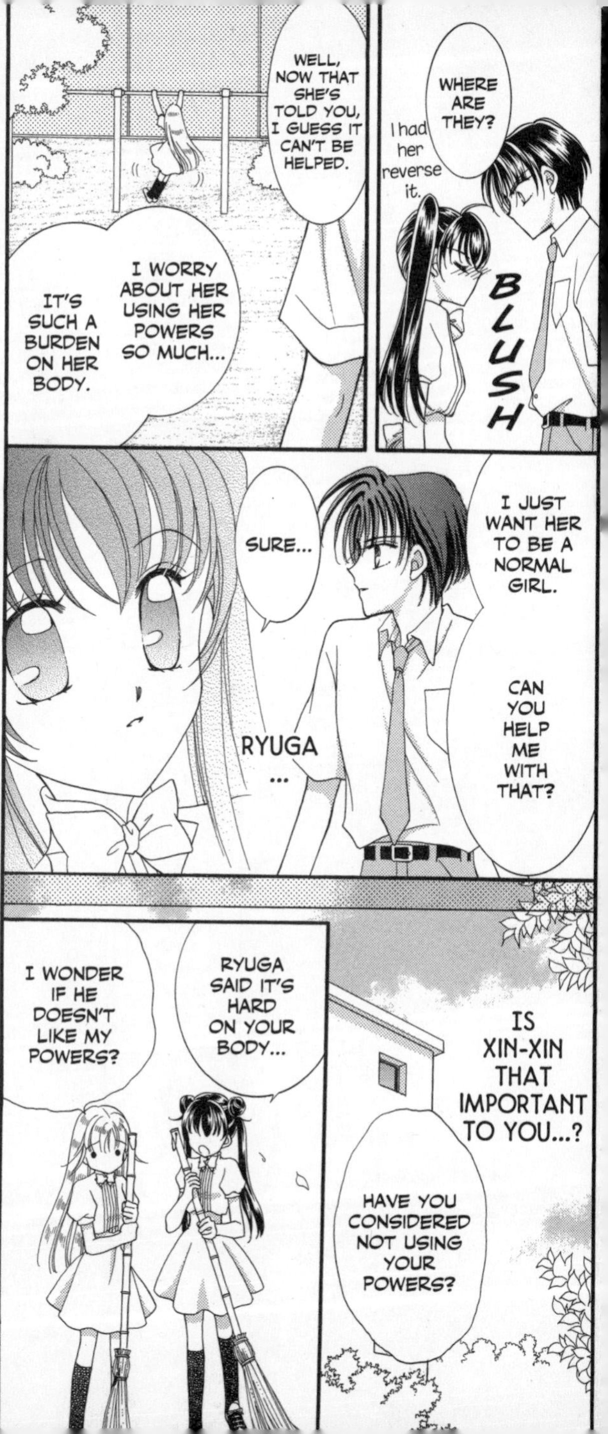
WHERE ARE THEY?
I had her reverse it.
BLUSH
WELL, NOW THAT SHE'S TOLD YOU, I GUESS IT CAN'T BE HELPED.
I WORRY ABOUT HER USING HER POWERS SO MUCH...
IT'S SUCH A BURDEN ON HER BODY.
I JUST WANT HER TO BE A NORMAL GIRL.
CAN YOU HELP ME WITH THAT?
SURE...
RYUGA ...
IS XIN-XIN THAT IMPORTANT TO YOU...?
HAVE YOU CONSIDERED NOT USING YOUR POWERS?
RYUGA SAID IT'S HARD ON YOUR BODY...
I WONDER IF HE DOESN'T LIKE MY POWERS?

13

I wanted to write a story about a star, so I wrote the story about Xin-Xin. Have you seen the Leonid meteor shower? They said it would be the best one in 30 years, so I was really excited. It was amazing! There were so many shooting stars, and I made tons of wishes! I hope I get to see it this year too!

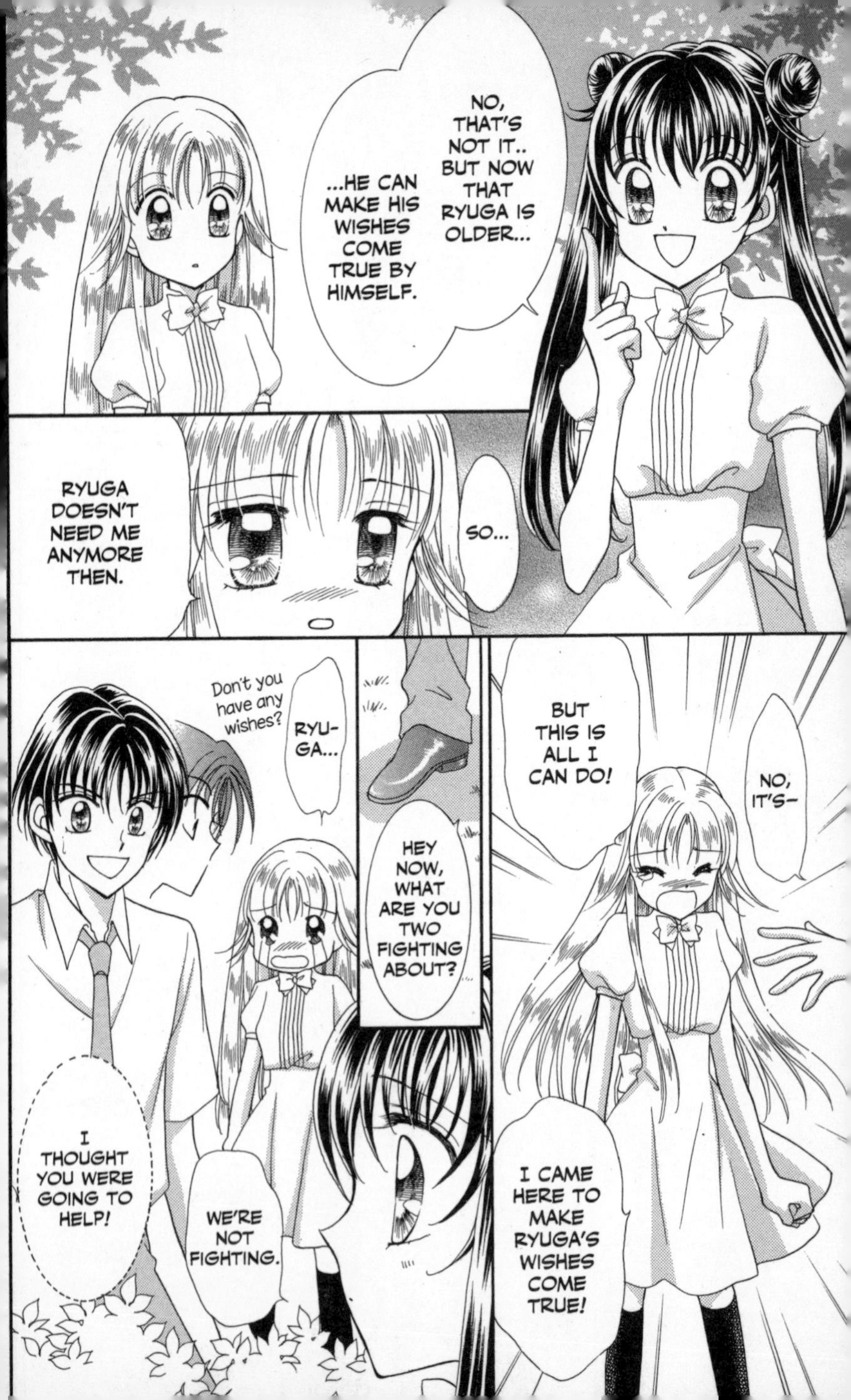
NO, THAT'S NOT IT.. BUT NOW THAT RYUGA IS OLDER...
...HE CAN MAKE HIS WISHES COME TRUE BY HIMSELF.
SO...
RYUGA DOESN'T NEED ME ANYMORE THEN.
NO, IT'S—
BUT THIS IS ALL I CAN DO!
I CAME HERE TO MAKE RYUGA'S WISHES COME TRUE!
HEY NOW, WHAT ARE YOU TWO FIGHTING ABOUT?
RYU-GA...
Don't you have any wishes?
WE'RE NOT FIGHTING.
I THOUGHT YOU WERE GOING TO HELP!

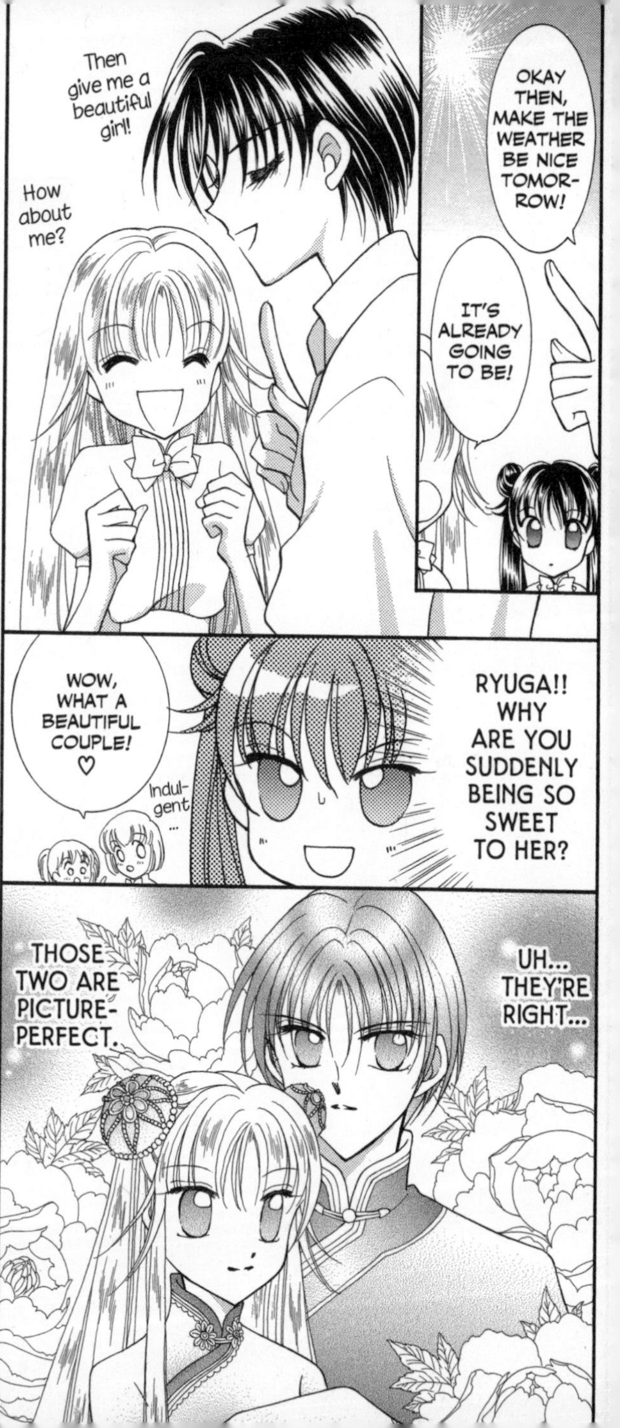
OKAY THEN, MAKE THE WEATHER BE NICE TOMORROW!
IT'S ALREADY GOING TO BE!
Then give me a beautiful girl!
How about me?
RYUGA!! WHY ARE YOU SUDDENLY BEING SO SWEET TO HER?
WOW, WHAT A BEAUTIFUL COUPLE! ♡
Indulgent...
UH... THEY'RE RIGHT...
THOSE TWO ARE PICTURE-PERFECT.

14

Speaking of stars (I'm pushing it ♁), this story reminds me of the old manga *The Giant's Star* about the guy who plays for the Tokyo Giants baseball team. I love the Giants, so I brought my parents and relatives along to a game this year when they were playing against Osaka. I'd been to the Tokyo Dome to see concerts before, but never to see a baseball game. It was so fun. They beat Osaka by a landslide! The only downer was that Matsui hit a home run when I was standing in line for the bathroom!

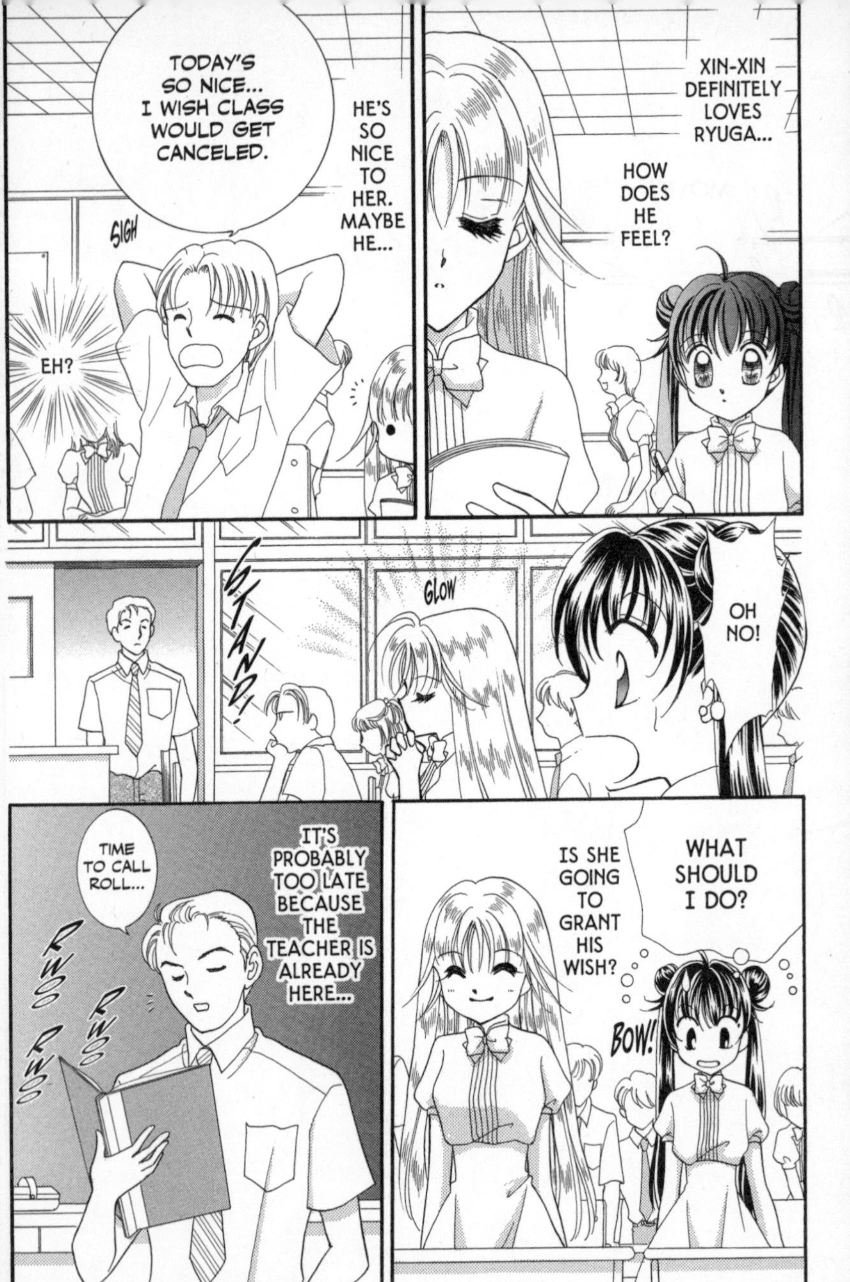
XIN-XIN DEFINITELY LOVES RYUGA...
HOW DOES HE FEEL?
TODAY'S SO NICE... I WISH CLASS WOULD GET CANCELED.
SIGH
EH?
HE'S SO NICE TO HER. MAYBE HE...
OH NO!
GLOW
STAND!
WHAT SHOULD I DO?
IS SHE GOING TO GRANT HIS WISH?
BOW!
IT'S PROBABLY TOO LATE BECAUSE THE TEACHER IS ALREADY HERE...
TIME TO CALL ROLL...
RWOO RWOO RWOO

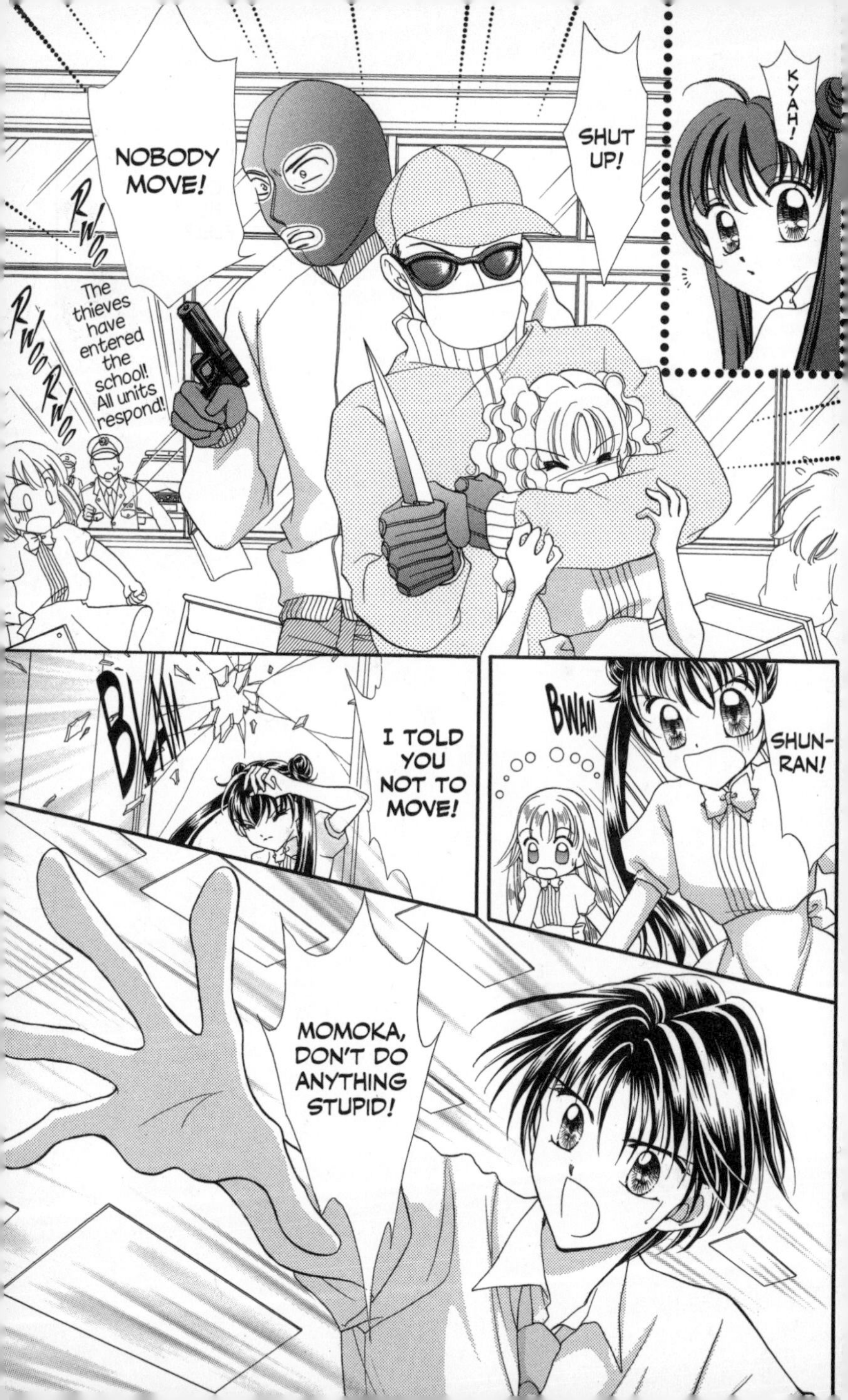
KYAH!
SHUT UP!
NOBODY MOVE!
RWOO
The thieves have entered the school! All units respond!
BWAM
SHUN-RAN!
BLAM
I TOLD YOU NOT TO MOVE!
MOMOKA, DON'T DO ANYTHING STUPID!

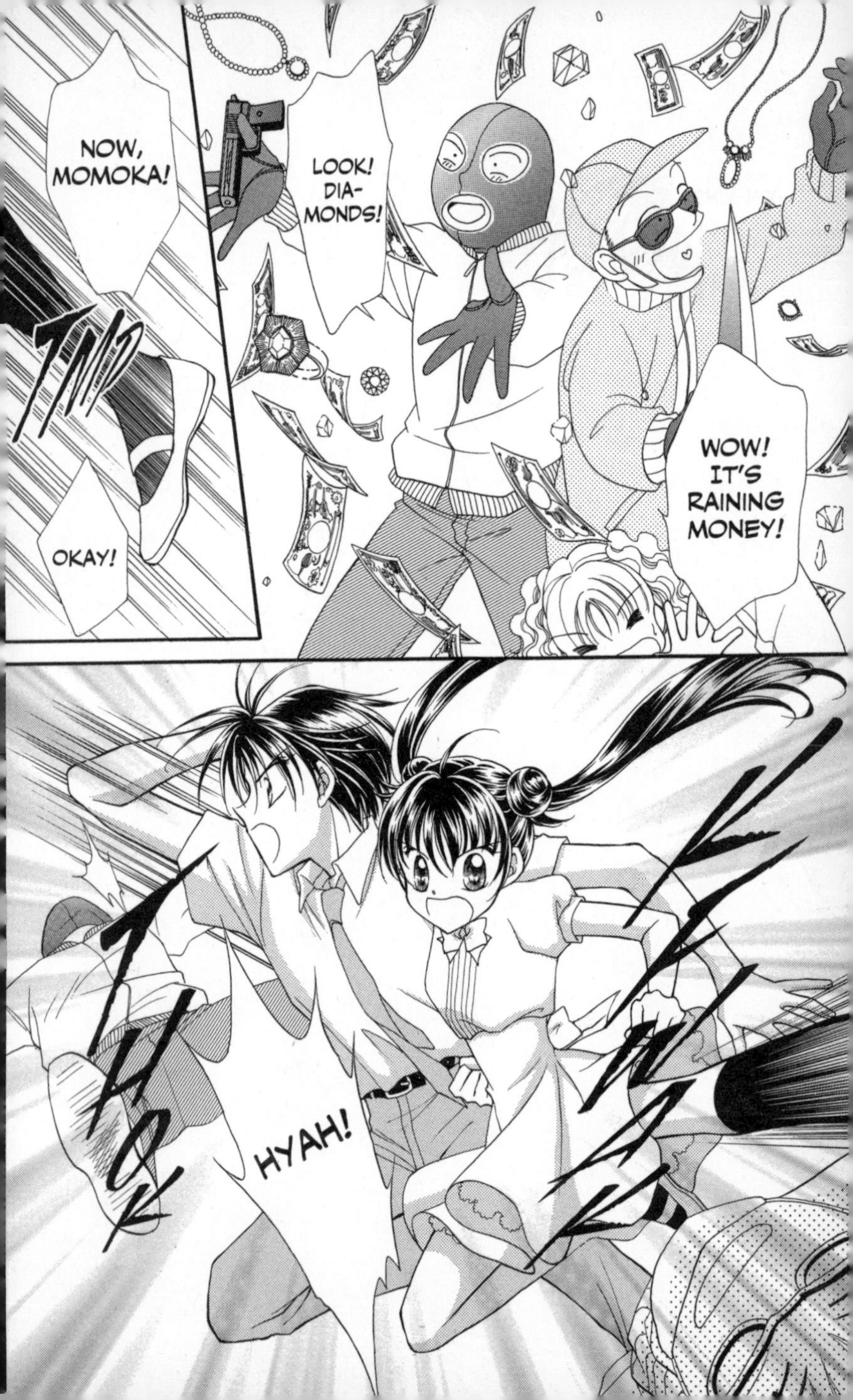
LOOK! DIA- MONDS!
WOW! IT'S RAINING MONEY!
NOW, MOMOKA!
OKAY!
HYAH!

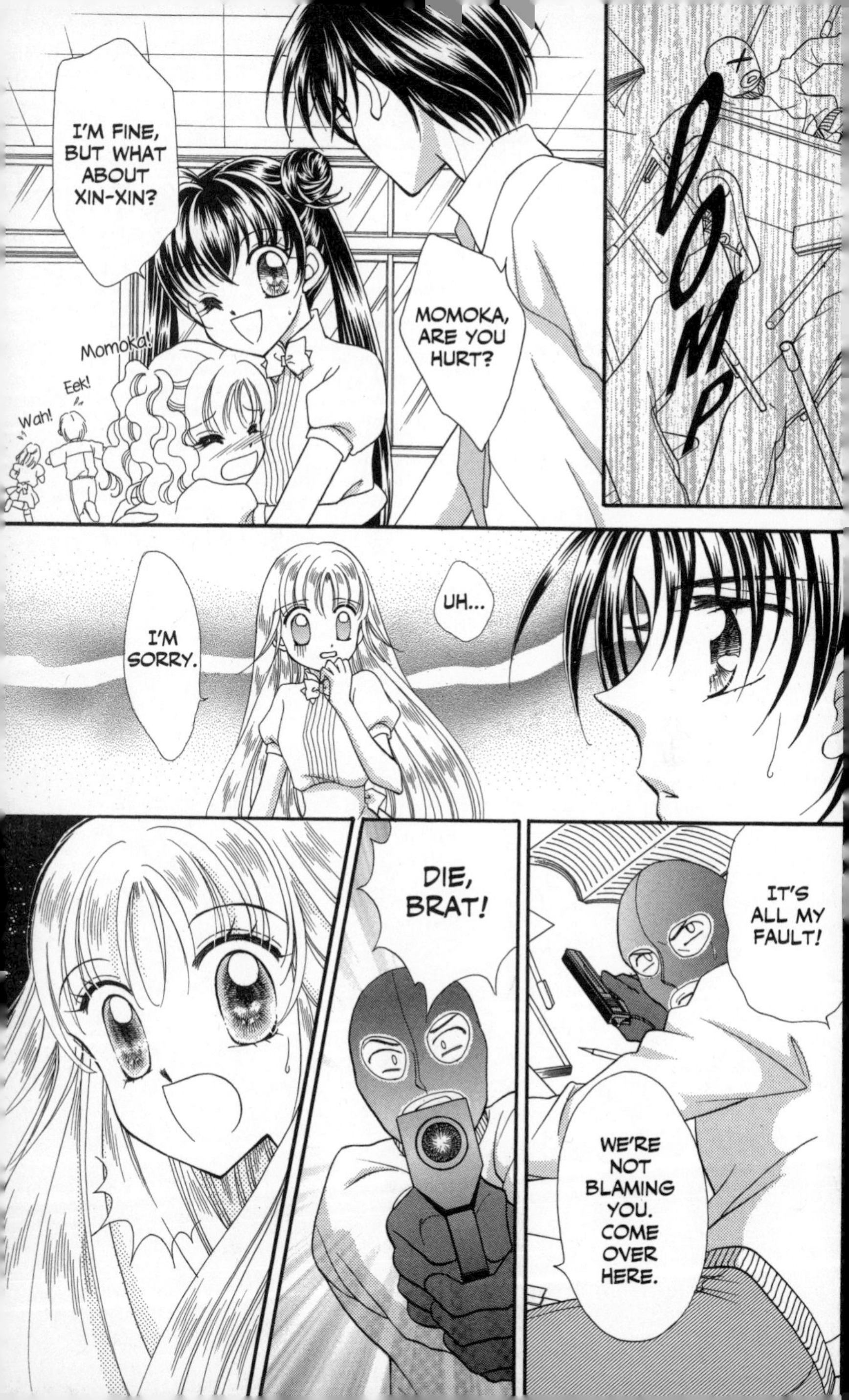
DOMP
MOMOKA, ARE YOU HURT?
I'M FINE, BUT WHAT ABOUT XIN-XIN?
Momoka!
Eek!
Wah!
UH...
I'M SORRY.
IT'S ALL MY FAULT!
WE'RE NOT BLAMING YOU. COME OVER HERE.
DIE, BRAT!

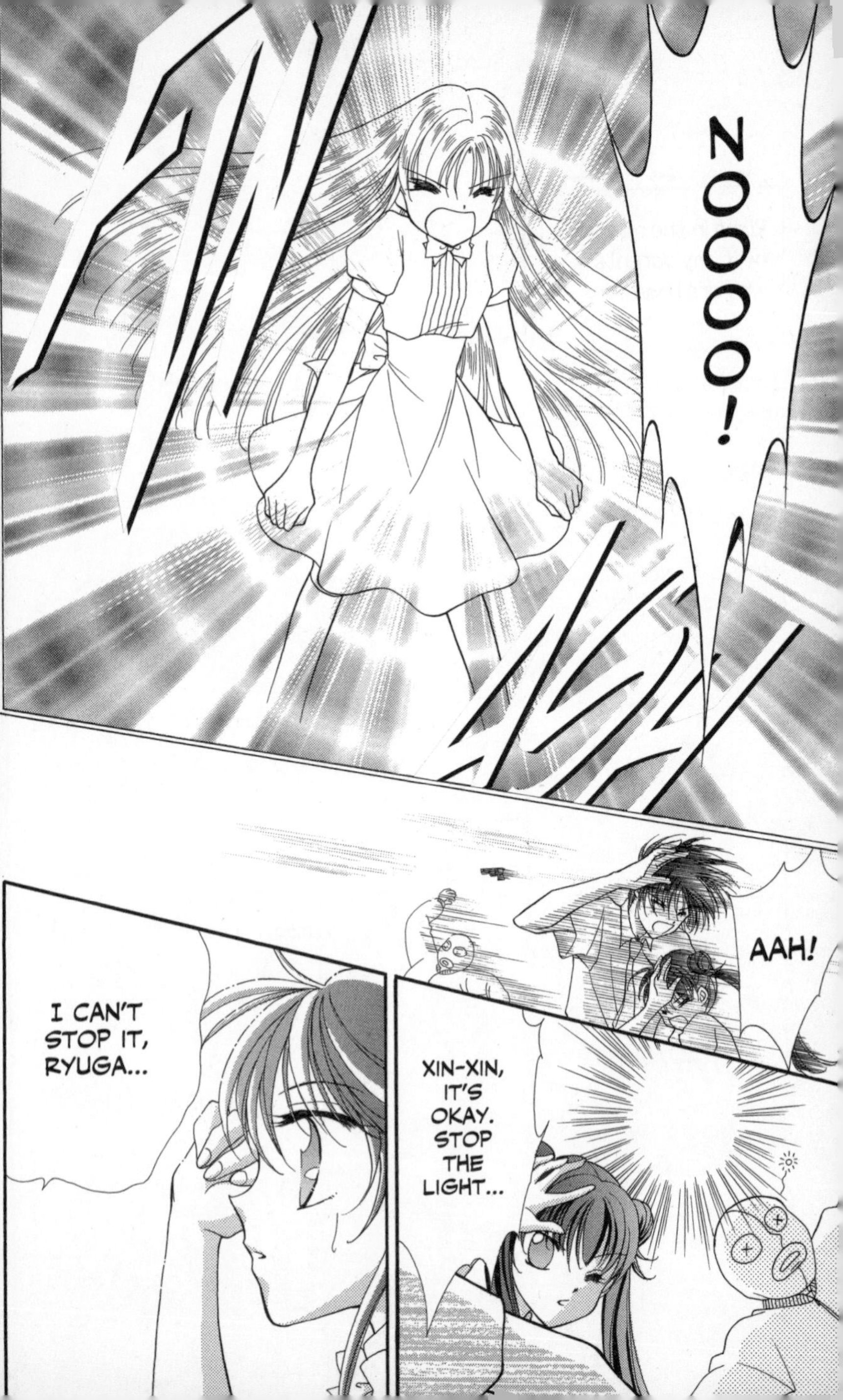
NOOOOO!
AAH!
XIN-XIN, IT'S OKAY. STOP THE LIGHT...
I CAN'T STOP IT, RYUGA...

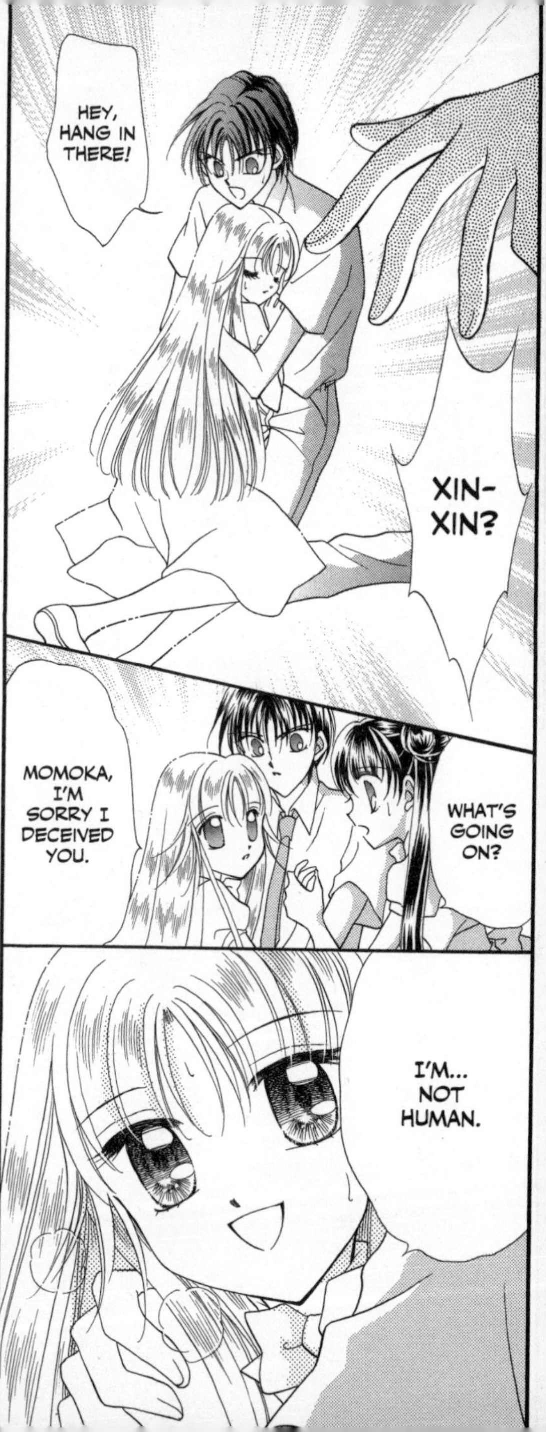
XIN-XIN?
HEY, HANG IN THERE!
WHAT'S GOING ON?
MOMOKA, I'M SORRY I DECEIVED YOU.
I'M... NOT HUMAN.

15

Right in the middle of it, my parents, who are huge fans of Osaka, started doing the Osaka cheer (especially Mom)! Apparently someone in the next row was doing the Tokyo cheer, so Mom got all worked up and started doing the Osaka cheer. ♪ How immature! But Dad bought Mom a bunch of Osaka stuff, so she was happy.

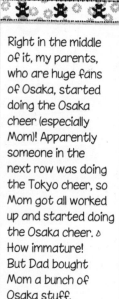

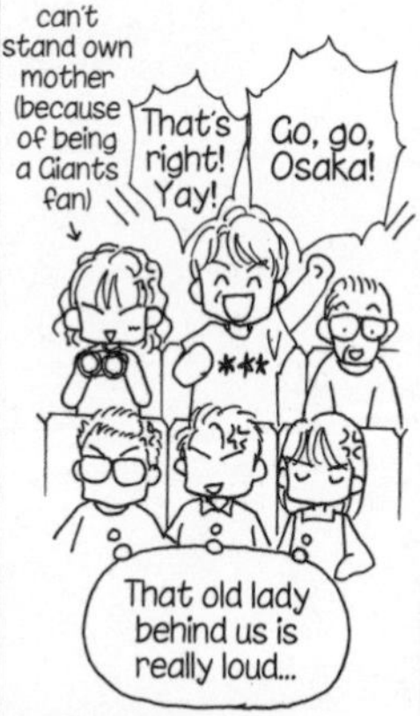
can't stand own mother (because of being a Giants fan)
That's right! Yay!
Go, go, Osaka!
***
That old lady behind us is really loud...

The melon ice cream they sold at the concession stand was great!

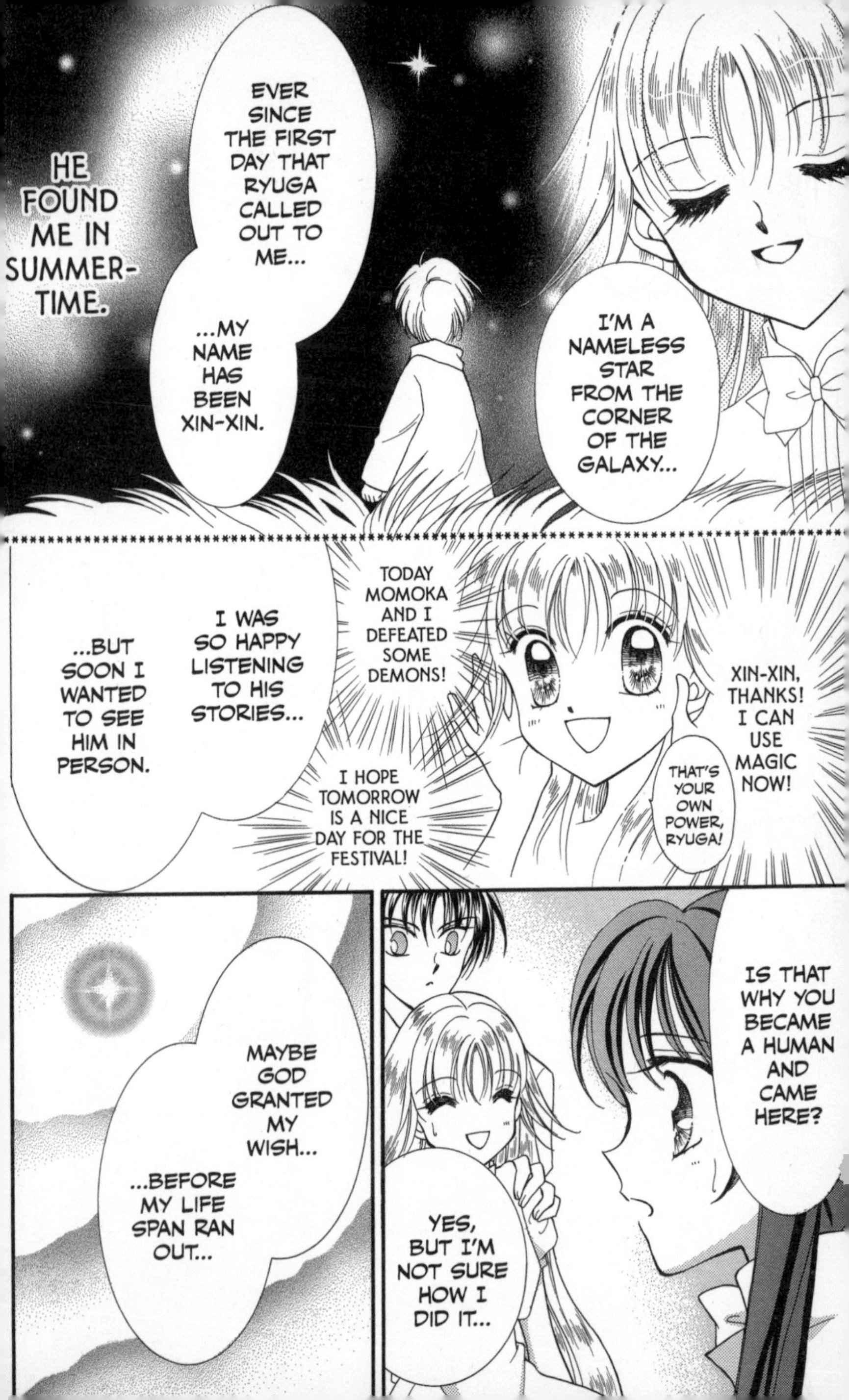
I'M A NAMELESS STAR FROM THE CORNER OF THE GALAXY...
HE FOUND ME IN SUMMER-TIME.
EVER SINCE THE FIRST DAY THAT RYUGA CALLED OUT TO ME...
...MY NAME HAS BEEN XIN-XIN.
XIN-XIN, THANKS! I CAN USE MAGIC NOW!
THAT'S YOUR OWN POWER, RYUGA!
TODAY MOMOKA AND I DEFEATED SOME DEMONS!
I HOPE TOMORROW IS A NICE DAY FOR THE FESTIVAL!
I WAS SO HAPPY LISTENING TO HIS STORIES...
...BUT SOON I WANTED TO SEE HIM IN PERSON.
IS THAT WHY YOU BECAME A HUMAN AND CAME HERE?
YES, BUT I'M NOT SURE HOW I DID IT...
MAYBE GOD GRANTED MY WISH...
...BEFORE MY LIFE SPAN RAN OUT...

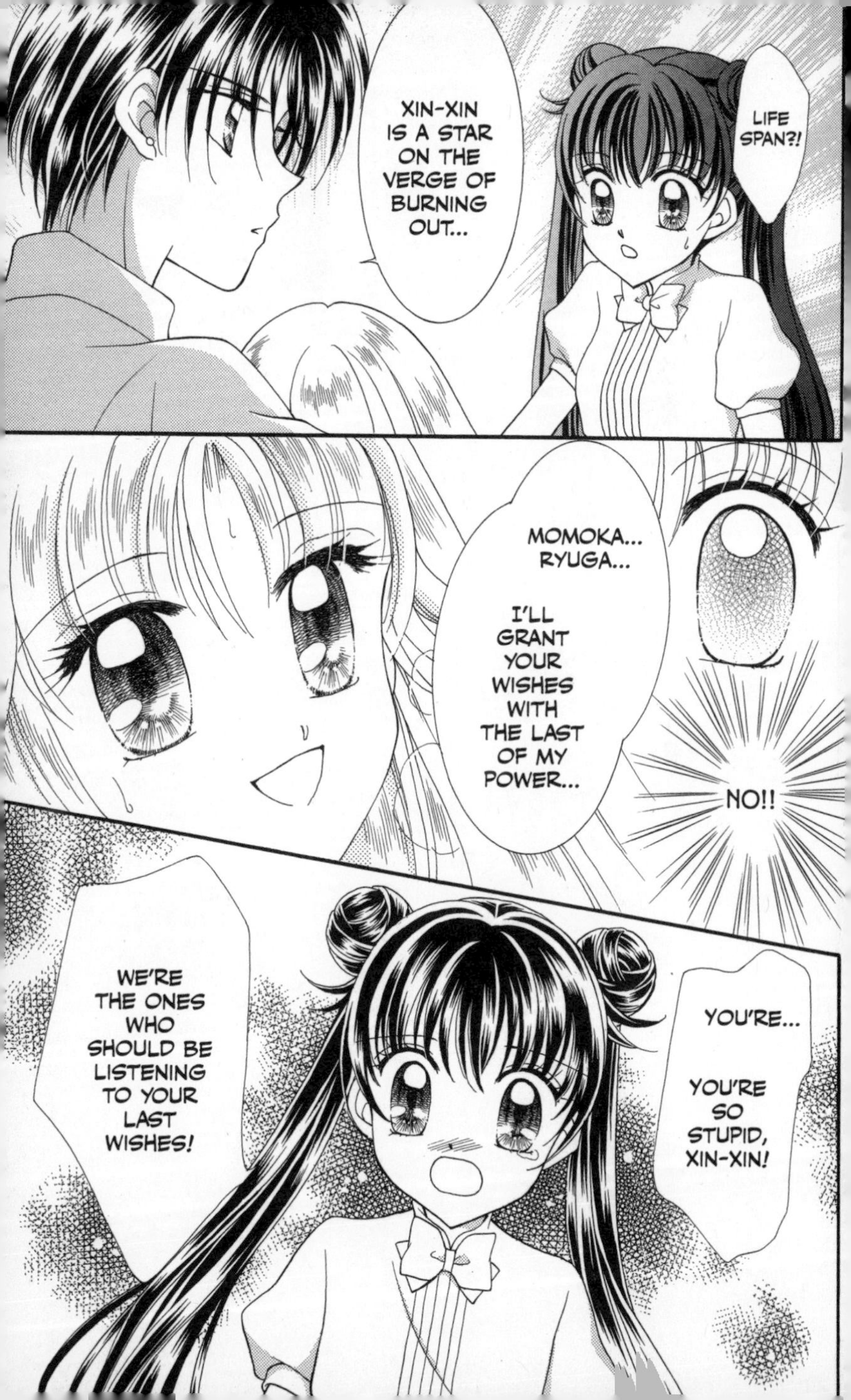
LIFE SPAN?!
XIN-XIN IS A STAR ON THE VERGE OF BURNING OUT...
MOMOKA... RYUGA...
I'LL GRANT YOUR WISHES WITH THE LAST OF MY POWER...
NO!!
YOU'RE...
YOU'RE SO STUPID, XIN-XIN!
WE'RE THE ONES WHO SHOULD BE LISTENING TO YOUR LAST WISHES!

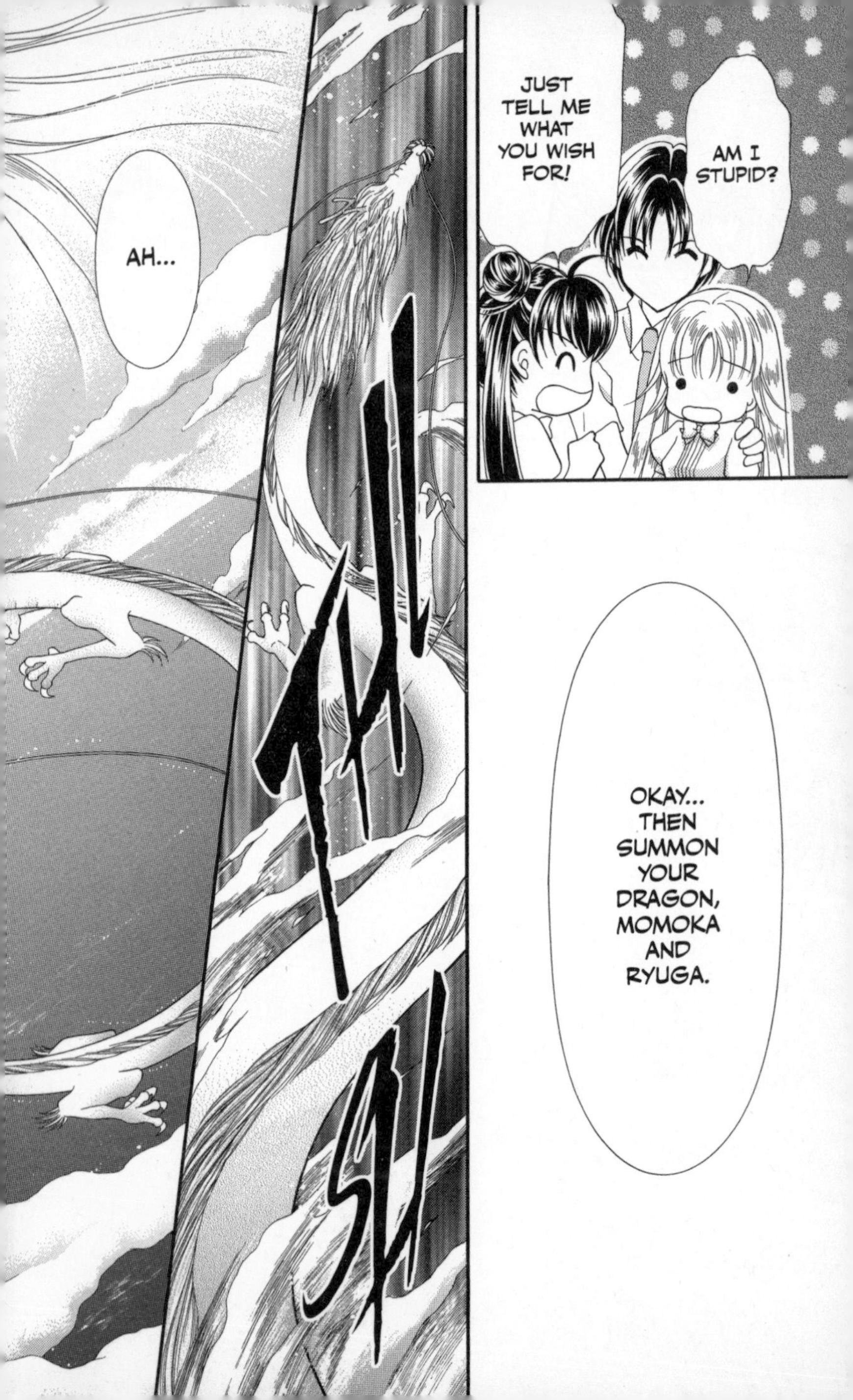
AM I STUPID?
JUST TELL ME WHAT YOU WISH FOR!
OKAY... THEN SUMMON YOUR DRAGON, MOMOKA AND RYUGA.
AH...

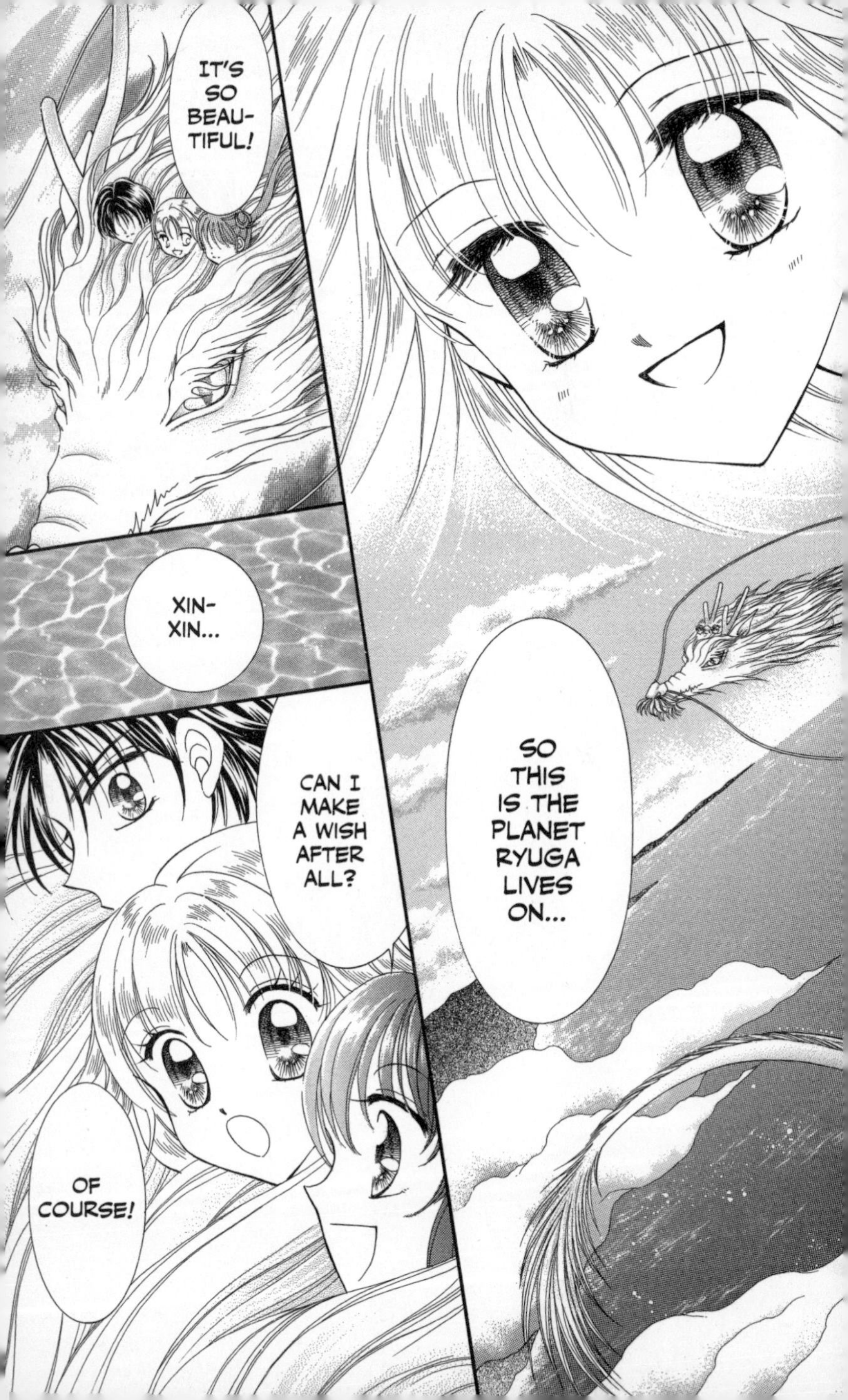
SO THIS IS THE PLANET RYUGA LIVES ON...
IT'S SO BEAU-TIFUL!
XIN-XIN...
CAN I MAKE A WISH AFTER ALL?
OF COURSE!

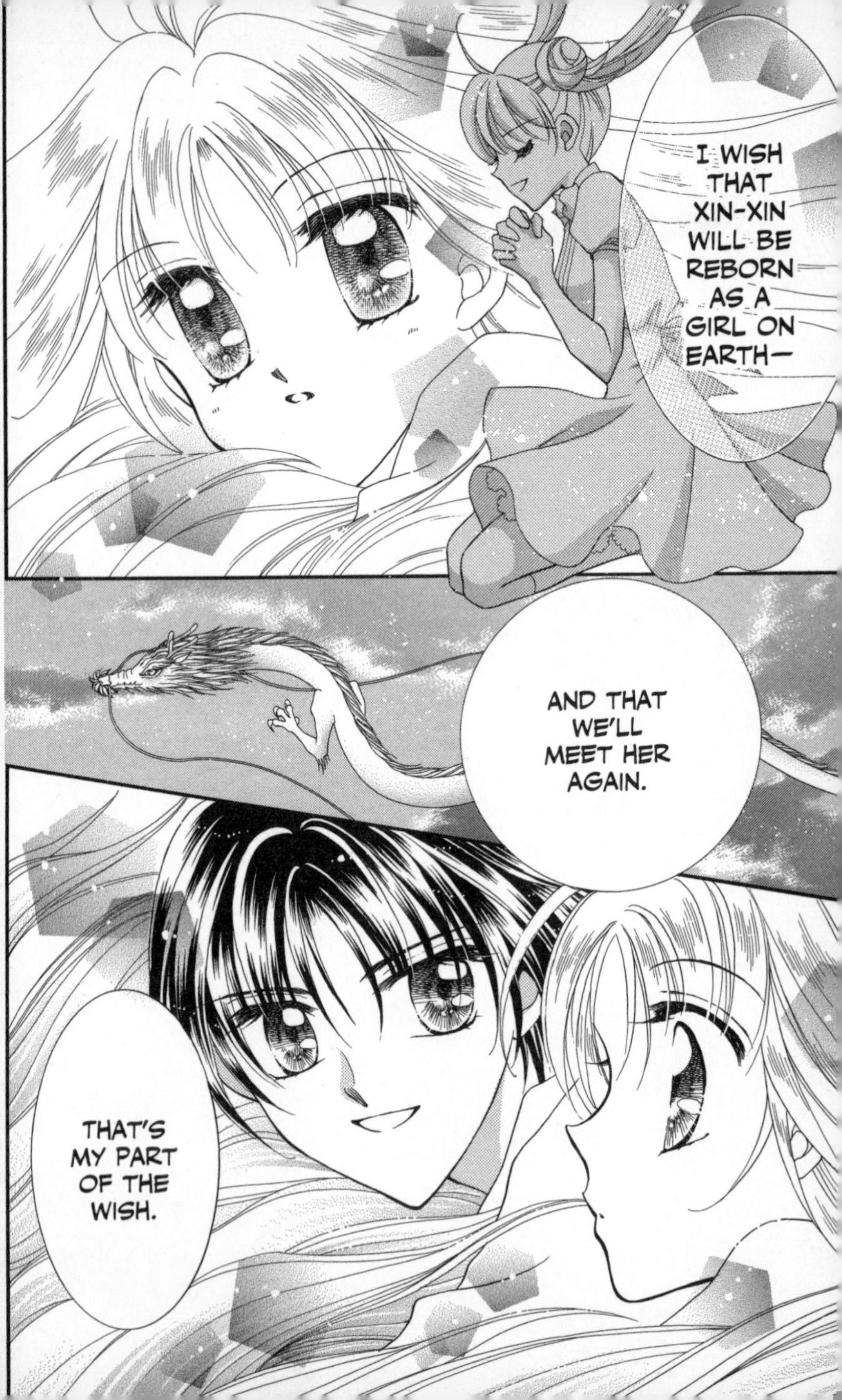
I WISH THAT XIN-XIN WILL BE REBORN AS A GIRL ON EARTH—
AND THAT WE'LL MEET HER AGAIN.
THAT'S MY PART OF THE WISH.

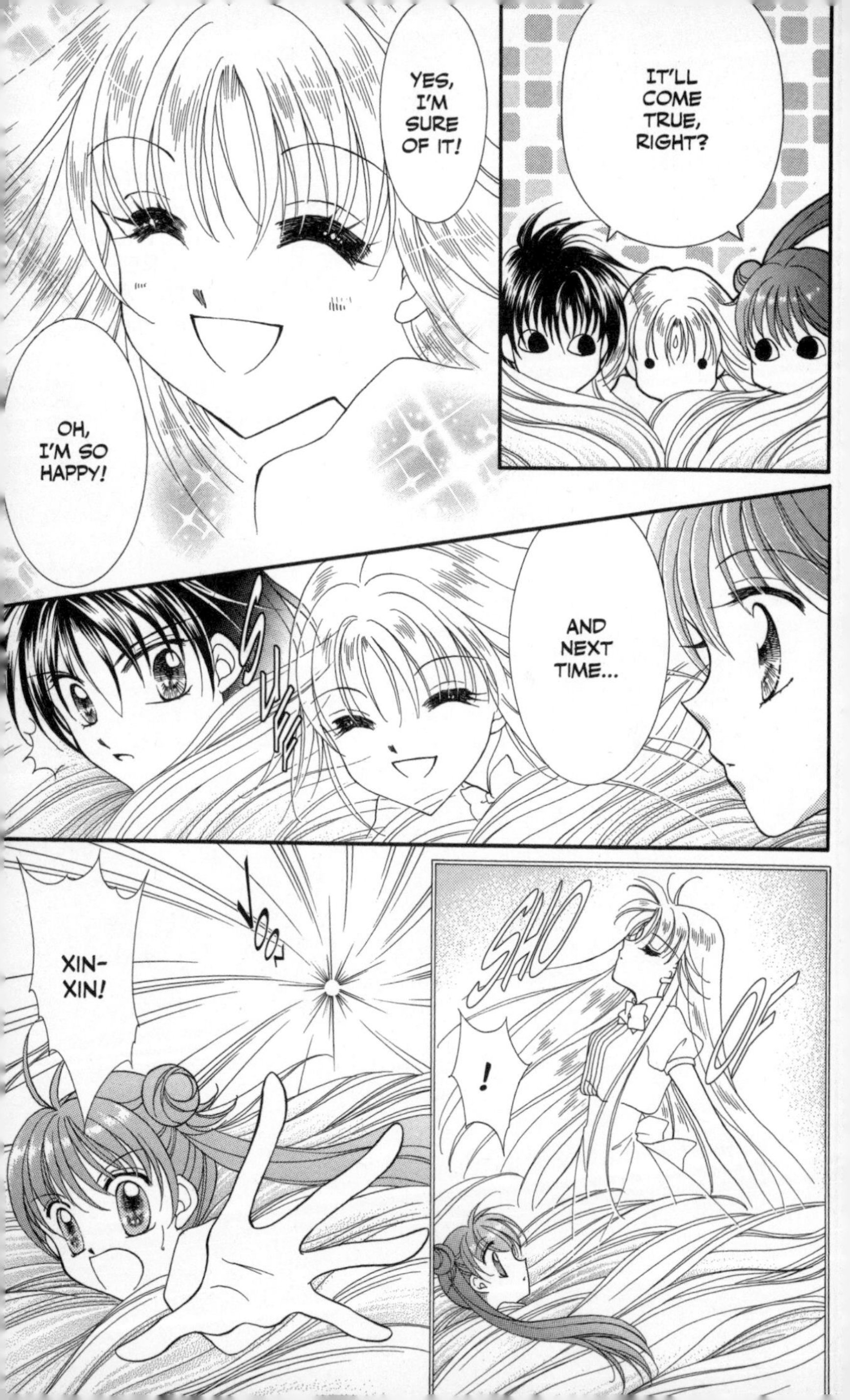
IT'LL COME TRUE, RIGHT?
YES, I'M SURE OF IT!
OH, I'M SO HAPPY!
AND NEXT TIME...
!
XIN-XIN!

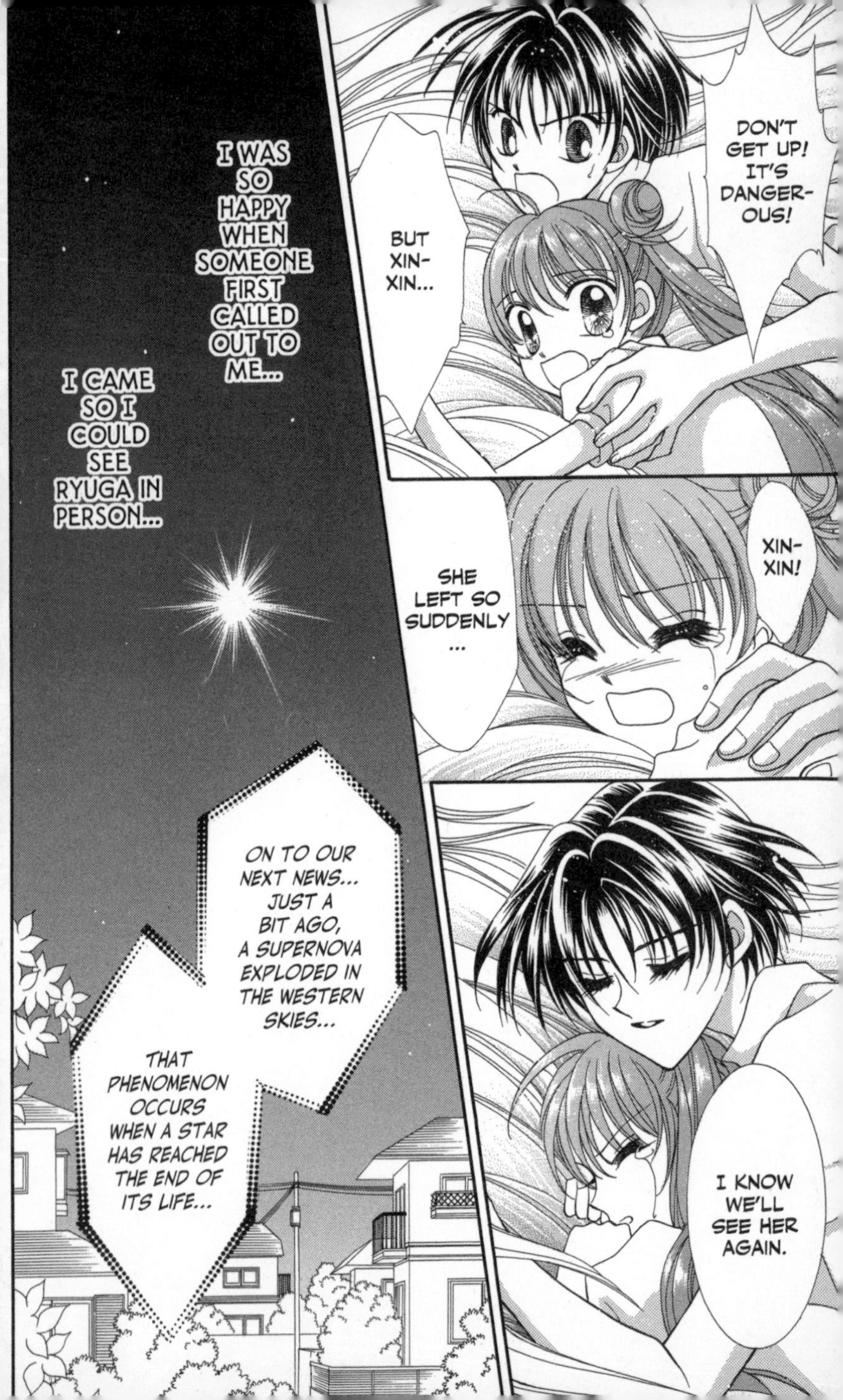
DON'T GET UP! IT'S DANGER-OUS!
BUT XIN-XIN...
XIN-XIN!
SHE LEFT SO SUDDENLY...
I KNOW WE'LL SEE HER AGAIN.
I WAS SO HAPPY WHEN SOMEONE FIRST CALLED OUT TO ME...
I CAME SO I COULD SEE RYUGA IN PERSON...
ON TO OUR NEXT NEWS... JUST A BIT AGO, A SUPERNOVA EXPLODED IN THE WESTERN SKIES...
THAT PHENOMENON OCCURS WHEN A STAR HAS REACHED THE END OF ITS LIFE...

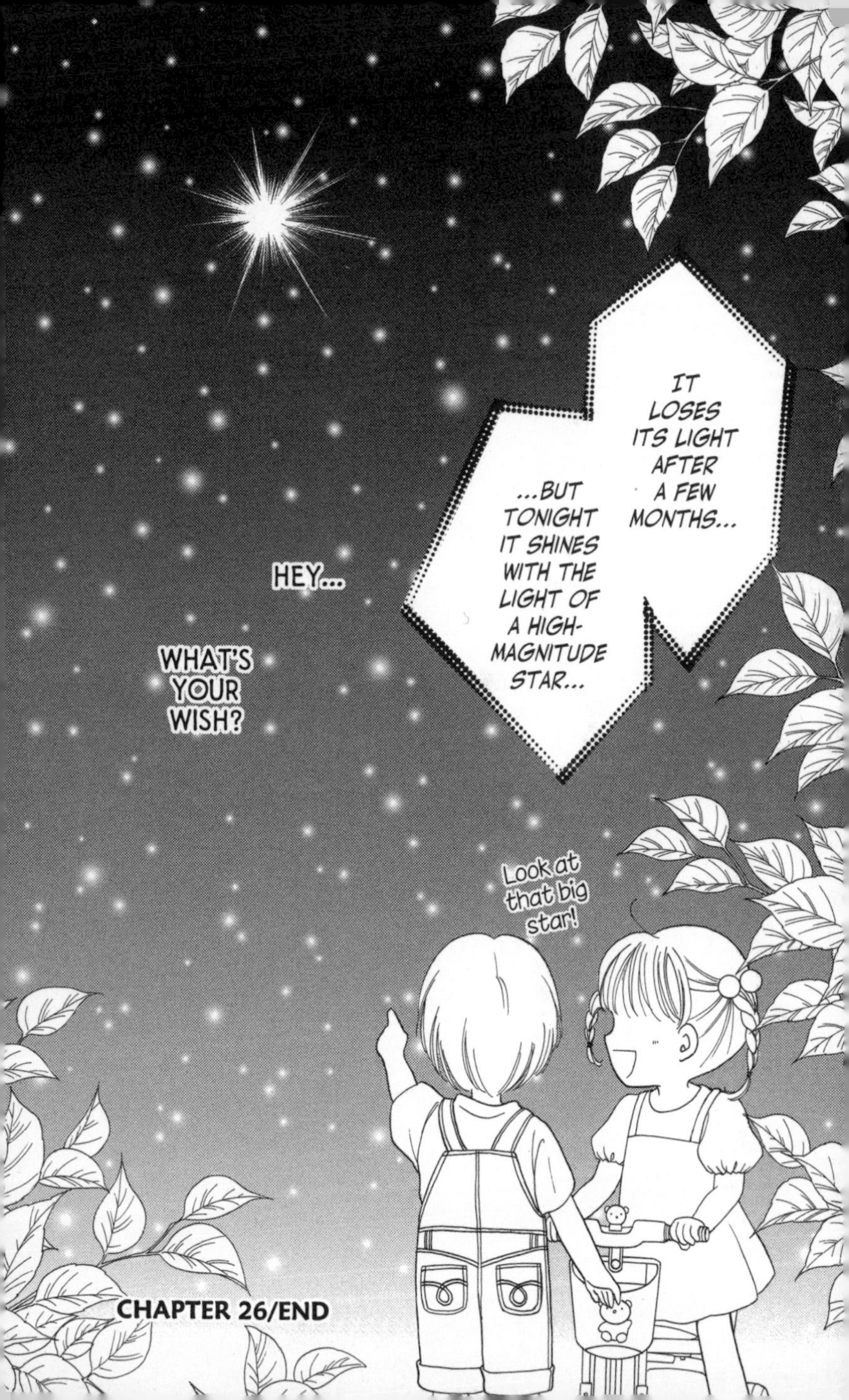
IT LOSES ITS LIGHT AFTER A FEW MONTHS...
...BUT TONIGHT IT SHINES WITH THE LIGHT OF A HIGH-MAGNITUDE STAR...
HEY...
WHAT'S YOUR WISH?
Look at that big star!
CHAPTER 26/END

ST.♥ DRAGONGIRL
Fan Art

Allyson L.

Lauren Morris

Nancy Thistlethwaite, Editor
VIZ Media
PO Box 77010
San Francisco CA 94107

ST.♥ DRAGON GIRL

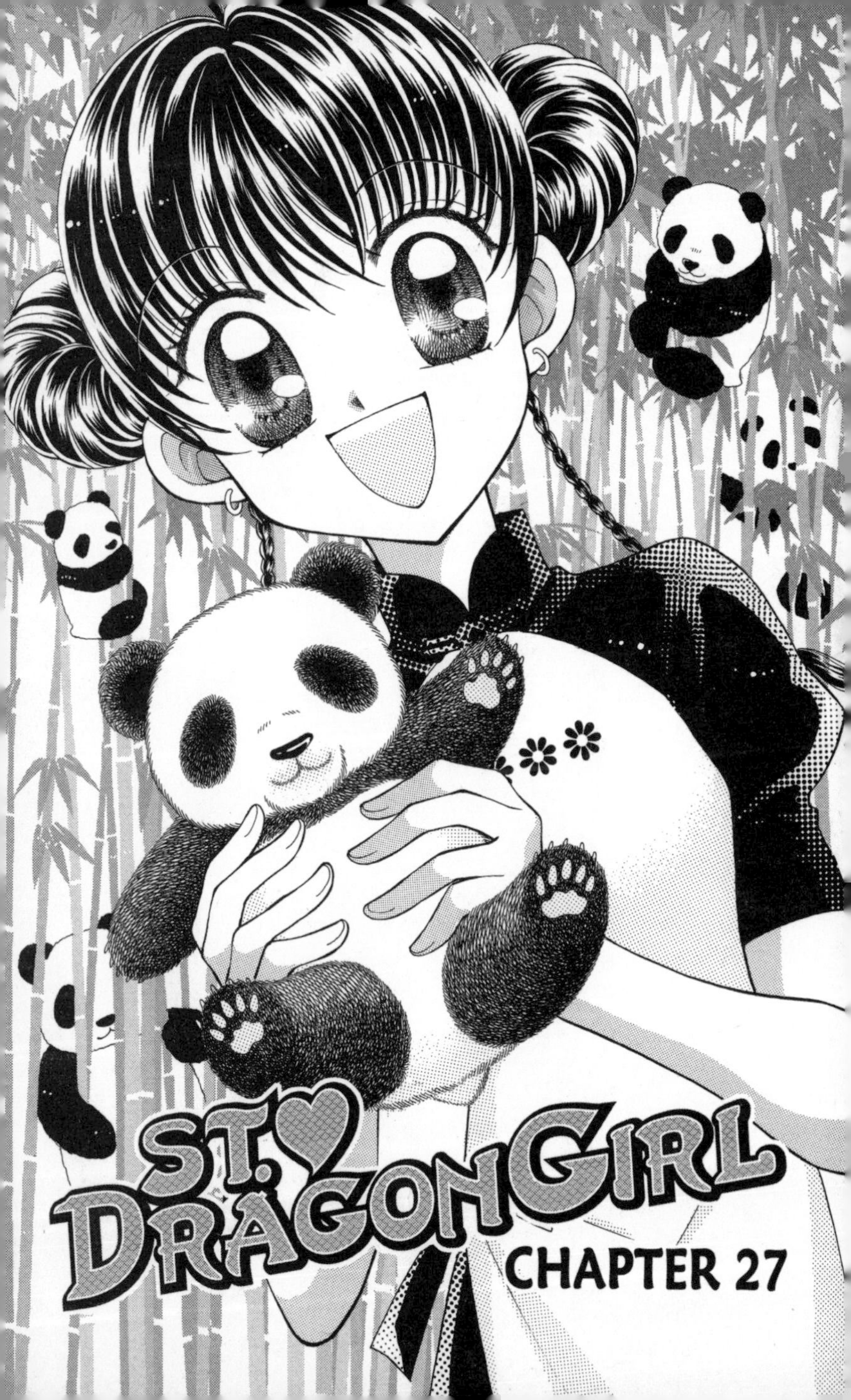
ST. DRAGON GIRL
CHAPTER 27

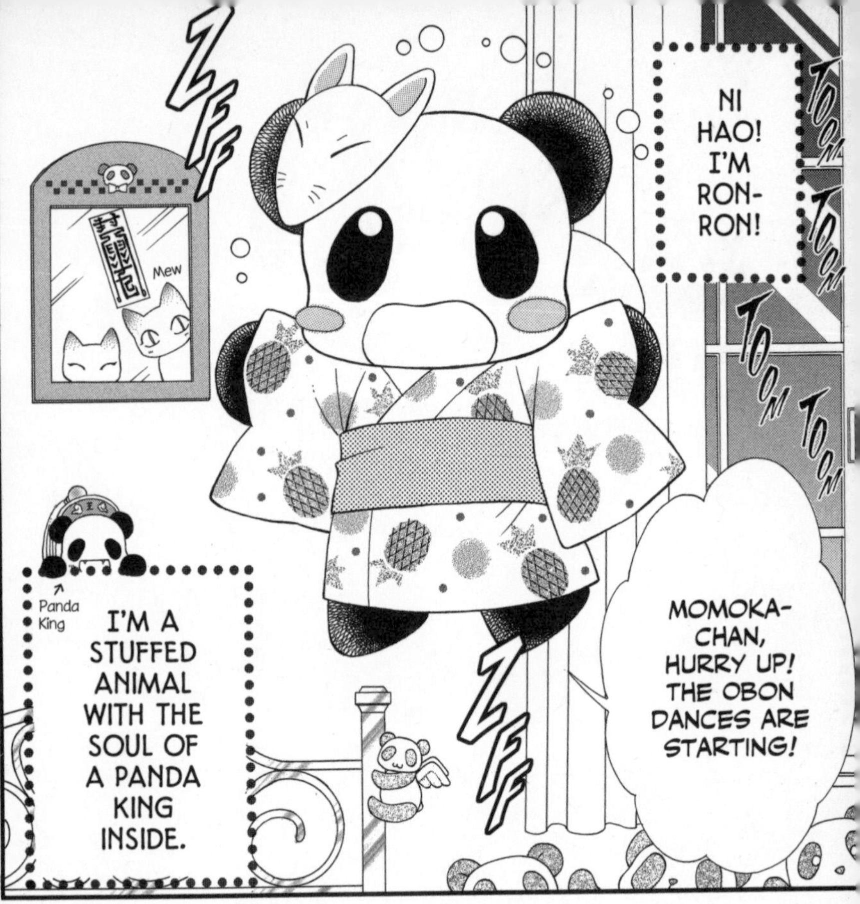
NI HAO! I'M RON-RON!
TOON TOON
TOON TOON TOON
MOMOKA-CHAN, HURRY UP! THE OBON DANCES ARE STARTING!
ZFF
ZFF
Mew
Panda King
I'M A STUFFED ANIMAL WITH THE SOUL OF A PANDA KING INSIDE.

When I went to Chinatown to do research the other day, I found a cute stuffed animal that looked like a gyoza. I missed the chance to buy it, but for some reason I couldn't forget about how cute it was! This time, however, I finally bought "Gyoza-chan"! There was a version wearing diapers, as well as a version on a pink key chain. I liked the white terry cloth version best though. ♡ It really soothes me! If you ever go to Yokohama's Chinatown, make sure you meet "Gyoza-chan"! I bought it at a shop close to the entrance of the marketplace.

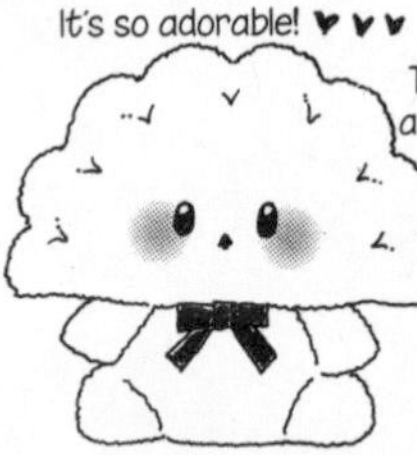
It's so adorable! ♥♥♥
There's a Dumpling-kun too!

↑ It's the one selling meat buns.

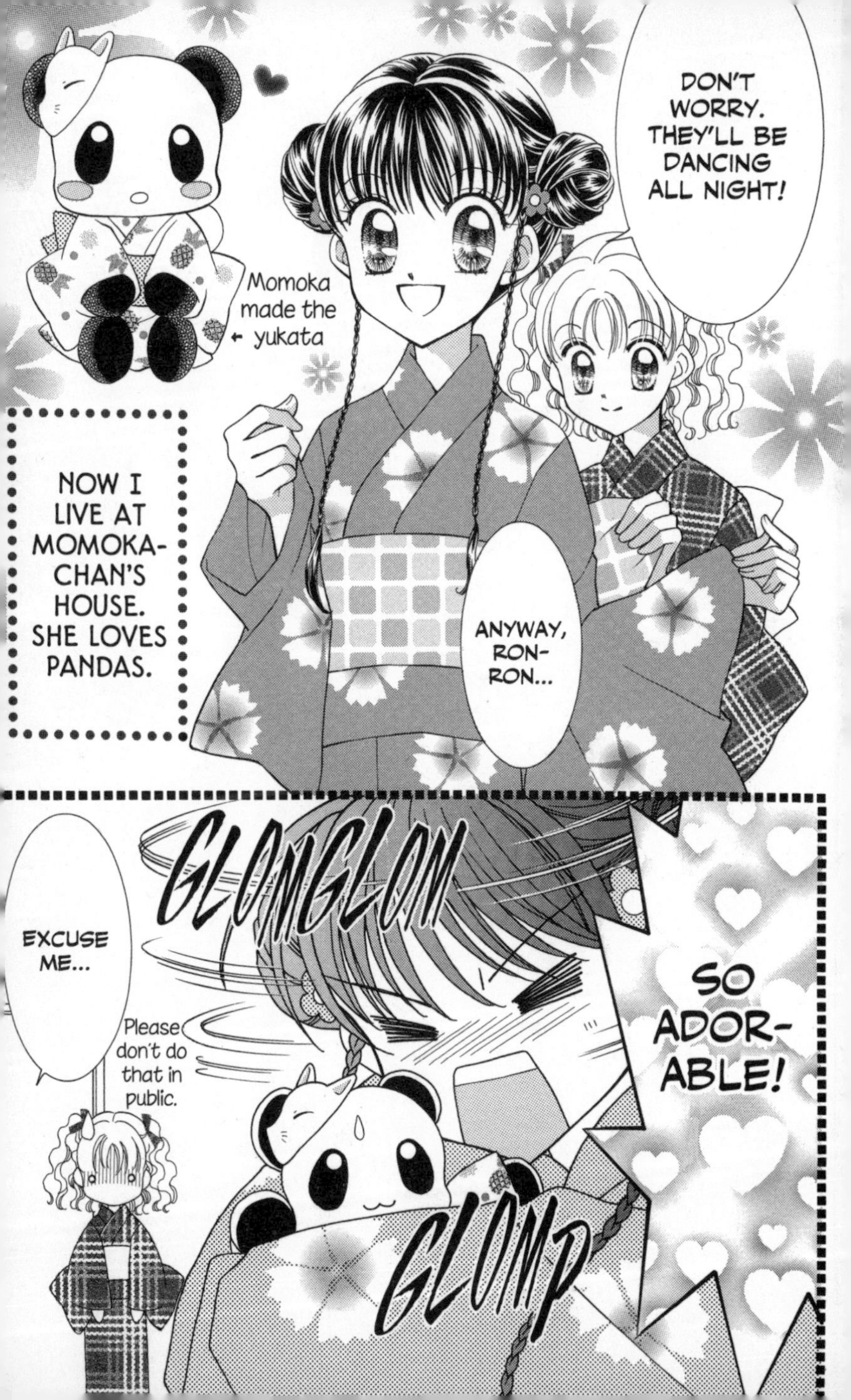
DON'T WORRY. THEY'LL BE DANCING ALL NIGHT!
ANYWAY, RON-RON...
Momoka made the ← yukata
NOW I LIVE AT MOMOKA-CHAN'S HOUSE. SHE LOVES PANDAS.
SO ADOR-ABLE!
GLOMGLOM
GLOMP
EXCUSE ME...
Please don't do that in public.

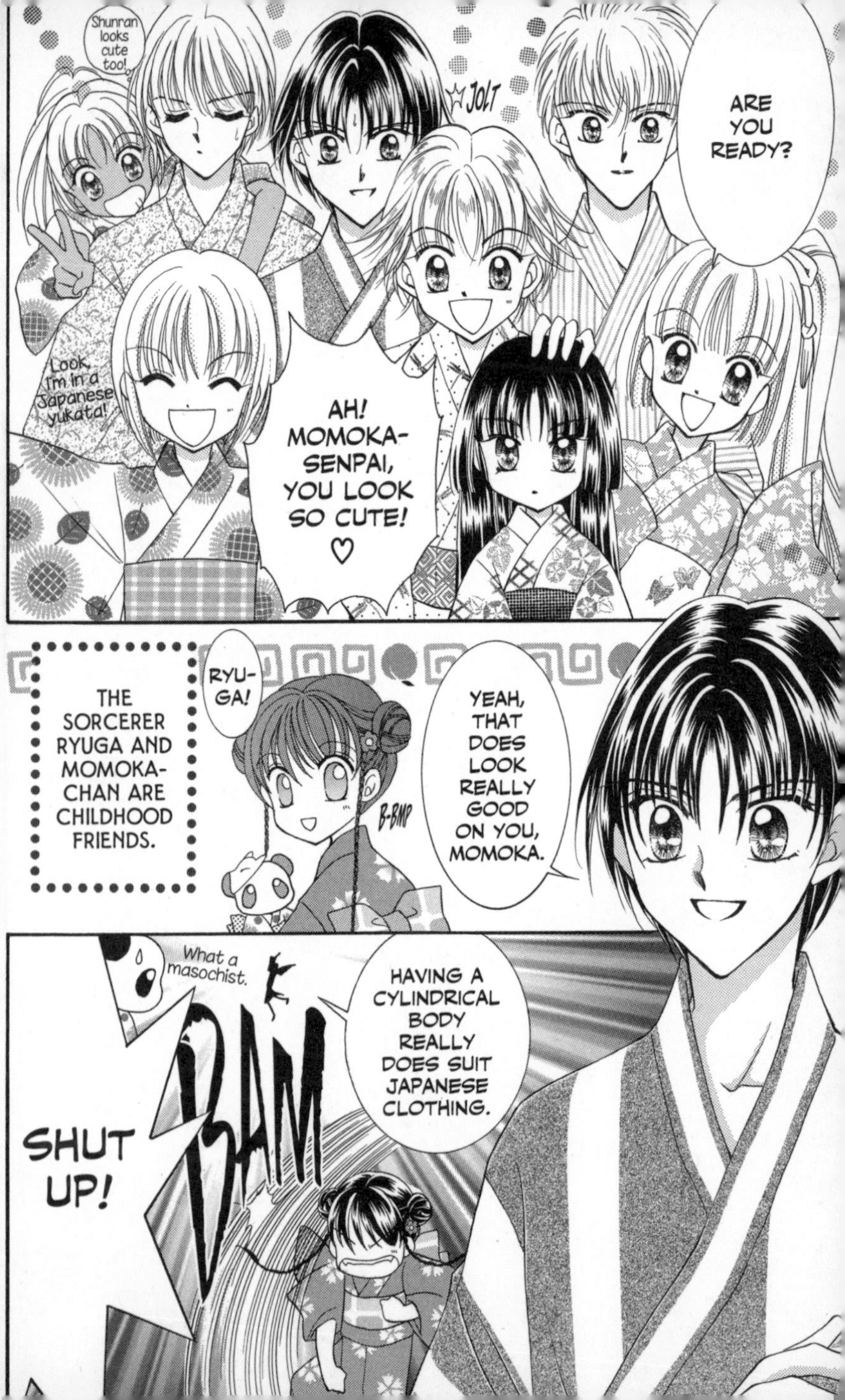
ARE YOU READY?
JOLT
Shunran looks cute too!
AH! MOMOKA-SENPAI, YOU LOOK SO CUTE! ♡
Look, I'm in a Japanese yukata!
YEAH, THAT DOES LOOK REALLY GOOD ON YOU, MOMOKA.
B-BMP
RYU-GA!
THE SORCERER RYUGA AND MOMOKA-CHAN ARE CHILDHOOD FRIENDS.
HAVING A CYLINDRICAL BODY REALLY DOES SUIT JAPANESE CLOTHING.
What a masochist.
BAM
SHUT UP!

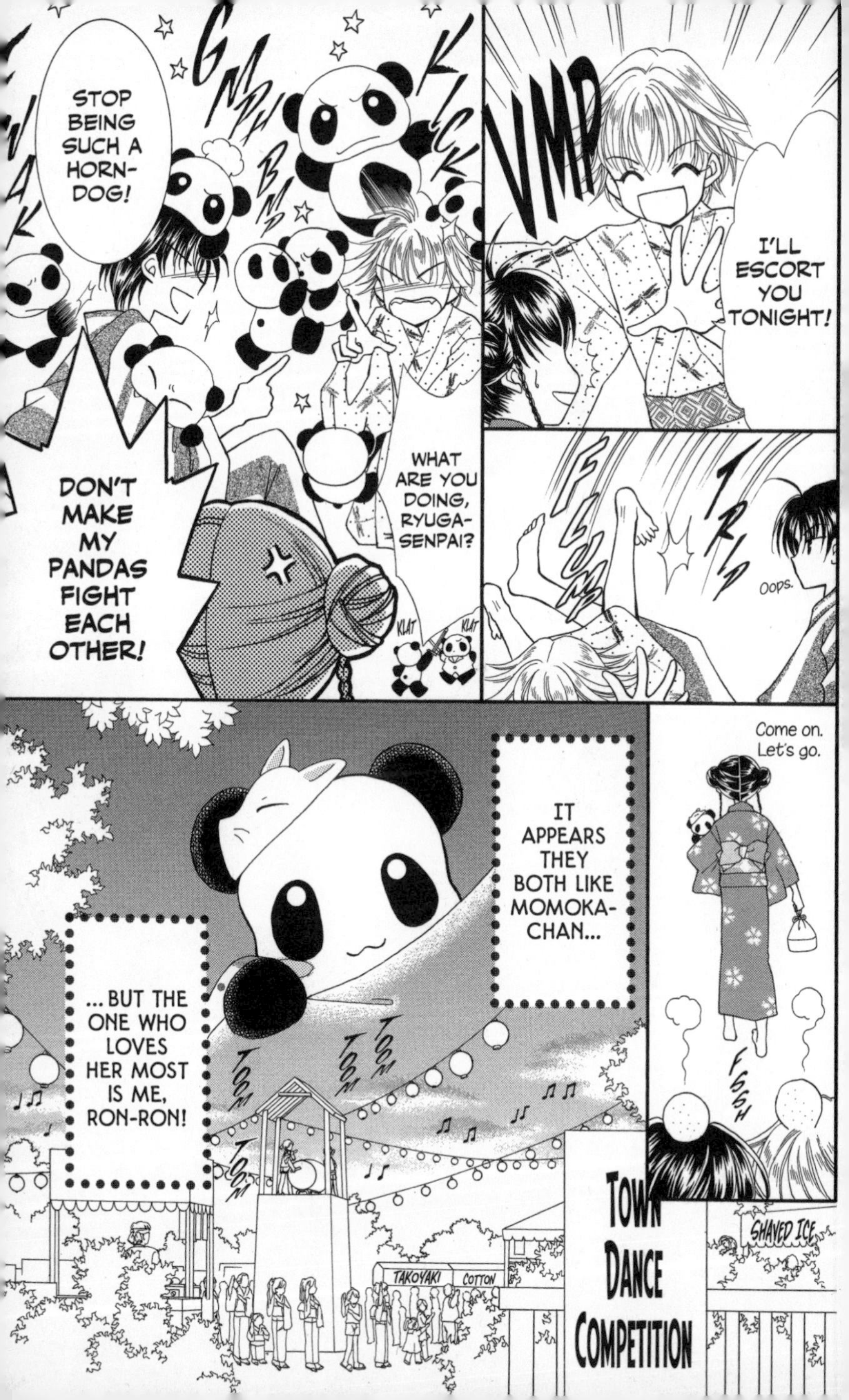
VMP
I'LL ESCORT YOU TONIGHT!
FLUMP
TRIP
Oops.
KICK
STOP BEING SUCH A HORN-DOG!
WHAT ARE YOU DOING, RYUGA-SENPAI?
DON'T MAKE MY PANDAS FIGHT EACH OTHER!
KLAT
KLAT
Come on. Let's go.
IT APPEARS THEY BOTH LIKE MOMOKA-CHAN...
... BUT THE ONE WHO LOVES HER MOST IS ME, RON-RON!
TOON
TOON
TOON
TOWN DANCE COMPETITION
SHAVED ICE
TAKOYAKI
COTTON

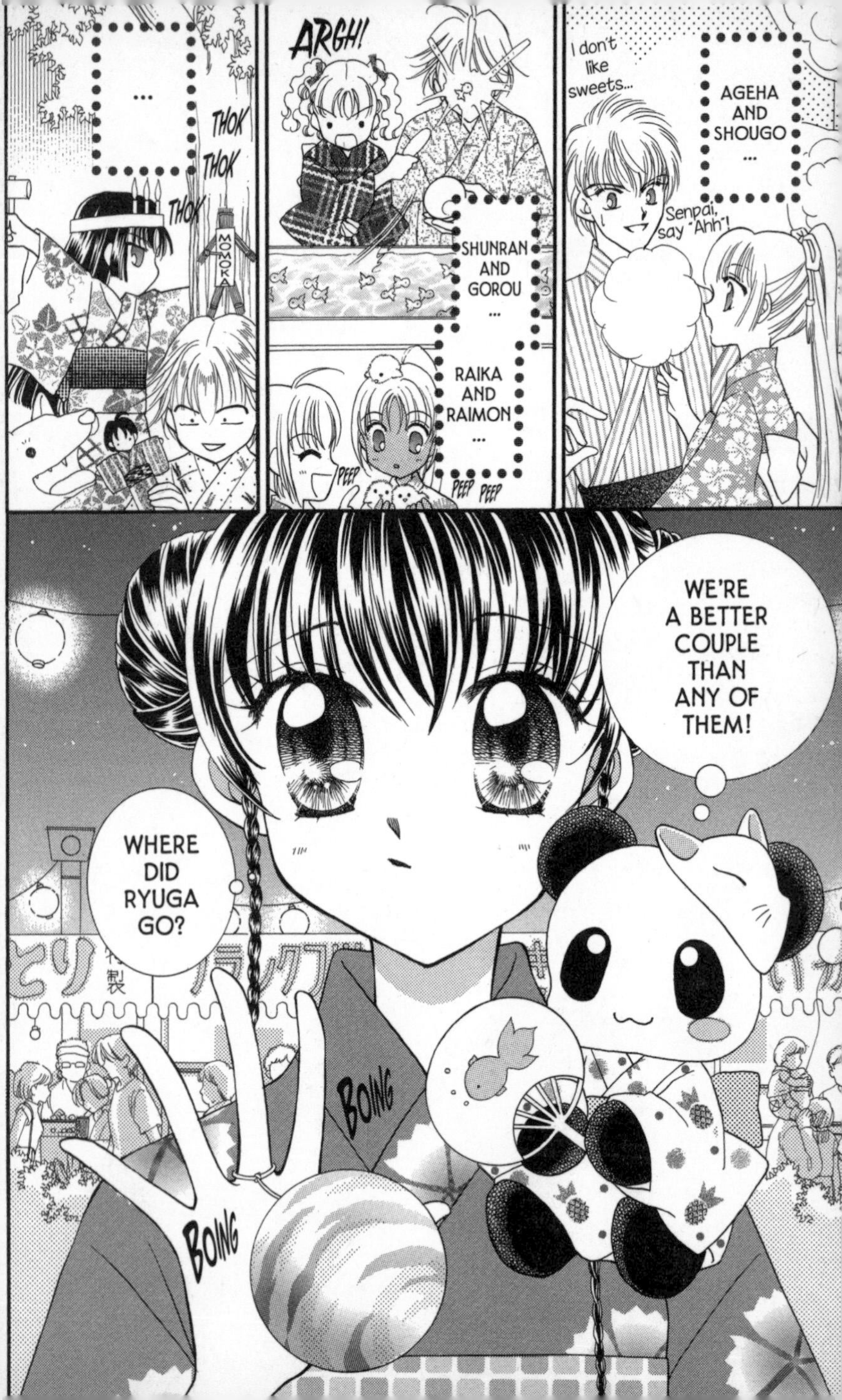
AGEHA AND SHOUGO ...
I don't like sweets...
Senpai, say "Ahh"!
SHUNRAN AND GOROU ...
ARGH!
RAIKA AND RAIMON ...
PEEP
PEEP PEEP
...
THOK
THOK
THOK
MOMOKA
WE'RE A BETTER COUPLE THAN ANY OF THEM!
WHERE DID RYUGA GO?
BOING
BOING

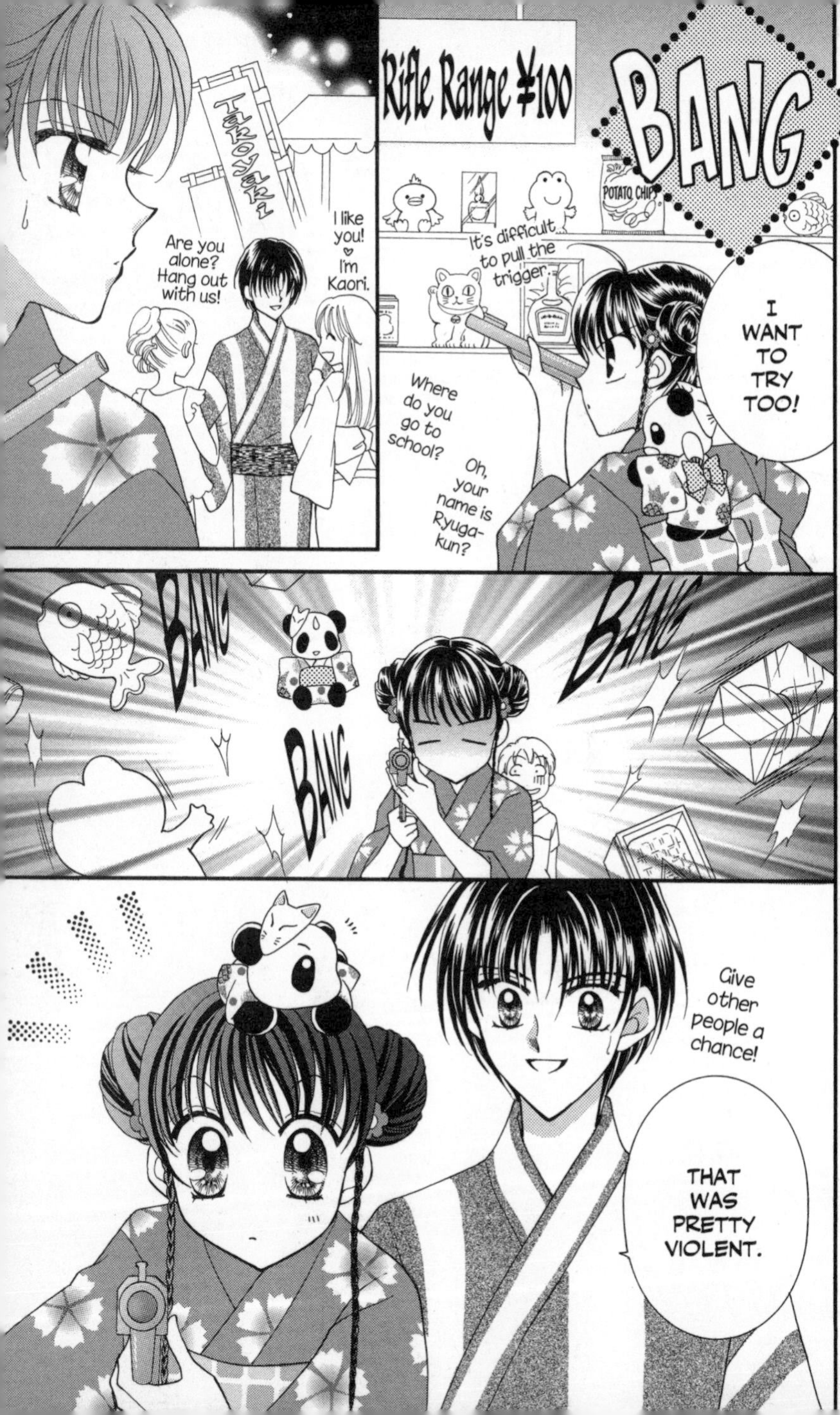
Rifle Range ¥100
BANG
POTATO CHIPS
I WANT TO TRY TOO!
It's difficult to pull the trigger.
Where do you go to school?
Oh, your name is Ryuga-kun?
Takoyaki
I like you! ♥ I'm Kaori.
Are you alone? Hang out with us!
BANG
BANG
BANG
Give other people a chance!
THAT WAS PRETTY VIOLENT.

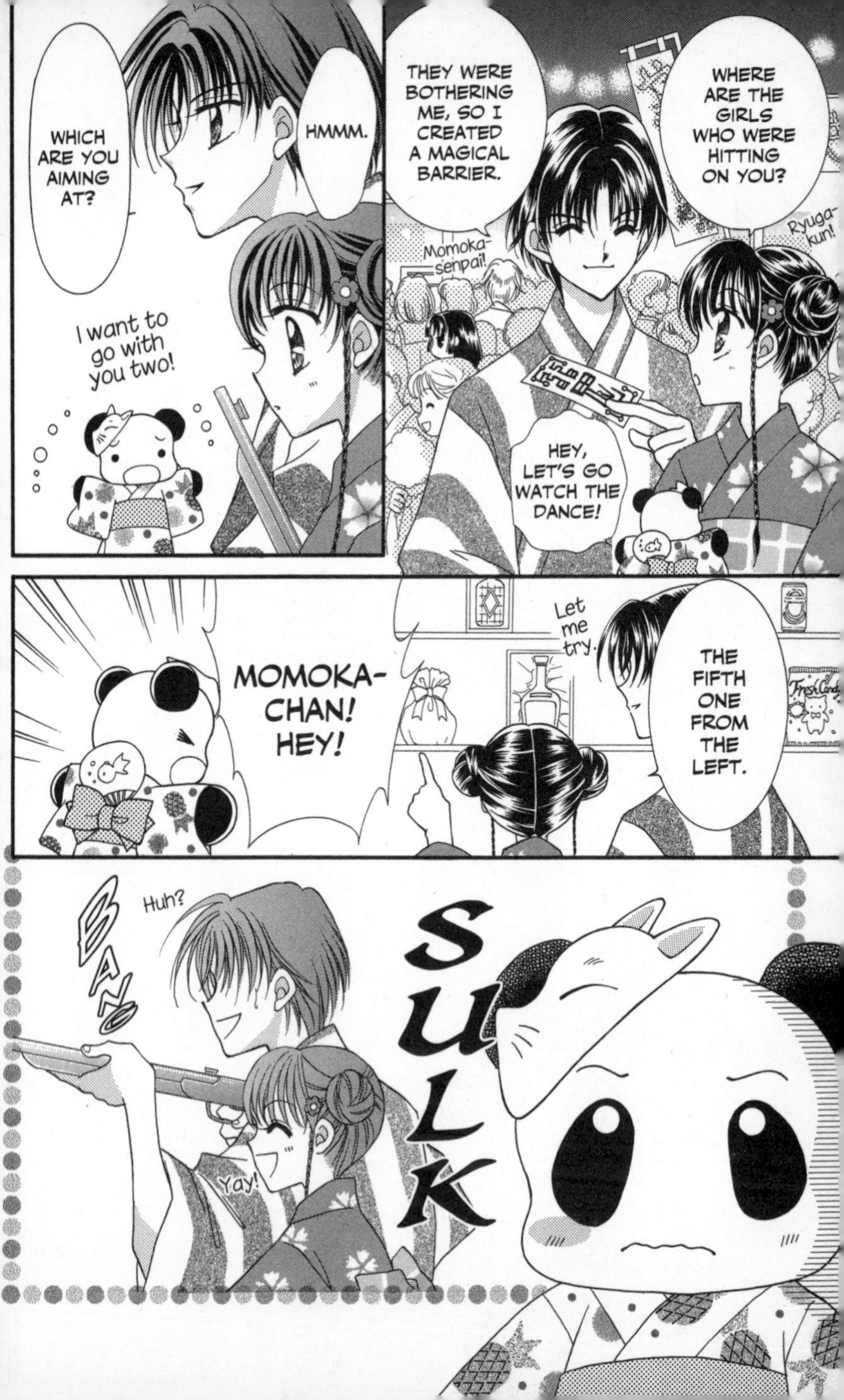
Ryuga-kun!
WHERE ARE THE GIRLS WHO WERE HITTING ON YOU?
THEY WERE BOTHERING ME, SO I CREATED A MAGICAL BARRIER.
Momoka-senpai!
HEY, LET'S GO WATCH THE DANCE!
HMMM.
WHICH ARE YOU AIMING AT?
I want to go with you two!
THE FIFTH ONE FROM THE LEFT.
Let me try.
MOMOKA-CHAN! HEY!
SULK
Huh?
BANG
Yay!

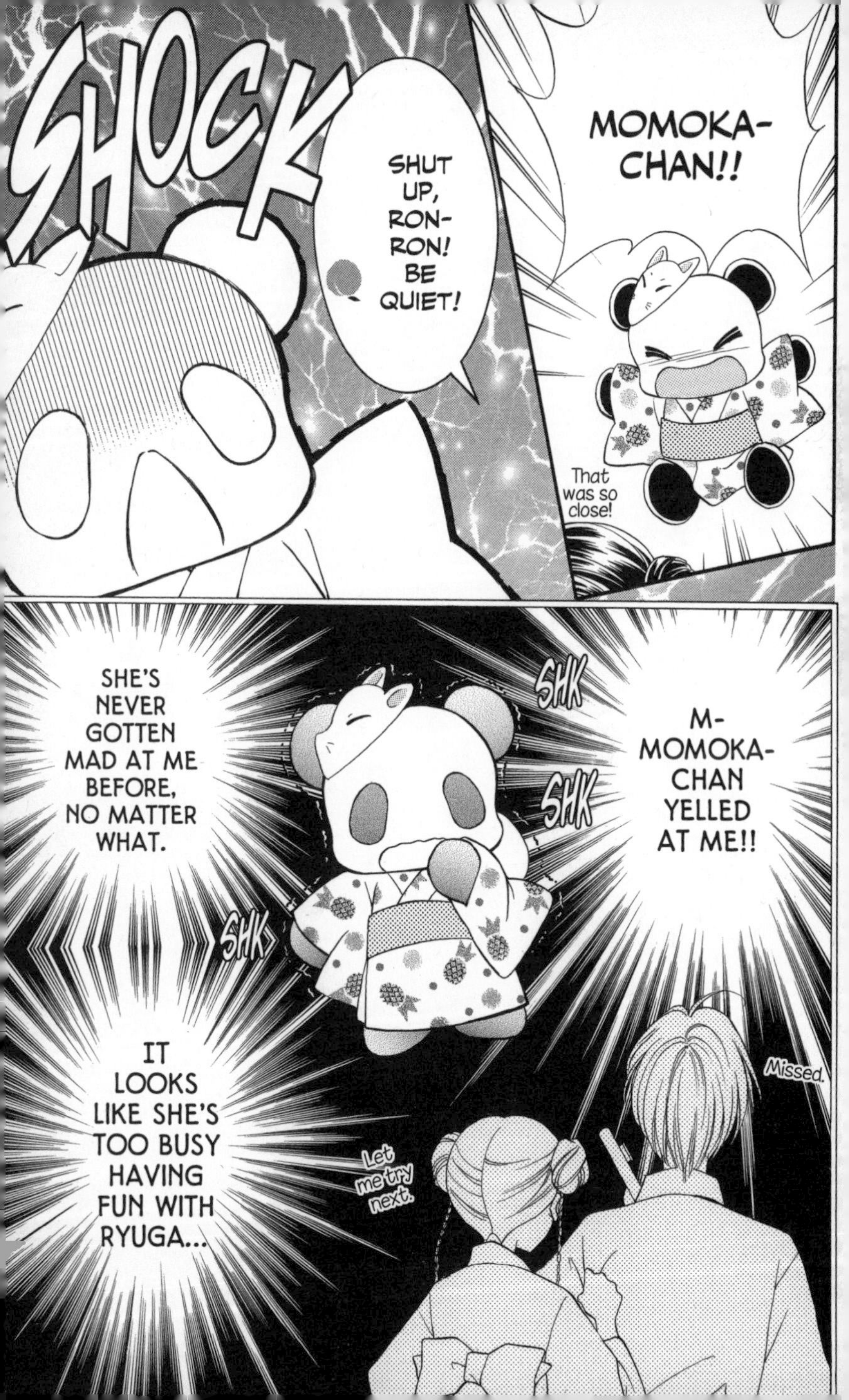

MOMOKA-CHAN!!
That was so close!
SHOCK
SHUT UP, RON-RON! BE QUIET!
SHK
M-MOMOKA-CHAN YELLED AT ME!!
SHK
SHE'S NEVER GOTTEN MAD AT ME BEFORE, NO MATTER WHAT.
SHK
Missed.
Let me try next.
IT LOOKS LIKE SHE'S TOO BUSY HAVING FUN WITH RYUGA...

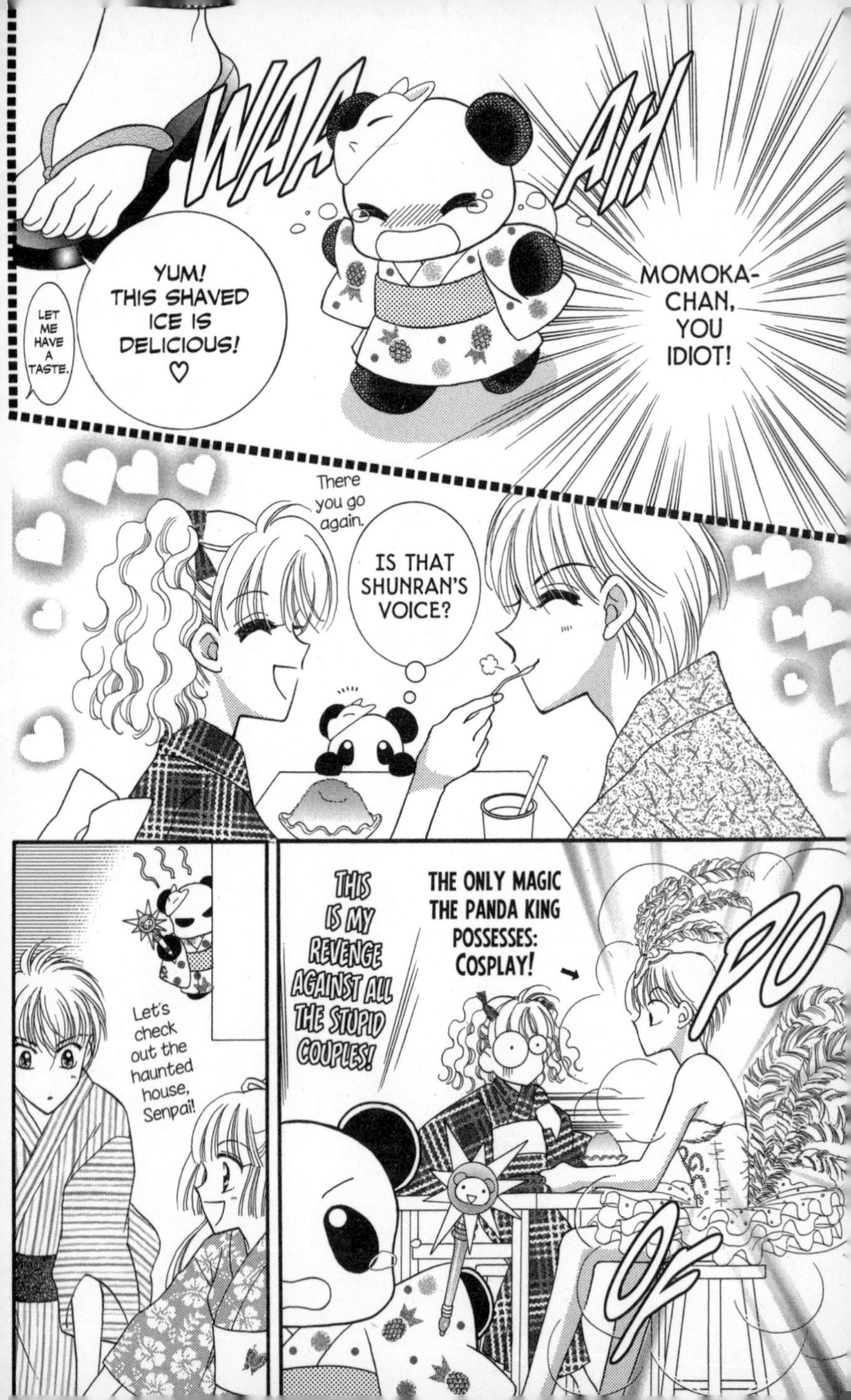
WAA AH
MOMOKA-CHAN, YOU IDIOT!
YUM! THIS SHAVED ICE IS DELICIOUS! ♡
LET ME HAVE A TASTE.
IS THAT SHUNRAN'S VOICE?
There you go again.
PO
THE ONLY MAGIC THE PANDA KING POSSESSES: COSPLAY!
THIS IS MY REVENGE AGAINST ALL THE STUPID COUPLES!
OF
Let's check out the haunted house, Senpai!

16

I had a lot of fun this summer. I went to see Shorinji Kenpo at the Tokyo Dome. It was called "The Circle of Life." Real Shorinji monks acted it out. The story was about monks who protected the palace from invaders by using kung fu. The emperor was so pleased that he asked the monks to become his guards in his royal court. He also asked them to teach him kung fu, but they refused. He became so enraged that he killed the monks. Only five young monks survived, and they vowed to build a new history for the Shorinji monks.

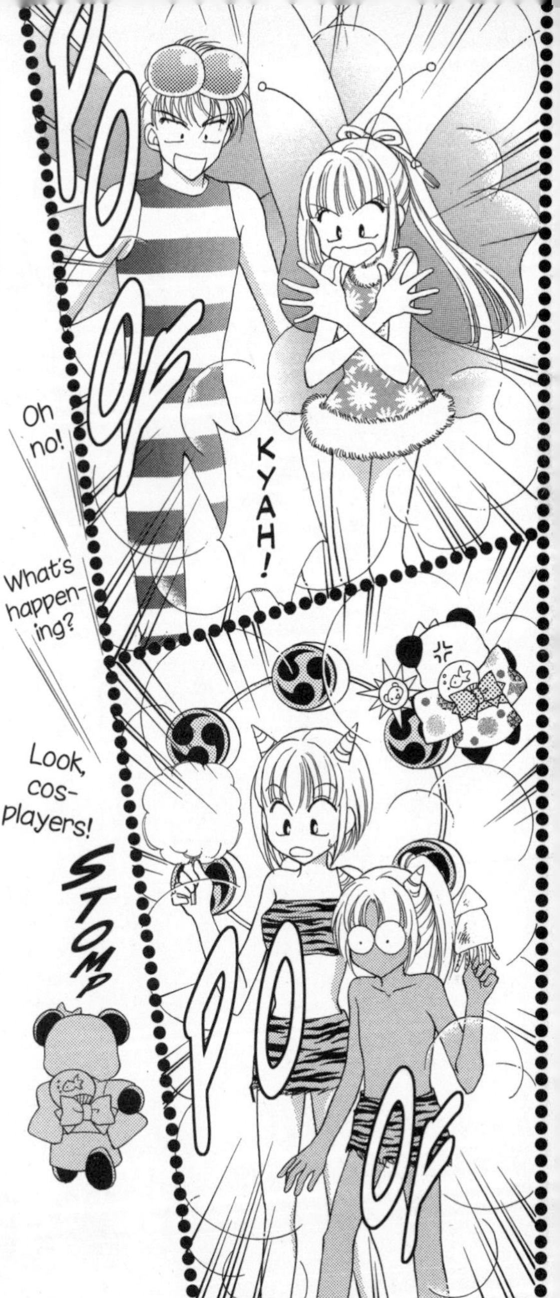

POOF
KYAH!
Oh no!
What's happen-ing?
Look, cos-players!
STOMP
POOF

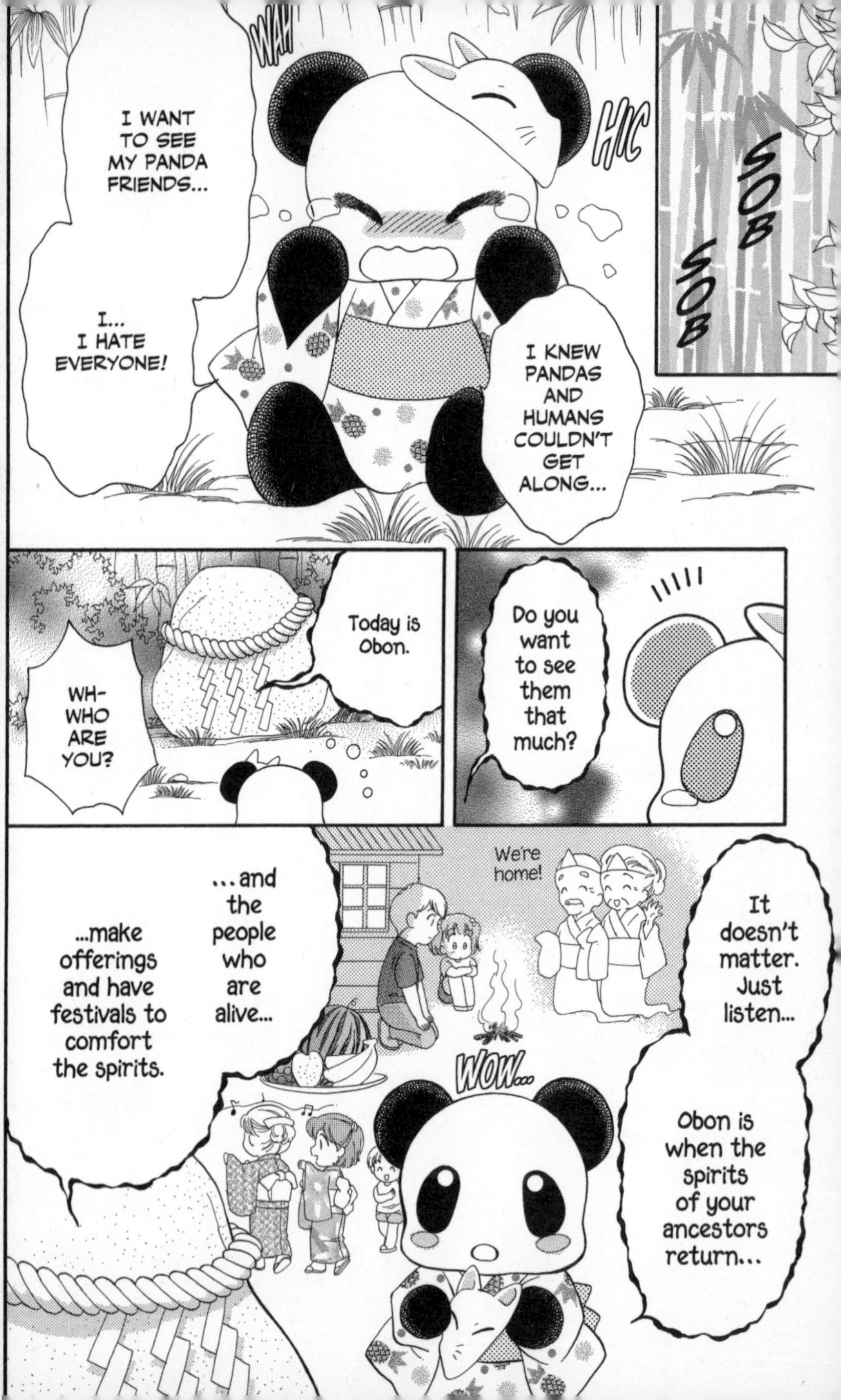
SOB
SOB
HIC
WAH
I WANT TO SEE MY PANDA FRIENDS...
I KNEW PANDAS AND HUMANS COULDN'T GET ALONG...
I... I HATE EVERYONE!
Do you want to see them that much?
Today is Obon.
WH- WHO ARE YOU?
It doesn't matter. Just listen...
Obon is when the spirits of your ancestors return...
We're home!
...and the people who are alive...
...make offerings and have festivals to comfort the spirits.
WOW...

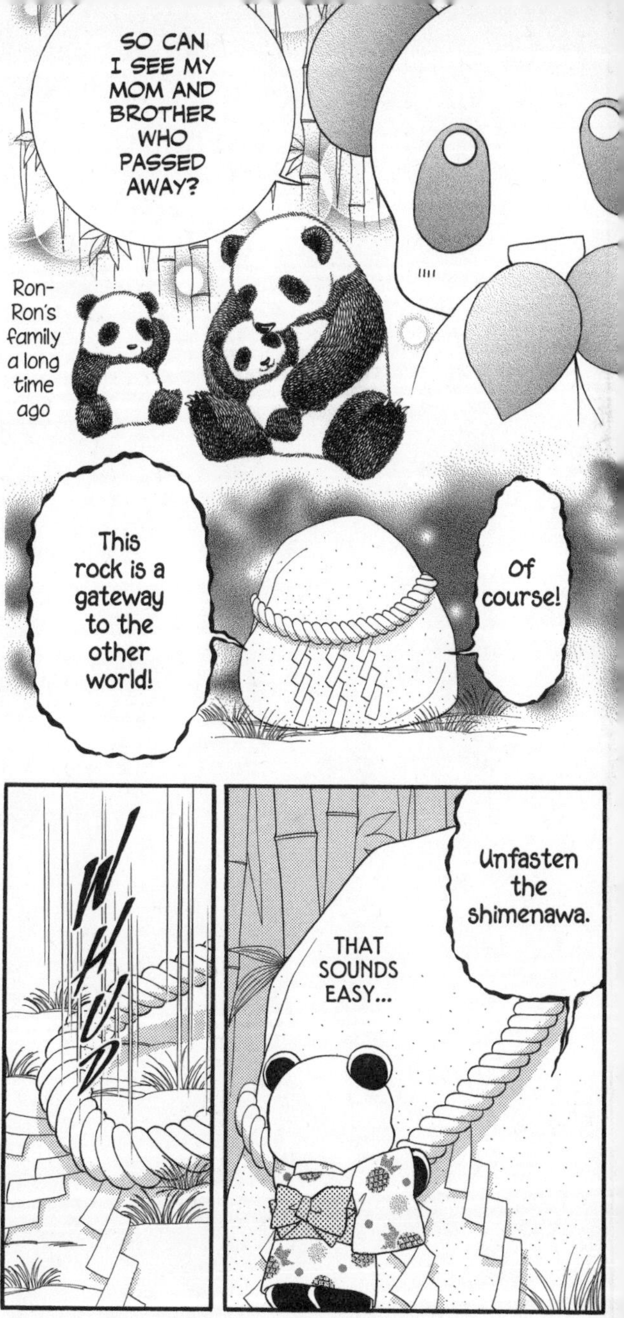
SO CAN I SEE MY MOM AND BROTHER WHO PASSED AWAY?
Ron-Ron's family a long time ago
Of course!
This rock is a gateway to the other world!
Unfasten the shimenawa.
THAT SOUNDS EASY...
WHUD

17

Seeing the monks do kenpo live was amazing. The five young boys who were monks were so cute, but I was surprised—they reminded me of anime characters. They were great at kenpo too.

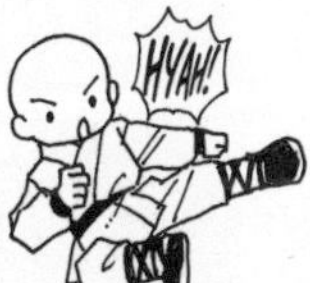
HYAH!

The youngest boy was probably 7 or 8, and I wonder if he'll serve Buddha for the rest of his life. I wonder if the monks will come next year as well. I bought a pamphlet and a video.

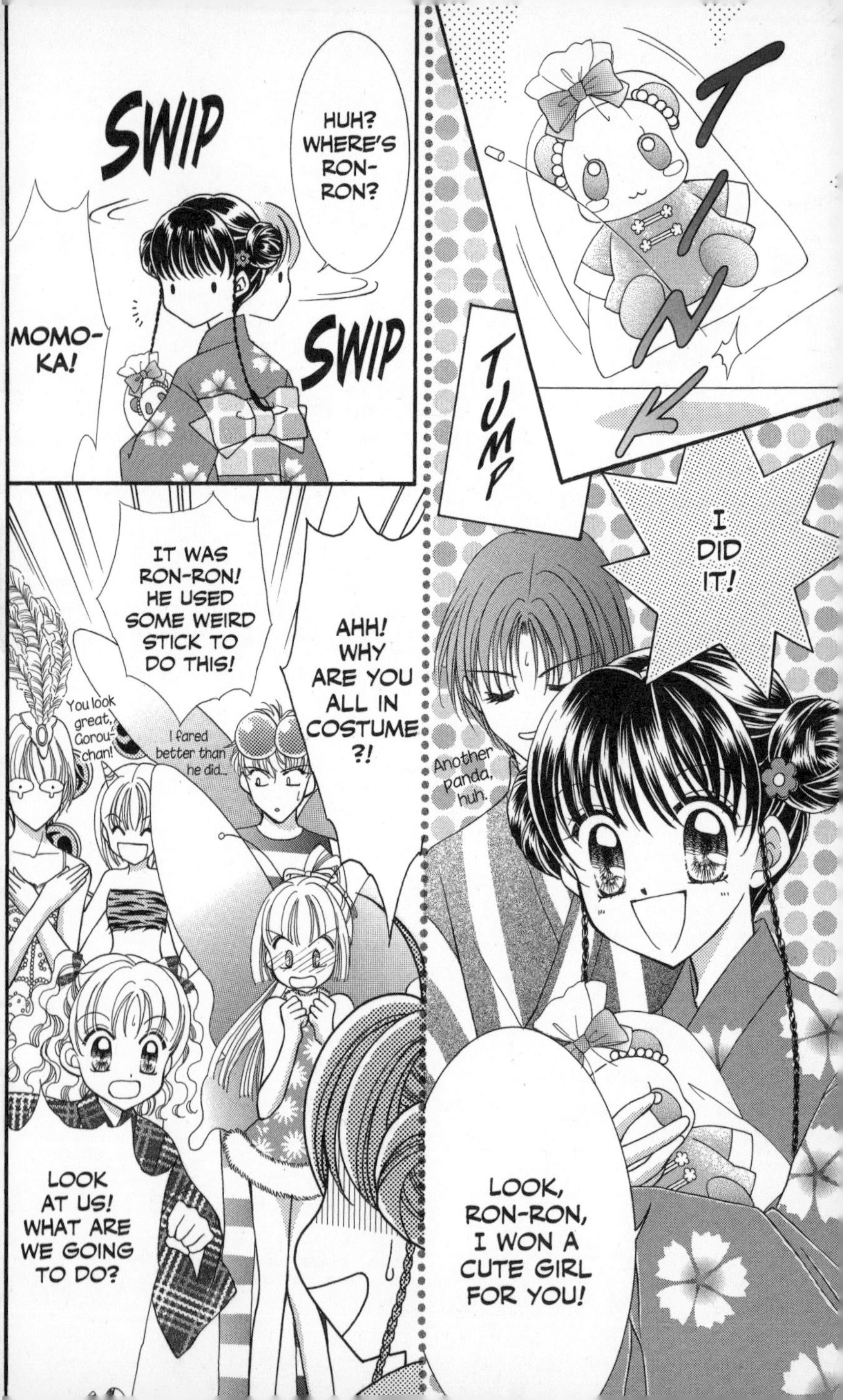
TINK
TUMP
I DID IT!
Another panda, huh.
LOOK, RON-RON, I WON A CUTE GIRL FOR YOU!
HUH? WHERE'S RON-RON?
SWIP
SWIP
MOMO-KA!
AHH! WHY ARE YOU ALL IN COSTUME?!
IT WAS RON-RON! HE USED SOME WEIRD STICK TO DO THIS!
I fared better than he did...
You look great, Gorou-chan!
LOOK AT US! WHAT ARE WE GOING TO DO?

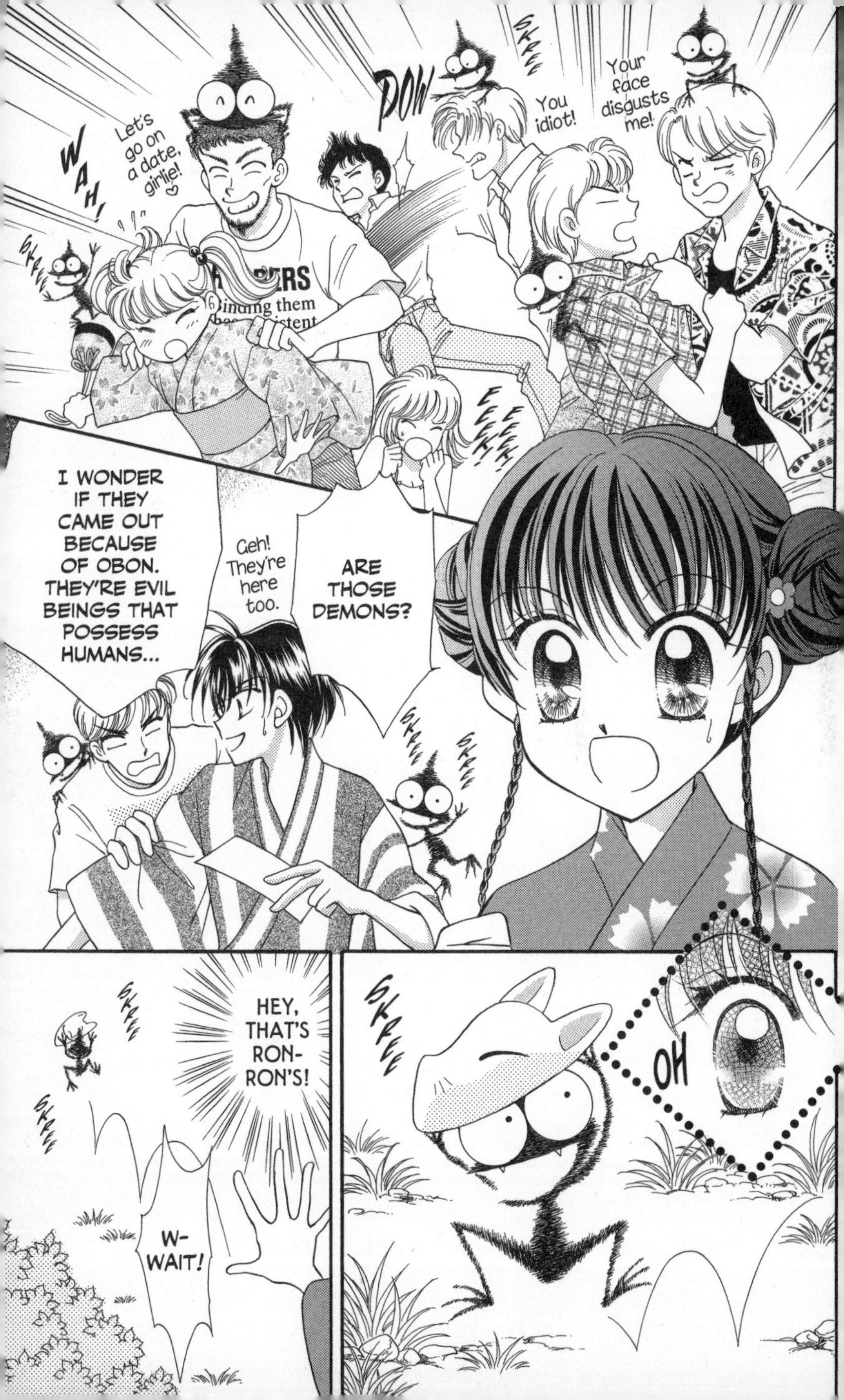
Your face disgusts me!
You idiot!
SKREE
POW
Let's go on a date, girlie! ♡
WAH!
SKREE
EEEK! EEEK!
ARE THOSE DEMONS?
Geh! They're here too.
I WONDER IF THEY CAME OUT BECAUSE OF OBON. THEY'RE EVIL BEINGS THAT POSSESS HUMANS...
SKREE
SKREE
SKREE
OH
HEY, THAT'S RON-RON'S!
SKREE
SKREE
W-WAIT!

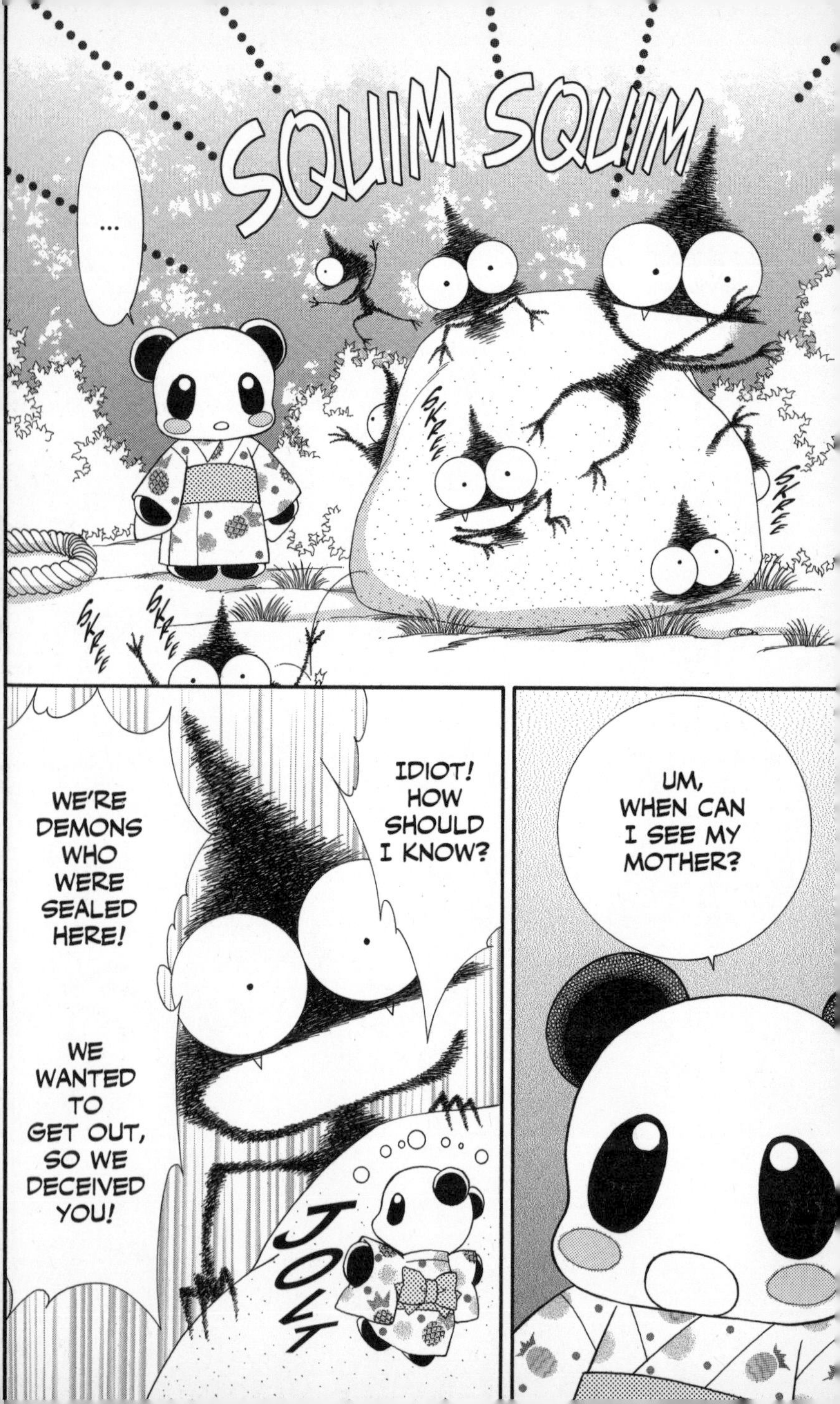
SQUIM SQUIM
...
SKREE
SKREE
SKREE
SKREE
UM, WHEN CAN I SEE MY MOTHER?
IDIOT! HOW SHOULD I KNOW?
WE'RE DEMONS WHO WERE SEALED HERE!
WE WANTED TO GET OUT, SO WE DECEIVED YOU!
JOLT

18

This is the last sidebar. In honor of the sixth volume, I'm giving away souvenirs from Chinatown. If you want any, please request them in your fan letters. The deadline is November 30, 2002. Once I read the letters, I'll decide who gets them.

Thanks for reading this far. I'll see you in volume 7!

BOW

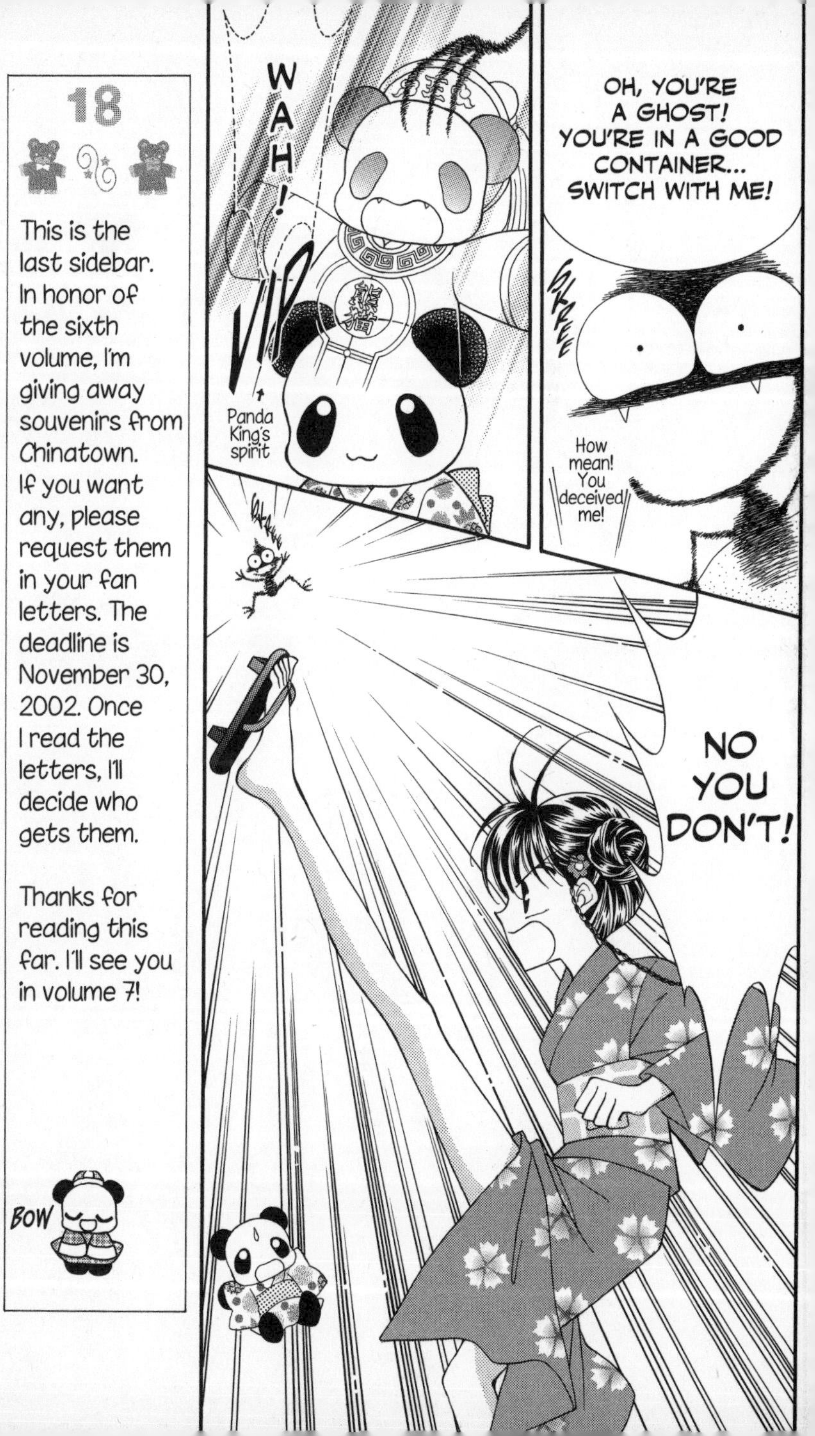
OH, YOU'RE A GHOST! YOU'RE IN A GOOD CONTAINER... SWITCH WITH ME!
SKREE
How mean! You deceived me!
WAH!
VIP
Panda King's spirit
NO YOU DON'T!

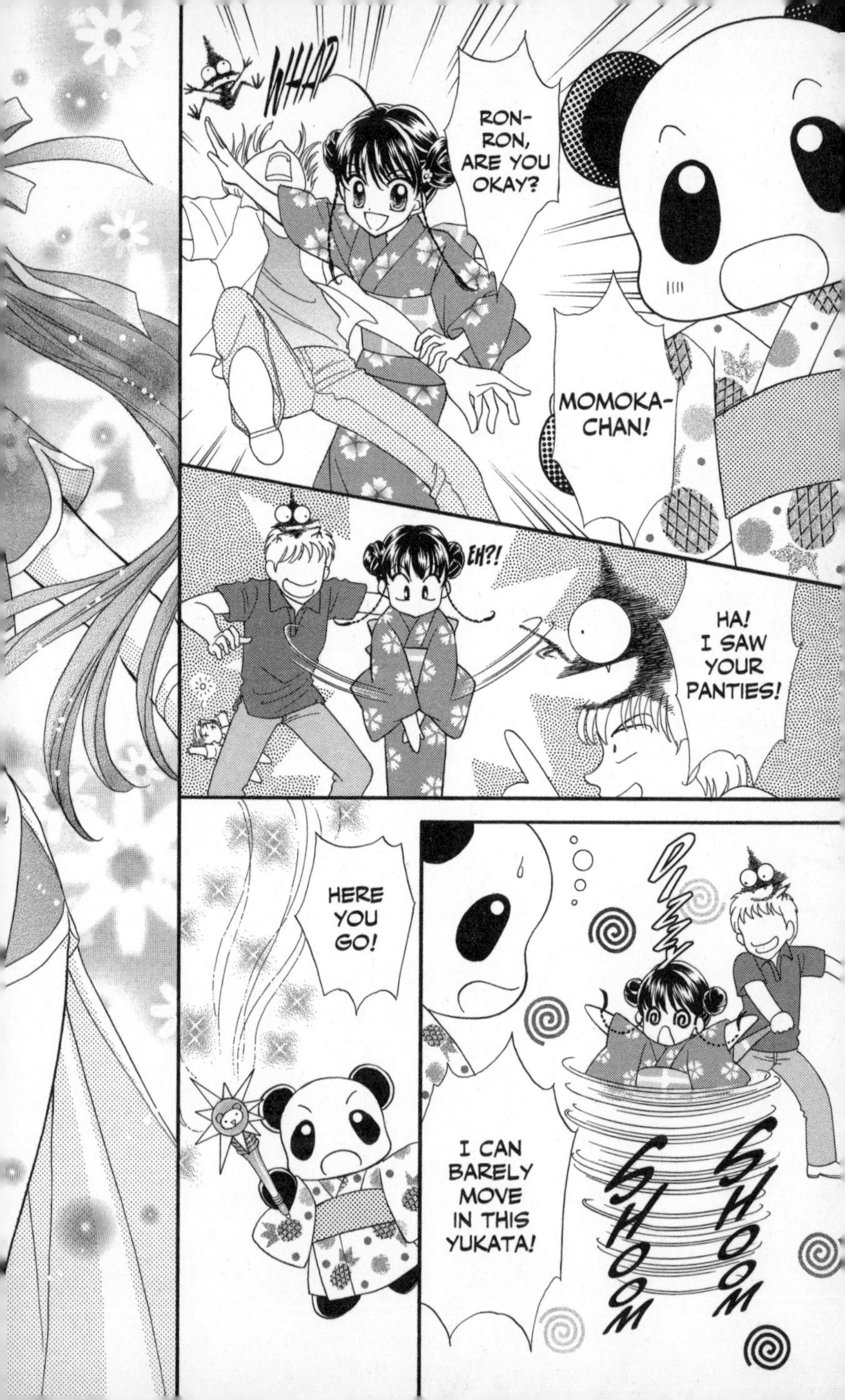
WHAP
RON-RON, ARE YOU OKAY?
MOMOKA-CHAN!
HA! I SAW YOUR PANTIES!
EH?!
I CAN BARELY MOVE IN THIS YUKATA!
SHOOM
SHOOM
HERE YOU GO!

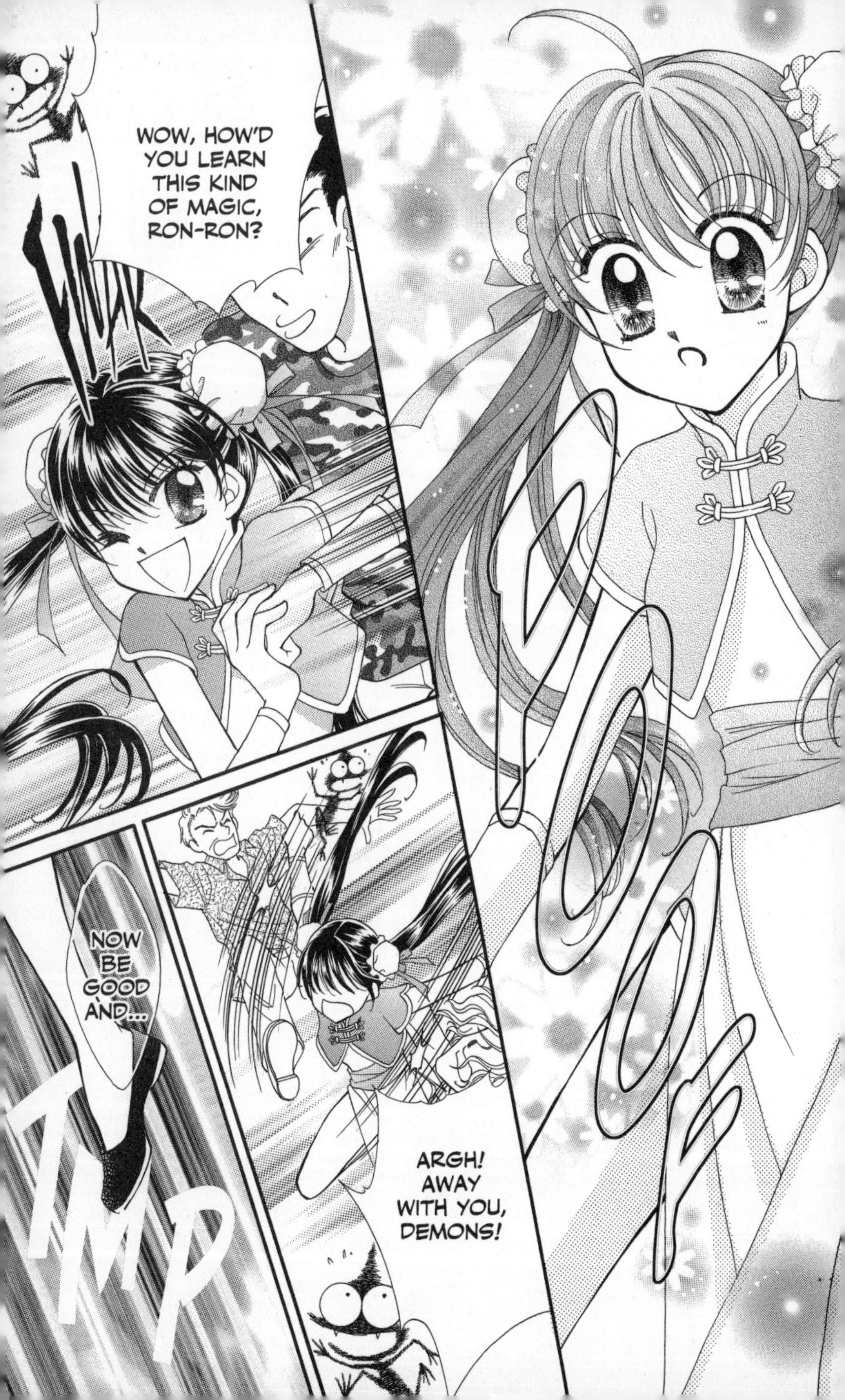
WOW, HOW'D YOU LEARN THIS KIND OF MAGIC, RON-RON?
ARGH! AWAY WITH YOU, DEMONS!
NOW BE GOOD AND...

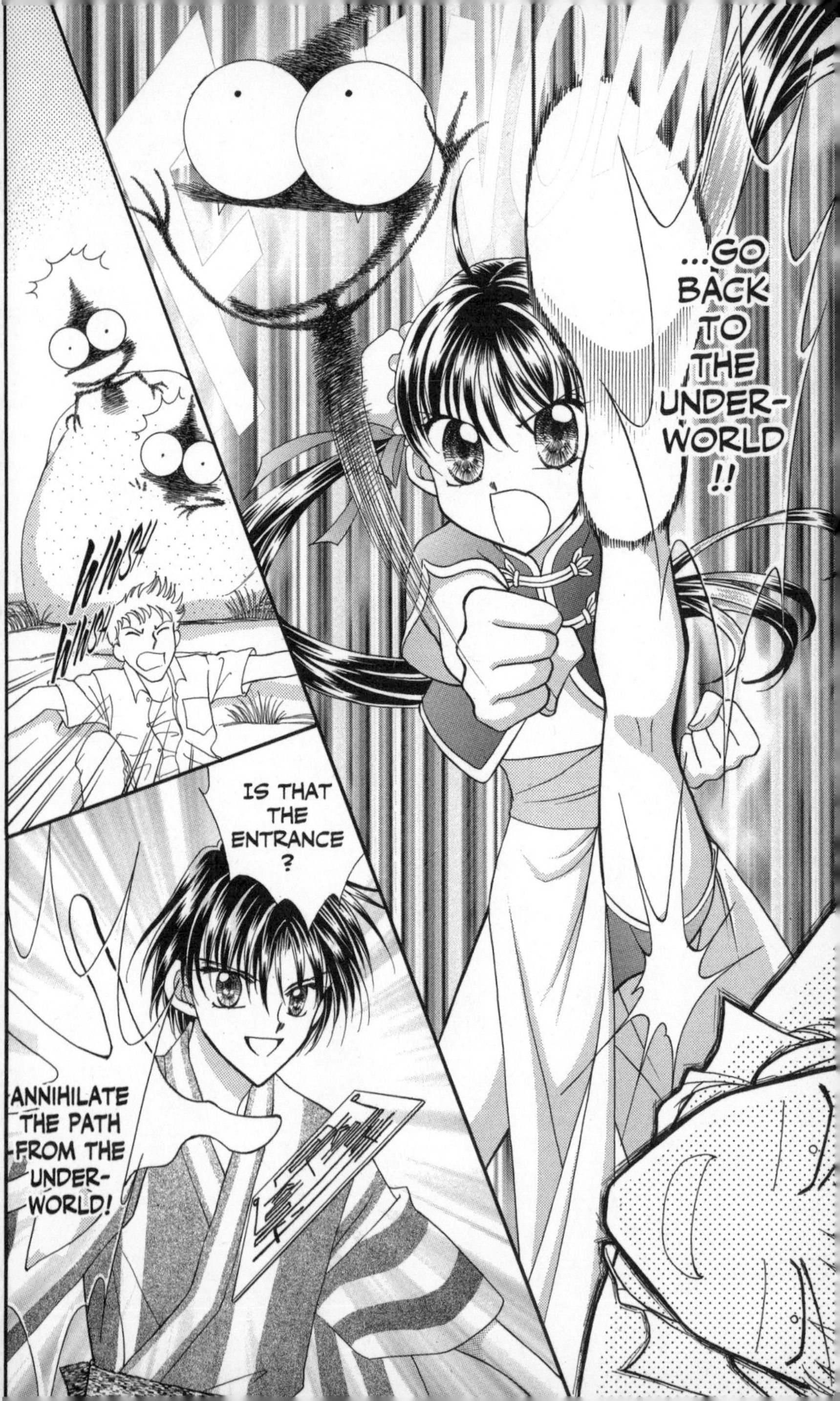
...GO BACK TO THE UNDER-WORLD !!
WHISH
WHISH
IS THAT THE ENTRANCE ?
ANNIHILATE THE PATH FROM THE UNDER-WORLD!

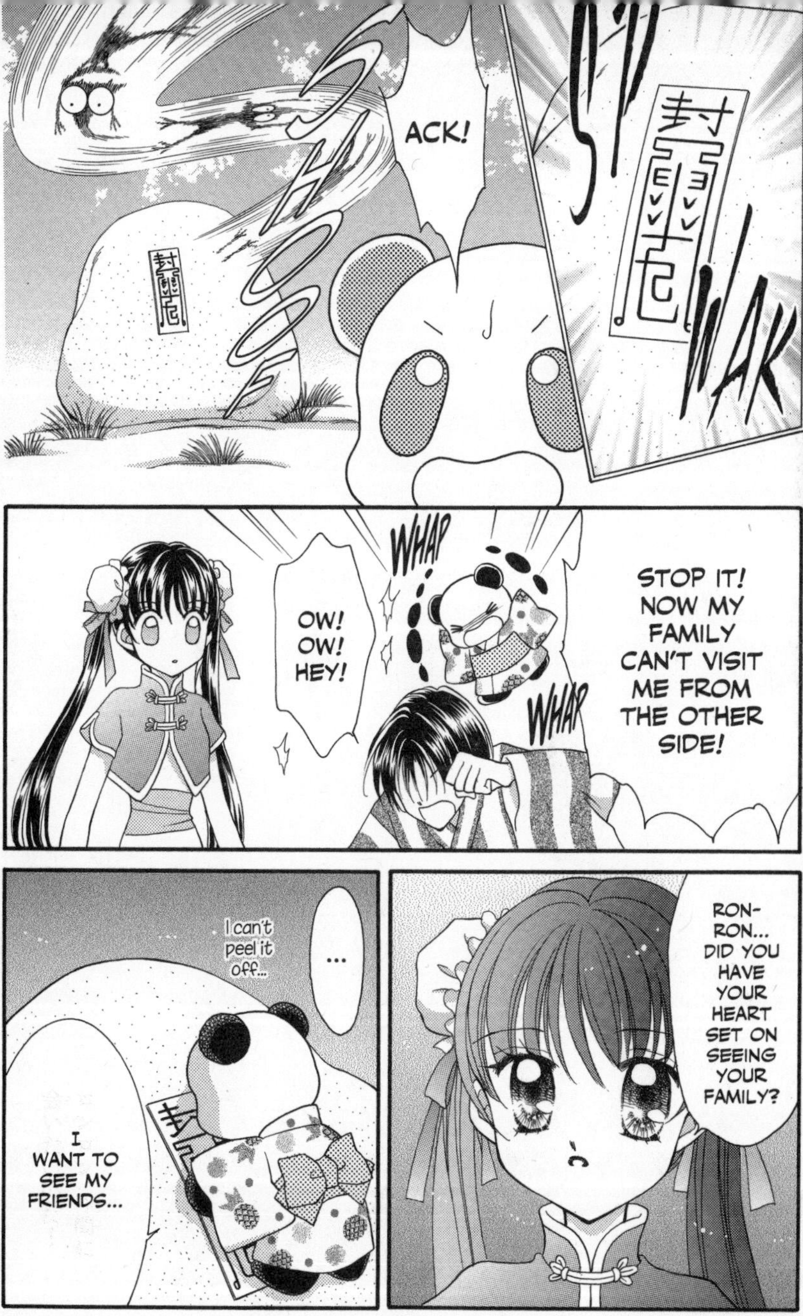
SP
WAK
ACK!
STOP IT! NOW MY FAMILY CAN'T VISIT ME FROM THE OTHER SIDE!
WHAP
WHAP
OW! OW! HEY!
RON-RON... DID YOU HAVE YOUR HEART SET ON SEEING YOUR FAMILY?
...
I can't peel it off...
I WANT TO SEE MY FRIENDS...

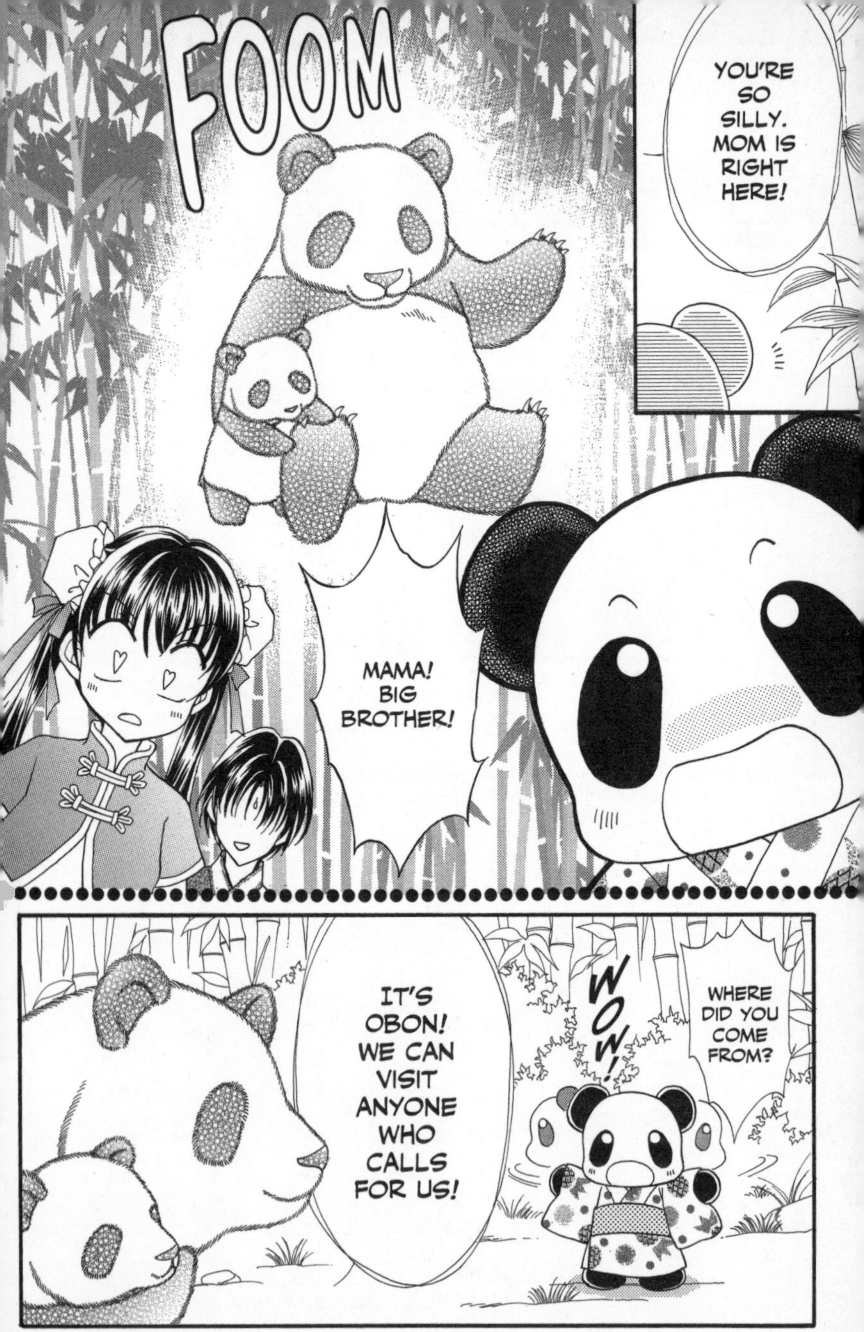
YOU'RE SO SILLY. MOM IS RIGHT HERE!
FOOM
MAMA! BIG BROTHER!
WHERE DID YOU COME FROM?
WOW!
IT'S OBON! WE CAN VISIT ANYONE WHO CALLS FOR US!

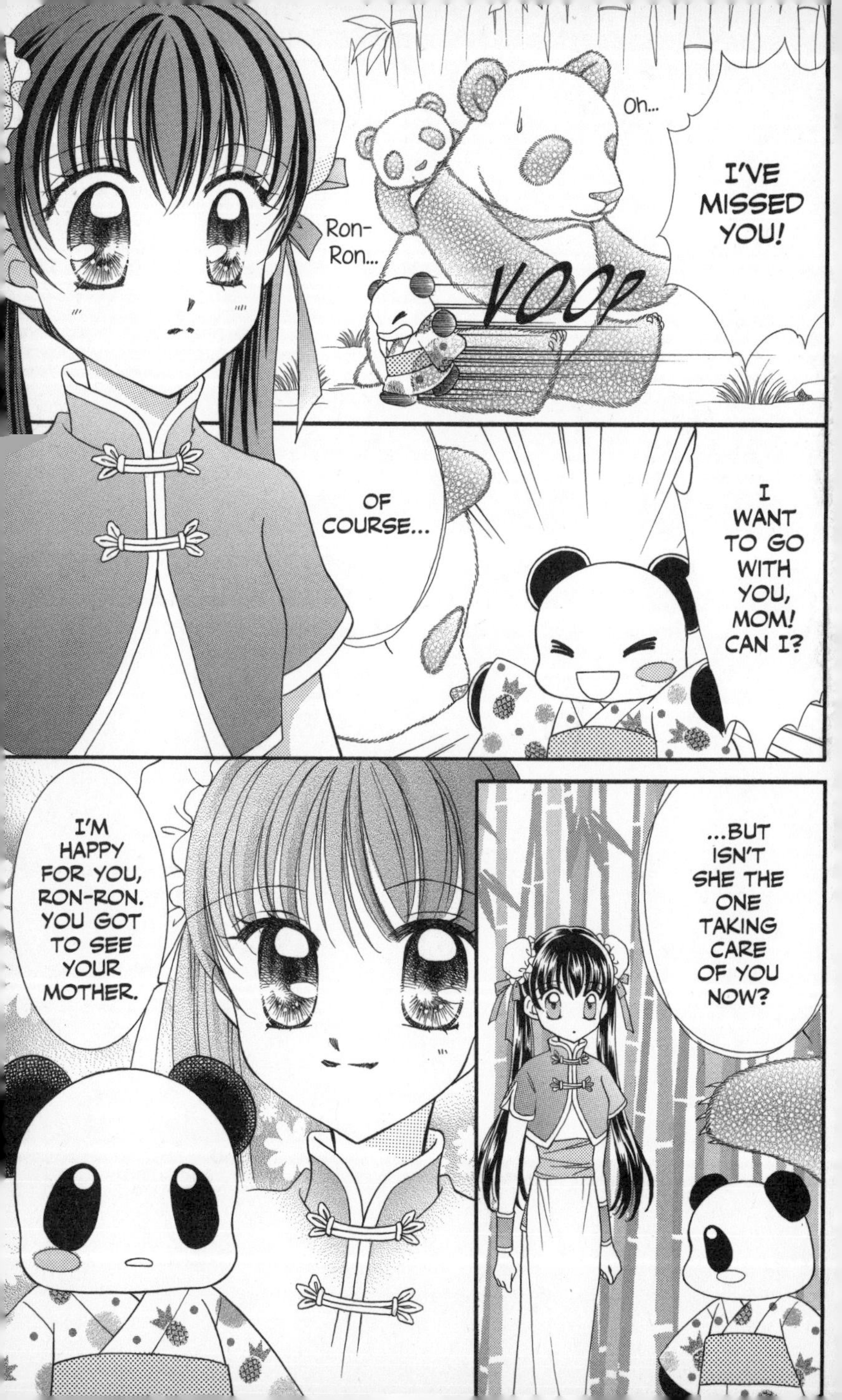
I'VE MISSED YOU!
Oh...
Ron-Ron...
VOOP
I WANT TO GO WITH YOU, MOM! CAN I?
OF COURSE...
...BUT ISN'T SHE THE ONE TAKING CARE OF YOU NOW?
I'M HAPPY FOR YOU, RON-RON. YOU GOT TO SEE YOUR MOTHER.

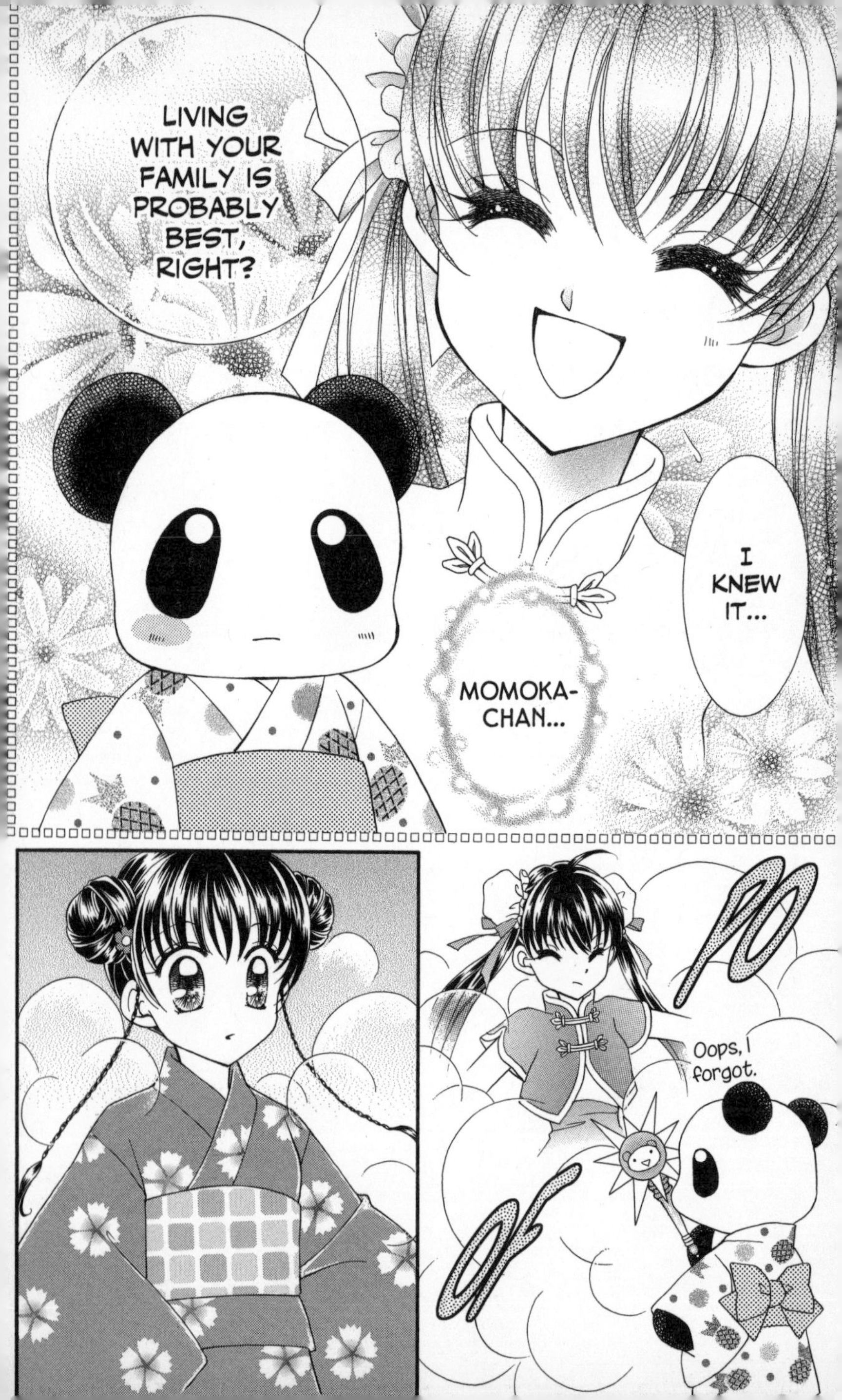
LIVING WITH YOUR FAMILY IS PROBABLY BEST, RIGHT?
I KNEW IT...
MOMOKA-CHAN...
Oops, I forgot.

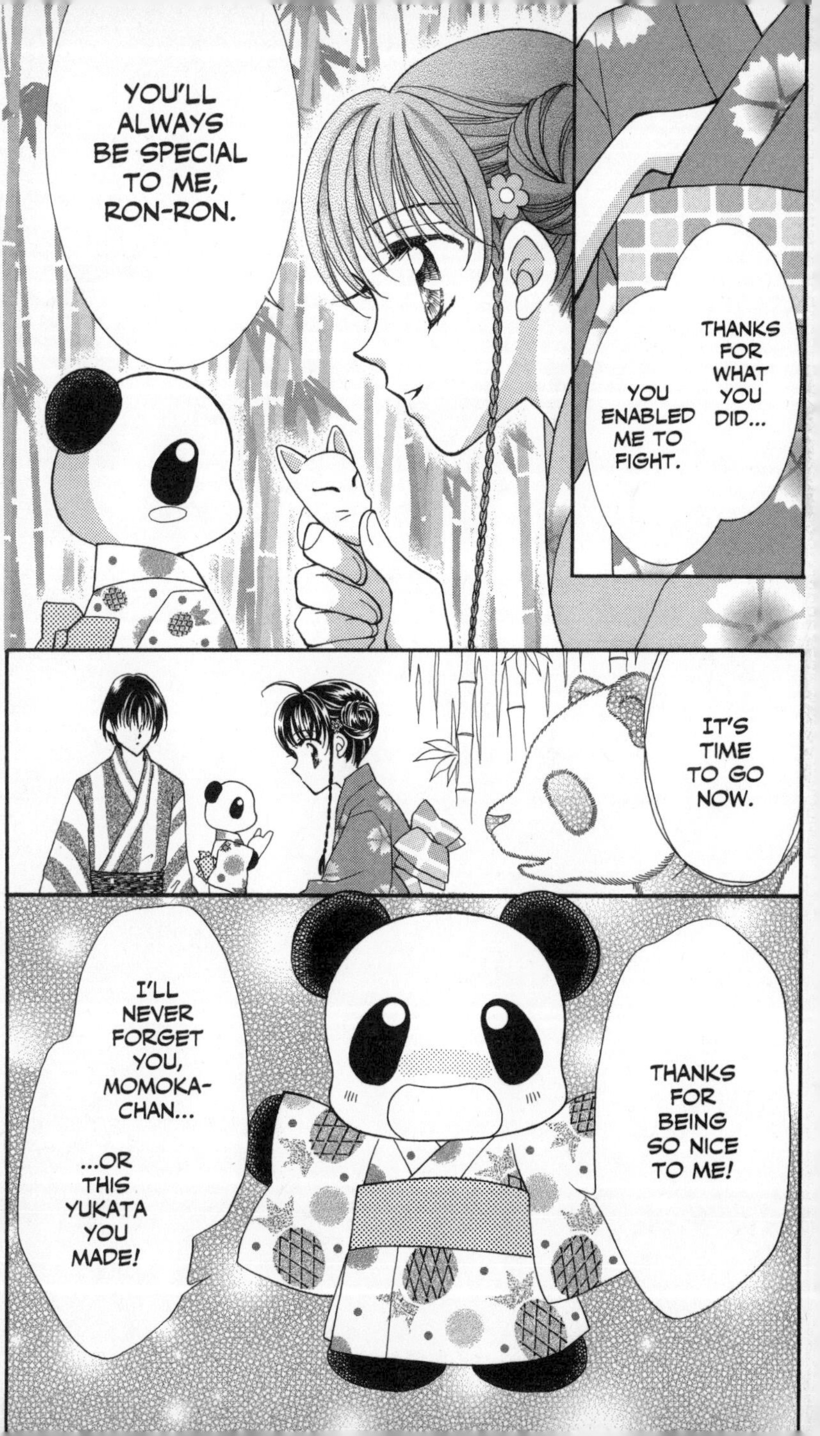
THANKS FOR WHAT YOU DID...
YOU ENABLED ME TO FIGHT.
YOU'LL ALWAYS BE SPECIAL TO ME, RON-RON.
IT'S TIME TO GO NOW.
THANKS FOR BEING SO NICE TO ME!
I'LL NEVER FORGET YOU, MOMOKA-CHAN...
...OR THIS YUKATA YOU MADE!

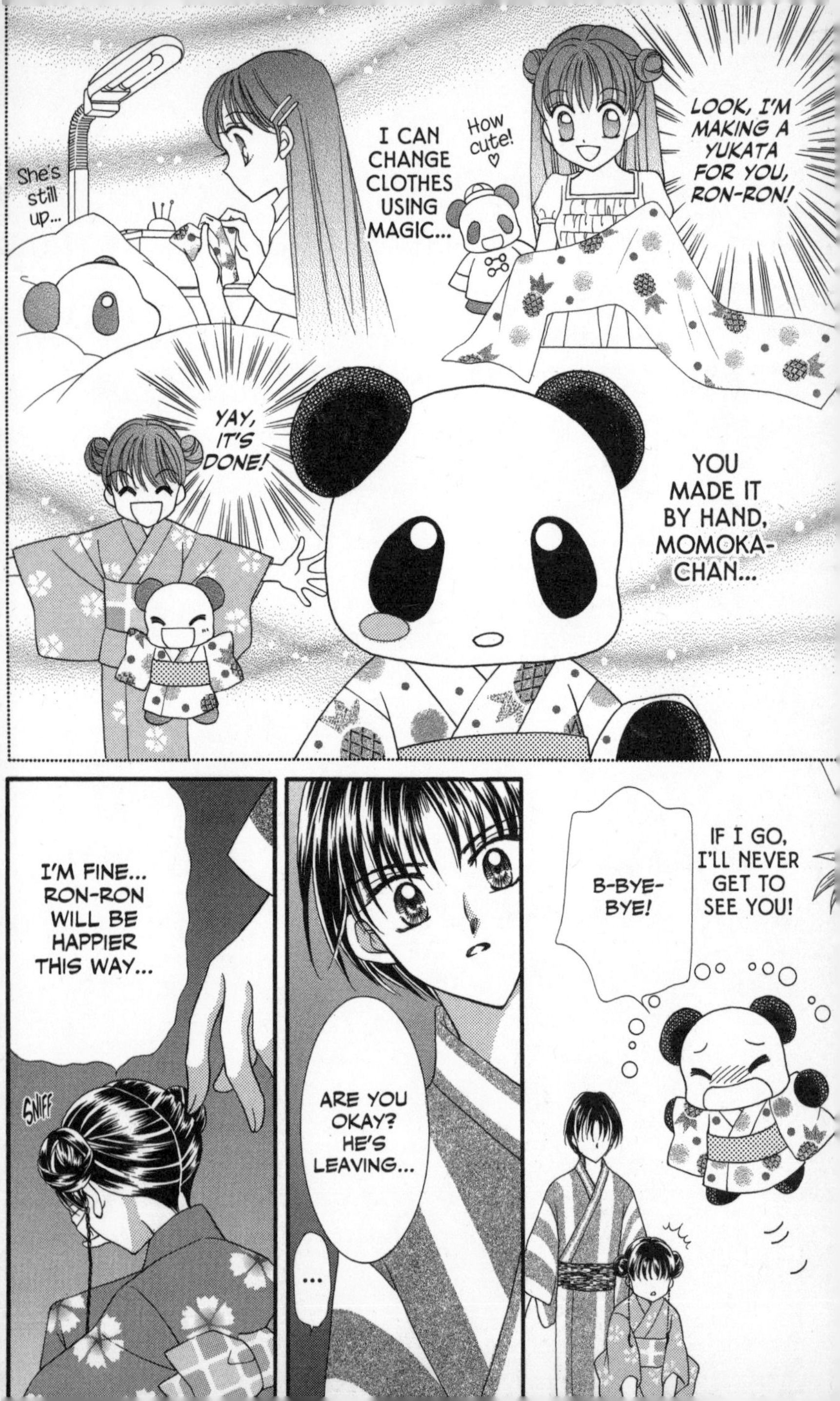
LOOK, I'M MAKING A YUKATA FOR YOU, RON-RON!
How cute! ♡
I CAN CHANGE CLOTHES USING MAGIC...
She's still up...
YAY, IT'S DONE!
YOU MADE IT BY HAND, MOMOKA-CHAN...
IF I GO, I'LL NEVER GET TO SEE YOU!
B-BYE-BYE!
ARE YOU OKAY? HE'S LEAVING...
...
I'M FINE... RON-RON WILL BE HAPPIER THIS WAY...
SNIFF

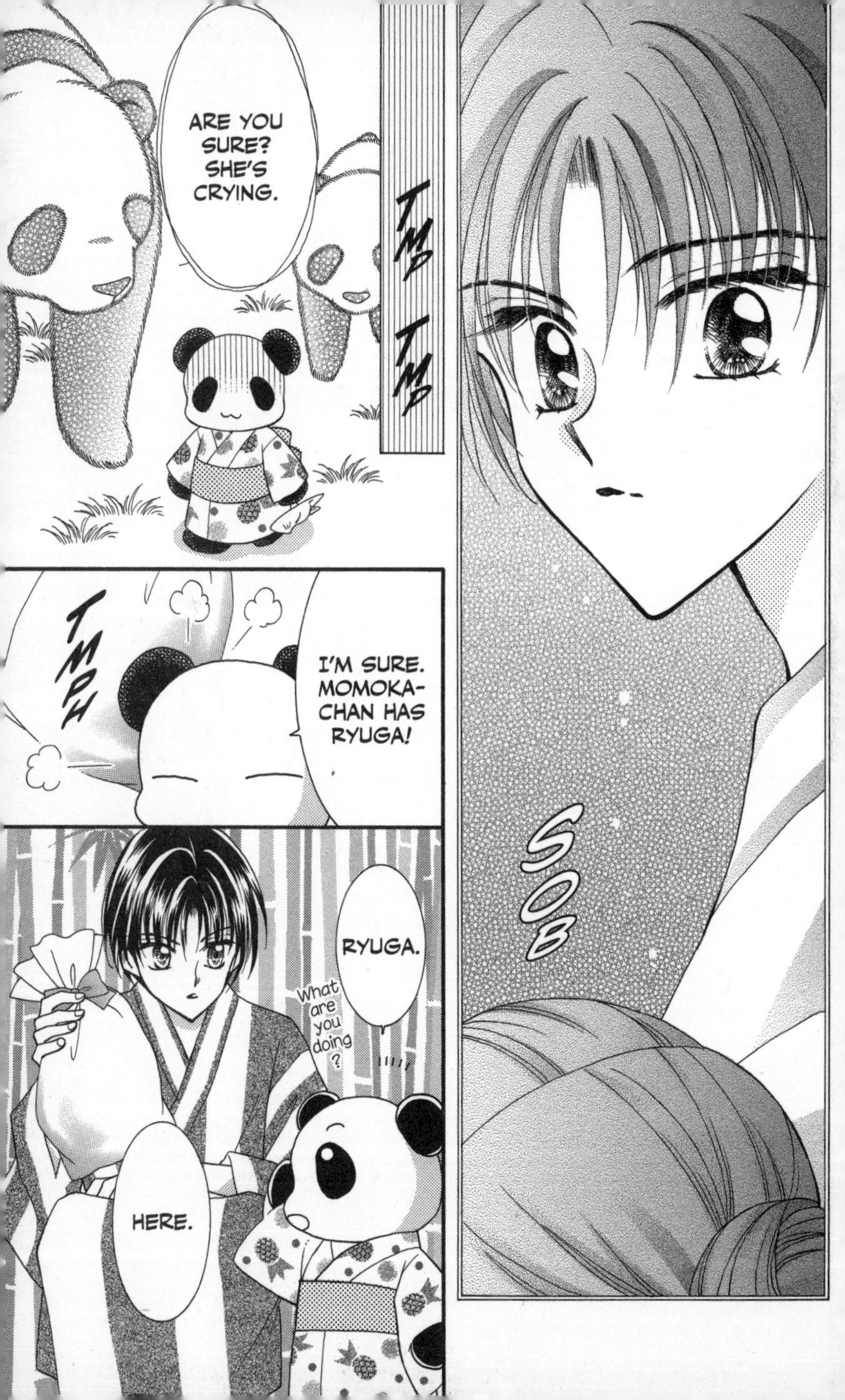
SOB
TMP TMP
ARE YOU SURE? SHE'S CRYING.
I'M SURE. MOMOKA-CHAN HAS RYUGA!
TMPH
RYUGA.
What are you doing?
HERE.

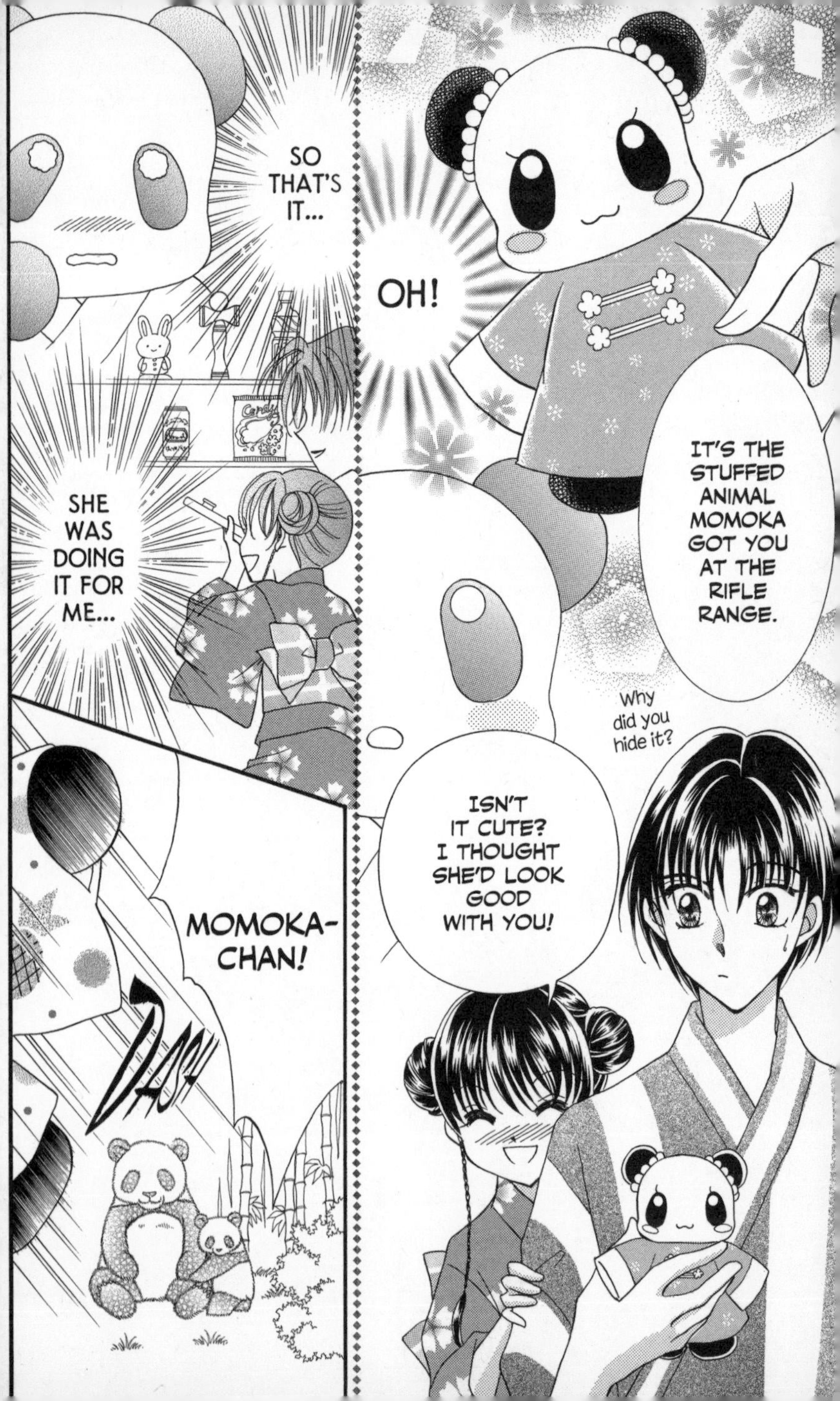
IT'S THE STUFFED ANIMAL MOMOKA GOT YOU AT THE RIFLE RANGE.
Why did you hide it?
ISN'T IT CUTE? I THOUGHT SHE'D LOOK GOOD WITH YOU!
OH!
SO THAT'S IT...
SHE WAS DOING IT FOR ME...
MOMOKA-CHAN!
DASH

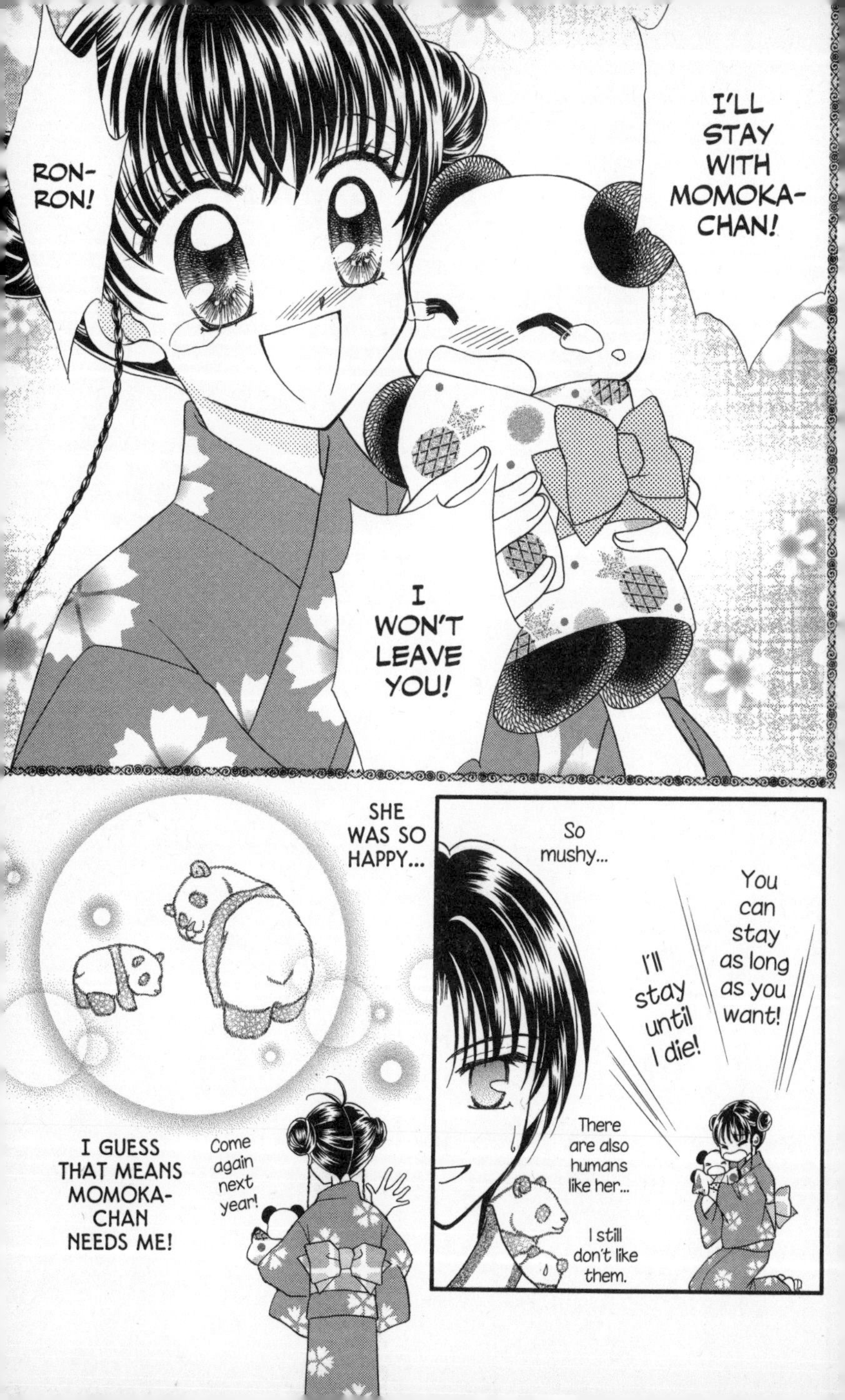
I'LL STAY WITH MOMOKA-CHAN!
RON-RON!
I WON'T LEAVE YOU!
So mushy...
You can stay as long as you want!
I'll stay until I die!
There are also humans like her...
I still don't like them.
SHE WAS SO HAPPY...
Come again next year!
I GUESS THAT MEANS MOMOKA-CHAN NEEDS ME!

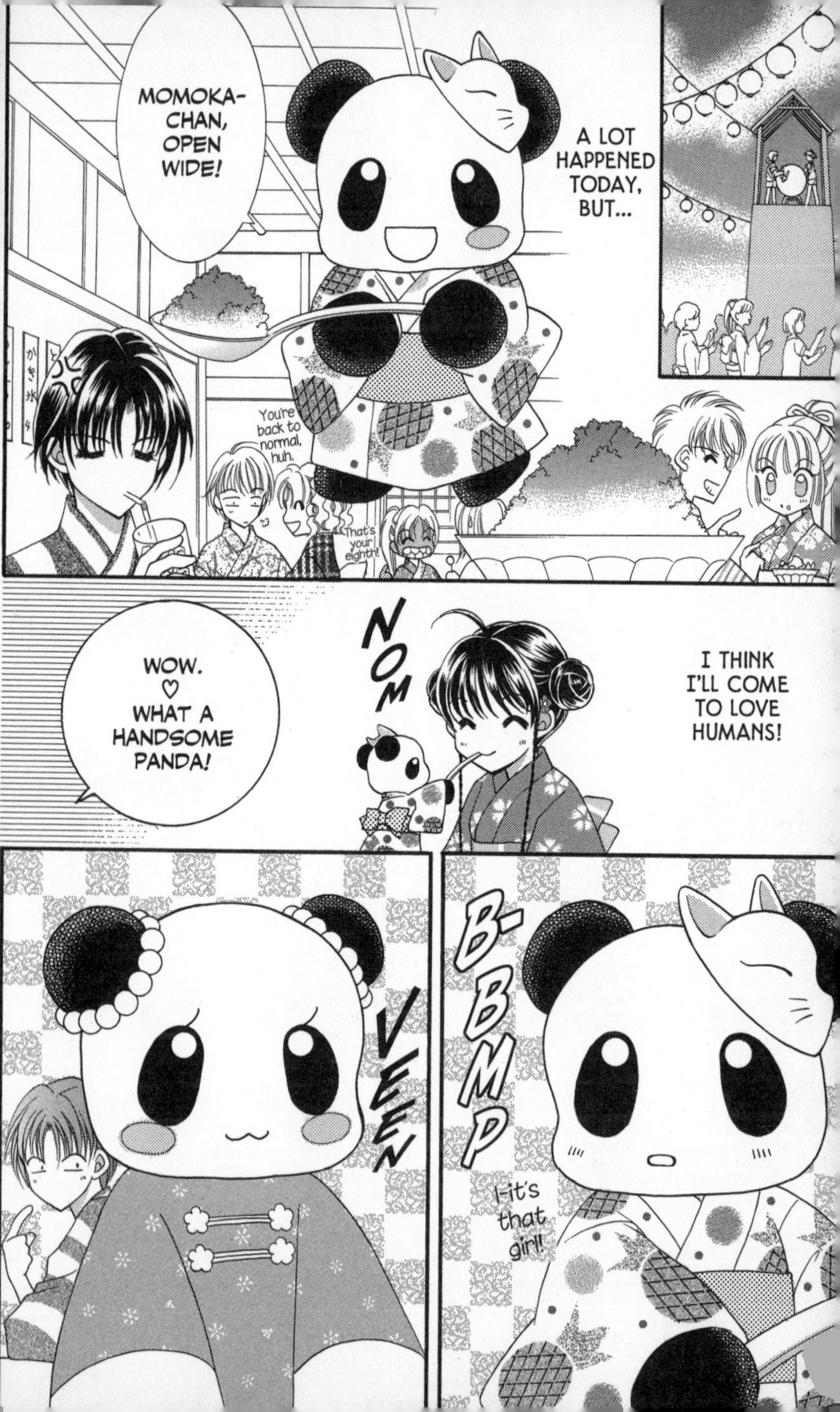

A LOT HAPPENED TODAY, BUT...
MOMOKA-CHAN, OPEN WIDE!
You're back to normal, huh.
That's your eighth!
I THINK I'LL COME TO LOVE HUMANS!
NOM
WOW. ♡ WHAT A HANDSOME PANDA!
B-BMP
I-it's that girl!
VEEN

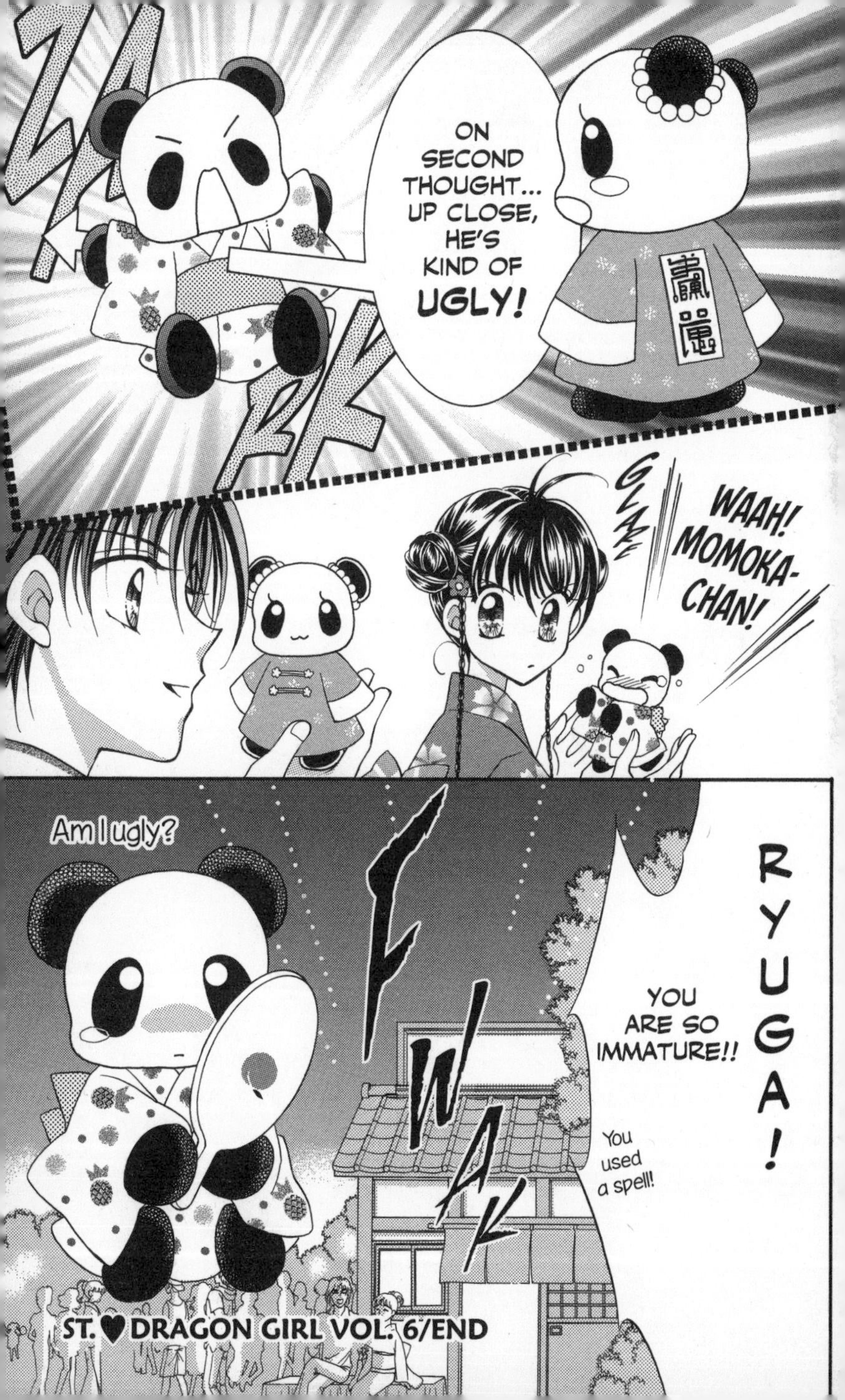
ZA
ON SECOND THOUGHT... UP CLOSE, HE'S KIND OF UGLY!
KK
WAAH! MOMOKA-CHAN!
GLARE
RYUGA!
YOU ARE SO IMMATURE!!
You used a spell!
FWAP
Am I ugly?
ST. ♥ DRAGON GIRL VOL. 6/END

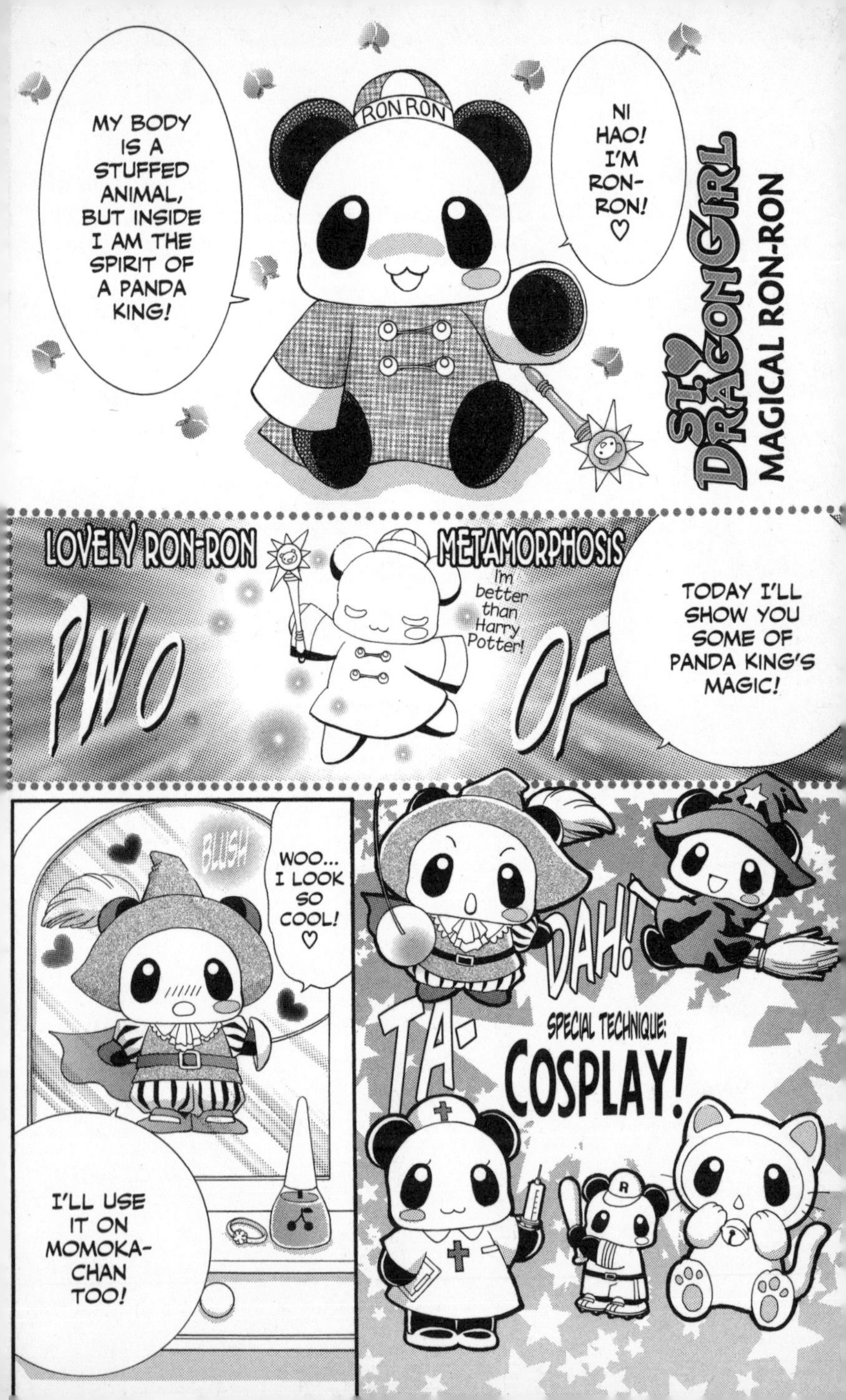
ST. DRAGON GIRL
MAGICAL RON-RON
NI HAO! I'M RON-RON! ♡
MY BODY IS A STUFFED ANIMAL, BUT INSIDE I AM THE SPIRIT OF A PANDA KING!
TODAY I'LL SHOW YOU SOME OF PANDA KING'S MAGIC!
METAMORPHOSIS
LOVELY RON-RON
OF
I'm better than Harry Potter!
PWO
DAH!
TA-
SPECIAL TECHNIQUE: COSPLAY!
WOO... I LOOK SO COOL! ♡
BLUSH
I'LL USE IT ON MOMOKA-CHAN TOO!

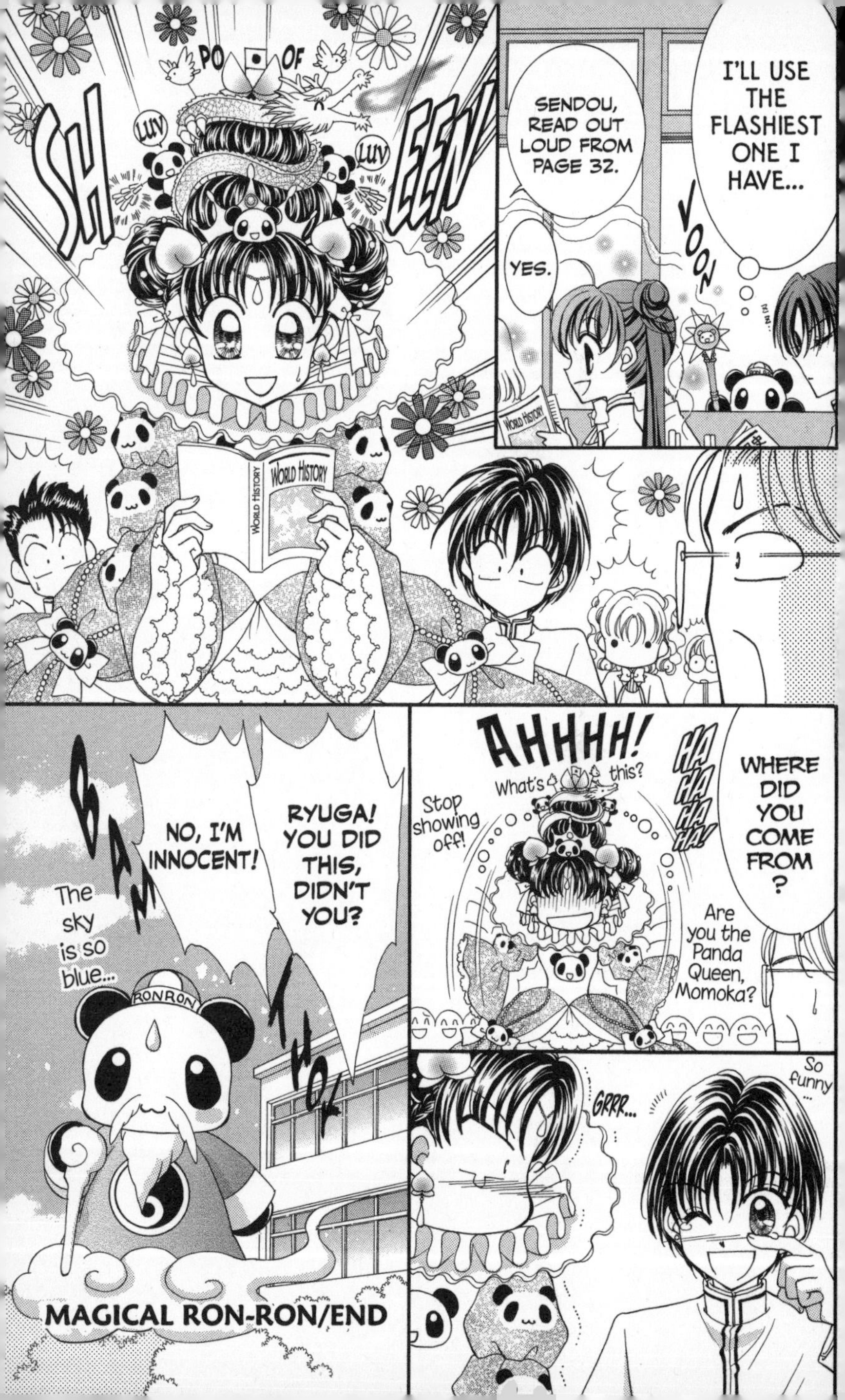
I'LL USE THE FLASHIEST ONE I HAVE...
SENDOU, READ OUT LOUD FROM PAGE 32.
VOOON
YES.
WORLD HISTORY
SH
EEN
PO
OF
LUV
LUV
WORLD HISTORY
WORLD HISTORY
WHERE DID YOU COME FROM?
HA HA HA HA!
AHHHH!
What's this?
Stop showing off!
Are you the Panda Queen, Momoka?
So funny...
GRRR...
RYUGA! YOU DID THIS, DIDN'T YOU?
NO, I'M INNOCENT!
BAM
THOK
The sky is so blue...
RONRON
MAGICAL RON-RON/END

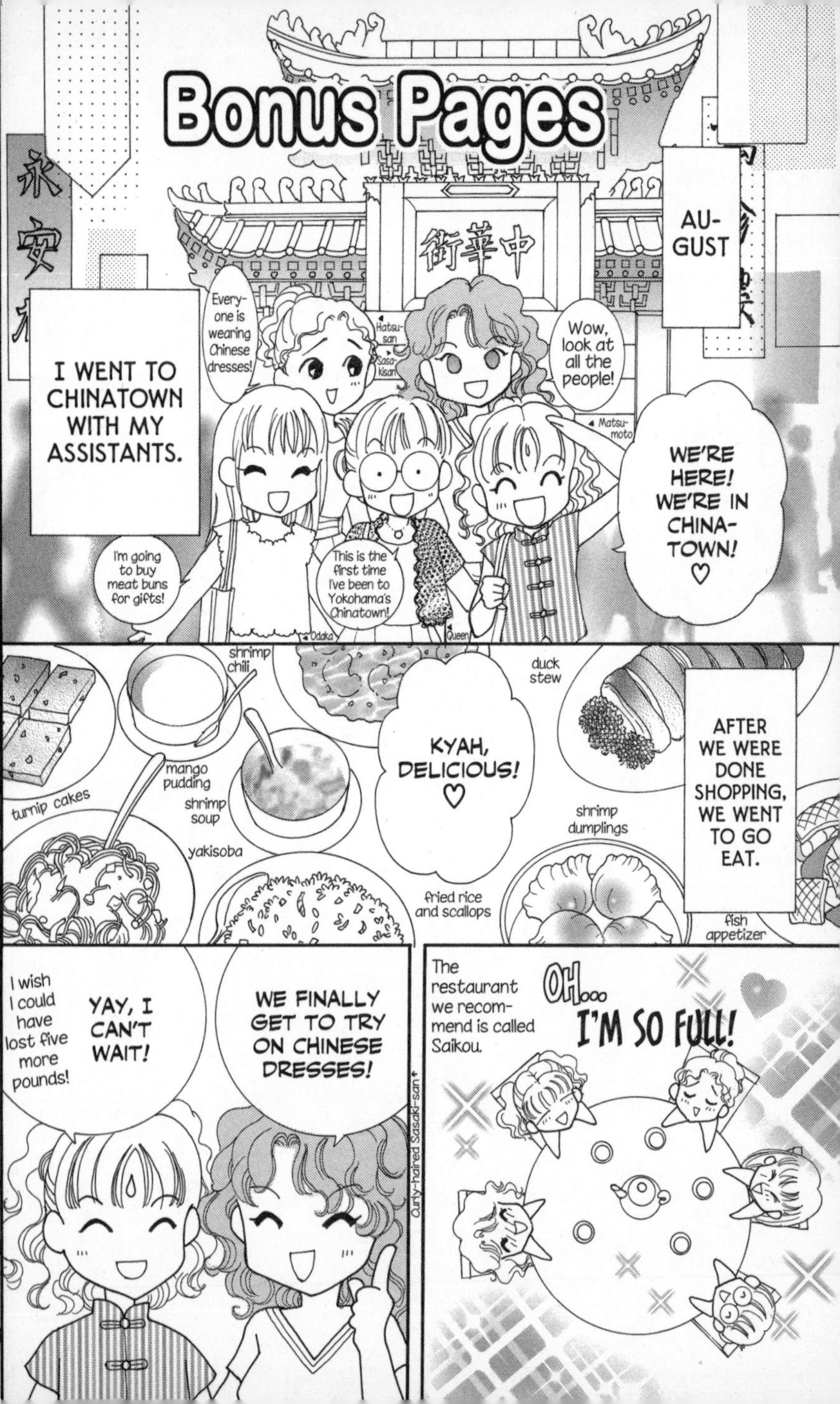
Bonus Pages
AU-GUST
WE'RE HERE! WE'RE IN CHINA-TOWN! ♡
Wow, look at all the people!
Matsu-moto
Sasa-ki-san
Hatsu-san
Every-one is wearing Chinese dresses!
I WENT TO CHINATOWN WITH MY ASSISTANTS.
Queen
This is the first time I've been to Yokohama's Chinatown!
Odaka
I'm going to buy meat buns for gifts!
AFTER WE WERE DONE SHOPPING, WE WENT TO GO EAT.
fish appetizer
duck stew
shrimp dumplings
KYAH, DELICIOUS! ♡
shrimp chili
fried rice and scallops
mango pudding
shrimp soup
yakisoba
turnip cakes
The restaurant we recom-mend is called Saikou.
OH... I'M SO FULL!
Curly-haired Sasaki-san
WE FINALLY GET TO TRY ON CHINESE DRESSES!
YAY, I CAN'T WAIT!
I wish I could have lost five more pounds!

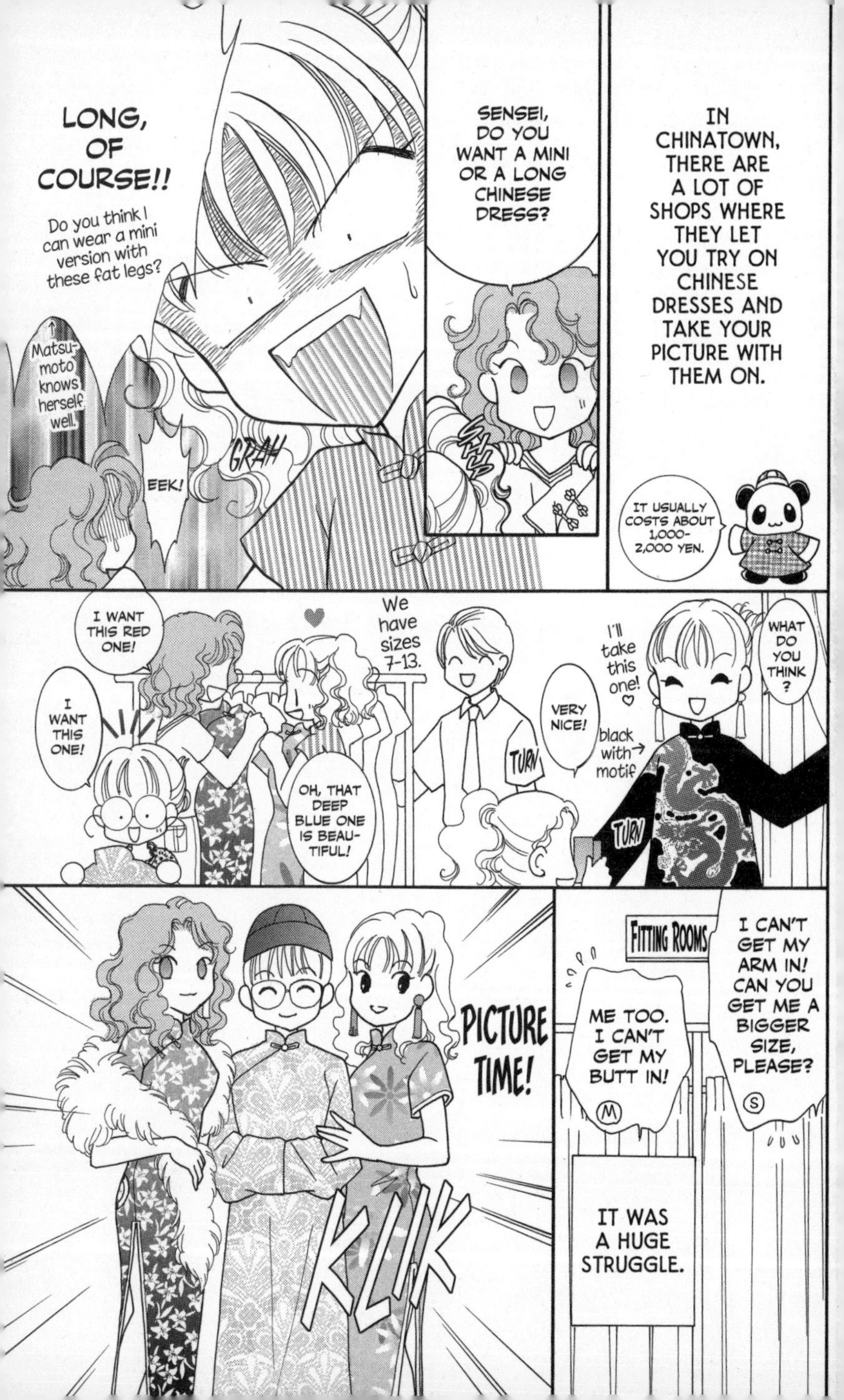
IN CHINATOWN, THERE ARE A LOT OF SHOPS WHERE THEY LET YOU TRY ON CHINESE DRESSES AND TAKE YOUR PICTURE WITH THEM ON.
IT USUALLY COSTS ABOUT 1,000-2,000 YEN.
SENSEI, DO YOU WANT A MINI OR A LONG CHINESE DRESS?
LONG, OF COURSE!!
Do you think I can wear a mini version with these fat legs?
GRAH
EEK!
↑ Matsumoto knows herself well.
WHAT DO YOU THINK?
I'll take this one! ♡
black with motif
TURN
VERY NICE!
TURN
We have sizes 7-13.
OH, THAT DEEP BLUE ONE IS BEAUTIFUL!
I WANT THIS RED ONE!
I WANT THIS ONE!
FITTING ROOMS
I CAN'T GET MY ARM IN! CAN YOU GET ME A BIGGER SIZE, PLEASE?
S
ME TOO. I CAN'T GET MY BUTT IN!
M
IT WAS A HUGE STRUGGLE.
PICTURE TIME!
KLIK

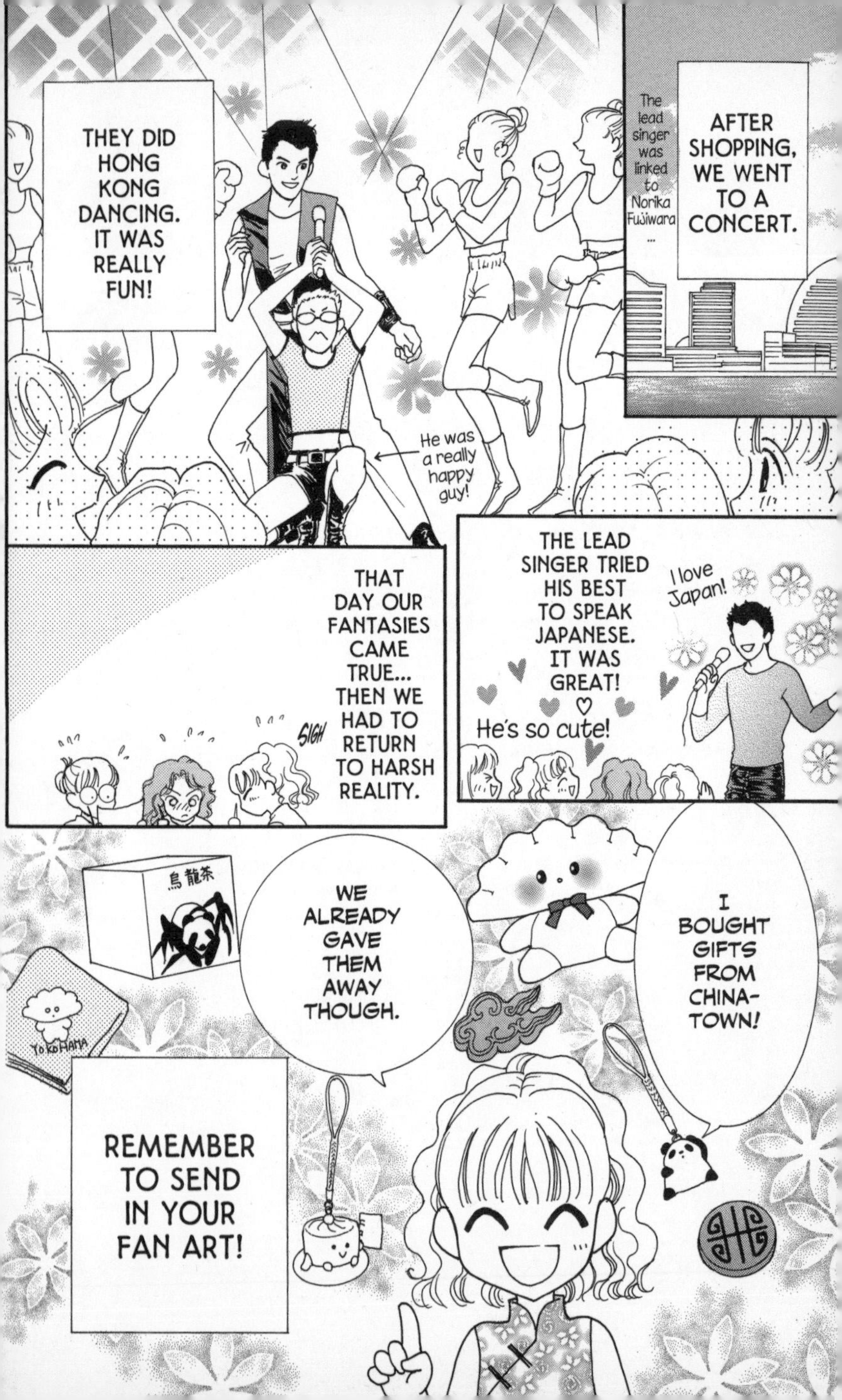

AFTER SHOPPING, WE WENT TO A CONCERT.
The lead singer was linked to Norika Fujiwara...
THEY DID HONG KONG DANCING. IT WAS REALLY FUN!
He was a really happy guy!
THE LEAD SINGER TRIED HIS BEST TO SPEAK JAPANESE. IT WAS GREAT!
I love Japan!
He's so cute!
THAT DAY OUR FANTASIES CAME TRUE... THEN WE HAD TO RETURN TO HARSH REALITY.
SIGH
I BOUGHT GIFTS FROM CHINA-TOWN!
WE ALREADY GAVE THEM AWAY THOUGH.
烏龍茶
YOKOHAMA
REMEMBER TO SEND IN YOUR FAN ART!

HONORIFICS

In Japan, people are usually addressed by their name followed by a suffix. The suffix shows familiarity or respect, depending on the relationship.

Male (familiar): first or last name + kun
Female (familiar): first or last name + chan
Adult (polite): last name + san
Upperclassman (polite): last name + senpai
Teacher or professional: last name + sensei
Close friends or lovers: first name only, no suffix

TERMS

A *shimenawa* is a rope used to cordon off consecrated areas, or as a talisman to ward off evil.

Obon is a period in summer that honors the spirits of deceased ancestors.

No matter how many times I go to Yokohama's Chinatown, it's still fun. Meat buns, sweets, toys, Chinese dresses, feng shui goods, etc. I want to buy everything I see! I can spend only one day there when I go, but I always come back revitalized. ♥

—Natsumi Matsumoto

Natsumi Matsumoto debuted with the manga *Guuzen Janai Yo!* (No Coincidence!) in *Ribon Original* magazine. *St. ♥ Dragon Girl* was such a hit that it spawned a sequel, *St. ♥ Dragon Girl Miracle*. Her other series from *Ribon* include *Alice kara Magic* and *Yumeiro Patisserie*. The popular *Yumeiro Patisserie* was made into an animated TV series in Japan. In her free time, Natsumi studies Chinese and practices tai chi. She also likes visiting aquariums and collecting the toy prizes that come with snack food in Japan.

St. ♥ Dragon Girl
Vol. 6
Shojo Beat Edition

STORY AND ART BY | **Natsumi Matsumoto**

English Adaptation | **Heidi Vivolo**
Translation | **Andria Cheng**
Touch-up Art & Lettering | **Gia Cam Luc**
Design | **Fawn Lau**
Editor | **Nancy Thistlethwaite**

VP, Production | **Alvin Lu**
VP, Sales & Product Marketing | **Gonzalo Ferreyra**
VP, Creative | **Linda Espinosa**
Publisher | **Hyoe Narita**

SAINT DRAGON GIRL © 1999 by Natsumi Matsumoto. All rights reserved. First published in Japan in 1999 by SHUEISHA Inc., Tokyo. English translation rights arranged by SHUEISHA Inc.

The stories, characters and incidents mentioned in this publication are entirely fictional.

Printed in Canada

Published by VIZ Media, LLC
P.O. Box 77010
San Francisco, CA 94107

10 9 8 7 6 5 4 3 2 1
First printing, March 2010

www.viz.com

PARENTAL ADVISORY
ST. ♥ DRAGON GIRL is rated T for Teen and is recommended for ages 13 and up. This volume contains mild violence.
ratings.viz.com

www.shojobeat.com

Tell us what you think about Shojo Beat Manga!

Our survey is now available online. Go to:

shojobeat.com/mangasurvey

Help us make our product offerings better!